CFO Insights

CFO Insights

Delivering High Performance

Michael Sutcliff and Michael Donnellan

John Wiley & Sons, Ltd

Preface

This book has been written to help business executives understand the finance and performance management capabilities required to create and sustain high performance. The combination of research results, case studies, finance executive interviews, and summary insights provides a rich base of knowledge for determining where an organization should prioritize its efforts, so as to build the capabilities required to optimize future success.

CFO Insights: Delivering High Performance covers multiple aspects of the journey to high performance. We analyze how and why high performers consistently outpace their peers over a sustained timeframe across business cycles, industry disruptions, and changes in leadership. We examine the characteristics and attitudes of the leaders among finance executives. We look at the strong correlation between a high-performance business and mastery of five finance capabilities: value-centered culture, enterprise performance management, finance operations, capital stewardship, and enterprise risk management. We explore each of these capabilities in detail and demonstrate their importance, both to the evolving finance function, and overall enterprise strategy and performance. In addition, we look at the characteristics of high-performance organizations in the public sector. And finally, we discuss achieving high-performance finance in some of the most dynamic regions in the world, including Eastern Europe, Japan, and China.

Our research has been conducted under the direction of the Accenture Institute for High Performance Business. The process started with identification of a set of companies across industries and geographies that consistently outperformed their peers over multiple economic cycles. We looked at those high-performance businesses to understand if their ability both to generate and sustain high performance was linked to their capabilities in the area of finance and performance management. We found a 70% plus correlation existed between those companies assessed as being masters of finance and the companies that were high performers in their industries.

Finance executives of high-performance businesses often operate outside of their traditional roles of managing the finance operations. They engage with the senior executive teams to identify where value-creating opportunities exist, and how resources should be allocated to capture them. They help the management team actively plan and deliver those value opportunities across the business. But finance executives also have to respond to an ever-increasing demand around regulatory controls, reporting requirements and adoption of new International Financial Reporting Standards (IFRS). This demand is expected to increase over the next several years and exacerbate the recent trend of increased costs for basic controllership and financial reporting processes. With the first rise in basic transaction processing that we have seen in the last thirteen years, finance executives have to balance the investment demands to create new capabilities that generate value across the business. This book provides a framework to assist finance executives in balancing the pace and mix of investments across five key finance capabilities required to generate and sustain high performance.

We are witnessing a continuing shift in the shape of finance and its footprint across the enterprise. We are also seeing a change in the way the finance leadership team engages with the business and the broader ecosystem of company networks. As companies collaborate more closely across industries to deliver products and customer services around the world, the focus of performance management has shifted beyond the walls of a single organization to the broader challenge of managing across multi-company value chains. This presents significant challenges to the legacy finance operating model.

Finance executives spend increasing amounts of time responding to the pressures that global business models bring to their industries. The finance leadership team has a pivotal role in making sure that they pace the rhythm of change in finance to match the required degree of change at the enterprise level through the deployment of appropriate operating models. As companies struggle to understand how they should source globally and deliver against competitors with different regulatory pressures and cost structures, the finance executives have a key role to play in helping business unit executives craft competitive responses.

The high-performance finance framework discussed in this book has been tested through the lens of the global CFO through interviews with over 250 senior finance executives. We have documented their multiple transformation journeys in terms of how they are shaping their own capability model as well as setting the breadth, depth and pace of change that is in keeping with the rhythm of their businesses. Our research reveals that they are all going down a similar path even as they start at different points and pursue their own priorities and particular areas of focus.

This book includes a series of metrics and insights from The Hackett Group, in an effort to provide the latest information from their database of finance operating cost and best practice trends. The Hackett Group benchmarking methodology and database together are recognized as the "gold standard" to define and measure how finance cost structures and best practices have changed over time. The Hackett Group perspectives provide details on where finance organizations are positioned today, and how that has changed over time.

The framework presented in this book has been validated as applicable across multiple industries and geographies. The framework defines the finance and performance management capabilities that an organization must possess to create and sustain high performance over time. We provide illustrations of the different approaches companies have chosen to build those capabilities, depending upon where the business is today and how quickly it needs to change to stay competitive. This book will help finance executives prioritize where and when they build new capabilities in their business to achieve high performance in a globally competitive environment.

We would like to express our deep thanks to the outstanding finance executives who shared their insights and experience with us: Fan Cheng of Air China; Joao Castro Neves of AmBev; Darren Jackson and Susan Grafton of Best Buy; Russ Taruscio of BP; Ken Hanna of Cadbury Schweppes; Dave Burritt and Steve Guse of Caterpillar; E. Follin Smith of Constellation Energy; Dave Lloyd of Corus; Jim Schneider of Dell; Nick Rose of Diageo; Stephen Ferraby and Stuart Young of Exel; Lauralee Martin of Jones Lang LaSalle; Graham Skeates of Prudential; Colin Sampson, Peter David, Peter Rasper and Hans-Dieter Scheuermann of SAP; Goh Choon Phong of Singapore Airlines; Seck Wai Kwong of Singapore Exchange; Jim Eschweiler of Starbucks; Mitch Blaser of Swiss Re; Bob Young of Teradata; Pat Erlandson of UnitedHealth Group; and Kathleen Turco of the US General Services Administration. These individuals not only confirmed our research, but also demonstrated the continuing contributions that innovative finance teams are making to their enterprise.

We also wish to thank the many members of our global Accenture team for their support and contributions: Tim Breene, Chapter 1; Scott Mall, Chapter 2; Paul Boulanger & Gordon Stewart, Chapter 3; Chris Rutledge, Chapter 4; Dan London & Brian McCarthy, Chapter 5; Tony Masella & Stefania Bassi, Chapter 6; John Ballow & Robert Smith, Chapter 7; Maged Fanous & David Rombough, Chapter 8; Rowan Miranda, Chapter 10; Steven Culp, Manfred Ebling, Karsten Schlageter & Luiz Ferezin, Chapter 11; Mauro Marchiaro, Chapter 12; Matt Podrebarac & Andy Hui, Chapters 13 & 15; Mitsuo Isaji, Chapter 14.

We also give special acknowledgement to our external contributors and to the team that helped us put this publication together. We would like to thank Richard T. Roth, Chief Research Officer of The Hackett Group. In addition, special thanks go to Rosanne Williams, Director of Research & Innovation for the Accenture Finance & Performance Management (F&PM) service line, Deborah Hinson, Director of Marketing for the Accenture F&PM service line, and their team (Haralds Robeznieks, Kerri Ann McElroy, Karin Abarbanel, Deanna Finley and others) for their efforts and contribution on our behalf.

Contents

Contents

Acronyms/ Abbreviations

ABC	Activity Based Costing
AGA	Association of Government Accountants
AP	Accounts Payable
AR	Accounts Receivable
ASSC	Accounting Shared Services Center
BPO	Business Process Outsourcing
CAGR	Compound Annual Growth Rate
CAPEX	Capital Expenditure
CEE	Central & Eastern Europe
CEO	Chief Executive Officer
CFO	Chief Financial Officer
CIS	Commonwealth of Independent States
COO	Chief Operating Officer
CRM	Customer Relationship Management
DR	Depository Receipts
DSO	Days Sales Outstanding
EBITA	Earnings Before Interest, Tax & Amortization
EBITDA	Earnings Before Interest, Tax, Depreciation & Amortization
EDI	Electronic Data Interchange
EH&S	Employee Health & Safety
EITF	Energy Issues Task Force
EMEA	Europe, Middle East and Africa
EPM	Enterprise Performance Management
EPS	Earnings Per Share
ERM	Enterprise Risk Management
ERP	Enterprise Resource Planning
EU	European Union

EVA®	Economic Value Added
EVM	Economic Value Model
EVP	Executive Vice President
F&A	Finance & Accounting
FASB	Financial Accounting Standards Board
FDI	Foreign Direct Investment
FIFO	First-In-First-Out
FMCG	Fast Moving Consumer Goods
FMP	Financial Management Program
FP&A	Financial Planning & Analysis
GAAP	Generally Accepted Accounting Principles
GDP	Gross Domestic Product
GDS	Global Data Services
GL	General Ledger
GNP	Gross National Product
IAG	Internal Audit Group
IAS	International Accounting Standards
IFRS	International Financial Reporting Standards
IMF	International Monetary Fund
IPO	Initial Public Offering
IR	Investor Relations
IRR	Internal Rate of Return
IT	Information Technology
JV	Joint Venture
KPI	Key Performance Indicator
LIFO	Last-In-First-Out
M&A	Mergers & Acquisitions
MIFID	Markets in Financial Instruments Directive
MPA	Multidimensional Profitability Analysis
MRO	Maintenance Resource Operations
NIEs	Newly Industrialized Economies
NIST	National Institute of Science and Technology
NOPLAT	Net Operating Profit Less Adjusted Taxes
NPV	Net Present Value
NRV	Net Realizable Value
NYSE	New York Stock Exchange
OECD	Organization for Economic Co-operation and Development
OLA	Operating Level Agreement

---

[1] ® Stern Stewart & Co.

P&L	Profit & Loss
PBF	Planning, Budgeting and Forecasting
PDA	Personal Digital Assistant
PE	Price Earnings
PMA	President's Management Agenda
PSV	Public Sector Value
R&D	Research & Development
RAP	Russian Accounting Principles
RAS	Russian Accounting Standards
RFID	Radio Frequency Identification
ROCE	Return On Capital Employed
ROI	Return On Investment
ROIC	Return On Invested Capital
RR	Rate of Return
SAR	Special Administrative Region
SBS	Shared Business Services
SBU	Statutory Business Unit
SEC	Securities and Exchange Commission
SKU	Stock Keeping Unit
SLA	Service Level Agreement
SOEs	State-Owned Enterprises
SOX	Sarbanes-Oxley Act
SSC	Shared Service Center
SVP	Senior Vice President
TEP	Total Economic Profit
TRS	Total Return to Shareholders
US	United States
UK	United Kingdom
VAT	Value-Added Tax
WACC	Weighted Average Cost of Capital
WTO	World Trade Organization

CHAPTER 1

What it Takes to be a High-Performance Business

PURSUING EVER-HIGHER LEVELS OF PERFORMANCE

Today's global business environment is marked by unprecedented complexity, uncertainty, and competition. Why are some companies able to increase shareholder value despite these challenges? How do they continue to thrive and innovate, year after year, regardless of disruptive industry shifts and unpredictable circumstances? What sets these companies apart?

By definition, few companies are able to consistently outperform their peers over multiple economic cycles. In an extensive research project, Accenture analyzed the high performers to determine what set them apart from the rest. Among many variables, we examined whether the ability to both generate and sustain high performance was linked to an organization's capabilities in finance and performance management. Not surprisingly, we found a strong correlation between those companies that were masters of finance and those that were high performers in their industries.

We also discovered that chief financial officers (CFOs) in these high-performance businesses are operating outside of their traditional roles. Instead of managing routine finance operations, they are much more engaged with their senior executive teams in helping to identify value-creating opportunities and in supporting the business in leveraging those

1

opportunities. Such changes are exemplified in the leadership of Dave Burritt, Caterpillar's CFO, as the story of his effort and success demonstrates.

THE LINK BETWEEN FINANCE MASTERY AND HIGH PERFORMANCE AT CATERPILLAR

Dave Burritt, CFO
Caterpillar Inc.

Dave Burritt is a keen advocate of high-performance finance. His $30+ billion company is one of 600 enterprises worldwide in the intensely competitive industrial equipment industry. Buoyed by strong global demand for its products and services, Caterpillar is successfully contending with major challenges: rapidly accelerating commodity prices (steel prices have increased from $387/ton to $877/ton since 2002 and crude oil is now trading close to record price levels), hypergrowth in China and across Asia, and tightening regulatory standards for hydrocarbon emissions.

Along with Caterpillar, a small group of companies in the industrial equipment sector excel in managing change and creating value. Among these top performers are Kone, ITT, Cooper Industries, Sandvik, and Danaher. Collectively, they stand out from the crowd in the total returns they have delivered to shareholders.

Among these companies, we have chosen to focus on Caterpillar for three reasons. First, its distinctive franchised selling model, supported by its CFO's commitment to innovative finance strategies. Second, its consistently superior profitability, as measured by a 50%+ growth in revenues since 2002. And last, because Caterpillar continues to reinforce and extend its outstanding leadership position as the world's largest engine manufacturer and one of the most strategically astute players in its industry.

We asked Dave Burritt to describe Caterpillar's current outlook and where he sees the company heading over the next couple of years. "Right now," he noted, "we are in the sweet spot of the economic cycle and our business model. Our numbers have just skyrocketed. While past performance is no guarantee of future success, last year was remarkable: we delivered an 85% increase in profits and a 33% increase in sales. Historically, we have to go back to 1947 to find percentage increases in sales and

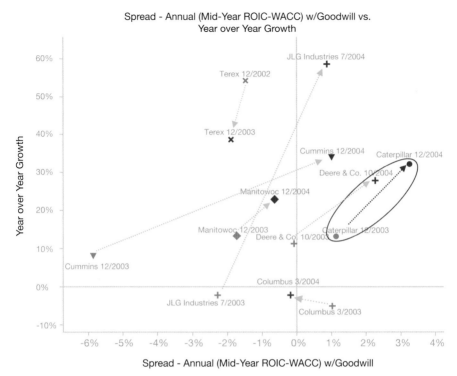

Figure 1.1 *Caterpillar's performance relative to its peers*
Source: Accenture analysis

revenue like these. While winning market share in an upturn, we've also responded exceptionally well to some serious industry issues.

"Who knows how long the current market will last? Whatever happens, we are going to be prepared for the future. We're spending a lot of time on increasing our flexibility, on scenario planning if you will, so that we can take advantage of the continuing upturn while also modeling possible responses if things shift and turn against us. We're raising the bar, looking at our metrics and repositioning the business. We are setting lower breakeven targets across the company and measuring them at the individual business-unit level.

We reach $30 billion in sales and revenue two years early, but haven't hit our return-on-sales metric. We'll have a lot of work to do in the short term. Over the long term, we plan to reframe our metrics. They need to be more asset-based and more value-based – and to reflect a stronger emphasis on cash. Eventually, we want a totally value-based management environment."

Dave went on to explain his leadership posture and how he and his senior finance team are supporting Caterpillar's drive to push its performance to the next level. "We're working this issue very hard," Dave commented. "We have restructured our entire finance organization. Until recently, it consisted of traditional accounting, treasury, tax, and investor relations departments. But today, we've added new functionality, such as our Strategic Consulting Organization, which works closely with our company's Executive Office and Strategic Planning Committee. Our finance resources now include Product Source Planning, a group that focuses on our vision for the future and our global footprint by identifying the investments we should be making around the world. Then we have our M & A team, which is charged with searching out opportunities in adjacent space.

"Finally, we have very rich and deep thought leadership in our organization. Our Business Strategic Support Group has a very strong knowledge of economics, but it also leads our initiatives in competitive intelligence, market research, and product and technology innovation. This group helps us monitor our competitors' global footprints so that we know what actions they're taking and how to respond. The goal is to be able to drill down into our competitors' statements as well as our own. This gives us greater granularity and connectivity. We have all the pieces in place to enable our company to become a 'master of the business.' As we strengthen our ability to team across the organization, we see a marvelous opportunity to point Caterpillar's leadership towards new pools of value – areas where we can leverage our strategic assets to out-compete our industry peers."

Caterpillar has been improving performance year after year. We asked Dave to identify the factors that have propelled his company to ever-higher levels of achievement. "If we go back to the 1990s," he explained, "the most significant event for us was our decision to restructure the company into individual business units. At the time, we had reached about $10 billion to $11 billion in sales and our business units were, in effect, operating as cost centers. We decided to push authority and full P&L accountability down to the business-unit level. This really made a huge difference.

"I believe that the other significant factor is the mindset that we have now as a Six Sigma company. This has given us discipline, structure, and a common language to achieve shared goals on big projects. It is helping us with our quality and growth, helping us control costs, and helping us with innovation. Currently, we have over 500 breakthrough projects in development. Our mission is to attain world-class status.

We measure our progress with a lot of rigor. Every month we reconcile ongoing results with our bottom line. For us, the brand of Six Sigma is rugged, tough, reliable, durable, enduring, disciplined. It's a great cultural fit with our business."

In the late 1990s, Caterpillar introduced value-based management into its European finance operations. Dave led that initiative, so we asked him to explain the rationale behind it. *"We saw an opportunity to improve people's understanding of the business and help them focus on what drives value for Caterpillar. I think we were successful in educating people and in putting in place a framework. I believe that the strong value-creating metrics within our Six Sigma model have become the enduring legacy of that project. We folded what we learned from our value-based management initiative into the rollout of Six Sigma, so that the numbers generated from Six Sigma projects capture true performance. Our strategic selection filters use a value-based approach, so that new projects are screened to ensure that they'll deliver the greatest value for Caterpillar. Some units are better at this than others, but today, everyone takes potential projects and drops them into this filter. So I would say that the value-based management work that we did in Europe became a good foundation for our deployment of Six Sigma metrics that are very robust.*

"Some of the things we talk about at Caterpillar are meaning, action, structure, and truth (MAST). Meaning is the burning platform for us. We are good at painting a picture of why something's important and getting people all fired up about it. We take action We're a results-oriented organization. We know how to move forward and make things happen. Structure involves process, people, and resources. When we trip and fall, it's usually because we didn't do a good job of putting the right structure in place. Finally, there's the truth. For us, this is about capturing value in a quantifiable way that reconciles with SEC published reporting. When people see the numbers coming out of any project or initiative, we want them to know that those numbers are accurate, reconciled, auditable, and enduring. If you don't have truth in your numbers, your structure will fall apart. If you don't have a strong structure – the resources and the people to get something done – you won't take any action. The result? You won't be able to achieve the meaning or the burning platform that you aspire to."

CFOs today are confronted with competing priorities. On the one hand, finance activity has never been more intensely focused on conventional technical accounting issues, basic financial management, and corporate governance. On the other *hand, even as demands for core finance capabilities are escalating, CFOs are being asked to operate far beyond traditional boundaries and become directly involved in leadership, strategy, and execution. We asked Dave to comment on balancing these divergent finance agendas. "The majority of my time is focused on the question, 'What does value look like from a stockholder's perspective?' – and on helping to create and execute strategies to keep us on an upward performance curve. We are increasing our transparency to support these efforts.*

"For example, we've completely revamped our reporting. We've moved all supplemental information to our Web site, tabulated our published information to enhance readability, and added bucket or waterfall charts to capture our corporate outlook. We've also added a Q&A document to help people understand our business better and to reinforce our key messages, headlines, and proof points. When the investment community sees into our business with more depth, it understands the issues that we need to fix as well as the things that we're really good at. Instead of just giving numbers, this new reporting approach reflects all the dimensions that we see. It also provides targets for us to aspire to.

"I also work with our economists on competitive intelligence and with our Strategic Planning Committee. However, the lion's share of my time is spent on people issues – helping my direct reports better integrate their functions with one another. A good bit of time is devoted to succession planning: who we need to develop and who we need to move around the world. Overall, I'd say that my time revolves around managing the critical success factors for my organization – and making sure we have the right people in the right place at the right time.

"We are refocusing our finance organization on this notion of 'being world class or finding somebody else to do it for you.' We are creating greater alignment with both short-term results and the drivers of sustainable long-term value creation for our entire company. We want everyone focused on stockholder value, improved cash flow, and greater profitability. We also want to make sure that we're offering the great leadership training provided by Six Sigma."

Dave Burritt's experience at Caterpillar clearly demonstrates how and why finance has come to play a pivotal role in driving corporate performance. Dave's dynamic approach also illustrates the many ways in which forward-thinking chief financial officers are reshaping their finance organizations to meet rapidly evolving global challenges. As his comments suggest, Dave and his finance team are involved in every aspect of Caterpillar's operational, strategic, and value-driving agendas. His views confirm our findings on the rapid convergence of strategy with economics and finance.

In addition to this strategic thrust, however, CFOs face continuing pressure to handle the basic blocking and tackling of accounting and finance. Many fully expect their workloads to grow over the next several years. In particular, emerging regulatory and statutory reporting requirements created by the Sarbanes-Oxley Act (SOX) and the recently introduced International Financial Reporting Standards have dramatically increased complexity. The CFOs we interviewed also face tough capital allocation decisions. They must address rising costs for financial transaction processing, controls, and reporting – the first such increase in 13 years – while trying to invest in developing new capabilities that really drive their businesses forward.

We are witnessing a fundamental overhaul of the finance function and its footprint across the enterprise. The way that CFOs and finance leadership teams engage with alliance partners and the 'ecosystem' of company networks so vital to many industries is changing dramatically. As more and more companies collaborate more closely to deliver new products and services around the world, performance management has become more about managing an extended network of companies than simply managing vertically integrated enterprises. This presents significant challenges to the legacy finance operating model.

CFOs face major challenges in helping their organizations achieve high performance. They will be better prepared if they have a full understanding of what the task entails. In the remainder of this chapter, we explain the metrics that define a high-performance business, why scale alone is not the answer, and the three building blocks of high performance.

IDENTIFYING AND EVALUATING HIGH-PERFORMANCE BUSINESSES

The Accenture Institute for High Performance Business has analyzed the performance of hundreds of leading organizations worldwide across multiple industry sectors[1]. One of the key objectives of our research is to help companies understand and methodically emulate these model enterprises – that is, *to learn from and apply their successful approaches*. From the outset, it has been our view that the drivers of high performance are identifiable and measurable – and that they can propel a company

- Airlines
- Aerospace and Defense
- Alcohol and Beverages
- Aluminum
- Automobile Suppliers
- Automotive
- Chemicals
- Computer and Peripherals
- Diversified Telecom
- Food Products
- Forest Products
- Health Plan Insurance
- Hotels
- Household Appliances
- Hypermarkets

- Industrial Equipment
- Media
- Oil & Gas: Integrated and Upstream
- Oil & Gas: Supermajors
- Office Electronics
- Personal & Household Products
- Pharmaceuticals
- Retail: Consumer Electronics Stores
- Retail: Drug Stores
- Retail: Fashion Apparel
- Retail: Home Improvement

- Semiconductors
- Software
- Steel
- Telecommunications Equipment
- Tobacco
- Utilities

Figure 1.2 *Industries analyzed in high performance research*

to new levels of growth regardless of history, circumstances, or industry dynamics. Equally important, we've determined that, with sufficient time and commitment, these drivers can be replicated.

High-performance businesses outpace their peers in total returns to shareholders, revenue growth, and spread performance (ROIC minus WACC) over three-year, five-year, seven-year, and fifteen-year time frames. They are rewarded with superior valuation multiples compared with their lower performing peers, and expectations about their future success are higher. They benefit from the perception, both internal and external, that they will continue to achieve stronger relative performance going forward, regardless of the trends and demands affecting their competitors and industries. Figure 1.2 identifies the industries that we have researched and analyzed.

Is industry a factor in high performance?

It is hard to overstate the importance of industry as a determinant of high performance. In fact, according to our findings, the dynamics of certain industries encourage the creation of long-term shareholder value. We are not referring here to the obvious benefits that a company derives from being part of a rapidly expanding industry sector – especially in a fast-growing geography such as China (see Chapter 15, *High-Performance Finance in China*). The influence that industry exerts is both more complex and elusive. To assess accurately true high performance, we modified our basic methodology to account for industry-specific factors.

In the global pharmaceutical industry, for example, stock price is based heavily on implied future value (that is, growth and profitability expectations) from drug R&D pipelines. As a result, we found it necessary to analyze projected value components of total return to shareholders to determine high-performance business attributes. In the utilities sector, where nimble adaptation to regulatory shifts is an attribute of high performance (see Constellation Energy, Chapter 7, *Capital Stewardship*), a 'market environment scorecard' was used to factor in the value of strategic positioning, adaptation to regulatory demands, and financial flexibility. In the industrial equipment sector, a very capital-intensive industry with a long business cycle, a 10-year total return performance screen was included along with standard 3-year, 5-year and 7-year reviews to establish relevancy.

There are also industries that have staked their perceived value on global scale and the successful amalgamation of different business models. A case in point is financial services, where universal providers now strive to offer bundled insurance, investment banking, asset management, and brokerage services to both institutional and retail customers (see Swiss Re in Chapter 4, *Value-Centered Culture*). From a capital markets perspective, companies in these industries define value creation at the corporate level, regardless of the particular mix of operational business models.

Certain industries have undergone radical structural change during the past decade, making the application of high-performance business criteria from even five years ago irrelevant. In these dynamic industries, we assessed high performance not only by applying peer benchmarking standards, but also by conducting longitudinal analyses of shifting industry conditions. In the United States (US) healthcare provider sector, for example, we evaluated companies over a 13-year period spanning three industry inflection points (see UnitedHealth Group in Chapter 2, *High-Performance Leadership*). Our research into this sector revealed that from 1990 to 2003, the fundamental drivers of high performance changed three times, from tightly managed care in the 1990–1995 period to product flexibility and open-plan models in the 1995–2000 period to administrative cost management in the 2000–2003 period.

Is scale an advantage in achieving high performance?

Does size matter? This is a question constantly posed by CFOs in a range of industries. Nitin Nohria, the Richard P. Chapman Professor of Business

9

Administration at the Harvard Business School – and co-author of the breakthrough business book, *What Really Works* – conducted a major study in which the impact of size on performance was explored. During the study, Professor Nohria and his colleagues analyzed more than 200 well-established management models employed over a 10-year period by 160 companies to identify successful management practices. Their conclusion: being big is no guarantee that a company will deliver superior business results over time. Despite this reality, the study found that many companies assumed that success depended on size – on their being the biggest player in their industry sector.

Professor Nohria also dismantled another myth concerning low cost. "You do have to pay attention to cost," he stressed, "but you don't have to be the lowest-cost player. Everyone doesn't have to be Wal-Mart and there are high-end retailers that are very successful in their space." He added, "You also don't have to delight the customer. You simply have to consistently deliver what you promise." In his view, the silver-bullet cures prescribed by most management thinkers over the past decade – such as downsizing, rightsizing, and total quality management – can't deliver positive results in every company because every company is different. "The ideas may be brilliant, but they aren't universal," Professor Nohria cautions: "Jack Welch's work to reinvent General Electric (GE) makes a great success story, but it's not a blueprint to follow if your company doesn't resemble GE."

For decades, scale-driven strategies and a preoccupation with market position have led companies to presume that size, by itself, delivers superior performance and sustained success. In the right context, scale does confer advantages, including increased production efficiencies, amplified purchasing power, and greater brand prominence. However, Professor Nohria's research underscores a sobering, but revealing, fact: scale alone does not assure a company's long-term competitiveness.[2]

The Corporate Strategy Board study, "Stall Points", states that of the 172 companies that spent time on *Fortune*'s list of the 50 largest companies between 1955 and 1995, only 5% were able to sustain a real, inflation-adjusted annual growth rate of more than 6% throughout their reign on *Fortune*'s list.[3] In addition, fewer than 5% of all publicly traded companies maintained total returns to shareholders that were higher than their industry peers during the 10-year period analyzed. From automakers to personal computer manufacturers, the list of companies that dominated their industries for a time – only to fade away as shifts in demand, technology or business models eroded their base – is a long one. As indicated

Using capital growth as a proxy for an increase in scale, the chart below plots the performance of the 50 US companies that grew their capital by the largest amount (in nominal dollars) in the past seven years. Only a select few companies were able to keep their market value growing on a pace with their capital growth (those at or above the line). Those that grew capital the most appear to have had the hardest time making their market value keep pace. Additional data showed that differences in the initial amount of capital grown did not appear to affect the results.

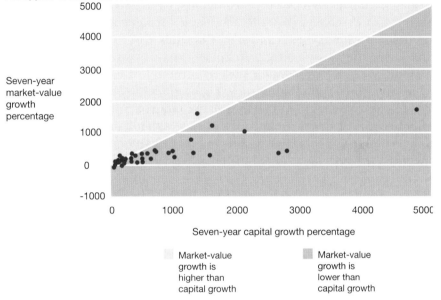

Figure 1.3   *The relation between scale and value creation*

in Figure 1.3, our research demonstrates that scale as an endgame strategy is, at best, unreliable in delivering high performance.

While size is important, our research confirms that it is not a prerequisite for high performance. Across industries, *the basis of competition is rapidly shifting from battles between companies to battles between networks of companies.* This shift is far-reaching in its impact, according to Marco Iansiti, the David Sarnoff Professor of Business Administration at Harvard Business School. As Professor Iansiti notes, competing successfully involves "exerting influence over vast networks of companies and managing assets you don't own." [4]

In today's global marketplace, size is being radically redefined. It is no longer simply an issue of scale; it's about strategic reach and alliance building. This is where the skills of the CFO come into play in understanding where and why alliances, joint ventures, and cooperative agreements

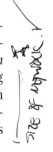

make more sense than the alternative and then in setting up the management processes and systems to support effective control and leadership. Caterpillar, for example, has entered the Chinese market via the joint venture route. Steve Guse, Caterpillar's Asia Pacific CFO, has been very involved in helping to establish operational management disciplines, financial management systems compliant with US Generally Accepted Accounting Principles (GAAP), and disciplined governance procedures. According to Steve, these control mechanisms are critical success factors that a company must get right from day one.

While vertically integrated scale is receding in value, network scale is steadily growing in importance. The combination of readily available technology and capital has pushed many industries in the direction of a fully networked structure in which even the simplest product or service is the result of collaboration among many different organizations. These business "ecosystems", based on interdependent relationships and networked capabilities, can confer powerful competitive advantage.

Companies such as Wal-Mart and Microsoft have realized this, and pursued strategies that not only aggressively further their own interests, but also promote their ecosystems' overall health. To this end, Microsoft and Wal-Mart – along with many other leading players, including American Express, eBay, Linux, and Nokia – have created platforms in the form of services, tools, or technologies, and allowed members of their business ecosystems to enhance their performance via access to these resources.

This is precisely the approach taken by London-based Symbian Ltd, a keystone company in the telecommunications industry. The company creates and licenses the Symbian OS platform, an operating system based on open standards for advanced mobile phones, also known as smart phones. Jointly owned by major telecom players, Symbian has grown by attracting new members to its flourishing business ecosystem. To date, it works with more than 250 partner technology companies and hundreds of application developers responsible for more than 4136 commercially available Symbian OS applications. Moreover, its platform dominates the global market. According to Gartner Dataquest[5], shipments of smart phones running Symbian accounted for more than 80% of all advanced mobile phones shipped in the third quarter of last year.

The result of cooperative strategies like Symbian's are complex, extended performance management systems that reach far beyond the internal boundaries of the traditional vertically integrated organization. The implications of operating in an interdependent business ecosystem, where size is not an endgame strategy, ripple throughout an entire organization and affect it at every level, from the CFO suite to functional teams engaged in R&D and product design. As Harvard's Professor Iansiti observes, "The minute you put technology in a product and begin to connect that [technology] to other products in a network, you create the linkages that have huge strategic importance." He goes on to add, "We have information technology everywhere: in phones, in cars, in appliances, in security management, and in our bodies. All this is becoming connected – and so are the companies that developed and produced the products in the first place."

HIGH PERFORMANCE AND ENTERPRISE VALUE CREATION

High-performance businesses effectively balance today and tomorrow, consistently delivering superior results and outperforming their peers over time – across business cycles, industry disruptions, and leadership changes. Through our research, we have determined that at the core of every company's ability to achieve high performance is what we call 'competitive essence' – the unique combination of business assets that shapes a company's ability to innovate, build competitive advantage over its rivals, succeed in today's markets, and position itself to capture new markets. What distinguishes high-performance businesses from their competitors is the way they develop and sustain competitive essence.

After analyzing the performance of hundreds of leading companies, we have identified three building blocks of high performance:

1 *Market focus and position*: the basis for exploiting growth opportunities and structural economic advantage through unique insights into current and future value.

2 *Mastery of distinctive capabilities*: the ability to create and exploit a set of hard-to-replicate capabilities that maximize differentiation and create value.

3 *High-performance anatomy*: the combination of factors that underpin distinctive capabilities and drive the ability to out-execute competitors.

High-performance businesses continually balance, realign, and renew these three building blocks to preserve and strengthen their competitive essence through a careful combination of insight and action. Figure 1.4

Understanding the Building Blocks of Success

1. **Market Focus and Position.** High-performance businesses seek unique insights into drivers of current and future value, anticipate changes and translate rapidly into differentiated operating models and business architectures.

   Moreover, high-performance businesses focus continuously on business model and service innovation, making markets rather than just riding them.

2. **Mastery of Distinctive Capabilities.** In addition to concentrating on market position and scale, top p also focus on mastering distinctive capabilities relevant to their target customers.

   Accenture research has thus far identified five areas of functional mastery: information technology; human and organizational performance; marketing and customer management; finance and performance management; and supply chain management.

3. **High-Performance Anatomy.** If distinctive capabilities can be thought of in terms of functional mastery, performance anatomy is about the organizational characteristics that underpin these capabilities. High-performance businesses unleash the organization's energies and core competencies; accelerate insight into action to out-execute competition; and manage the balance between today and tomorrow.

   Performance anatomy is not just a fancy term for culture. It is determined by the mindset top management brings to such diverse areas as strategy, planning and financial control, leadership and people development, performance management and use of information technology.

Figure 1.4 *The building blocks of high performance*

describes the three building blocks and their components, which are explored in greater detail in the next section.

Market focus and position

The first building block of high performance reflects a company's capacity for maximizing growth opportunities and structural economic advantages. High performers understand the dynamics of their industries better than their competitors and successfully manage the creation of value through appropriate strategies. Every company has some level of appreciation for the intrinsic value of good strategy. What sets high performers apart is what they see as the best means for creating value and how they perceive the role of strategy in generating it.

In many professions, such as medicine and the law, determining the right course of action is frequently a matter of determining the right answer to myriad smaller questions. In business, good decision making about market focus and position is likewise made up of good component decisions. Our ongoing research into high-performance business reveals that market focus and position are optimized when companies concen-

14

trate first on getting the right answers in three critical areas of strategic decision making.

1 How to manage for today and tomorrow

For high performers, good choices are rooted not only in their present capabilities but also in those they can readily develop. Because of the risks of scaling through acquisition, high performers know they must maintain a constant emphasis on organic growth, at every level of scale and industry maturity. Maintaining organic growth over time, however, is not easy. Deciding to broaden a company's scope into new businesses, or to increase its reach into related markets or new geographies, must be based on intelligent assessments of numerous factors.

Yet in high performers we see a characteristic wisdom to filter their opportunities – before making a decision – constantly and carefully through two important screens: the limits of their capabilities, and a perspective of multiple horizons of strategy. We have observed these organizations to be what we might call "realistic dreamers." They push themselves to the limits of their capabilities, but not beyond.

Every organization has a frontier of "doability" in its strategy and visioning, and high performers have an intuitive sense of where that frontier lies. For example, Toyota Motor Corporation, once known mostly for its compact sedans, successfully extended its frontier and now enjoys great success with its Lexus luxury brand. Another example is Microsoft Corporation, which has been among the most adept at taking visionary strategic positions that are also, upon inspection, highly actionable because they leverage real existing capabilities.

Take Microsoft's Xbox. Moving into the gaming arena was a daring move when the company introduced its game console in 2001, a year after Sony's PlayStation 2 hit the market. But Microsoft believed it had the marketing and distribution strengths as well as the brand awareness to enable it to win in this market. Though the Xbox still has only a fraction of PlayStation 2's installed base, it did manage to outsell PlayStation 2 for the first time during the last quarter of 2004, signaling that Microsoft did not overshoot its capabilities in this space.

The ability to make the right decisions in this dimension is also based on a company's skill at managing, often simultaneously, across near-, medium-, and long-term time horizons. High performers make decisions that actively implement an overall strategy across multiple time horizons, even when those decisions require enormous additional investments that threaten to cannibalize their existing businesses. The secret in high performers is funding new businesses from the profits of cash cows when they are richest, not waiting until such funds have dried up. Microsoft, for example, has been effectively managing multiple horizons by using the cash flow from its core operating systems business to build a leadership position in desktop applications, and has done so with offerings like Office and Internet Explorer, as well as in related ventures like Xbox, MSN and server applications.

2 How to best parent operated businesses

High performers choose highly distinctive value-added activities for their corporate cores, and then build or acquire a set of businesses uniquely able to benefit from the core and the other business units. Procter & Gamble, for example, shares leadership capabilities, a strong brand, marketing expertise, a shared distribution network and deep skills in new product development throughout the company, to the benefit of all units. 3M has a distinctive capability in research and development that it spreads across its business units.

Parenting in high-performance businesses is not a "bare minimum" or perfunctory approach only about supervision or shared services. These companies' executives are active leaders and drivers of change. Unlike average companies, high performers derive significant real competitive advantages from their corporate centers, and do so by design. Yet they also recognize that the role of the corporate center is not fixed but must evolve over time. Jack Welch may have become justifiably famous for his management of GE, but the real badge of accomplishment came from the fact that he actually tended the company through a number of distinct eras of management, successfully achieving different corporate agendas in each era. And Welch's last directive to successor Jeffrey Immelt is alleged to have been, "Blow it up!" – the same advice he had received from his predecessor 20 years earlier.

High performers also know that what their businesses need from a parent changes with the maturity of the business and its industry lifecycle, the changing structure and nature of the portfolio, external events and disruptive technologies. Because of constant changes in competitive circumstances, the acid test of parenting for high performers is not whether the core is adding value but whether it is still adding more value than an alternative parent company could.

3 How to compete through organization design

The best companies develop unique designs and leadership structures that reinforce their chosen sources of competitive advantage, rather than follow a formulaic design process from a textbook. High performers know their strength lies not in the labels on the organization chart but in the unique ways their organizations are able to execute that design. High performers do not create differences just for difference's sake, however.

One particular way these companies differentiate their organization design is by creating what business school professors Lynda Gratton and Sumantra Ghoshal have called "signature processes." Unlike best-practice processes, signature processes create distinctive advantage because they have grown as the company has grown, and are intimately connected to the passions of the executive team. Nokia provides an example of how a company can dominate its market through a signature organization design. Because Nokia's heritage is as a software technology company, the doctrines of standardization and reusability are deeply ingrained in its culture. Development is faster, and costs are lower, when software development occurs "modularly."

That modular philosophy eventually found its way into Nokia's organization structure; in the company architecture, business units and functions are comprised of modular teams of people with common competencies and skills. In the end, however, the real advantage of Nokia's approach, as high performers know, is the capacity for change – the increased organizational flexibility and agility such an approach allows.

Mastery of distinctive capabilities

The second building block of high performance involves creating and exploiting a unique set of capabilities. Whether in sports, the fine arts or business, mastery of a core skill, talent or competence is essential to achieving high performance. One needs to look no further than the Olympic Games to confirm this. Competence is a given – it is required to simply compete – but it is never enough to win the gold medal. Discipline, fierce commitment, and the determination to deliver their personal best are what distinguish Olympic champions from the rest of the field. In the business world, it is much the same. Competence is necessary, but not sufficient. Companies must have a command of business basics, such as technical accounting, business controls, and risk management. Here again, however, only the mastery and extension of distinctive capabilities provide sustainable competitive advantage.

Caterpillar offers a striking example of how core strengths can be tied to a differentiated customer experience to create a suite of distinctive capabilities. Its exclusive global dealer network constitutes a significant extension of the Caterpillar organization and brand, employing more than 100,000 people worldwide. The dealer franchise is not only the primary sales channel for the company, it also ensures that Caterpillar's customers experience consistently high standards in after-sales service and support at just about every location imaginable on the planet. It is this kind of asset utilization advantage, tied to the customer experience, that creates distinctive capabilities. It also results in a combination of well-deployed resources that competitors find very hard to beat.

For capabilities to produce superior business performance, they must not only be distinctive, they must be aligned and, in many cases, fully integrated. Companies must cultivate and combine their strengths in ways that create a defensible, hard-to-replicate formula for business success. By studying high-performance businesses, we have gained insight into what makes their capabilities truly distinctive and why developing them is critical to achieving sustainable superior performance. Five key attributes make the difference.

1 Customer centricity

A high performer defines what we call "a customer-centric algorithm for value creation." This is essentially a formula for doing business that translates into a big idea regarding customer needs – and the processes and resources necessary to satisfy those needs cost-effectively. Creating this blueprint for success requires a company to have deep customer relationships and insight. It also demands that it be creative in its use of resources to manage the costs of delivering exceptional value to both customers and shareholders.

In the airline industry, low-cost carriers have achieved great success with a value algorithm that combines cost savings in customer-facing processes with high asset utilization in operations. These processes, as reflected in their distinctive capabilities, include approaches such as providing a single class of service, using a uniform fleet of aircraft, and having employees serve multiple roles. The CFOs in most low-cost airlines understand the leadership role they need to play and know specifically where to focus their business-support resources. As a result, most have adopted an outsourced shared service model for passenger revenue accounting. This enables them to pool transaction processing operations using an industry service utility called Navitaire. Figure 1.5 illustrates the operating model used by low-cost airlines.

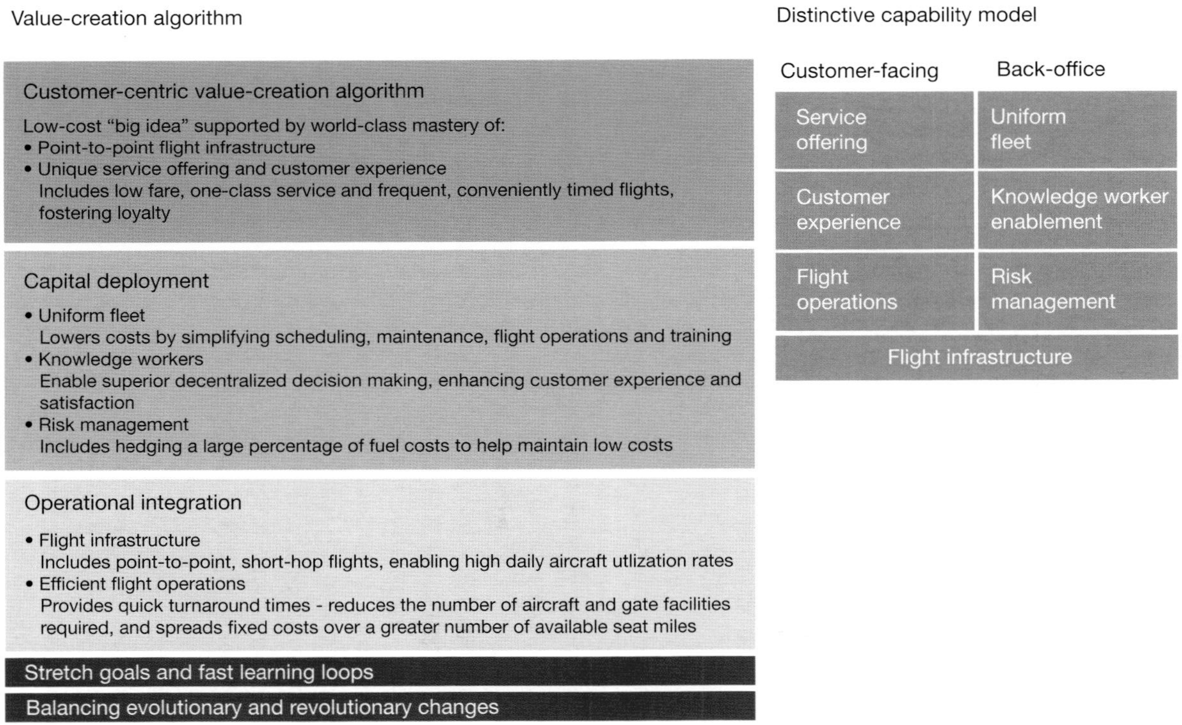

Value-creation algorithm

Distinctive capability model

Customer-facing	Back-office
Service offering	Uniform fleet
Customer experience	Knowledge worker enablement
Flight operations	Risk management
Flight infrastructure	

Customer-centric value-creation algorithm

Low-cost "big idea" supported by world-class mastery of:
• Point-to-point flight infrastructure
• Unique service offering and customer experience
Includes low fare, one-class service and frequent, conveniently timed flights, fostering loyalty

Capital deployment

• Uniform fleet
Lowers costs by simplifying scheduling, maintenance, flight operations and training
• Knowledge workers
Enable superior decentralized decision making, enhancing customer experience and satisfaction
• Risk management
Includes hedging a large percentage of fuel costs to help maintain low costs

Operational integration

• Flight infrastructure
Includes point-to-point, short-hop flights, enabling high daily aircraft utilization rates
• Efficient flight operations
Provides quick turnaround times - reduces the number of aircraft and gate facilities required, and spreads fixed costs over a greater number of available seat miles

Stretch goals and fast learning loops

Balancing evolutionary and revolutionary changes

Figure 1.5 *The operating model of low-cost airlines*

2 *Asset efficiency*

High performers are often fanatical about asset efficiency. At the same time, they know instinctively when and where investments will sustain a first-mover advantage in the face of copycat competitors. This commitment is critical. The US retail giant Wal-Mart, for example, is estimated to have invested more than $500 million in the early 1990s to create the infrastructure for its cross-docking system. This has proven to be money well spent since the investment has enabled Wal-Mart to deliver continued high performance. Capabilities around capital stewardship, which we explore in Chapter 7, are a strong focus for high performers. Such stewardship reaches beyond simple asset accounting and investment planning.

3 *Selectively integrated core processes*

High performers focus their operational integration efforts. They concentrate on connecting the core processes that support their formula for value creation. While many companies struggle to make *all* their processes connect, high performers try to integrate only those that truly matter to their business.

Though it may appear counterintuitive, high performers deliberately choose not to optimize selective parts of their businesses. They can make these tough choices because they have a clear understanding of their algorithm and a deep knowledge of what adds value. UnitedHealth Group, for example, has chosen not to deploy shared services for transaction processing because it has determined that "transaction processing" is not critical to competitive success in its industry sector.

Companies that don't understand their algorithms try to optimize everything, and fail to recognize the trade-offs in performance that must inevitably be made. Ultimately, they wind up abandoning their performance improvement strategy altogether because they try to optimize all the parts of the business as opposed to only those that really deliver high performance.

In contrast, Zara is a prime example of a company that understands and exploits the three building blocks of high performance. A leading clothing manufacturer and retailer headquartered in Arteixo, Spain, Zara bases its high performance on the mastery of supply-chain management. As a result, it has built supply chain logistics into its business strategy and has devoted significant attention to designing an integrated operating model around this core competence. This focus allows Zara to consistently set industry standards for time to market, order fulfillment, and customer satisfaction.

4 Stretch goals

High performers continuously improve their algorithms through stretch goals – objectives set just beyond a company's reach, so that it must strive to attain them. After a company has defined its formula for success, allocated the resources to build it, and launched it operationally, it must commit to the process of continuous improvement. The idea is to improve not incrementally but dramatically, by continually setting stretch goals that push performance to new levels. High performers achieve this by employing fast-learning loops – processes that quickly transform insights on how to improve their algorithm into actions that result in precisely those improvements.

Stretch goals yield the best results when they force employees to work smarter, not harder. Japan's Toyota Motor Corporation offers an important lesson on stretch goals. Long famous for its continuous improvement programs, Toyota recently launched a formal "stretch goals" initiative in its North American Parts Operations, the parts and accessories distribution arm of Toyota Motor Sales, USA Inc. Three goals were set: saving $100 million in distribution costs, cutting inventory costs by $100 million, and improving customer satisfaction by 50% – all at the same time.

Steven J. Spear, an assistant professor at Harvard Business School's Technology and Operations Management Unit, has studied Toyota for nearly a decade. His work focuses on "decoding Toyota's DNA" and on identifying the underlying principles that account for its consistent ability to outperform competitors. "Toyota hasn't figured out a silver-bullet solution. But it has figured out what to do to get much better much faster and across a broader range of processes and functions than anybody else in the industry," Professor Spear observes. "Moreover, it achieves competitive advantage through operations on the basis of its ability to learn more quickly and more consistently than competitors."

If BMW is the ultimate driving machine, as its advertising message asserts, then Toyota is the ultimate learning machine, contends Professor Spear. "It's Toyota's insatiable appetite for learning that allows it to achieve much higher levels of performance across quality, efficiency, productivity, flexibility and lead time." More important, Toyota management involves employees at all levels in its quest for perfection. What's more, it supports employees by supplying them with key data to help measure – and improve – their performance.

"By establishing stretch goals at every cut and slice of the organization, you have employees coming to work thinking how they can subtract two or three seconds from the assembly process," Professor Spear explains. He should know. As part of a Toyota team, he spent six months visiting many of the company's plants around the world. At first, he was amazed by the number of supervisors, managers, and team leaders involved in the company's continuous improvement process. He soon realized that what first appeared to be a bloated organization is really one that "fosters, facilitates and nurtures the constant drive to do better. These are the people who get employees to think about the two-to-three seconds they need to shave off production time. And once the employees get it down to 51 seconds, these are the same people who ask the question: 'If we got it to 51 seconds, then why can't we get it down to 47?'" Professor Spear adds.[6]

To demonstrate its commitment to doing whatever it takes, Toyota recently announced Global Vision 2010, a long-range program to reinvent itself. In launching the program, Toyota stated: "We realized we needed to develop a greater sense of urgency in our business. Success is good," it added, "but without urgency, serious weaknesses set in, customer focus declines, creative ideas dry up and before you know it you are in trouble." To avoid this dangerous scenario, Toyota keeps a keen eye on the market – even in the best of times.

5 *Dynamic algorithms*

Toyota's relentless drive for improvement keeps its algorithm alive and vibrant. The pace of change requires algorithms to be dynamic, which is why the fifth attribute that contributes to distinctive capability is often the hardest for companies to get right. This is because revitalizing the formula for success requires constant vigilance and keen marketplace awareness. High performers are particularly good at both adjusting this and dramatically redefining it as circumstances require. Moreover, they have the foresight to refresh component capabilities when the algorithm is faltering, but not yet failing.

In contrast, lower performers lack such foresight and flexibility. In many instances, they don't succeed because they give up on the formula too soon or hold on to one for too long. These businesses tend to see potential problems everywhere, a costly mindset that drains time and resources – and, ultimately, marks them for failure. Intel's legendary CEO Andy Grove identified this problem explicitly. In his book, *Only the Paranoid Survive: How to Exploit the Crisis Points that Challenge Every*

Company, Grove described how high performers can immediately spot the difference between a real and a perceived threat to their business – and react appropriately.

High-performance anatomy

High-performance anatomy, the third building block of high performance, is perhaps the most elusive characteristic that great companies display. This attribute can best be described as the unique way in which a company translates insight into action. We believe that high-performance anatomy is what empowers companies to excel in their drive to out-execute their competition. Think of it as a predisposition to perform at the highest level. It is the tangible expression of the "vision and values" of an organization, especially those of its founders.

High-performance anatomy informs a company's identity and infuses every aspect of its operations as they unfold across business cycles, industry disruptions, and changes in leadership. Distinct from culture and organization design, high-performance anatomy defines a company across five dimensions.

1 Action-oriented insight

High performers thrive on action-oriented insight, proactively creating and shaping markets based on the relentless pursuit of customer-valued innovation. In the process, they achieve a near-perfect balance between execution and market focus. High-performance businesses also have a sharp focus on intangible assets and often develop innovative models to manage and measure them. They are keenly aware that future performance is not always driven by, or dependent on, resources that appear on a conventional balance sheet. This mindset enables high performers to deliberately manage their agendas to ensure a balance between today and tomorrow. Thus they demonstrate mastery of the creative tension between organizational stability and the need to adapt to constant change.

High-performance businesses are not only focused on pleasing their customers and exceeding shareholder expectations, their disciplined ability to execute is also the envy of their competitors. High performers value and believe in rigorous execution – in the adherence to budgets and deadlines that foster mutual trust and reliability throughout the organization (See Figure 1.6).

2 Exceptional productivity

High-performance businesses achieve extraordinary levels of produc-

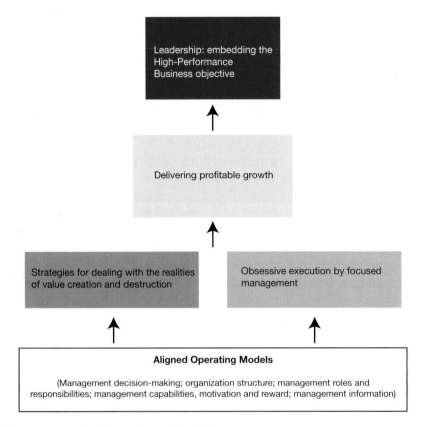

Figure 1.6 *Action-oriented insight*

tivity through the way they train, lead, and engage employees. All the CFOs featured in this book expressed a passion for developing people and their capabilities. High performers prove more effective than their competitors at exploiting the collective intelligence and motivation of their workforces. How? According to our research, there is a strong correlation between financial performance and the priority that organizations place on human capital development. For example, leading companies are far more likely than others to regularly measure the link between investments in people and business results. Moreover, their chief executive officers (CEOs) take a much more visible and direct role in people-development initiatives. In this way, high performers create what we call a "talent multiplier", which produces better results per dollar of investment in their workforces.

In the companies where we observed this trait, the CEO and CFO frequently take a visible and direct role in people-development initiatives. The goal is to cultivate employees who operate well above their title or level, magnifying their impact and individual contribution to workforce return on investment (ROI). The result: highly motivated employees who take the initiative – a multiplier effect that serves as a hard-to-imitate competitive advantage.

Take the Delaware-based MBNA Corporation, which issues credit cards to more than 50 million customers and manages assets worth more than $100 billion. Since its founding, the company has targeted upscale customers as part of "affinity groups" like dentists or association members, and set out to provide them with a superior customer service experience. The company's entire performance anatomy supports this mission and is reflected in every aspect of MBNA's operating style.

The company's talent multiplier can be seen in its careful recruiting of individuals who can be expected to excel in customer interactions. Recruiting is an intensive process that includes peer interviews to ensure fit. Behavior is reinforced by the company's generous benefits, and evidenced in its selection by *Fortune* magazine for five years in a row as one of the best companies to work for. MBNA's continuous renewal mindset is reflected in its requirement that all employees spend at least four hours per month "customer listening." "Customer satisfaction" scores are posted daily; individual incentives are tied to customer satisfaction, keeping the focus on ongoing, value-creating change. Even employee pay stubs are inscribed with the words "Brought to you by the customer." [7]

To create this type of deep commitment, aligning an organization's workforce with its strategic mission is essential. In our work with a wide range of companies, we have observed at least three successful approaches for accomplishing this. Some companies create alignment through the force of a strong and capable leader's personality. Other high performers achieve it through longtime collaboration within a core leadership team, such as those at Nokia and Walgreen Co. Alignment can also be created by infusing an organization with a shared sense of purpose. This is conveyed not through abstract mission or vision statements, but through leaders training leaders, active stewardship at all management levels, and the requirement that all employees personify the company's values in their daily work.

3 Information technology (IT) as a strategic asset
The third dimension of high-performance anatomy is the recognition

of IT's strategic value. High performers recognize IT as an enabler in generating innovation and new value creation. High performers regard information technology as a source of operational excellence and competitive advantage. They look beyond using IT as a tool for controlling costs, and view it as the means for capturing the business value of information. They are quick to adopt new technologies – and eliminate ones that don't work.

They also encourage employees to use IT intensively and creatively. There's not a big "rah-rah" celebration around the next technology initiative. And there's no hype or fancy names. The view that IT is a strategic asset is embedded in the company. Everyone in the organization sees it as a way of doing business. In contrast, poor performers allow their IT investments to be driven by replacement cycles. As a result, the lion's share of their IT investments is spent on running, fixing, and only incrementally improving existing systems, rather than on using them to deliver competitive advantage.

4 Meaningful performance metrics

Fourth, high performers manage a selective scorecard that is aimed at sustaining their competitive essence. This unique scorecard tracks critical tangibles, such as financial performance, but also emphasizes value-enhancing intangibles, such as employee motivation. High-performance businesses know specifically what drives their superior results and devise methods to measure what matters. Their performance metrics are broadly inclusive yet highly selective in their focus.

5 Effective change management

Fifth, high performers continually find ways to keep their organizations energized and employees on their toes. They do this by encouraging their employees to shoulder three simple but powerful responsibilities: doing their work well in order to accomplish key business objectives; improving the way their work is done by continuously striving to work smarter; and revolutionizing their work by seeking out the next wave of products and processes to boost performance. The CFOs interviewed for this book unanimously agreed that change is a constant that must be factored into any corporate agenda. Indeed, many of the CFOs we talked to said that change management was now a core competence of the finance professional.

CONTINUOUS IMPROVEMENT

High-performance businesses do not just expect success – they relentlessly pursue it through continuous improvement. They understand the dynamics of their industries better than their competitors and master their distinctive capabilities to achieve superior execution and results. In doing so, they successfully manage the creation of value. As we will see, the CFO plays a vital role in helping their companies develop the attributes that lead to high performance.

CFO INSIGHTS: LESSONS FROM THE MASTERS

There are three common building blocks to a high performance business, and the finance organization has a role to play in each of these.

- The first is market focus and position. Finance helps the company understand the economic fundamentals of its industry, how value is created – and how it is perceived by the rivals it competes with for investment capital. Finance uses insightful analytics to enable its enterprise to either defend or extend the market position it holds – and determine when to seize new opportunities in new markets.

- The second building block is the mastery of distinctive capabilities. Finance plays an active, front-line role in identifying and building these capabilities by participating in all major decision-making cycles. The CFO helps to determine which capabilities really make a competitive difference strategically. The finance team helps build these distinctive capabilities, whether they involve pricing effectiveness, a faster cash conversion cycle or more efficient use of capital.

- The third building block is what we call high-performance anatomy. From the CFO's perspective, supporting this area requires a focus on the performance management system embedded within an organization. Finance executives have a major role to play in making sure that their entire organization understands how to deploy robust systems to monitor what's going on in the business and how to deliver timely, accurate information to decision makers. Finance must also have the discipline to enforce resource allocation decisions and performance management requirements across the business.

REFERENCES

1 Accenture, Measuring High Performance, *Outlook Journal*, Sept 2004. http://www.accenture.com

2 Peggy A. Salz, Sustainable Business Success is Based on Three Key Building Blocks: Sharply Defined Strategies are Vital, *Wall Street Journal*, February 15, 2005. http://www.wsj.com

3 Corporate Strategy Board, Stall Points: Barriers to Growth for the Large Corporate Enterprise, *Corporate Advisory Board*, 1998.

4 Peggy Anne Salz, Size Alone Doesn't Spell Success: Networking Is Needed in the Interdependent Business Ecosystems of Today, *Wall Street Journal*, March 3, 2005. http://www.wsj.com

5 Roberta Cozza and Ben Wood, Market Share: Smartphones, Worldwide, 3Q04, *Gartner Dataquest*, December 22, 2004. http://www.gartner.com

6 Peggy A. Salz, Sustained Success Hinges on Mastering Key Business Functions and Creating Distinctive Capabilities, *Wall Street Journal*, April 19, 2005.

7 Tim Breene and Paul F. Nunes, Balance, Alignment and Renewal: Understanding Competitive Essence, *Outlook Journal*, February 2005. http://www.accenture.com

CHAPTER 2

High-Performance Leadership

HIGH-PERFORMANCE LEADERSHIP THROUGH THE LENS OF THE CFO

Pat Erlandson, CFO
UnitedHealth Group

In an industry faced with challenges, from escalating medical costs and employer demands, to identifying more affordable healthcare solutions to maturing markets, and intensive regulatory pressure, UnitedHealth Group (UnitedHealth) has thrived and risen to the top. In terms of total return to shareholders, UnitedHealth has consistently outperformed its peers – achieving robust revenue growth, increasing operating margins, and generating strong cash flow – all despite tumultuous industry conditions.

In UnitedHealth's 2004 Annual Report Letter to Shareholders, Chairman and CEO Dr. William McGuire states: "UnitedHealth Group has been – and will continue to be – an important innovator and advocate for addressing the issues of quality, affordability, accessibility and usability in health care." This is an organization with superb leadership. Its success can be traced not only to its focus on building shareholder value, but also to its role as an advocate committed to improving health care in our society. Pat Erlandson, UnitedHealth's CFO, is a valued, highly visible member of its outstanding leadership team. The contributions Pat's finance team has made to

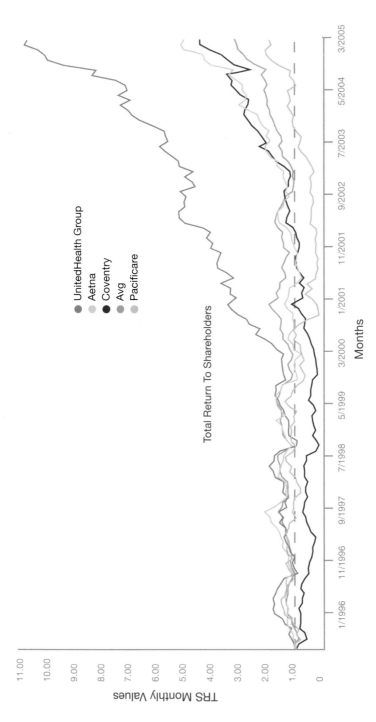

Figure 2.1 *UnitedHealth Group's performance relative to its peers.*
Source: Accenture analysis

UnitedHealth's results convincingly demonstrate the impact of a high-performance finance organization on a company's growth, profitability and returns to owners.

In 1997 – less than a decade ago – Pat Erlandson joined Minneapolis-based UnitedHealth Group Inc. at the start of a financial climb that has elevated this understated healthcare company to a top five ranking on the BusinessWeek Top 50 for the past three years.[1] Previously a partner with Arthur Andersen, Erlandson joined UnitedHealth Group as a vice president in charge of planning, process and information channels. Now CFO of an organization that has grown from less than $10 billion in annual revenues in the mid 1990s to $45 billion, Erlandson has a unique perspective on high-performance leadership. Listening to this Minneapolis native, one could easily get the impression that the timing of his joining UnitedHealth Group was simply coincident with the start of the company's surge in growth. However, as the story unfolds, it becomes increasingly evident that both Erlandson and his finance team have been key factors in helping UnitedHealth Group grow into a healthcare giant serving more than 55 million Americans, and handling more than $60 billion in annual healthcare spending.

About six months before Pat Erlandson came to UnitedHealth Group, CEO Bill McGuire hired current President and Chief Operating Officer Steve Hemsley as his partner in the UnitedHealth office of the Chair. Bill and Steve were busy assessing the strategic assets acquired and developed by UnitedHealth and recruiting other top members of their leadership team. Starting in 1997, Erlandson supported these executives as they formulated a high-performance journey that began with a fundamental reassessment of UnitedHealth's structure. As Erlandson recalls: "1997 was significant because we began to align the businesses to the markets in a way that was very different. We realigned our leadership, assets and competencies into five distinct, fully functional and accountable operating segments focused on large distinct health care markets. The idea was to organize our capabilities in a far more focused way to serve these markets in a distinctive, measurable, accountable value-added way."

Initially, Erlandson viewed his role as the implementer of Bill McGuire's and Steve Hemsley's vision. As he recalls: "My first job was to take the vision and help turn it into reality." There were three major components to this implementation. First, UnitedHealth Group took its combined organization – then known only as United-Healthcare – and its income statement, balance sheet, people, products capabilities and customers, and split them into five distinct entities. "We created five fully functional, freestanding businesses, each with its own CEO and management team and staff right down the line – IT, human capital, operations, legal and finance."

Next, Hemsley, Erlandson and his newly-assembled core finance team focused on creating stronger financial discipline by instituting a series of "Rules of the Road," internal controls, and management guidelines. In his view: "Getting everyone to interact according to the same set of values was vital."

Finally, Erlandson and his team created UnitedHealth Group's core governance bodies consisting of leadership from the newly-formed businesses and management processes for strategic, business, financial, capital, technology and human capital planning. These governance bodies and processes have evolved and still exist today. Erlandson believes that "It was necessary to formally define and clearly communicate these processes and governance bodies because we had an entire organization that was changing the way it did business, with people moving into new positions within these five newly-formed businesses. To add to the challenge, each of the newly-formed businesses had much more transparency in terms of their publicly reported results and accountability for delivering against our public commitments."

Throughout the late 1990s, UnitedHealth Group delivered steadily improving financial results, and Erlandson and the leadership team continued to build out the new organizational platform – including repeating this process to create a sixth free-standing business in 2002. As UnitedHealth grew, Erlandson received increased formal responsibility in finance. In 1999, he was promoted to corporate controller. As controller – and later as CFO – Erlandson has continued to focus on many of his early priorities, such as people development, and operational and capital performance management across all the businesses. UnitedHealth Group's revenue earnings, cash flows and return on equity continued to grow. By 2000, as Figure 2.1 indicates, the focused company from Minneapolis began distancing itself from the competition, especially in the area of total return to shareholders.

Asked to explain how UnitedHealth Group has been able to increase its stock price tenfold since 1998, Erlandson cites these factors. "First, a very clear, unwavering strategy of being a diversified health and well-being company, facilitating the organization of resources across the broad expanse of health care. Through the

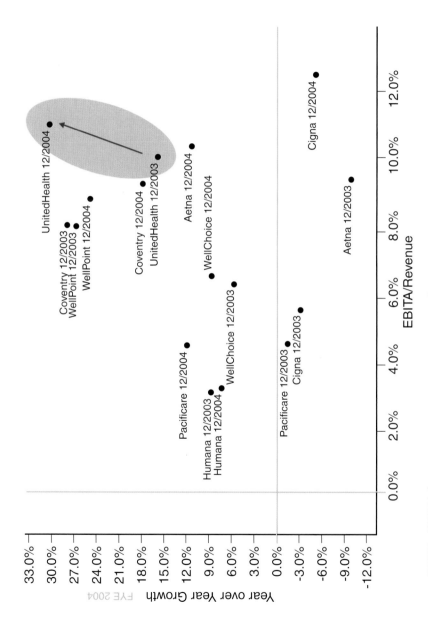

Figure 2.2   *UHG's EBITA/revenue vs year over year growth*
Source: Accenture analysis

leadership and strategy of Bill McGuire and Steve Hemsley, we aspired to be something much more than an HMO or a health insurer.

"The diversified health and well-being business has been built around three competencies:

- *networks and health advancement;*
- *technology-based, large-scale transactional capabilities; and*
- *knowledge and information.*

"All the things we have done have been an extension of this strategy. The more than 75 acquisitions made and integrated since the mid-1990s have enhanced our capabilities in these areas. Likewise, the organizational realignment we went through to create five independent, fully functional and separately accountable operating segments was an extension of this strategy.

"Another factor contributing to this success has been an intense focus on innovation and execution. We have invested heavily in technology-driven business improvements, spending in excess of $.25 billion on initiatives designed to automate transactions; replace labor intensive activities with technology while at the same time reducing cost and improving quality; create internet portals with our key constituents, including customers, employers, care providers and brokers to enable simpler electronic communication and commerce; establish large-scale databases, and one of the largest, most robust clinical databases. With respect to execution, as we have assembled the assets and built the capabilities noted above, we are relentless on driving strong operating results, managing our capital wisely, generating significant operating cash flows, continuing to invest in the business and returning excess capital and improving our returns to shareholders through share repurchase. The final three factors are people development, planning and performance management, and capital management." In his view, all are equally important to United-Health Group's high performance.

Listening to Pat Erlandson talk about people development, you sense that United-Health Group thinks about this area in a way that differs from most organizations. For example, Erlandson uses terms like "best available athlete" and behavior "DNA," and notes that 80% of UnitedHealth's executive leadership team hires in the past five years have come from outside the healthcare industry. Erlandson adds, "One of the keys to our success that began in the late 1990s had to do with the recruitment of exceptionally talented people from a wide range of industries rather than specifically from the healthcare field. We have a very strong pool of multidisciplinary talent here, and this continues to be a key ingredient in our success."

When it comes to developing finance capabilities, Erlandson has supported UnitedHealth's growth by attracting and retaining finance leaders who reflect the needs of the fast-paced, decentralized organization he helped shape back in 1997. Erlandson describes his finance leaders as "hands-on, detailed operators with a strong controls background who get their hands dirty, and truly understand the business. There is a strong orientation towards control. At the same time, we need them to balance the amount of control we oversee with their role as change agents." Erlandson's approach is both empowering and effective – and has been driven by a very small corporate finance group. As he puts it, "Almost everything has been embedded in the businesses, which has resulted in very strong finance people throughout our operations and a lean, cost-effective corporate finance team."

Planning and performance management has been and continues to be a key factor in UnitedHealth Group's exceptional growth story. To Erlandson, planning and performance management at UnitedHealth is all about "detailed work to develop a shared set of commitments. You can't run a business this broad and this transparent to the external market without establishing a joint commitment between corporate finance and our leadership teams in the businesses." In addition to shaping and launching UnitedHealth's core performance management processes in the late 1990s, Erlandson has continued to drive planning and performance management disciplines and behavior in UnitedHealth's business segments. Three key actions include 1) integrating planning and performance management with day-to-day execution, 2) defining performance management broadly to include business risk management, and 3) providing the right tools and finance support to UnitedHealth Group's businesses.

Erlandson describes his approach: "We are obsessed with delivering on commitments. We do a very good job of planning up front and then reinforcing this with rigorous controls emanating from the governance structure and management processes I described earlier. These include a disciplined planning process – and a very strong control and risk management process designed to help us identify problems and issues in their early stages, and then deploy mitigation activities within our planning process. Our risk management process is tied into our business planning *process so tightly that you almost can't separate the two, because a lot of business planning is identifying the obstacles that stand between you and what you want to accomplish, and then figuring out plans to mitigate those obstacles."*

In addition to people development and planning and performance management, Erlandson views capital planning and management as one of the most important factors in UnitedHealth Group's high performance. *"Since 1997, we have continued our strong operating performance, but we've become better stewards of our capital. I think this has driven the value you see coming through in the TRS (total return to shareholders) numbers."* Not surprisingly, Erlandson has made this area one of his top personal priorities: *"Capital management is where I spend most of my time: monitoring and being really engaged with the businesses as we manage working capital, optimize our capital structure with appropriate debt leverage, plan and monitor technology-enabled business investments and acquisitions to generate returns exceeding business specific weighted average cost of capital hurdle rates, managing to efficient regulatory capital levels and redeploying excess regulated capital, and using share repurchase as an efficient use of capital. Capital management is critical. Deploying investment across six businesses in an efficient and effective way is central to ensuring that we get good returns from each. These are decisive factors that have enabled us to continue to experience strong, sustained growth from $17 billion in revenues in 1998 to $45 billion today."*

While personally involving himself in the capital management process, Erlandson has also helped drive high performance by strengthening capital management skills within his finance organization. As he notes: *"One of the key areas of competence we developed was our ability to deal with large capital projects while maintaining a focus on delivering projected return on capital. We had to build project finance analytical teams as well as project management teams. We put in place a project finance management oversight team that goes beyond project management. It establishes an end-to-end process that revolves around a very solid business case. It plans and tracks capital investment, capital returns, internal rate of return, etc. – and monitors and communicates all this."* Consistent with his overall approach to enhancing finance capabilities, Erlandson has built up these skills where they need to be – in UnitedHealth's businesses. He notes: *"We have only a few people in corporate. Our corporate finance team is charged with sharpening finance skills in the businesses that have responsibility for operational execution."*

As Erlandson looks back on his time with UnitedHealth Group, he is pleased to see that many of the early programs he helped McGuire and Hemsley establish are still around in even more robust and useful forms. He also appreciates the way his finance organization has evolved over time to meet the changing needs of United-Health's diverse markets.

As recounted by Pat Erlandson, UnitedHealth Group's journey to becoming a high-performance business is both impressive and enlightening. How a relatively small healthcare company based in Minneapolis moved to No.1 on *Fortune* magazine's 2005 list of the Most Admired Health Care Companies[2] is testimony to the importance of thinking innovatively, focusing on the basics, and giving people the tools, the incentives, and the room to succeed.

This chapter describes the UnitedHealth Group and Pat Erlandson's approach in great depth, not only because his company has achieved exceptional growth, but because Erlandson himself exemplifies high-performance finance leadership in action. First and foremost, this dynamic CFO has played a pivotal role in leading a high-performance finance team in evolving UnitedHealth Group to enable it to deliver against increasingly ambitious performance targets. Second, Erlandson and his team introduced greater financial discipline and a robust governance structure to UnitedHealth to promote shared values, transparency, and accountability. Next, Erlandson supported UnitedHealth's growth by building a corps of skilled, hands-on finance executives who have played leadership roles in embedding finance expertise throughout UnitedHealth's operations. And finally, Erlandson has consistently displayed an expansive view of his role as CFO – allowing that role to evolve as his company reshaped itself. From an early focus on core financial issues, over time he has devoted increasing attention to people development, performance management, and capital stewardship.

What is it about high-performance leaders that makes them stand out? How should you be thinking about your own evolving finance role and your ability to be a high-performance leader?

Unlike so many "how to" leadership books written over the past decade, the focus here is not on approaching high-performance leadership from a prescriptive, "one size fits all" standpoint. Our experience and research have demonstrated that there are many different paths to becoming an effective finance leader in a high-performance business. The CFOs we spoke with achieved this goal by improving their individual abilities as finance executives and by developing the full capabilities of their finance organization. In your role as a finance executive, our goal is to help you better anticipate, decipher, and manage the opportunities to achieve exceptional performance.

If you're already a CFO, imagine you have just taken over as CFO at a new company twice the size of your previous employer. If you're an aspiring CFO, imagine that you have just been promoted to this position at your company. In either case, what is your first order of business?

CASE STUDY
Beginning the journey to high performance

In early 2002, the situation facing Follin Smith, Executive Vice President, CFO and Chief Administrative Officer of Constellation Energy Group (for a more extensive interview, see Chapter 8), was somewhat similar to the scenarios described above – with a large dose of industry upheaval thrown into the corporate mix. Constellation had just brought in Smith as its first-ever externally recruited CFO. It was January and the outlook was chilly: Enron had just crashed and the investment community was predicting the implosion of the deregulated energy industry. What to do?

Smith began at the starting point of any high-performance journey – by developing a detailed understanding of how her company was going to make money – and then articulating that understanding clearly and decisively. In this case, her audience was a deeply skeptical investment community. She and Constellation Energy's new CEO were making their presentation at a tense time, when the Enron situation had raised serious questions about the future of other companies in the energy sector. Working together, she and her CEO gave an extremely detailed picture of their company's direction and resources. Their transparent, meticulous approach fostered confidence in Constellation's direction at a time of intense industry upheaval.

As important as visions and three-year plans are, high performance ultimately depends on the ability to deliver against near-term results based on your existing business model. A CFO who has a deep understanding of his/her company's business, competitors' businesses, and industry value chains can be invaluable to a CEO. With a CFO like this at the finance helm, a company's chief executive can spend more time focusing on strategic planning and future growth opportunities.

One of the popular mantras in finance today is the call for CFOs to "maximize growth." The CFO of a global beverage company put into perspective why the call to *optimize* growth may be more on point, when he noted that "growth opportunities must be balanced with fiscal rigor" (see Chapter 8, *Enterprise Risk Management)*. This CFO's insightful comments highlight the risks of being seduced into overly rapid, reactive, pressurized growth. The distinction between *maximizing* and *optimizing* growth is subtle, but important. The push to *maximize* growth frequently results in indiscriminate, artificially accelerated expansion: growth for the sake of growth. This type of growth is often externally driven. In contrast, *optimizing* growth suggests a different path – one in which a company chooses strategic, astutely timed, well-paced expansion. This type of growth tends to be organic and internally generated.

We believe it is the CFO's responsibility to help his/her company optimize growth *and* total shareholder returns. This balancing requires some important trade-offs, which we will discuss later. Nevertheless, the starting point for optimizing growth and total shareholder returns is your *mindset*: how you view your business and your finance organization in relation to that business.

As Pat Erlandson of UnitedHealth Group vividly demonstrated, high-performance CFOs tend to think differently about both their businesses and the role that finance plays in contributing to corporate growth. In our CFO interviews, we've observed an "outside-in" mentality. Exceptional finance leaders view finance through the lens of the competitive business space – *not* the other way around. They are able to step outside the confines of their discipline and see their role from a broader perspective. This mindset helps finance *stay in rhythm with the business* – a key attribute of high-performance finance.

Staying in rhythm with the business begins with an in-depth understanding of an enterprise's value chain and operating model. This grasp of broader operating dynamics is exemplified in Bill McGuire, Steve Hemsley and Pat Erlandson's decision to infuse finance resources into UnitedHealth Group's independent businesses. The "hands on" knowledge that results from this approach enables finance leaders to anticipate the needs of their business, build capabilities in time to support those needs, and avoid wasting precious resources on capabilities that their business does not need or is not ready for. High-performance leadership from the perspective of the CFO is not always about building a world-class finance organization. In fact, this may be completely the *wrong* strategy for a business at a particular point in time. High-performance finance leaders focus on supporting business growth, creating value, and exploiting opportunities, *not* on inwardly focused, functional agendas.

CASE STUDY

Pacing the introduction of new finance approaches

Since the late 1990s, one global metal producer has completed international acquisitions and spin-offs, shifted its emphasis to the more consumer-oriented downstream part of its business, and increased its annual sales significantly. While supporting all these initiatives, the CFO and his finance organization were simultaneously driving an EVA® program out into the business, converting to US GAAP, adopting Sarbanes-Oxley (SOX) for 700 reporting entities, and instituting value-based management principles.

It is value-based management that has had the biggest influence on how executives view their business. As the CFO points out, "It's basically a fact-based analysis. We determine the fundamental value drivers of each business from a business standpoint, a market-standpoint, and a competitor standpoint to establish whether or not the business can earn its cost of capital, and maximize investment returns over and above that. Once we've analyzed this, we can figure out whether or not we are managing it correctly, whether we can change our competitive posture, and how to define our source of competitive advantage."

To better understand how finance has evolved to support the needs of the business, we asked the CFO to describe perceptions of finance leadership today compared with the late 1990s. According to him, the way business executives perceive finance is "totally different." He goes on to say, "Historically, finance was considered an administrative support function for reporting purposes. Today, the finance function operates very differently. Each finance director is now the 'financial conscience' for the head of each business. He is the one who makes sure that the business leader understands the value drivers and can see where the business is creating value or is destroying value. The proof of the pudding is the people reviews we conduct every year with each business president. In all cases, the finance director of each business is clearly the number two person. This was not the case before."

The CFO ends his discussion by talking about the importance of not moving too fast as a business, while also providing a friendly reminder to us as consultants about the importance of timing. Looking ahead, he notes, "Our next evolution is to move to the shared services model – it's a 'no-brainer.' However, this was not the right approach in recent years, when the focus was on M&As and restructuring. Who wants to talk about shared services when you're spinning off a business that's been in the company for 40 years? You've got to put things into perspective and stay focused."

MAINTAINING FISCAL DISCIPLINE IN THE FACE OF TRADE-OFFS

Earlier, we referred to the trade-offs that must be balanced in any drive to optimize growth and total shareholder returns. These include short vs long-term results, innovation vs controls, and growth vs capital discipline. Very few companies – high performance or not – can escape the need to make difficult decisions around these issues. Constellation Energy Group, however, has figured out how to use its market position to minimize the tensions that these kinds of trade-offs can trigger.

As Executive Vice President, CFO and Chief Administrative Officer, Follin Smith explains: "We've been able to do both: invest for the long-term while delivering current results because we're in such an enviable market situation. Why are we there? Because we've seen an opportunity when nobody else has seen it. Anecdotally, what we're hearing on both the wholesale and retail side is that our competitors are losing out to us in places where they have no margin. And we know we're making historic margins. It's like Dell pulling together all the logistical elements and putting together a commodity product – and then selling it in such a superior way that no one can compete with it from a cost perspective. Dell can pass on lower costs to the customer, which helps it take more market share and gets this virtuous cycle going so that it can lower its cost per unit. We think we've entered that virtuous cycle in our wholesale arm."

As demonstrated by Pat Erlandson at UnitedHealth Group, one of the keys to maintaining financial discipline in the face of challenging trade-offs is establishing rigorous governance bodies and capital management oversight groups. Although the C-suite handles many trade-off decisions – certainly the larger ones – individuals at all levels of an organization are faced with tactical trade-off choices on a daily basis. How does a CFO help instill an appreciation for these types of trade-off within the finance function and throughout his/her organization?

The CFO of a global metals producer found that a well-known capital metric helped his cause. EVA® has been a very useful tool in helping people throughout his company understand the value drivers underlying decisions. "I think everybody understands the EVA® calculation," notes the CFO, "and the relationship between their activities and the cost of capital." By embedding this within his company, the CFO has helped ensure that decisions at every level will be made in a fact-based, value-focused way. For the CFO of a global beverage company, corporate values are the touchstone of the decision-making process, especially in new regional markets like India and China. As he notes, "In this part of the world you can operate in a number of ways that are unique to the region, but at the end of the day, there is a defined way that our company does business."

THE CFO AS CHANGE AGENT AND TEAM BUILDER

Regardless of the approach used, the comments above highlight the role of the CFO as a change agent, both within the finance function and within a company as a whole. In our experience, high-performance leaders in finance not only have a strong personal drive to excel, they also have the ability to reach out and motivate. While they are almost always outstanding individual contributors, these exceptional CFOs also distinguish themselves by their ability to lead through others. Additionally, they tend to define their roles broadly and fluidly in response to the evolving needs of their total business. Finally, they are self-aware enough to seek out and secure complementary skills in building their finance leadership teams. The core message: If you want to be a greater force for change in your company, your focus should not be limited to improving yourself; it should encompass improving the primary tool at your disposal – your finance organization.

Consider the view of Bob Young, the CFO of Teradata: "There are a lot of perspectives about what a CFO is. However, if you ask the most effective CFOs how they think about their role within their organizations, it's a lot broader than simple accounting. A transformation is taking place in the role of the CFO. One of the interesting things I do is help sell our products. Because I'm a user I go out and talk to other CFOs about our product offerings. I'm seeing that CFOs have started to figure out that their role is changing. They need to adapt their personal behavior and time allocation, as well as the skills in their organization, to help deliver more broadly based services to their organizations."

As his comments indicate, Bob Young thinks very expansively about his role as CFO. In addition to overseeing his company's finance resources, he is knowledgeable enough about its product offerings to actually sell products to other CFOs. He brings his finance background to his customer relationships and his deepening understanding of Teradata's front-line business activities to his finance work. Underscoring his point about the CFO's changing role is the fact that Young was given responsibility for pricing at Teradata, and has built up a pricing center of excellence at the company.

After a CFO assesses the potential for broadening his/her role, the next logical area to focus on is the finance leadership team. BP's Director for Strategy Accounting Services, Russ Taruscio, summarizes the importance of team building by saying, "In my view, having a strong CFO and senior finance leadership team is critical to BP's success in becoming one of the most powerful and wealthiest companies in the world."

For Pat Erlandson of UnitedHealth Group, his role as CFO and the responsibilities of his top finance team are carefully delineated. As Erlandson explains, "We give divisional CFOs the autonomy to run their businesses in partnership with their respective CEO and COO. From a personal perspective, I really have almost no responsibility for financial reporting because I have a very strong controller, and very strong tax and treasury leaders. So my focus is very much on planning, measurement, and accountability – and on understanding the businesses well enough to work with them to set very aggressive commitments and then make sure that they are achieved. Capital management is where I spend most of my time now."

The CFO of a global metals producer has had a major impact on his company's growth through his deep involvement in building its finance capabilities. The finance team he built grew along with the company, from fewer than 100 to almost 2000 people around the world. The CFO was very involved in hiring senior finance executives from a range of industries to help drive global expansion. As he observed, these executives were hired not just as "subject matter experts, but as change agents." According to the CFO, their abilities in this arena have been instrumental in the company's success.

RECRUITING AND RETAINING TALENT: A CFO IMPERATIVE

Attracting and retaining top finance talent has become an increasingly critical issue – and surfaced as a key concern among the CFOs we interviewed. Two recent trends are driving this towards the top of the CFO agenda. Externally, the market for top finance talent has heated up with the advent of new regulations, such as SOX. The finance function's increasing complexity has made it more challenging and expensive to find and recruit new talent. Retaining exceptional executives is also an issue, due in part to the surge in business process outsourcing (BPO). As more and more finance organizations adopt BPO, many CFOs are wondering where they will find their next generation of leaders.

CFO Bob Young analyzes the people development challenges brought on by outsourcing: "A lot of companies who have used outsourcing to attack their cost structure have simply stopped recruiting finance people in any quantities. This creates an imbalance in your experience levels, because you have a gap – maybe 3, 4, or 5 years – in which you haven't hired anybody of consequence. As a result, in some cases, you have senior people doing junior-level jobs. Some day we're going to pay for this."

Young goes on to talk about the shifting proportion of decision-support roles vs transaction processing roles brought on by outsourcing: "I think it's both a problem and an opportunity. As you rotate more of your human capital into decision support, you can have a resource gap. Technical accounting does not necessarily transfer into more strategic areas. So I think we've got a training and recruitment challenge."

No one solution can completely address the recruiting issues that CFOs face. However, there are several factors to weigh as you think about your people development programs and practices.

First, consider the degree of structure around your development programs and determine whether it is adequate or not. If most of your training is informal and "on the job," you risk losing top talent by not investing in their future development. For example, the CFO of a global beverage company made special note of his company's formal training program, which operates on two levels, regional and international. In the regional program, promising future leaders are trained in a wide range of areas, from corporate values to strategic decision making. At the international level, the company's CFO is directly involved in the program's planning and execution. This top management commitment is key to successful recruitment.

Second, adopt a strong point of view about the finance leaders and capabilities that you want to develop – and then structure your program to reflect this. UnitedHealth Group's Erlandson notes: "Back in 1998–99, we did our massive reengineering effort largely through our operational and functional leadership, but we didn't have critical change management and program management capabilities in-house at the time. We knew that the company was going to rapidly and continuously evolve. Therefore, we decided to build those kinds of capabilities into our finance team. We proactively developed them, making change management a core competence in finance at UnitedHealth."

Finally, if a large number of your finance processes are outsourced to a third-party provider, consider a joint talent development program. As Teradata's CFO, Bob Young notes: "Having a joint talent development scheme sounds like a good idea. It may be that everyone on the client side doesn't need to rotate through a shared service center, but there is a set of people that needs the hard-core, hands-on transaction accounting experience so that they understand how it works and what it takes to get it done. Clients always need people who understand how outsourcing operates."

In addition to developing capabilities within their finance teams and training future finance leaders, one of the ways that high-performance finance executives lead through others is by helping to infuse finance acumen throughout their organizations. We saw Pat Erlandson do this at UnitedHealth Group. It's also a priority for Teradata's Bob Young: "I think there's an overlap in the skills that brand managers and really competent financial analysts need. They both need a core set of shared skills. The career finance person may have a deeper set to rely on, but it's very hard for us to engage with a brand manager who doesn't have basic finance skills. If this financial base doesn't exist, then an engagement is going to be impaired." Young formally helps build in this knowledge across Teradata through the formal cross-pollination of his finance personnel with executives in other functions.

MAXIMIZING YOUR OPPORTUNITIES FOR IMPACT

Exceptional CFOs look beyond their individual finance skills in building their finance team's capabilities and increasing finance acumen throughout their enterprise. This expansive view enables them to contribute fully and lastingly to their companies' success. In closing, we would like to focus on *you* – in your evolving finance role – and how to maximize your opportunities for contributing to the success of your business. Blythe McGarvie, the President of Leadership for International Finance, has developed a framework for leadership effectiveness called the "FISO Factor" that many business executives find useful. McGarvie's "Fit In, Stand Out" model is based on the concept that two drivers power business leadership: integration (fit in) and transformation (stand out).

According to McGarvie, mastering these two leadership-building drivers will enable you to build the support required to take your company beyond the status quo. To become an effective, influential change agent, says McGarvie, you must first establish a credible and respected leadership platform. Only from this solid foundation can you effectively advocate change and promote transformation. The FISO leadership framework is outlined below.

Fitting in is the process of integrating oneself into the culture and structure of a company. It involves discovering the distinctive ways in which things get done and acting as a team player – someone who is viewed as dependable, possessing valued skills, and committed to group goals. To "fit in" refers to the ability to support, maintain, and work within existing systems.

Standing out is the process of becoming an advocate for change and mobilizing resources to promote organizational transformation. It involves knowing how and when to take the lead, trigger change, and push the bound of performance to achieve successful enterprise growth. To "stand out" means to lead the system beyond its established boundaries.[3]

Within this chapter and throughout this book, we offer numerous examples of CFOs who have learned to work within the cultural bounds of their organizations while also honing their ability to stretch those boundaries and move beyond them to promote growth and resilience. Their experiences highlight the importance of building a solid base of support before undertaking broad change programs. Leading a major transformation demands meticulous timing and planning. The CFO insights and experiences captured in our interviews offer valuable guideposts for understanding when to "fit in" and when to "stand out" so that you and your finance organization can stay in solid rhythm with your business – and propel it to high performance.

CFO INSIGHTS: LESSONS FROM THE MASTERS

- High-performance CFOs build a reputation that can be extended to their finance teams by developing a robust, resilient personal platform. That platform is based on their ability to earn trust within their organization for both their finance acumen and their deep understanding of the value drivers of their business.

- Building on the solid foundation they've created, high-performance CFOs pace change within their finance organization to the rhythm of change within their enterprise. They know when to "fit in" and integrate within existing systems – and when to "stand out." When needed, they provide a counterintuitive point of view and challenge conventional wisdom in order to promote growth and drive through better results in their enterprise.

- Effective CFOs excel at leading through others. They extend their platform to the entire finance organization. They give priority to recruiting talented people with diverse backgrounds and perspectives. They are deeply committed to developing their finance talent pool and extending the capabilities of their finance organization beyond the basic blocking and tackling of accounting and reporting.

- High-performance CFOs devote significant resources to assembling a team that not only drives superior execution and results in their finance organization, but whose members can act as change agents and trusted advisors. These finance advisors know how to mobilize the business-support resources needed to produce better, more informed decision making – and to create and capture value across their enterprise.

REFERENCES

1 BusinessWeek, Top 50, 2005. http://www.businessweek.com

2 Fortune, America's Most Admired Health Care Companies, 2005. http://www.fortune.com

3 Blythe McGarvie, *Fit In, Stand Out: Mastering the FISO Factor*, McGraw-Hill, October 2005. http://www.FISOFactor.com

CHAPTER 3

Masters of Finance Framework

DELIVERING OUTSTANDING GROWTH AND PROFITABILITY

Jim Schneider, Senior Vice President and CFO
Dell Inc.

Dell continues to redefine the competitive rules of play in the many industries and customer segments it serves. It is recognized as the global leader in the direct-sale computer market and as an innovator in online sales and supply chain effectiveness. Its ability to pioneer new business models as a means of delivering superior growth, profitability, and returns on investment is well documented.

Globalization, value chain complexity, accelerated change, technology obsolescence; flexibility in cost structure – these are some of the pressing industry issues that Dell has successfully managed by focusing on the right business imperatives.

Since 1996, Dell has delivered double-digit revenue growth and excellent TRS, consistently outpacing its peer group (see Figures 3.1 & 3.2). Dell's strong spread performance and underlying "best in class" ROIC are clear indicators of management's ability to generate exceptional investor returns. We've chosen to feature Dell here as both a high-performance business and a widely recognized "master of finance."

Jim Schneider, Dell's SVP and CFO, shared his thoughts with us on how his fast-paced industry affects the way he and his team engage with the business. "Dell's

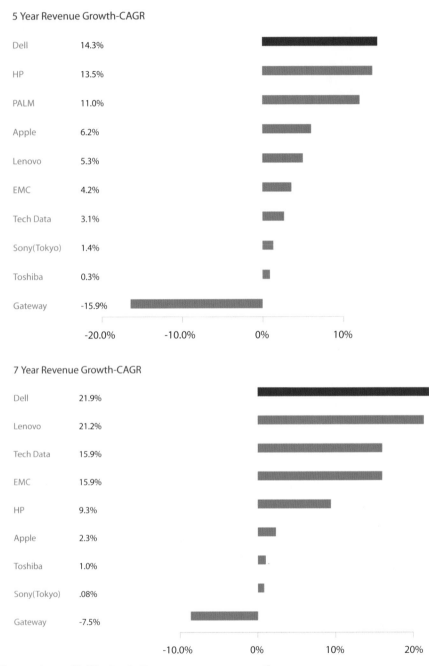

Figure 3.1 *Dell's 5- & 7-year revenue growth*
Source: Accenture analysis

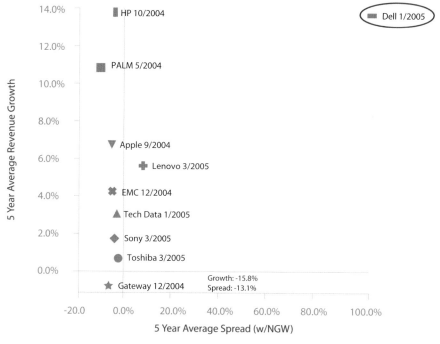

Figure 3.2 *Dell's performance relative to its peers*
Source: Accenture analysis

finance capabilities are tightly integrated with our overall enterprise strategy. This is predicated on leveraging the Dell 'direct' business model for the markets that we can dominate. Since the mid-1980s, we have grown from a start-up company to one that is now worth more than $100 billion with strong market positions across the globe. Today, one in six PCs shipped in the world is a Dell; in the US market, it's one in three.

"During our formative years, we developed strong finance capabilities and competencies that go beyond the basic block and tackling of accounting and finance. These continue to mature and evolve as the business grows. Our most widely publicized finance capability is our working capital management process. Dell differs from its competitors in that we make every single machine to a specific order while the rest of the industry produces them to match a sales forecast. The advantages of our model are tangible and enormous. For instance, we carry only five days of inventory.

"In the finance area, our low-cost operations and partnering approach reinforce a deeply embedded value-centered culture. Finance is a trusted business partner and is intimately involved in strategic, tactical, and operational decision making. We continue to develop our business analytical capabilities based on the principle of what we call 'profit pools.' End-to-end process connectivity enables us to provide real-time reporting to all our front-line management teams. This has been called 'frictionless commerce.' Lastly, we are immensely proud of the high-caliber talent of our finance professionals.

"Dell has built strong finance operations based on deployment of the shared services model; we believe that this is a prerequisite for finance mastery. Efficient, effective transaction processing means that our controls are both robust and resilient. As a result, we avoid the issues that distract other companies because their finance processes and systems are fragmented.

"At Dell, transaction is embedded in everyday operational activity and highly automated via service centers in Slovakia, Panama, China, Morocco, and India. These centers have standard processes built into their DNA. We have strong internal controls and a robust compliance environment, but they do not take over the finance agenda to the exclusion of higher finance capabilities."

Jim described Dell's strong value-centered culture: "Our DNA promotes an expectation of great performance from our people and this value is a norm. All new hires are brought to our headquarters in Austin, Texas, for 90 days, where we instill our culture in them from day one. We have a constructive passion for winning in everything we do. Continuous improvement is basic to our culture. It's reflected in how we build a global workforce with diverse backgrounds and skills – and how we maintain the highest standards of integrity, develop leaders, and encourage personal accountability.

"Finance is a trusted business partner and our finance professionals have a seat at the table when key decisions are made. Our executive committee meetings have presentations from several finance folks, and their visibility is very high. We believe that our business decision-making framework and our ability to execute at speed are among our most important capabilities. Our profit pool approach is central to our decision-making framework. We assess the profit (not revenue) available in a market segment and draft concrete plans to capture a healthy portion of the profit pool, discounting the pool for the competitive impact of 'the Dell Effect' that typi-

cally occurs when we enter a market. Only when there is strong confidence in the plan to capture the profit pool do we move. But when we decide to move, we do so rapidly.

"At Dell, decisions are made rapidly – even if we don't have complete data. We get the best data we can and do not drag the process out waiting for perfect information. Dell is a relatively flat organization. We don't need to go through layer upon layer of approvals to get something done.

"Compared with other companies, we move very quickly. One example was our speed to market on personal digital assistants. Early on, we moved slowly while our competitors wasted a lot of money in defining the market. We've capitalized on this by entering a more defined market at a much lower price point. Timing market entry has been a very valuable tool for Dell in efficiently capturing the maximum share of targeted profit pools.

"We demand exceptional granularity from our data warehouse, which enables us to provide real-time reporting. We pull the latest information into a dashboard every morning at 6 a.m. This gives us field-specific intelligence about margins and our product line sales, which is vital since demand, supply, and competitive patterns change daily. Top executives can review order dollars and units by region, in about eight categories straight away, and can see if everything is OK or what they need to change. The level of granularity and transparency equips decision makers everywhere to spot trends and act before the competition has even noticed. Managing performance in this way is key to our success.

"Our reporting capability is not just about real-time information leveraging standardized processes. Due to our business model, we are closer to the customer and can see market changes faster than competitors – and we act on new information at speed."

The last area that Jim talked about was the high-caliber finance professionals that Dell is able to recruit, develop, and retain. "We are good at hiring and we promise good career progression to everyone who joins us. I would rather hire an MBA with general business skills and experience than an accountant. If you evaluated our finance operations staff and checked their résumés, you would see that a traditional accountant would be a good fit with only a few of our reporting roles. We want our executives to be creative thinkers who'll say, 'I want to move the business and *understand how it reacts.' This is much more important and interesting than simply crunching numbers and manipulating spreadsheets.*

"For a long time, people were attracted by our stock. We are now past our hyper growth phase and are more concerned about providing solid professional development. We do a lot of coaching, even at senior levels, to help people become better leaders. For example, in Asia we have a bridge initiative. Executives are required to be concerned about the careers of their four direct reports, and this cascades down through the organization. We are very competitive and are constantly evaluating how to maintain our edge. We realize that in the future we'll need better leaders and managers if we want to continue to be a high-performance business."

High-performance businesses like Dell typically have clearly defined strategies that align their finance operating models and capabilities with the success requirements of their respective industries. This chapter looks at the different paths that leading companies have taken to achieve finance mastery.

WHY IS FINANCE MASTERY IMPORTANT?

While not all high-performance companies exhibit exactly the same combination of distinctive characteristics, there is considerable commonality in the way that they deploy resources across the capability areas required for finance mastery. They exhibit similarities in the way that they deliver support to the business and integrate their agendas with overall enterprise strategy. CFOs in these exceptional companies play a critical role in matters of strategy, leadership, and execution, and are intimately involved in constantly redefining the future direction of their business. They and their finance organizations have become what Dave Burritt, the CFO of Caterpillar, describes in Chapter 1 as "masters of the business" – high-performance teams that are proactive rather than reactive, and influence results rather than simply being influenced.

CFOs face a wide variety of demands from multiple internal and external stakeholders. The requirements that they must meet to support high performance are becoming progressively tougher to deliver against (see Figure 3.3). In particular, the CFOs we interviewed told us that they are confronting competing priorities in two key arenas. They are being called upon to spend ever-higher proportions of their time on matters of strategy

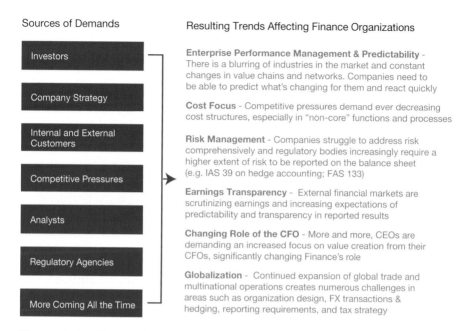

Sources of Demands

Resulting Trends Affecting Finance Organizations

Investors

Company Strategy

Internal and External Customers

Competitive Pressures

Analysts

Regulatory Agencies

More Coming All the Time

Enterprise Performance Management & Predictability - There is a blurring of industries in the market and constant changes in value chains and networks. Companies need to be able to predict what's changing for them and react quickly

Cost Focus - Competitive pressures demand ever decreasing cost structures, especially in "non-core" functions and processes

Risk Management - Companies struggle to address risk comprehensively and regulatory bodies increasingly require a higher extent of risk to be reported on the balance sheet (e.g. IAS 39 on hedge accounting; FAS 133)

Earnings Transparency - External financial markets are scrutinizing earnings and increasing expectations of predictability and transparency in reported results

Changing Role of the CFO - More and more, CEOs are demanding an increased focus on value creation from their CFOs, significantly changing Finance's role

Globalization - Continued expansion of global trade and multinational operations creates numerous challenges in areas such as organization design, FX transactions & hedging, reporting requirements, and tax strategy

Figure 3.3 *Demands on finance organizations*

and leadership while also being asked to intensify their focus on finance and accounting basics in response to heightened regulatory scrutiny and transparency issues.

Companies must move past these hurdles to deliver value. Does finance mastery really generate additional value? Consider the case of Marriott, a global lodging provider. This finance master recognized the need for, and developed, a world-class finance leadership team. This team fostered a value-centered culture throughout its enterprise that emphasized superior execution and results. In doing so, finance became an intimate business partner to all areas of Marriott's diverse operations. The company's finance functions are fully aligned with its growth and profitability objectives. With finance comfortably seated at the leadership table, Marriott said it expects revenue per available room growth of 8% to 10% in 2005 and 7% to 9% in 2006, leading to earnings per share of $2.58 to $2.61 in 2005 and EPS of $3 to $3.10 in 2006, excluding results from its synthetic fuel business.

THE FIVE CAPABILITIES THAT LEAD TO FINANCE MASTERY

Accenture's research has uncovered five key finance capabilities among companies that we have identified as "masters of finance." These capabilities, all directly linked to achieving superior business performance, can be thought of as five pillars supporting an organization's finance structure (as shown in Figure 3.4).

What we found to be unique among all the high performers we studied was that they were developing what we have called *extended capabilities*, as defined by the framework below, and beyond the basic block and tackling of accounting, controlling and risk management. The high-performance companies that we analyzed all exhibit a distinctive set of extended capabilities. Not all companies deploy their resources or prioritize their focus on specific capabilities in the same way. Each organization is on a unique journey and its priorities change over time as it masters the deployment of particular sets of competencies. For example, as a company moves into a steady-state mode after lifting the performance of finance operations, its focus will shift from enhancing finance operations to the creation of new, extended capabilities in one or more other high-performance arenas, such as capital stewardship or risk management.[1]

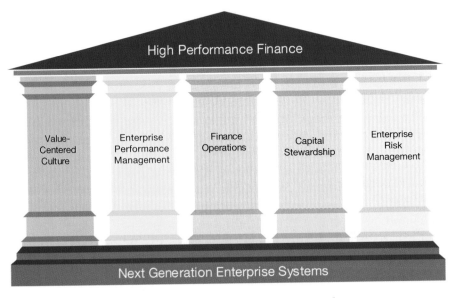

Figure 3.4 *The high-performance finance framework*

Mike Sutcliff notes:

> "The finance organization recognizes that it needs to control the business, effectively manage risks, report financial results, and provide transparency into the cost drivers and potential results of the business. These activities require infrastructure and resource capability. At the same time, the finance organization has to flex with the business as it moves into new markets, occupies new competitive space, or develops new capabilities to compete differently in the future. The challenge for finance is balance: investing in control infrastructure and reporting capabilities while deploying the resources needed to develop the new capabilities that support business growth."

In short, finance must balance today's requirements for operating cost leadership with the longer term goal of finding and supporting business growth opportunities. In this section, we introduce the five key capabilities and 21 related core competencies that drive high-performance finance. Each finance capability and the competencies associated with it are analyzed more fully in later chapters.

Value-centered culture

Value-centered culture optimizes the delivery of value to multiple stakeholders through conscious decisions on which strategies are pursued and how resources are deployed. It infuses an organization with financial acumen, governance, and discipline, so that everyone's behavior is consistently focused on the common objective of delivering sustainable and superior total shareholder returns. This culture provides a fact-based environment and the management processes required to identify new value creation opportunities. It also possesses the discipline to manage and act on those opportunities. Value-centered culture includes the ability to balance the delivery of current value with the investments required to develop future value. The related competencies underlying this capability are these.

- *Finance management/governance*: establishing effective controls and the management processes required to enable effective decisions across the entire organization.

- *Finance skills development*: attracting and developing the talent pool necessary to implement finance and performance management processes, and create analytics to support the business.

- *Change management*: developing the skills and confidence to lead business transformation.

Building a value-centered culture is a rewarding, but demanding process. Mike Sutcliff comments: "As finance executives move beyond transaction processing into the value creation agenda of the business, they face the challenge of influencing a wider group of people who need the basic financial skills to talk about value and identify new opportunities emerging across the business. There is a lot of work to be done to embed those skills throughout an organization, so that people become very comfortable having a fact-based discussion about the business and where it's headed. At the same time, finance executives need to be flexible and understand not only their own company's strategy, but what the other players in the industry are doing. They need to understand where industry lines are blurring to create an inflection point that will allow them to come up with new value innovation ideas".[2]

The unique and differentiated approaches to becoming a value-centered organization are discussed in Chapter 4.

Enterprise performance management (EPM)

EPM enables an organization to understand and refocus its competitive position in order to maintain its industry leadership. Exercising this capability enables management to measure performance at all levels of detail and to accelerate the transformation of insight to action. EPM helps organizations make better, timely decisions to ensure optimal resource allocation on a consistent basis with the goal of maximizing sustainable shareholder value. The competencies related to EPM are these.

- *Shareholder value targeting*: understanding and identifying value-creation opportunities and threats across the enterprise.

- *Portfolio assessment and target setting*: evaluating portfolio options and selecting opportunities for the deployment of both capital and expenditure to achieve a balanced set of stretch targets.

- *Planning and forecasting*: integrating internal and external data to generate driver-based forecasts that accurately predict performance results calibrated by economic value under multiple scenarios.

- *Performance management and reporting*: capturing and reporting enterprise performance information required to support value-creating analysis, insight, and decision making.

- *Investor relations*: maintaining clear, open communication with the investor community to build trust, ensure earnings transparency, avoiding surprises and sustaining confidence in the executive management team.

We examine enterprise performance management in detail in Chapter 5.

Finance operations

Finance operations focus on cost and efficiency in operations and processes through ERP, shared services or outsourcing. Related competencies are these.

- *Transaction processing*: providing maximum efficiency in core finance functions (accounts payable, general ledger, etc.) – increasingly delivered through shared services or outsourcing.

- *Financial and regulatory reporting*: accurately and fully capturing regulatory and tax reporting requirements from a transactional and systems perspective.

- *Management reporting*: delivering comprehensive data for management decision making – a technology and transaction-driven capability (analysis capabilities are part of EPM).

- *Internal control*: providing the disciplined oversight of financial, accounting, and audit systems required for business support – and to avoid liability, fraud and unnecessary risk exposure.

BP exemplifies world-class finance operations. Russ Taruscio, Director for Strategy Accounting Services, explains: "In my view, having a strong CFO and senior leadership team is critical to BP's success in becoming one of the wealthiest and most powerful companies in the world. In finance control and accounting, we are focused on three critical features. The first is the delivery of consistent, reliable and timely management information. Without that, the business people can't make reliable decisions, and so we take that as a very important activity. The second is providing a control environment that allows BP to be trusted internally and externally. The environment today certainly has changed from what it was a few years ago – not that having a controlled environment is less important, but it's critical that we are a trusted company and creating that trust is a key aspect of the roles of the controller, CFO, and senior management. Lastly, we are focused on delivering accounting services cost-effectively. We want accounting services that deliver reliable data into the management information system at a cost that allows us to be competitive. As competition increases, we think that's critical."

Finance operations are explored in Chapter 6.

Capital stewardship

Capital stewardship is the ability to deploy, preserve, and build capital resources by managing the income statement and balance sheet in an integrated way to maximize returns to shareholders. Competencies related to capital stewardship include the following.

- *Capital investment*: effectively managing financial investments not required to fund day to day operations with the goal of maximizing long-term financial resources and flexibility.

- *Capital structure oversight*: maintaining a dynamic balance between debt and equity to finance investments and growth strategies.

- *Working capital and balance sheet management*: managing cash from operations and the balance sheet, at the right capital charge, to sustain superior operating performance.

- *Tax management*: proactively managing tax liability and associated risks based on access to a trail of solid, timely data for quarterly/ annual financial statements, tax returns and audits.

- *Intangibles management*: recognizing, managing, and leveraging the value of intangible capital and off-balance-sheet transactions (i.e., operating leases, take or pay contracts, etc.).

Pat Erlandson, CFO of UnitedHealth Group describes the importance of capital stewardship to his company: "Our capital management process helps us figure out how best to deploy scarce resources. Capital management is critical in this business. Deploying investment across five businesses with $45 billion in revenues in an efficient and effective way is central to making sure that we get good returns across each of these businesses. Our capital management process is a decisive factor in enabling us to experience strong, sustained growth, from $400 million of revenues in 1989 to $17 billion of revenues in 1998 to $45 billion today. If you include our capital expenditures and our non-capital expenditures (what we call our research and development costs), then over the last five or six years, we've spent over $2 billion. That's between $400 million and almost $700 million a year. Importantly, in 1998 we began buying our shares back. We started this because it represents very good value. So I think that we've not only continued strong operating performance, but we've also become much better stewards of our capital. This has driven the value that you see coming through in the TRS numbers."

Chapter 7 illustrates the benefits of investing in capital stewardship and demonstrates the strong link between capital management and stock performance.

Enterprise risk management (ERM)

ERM is the monitoring and managing of financial and non-financial risk across an enterprise's portfolio of assets in support of its strategic objectives. Enterprise risk management is an increasingly important finance function and has risen to the top of the CFO's agenda. CFOs must tailor their finance organizations' approaches to risk management to best meet their enterprises' business needs. Competencies related to enterprise risk management are these.

- *Financial risk management*: accurately calculating and proactively evaluating market, liquidity and credit exposures.

- *Business risk management*: assessing risks related to planning and management processes supporting an enterprise's business plan/model. Focuses on evaluating the impact of external and internal variables, such as market dynamics and economic cycles.

- *Operational risk management*: effectively measuring and assimilating risks arising from processes, logistics, technologies and systems adopted by operating entities. Insurance risk is a subset of this component of enterprise-wide risk management.

- *Event risk management*: managing exogenous considerations, such as natural disasters, governmental or quasi governmental policies and regulations. Basel II, Sarbanes-Oxley Act (SOX), and war are prime examples of external events and circumstances that exert cross-industry impact.

Regulatory change and the associated requirements for compliance are inducing organizations to embrace more comprehensive approaches to risk management. Lauralee Martin, EVP/CFO of global finance for Jones Lang LaSalle, a global real estate service provider, commented that her company has implemented a global operating committee for risk review. The committee, Lauralee says, "determines whether the risk is isolated or whether we need to address it in a broader way. The question we always ask is, 'Can we address the risk at the source?'"

In Chapter 8, we examine the specific risk management needs of businesses and the differentiating capabilities used to mitigate risk in a constantly changing world of risks and rewards.

The five distinctive capabilities described above – and their associated competencies – set high performers apart from their competitors and position them to prosper in challenging economic environments while peer companies struggle. High-performing finance organizations also effectively address four imperatives. Masters of finance excel at 1) managing for value, 2) fostering a value-centered culture across the enterprise, 3) appropriately investing in and leveraging technology, and 4) developing a talent pool of professionals who combine deep finance skills with intimate, hands-on knowledge of front-line business operations.

1 Managing for value

Financial markets often do not value companies as highly as management and shareholders would like, leaving many top executives wondering how to increase their company's market value. Simply improving earnings per share won't work. The market prices stocks based on expectations of future cash flows adjusted for risk, not on traditional accounting metrics. Shareholder value targeting is about focusing on the long-term value drivers – financial and non-financial, tangible and intangible.

Finance management must be able to discern the drivers of current and future value, slice and dice business components, and then disaggregate data down into value driver trees so that strategic, tactical, and operational decisions can be calibrated in economic terms. Not only is this crucial to maximizing shareholder returns, it also enables the finance organization to help the enterprise respond more effectively to changing business conditions.

2 Fostering value-centered culture across the enterprise

Our research has demonstrated that an enterprise with a value-centered culture motivates and enables employees to make and quickly act upon decisions that create shareholder value. Such a culture removes many of the normal barriers to change and gets everyone marching in step, in the same direction, adhering to the same agenda and the same priorities.

A value-centered culture forms part of the high-performance anatomy. Creating and sustaining a value-centered culture within their finance function and then extending it across their enterprise is considered by CFOs to be the single most critical element for success.

3 Appropriately investing in and leveraging technology

Organizations need to understand their process and technical capabilities. They must be able to advance to the next technology capability level and the next operating model before their competitors have even anticipated the next wave of change. Leading companies deploy fit-for-purpose, right-sized technology. They invest in business analytics tools related to enterprise performance management. These tools help executives make better decisions about resource allocation and demonstrate a company's short- and long-term value to shareholders. Leading companies continually invest in technology at above-industry-average rates and secure higher returns than their counterparts.

4 Developing a talent pool of professionals

To exert maximum impact on their organization, finance practitioners require not just the technical skills of the accounting trade, but also core business skills. They must be able to think innovatively – not just about costs, revenues, and budget performance, but also about capital stewardship and employing advanced analytical techniques to predict change. Leading companies have refocused their acquisition of finance talent to attract people with diverse backgrounds. They have launched innovative job rotation programs, both inside and outside of finance, to build core business skills and cross-fertilize capabilities. And they have developed training programs, both formal and informal, aimed at fostering the distinctive talents of their finance professionals. But above all, finance leaders have succeeded in attracting talented professionals who can truly make a difference to their companies by creating a culture in which "finance is the place to be" to advance in the business.

The CFOs we spoke with unanimously agreed that finance plays a pivotal role in enabling organizations to become high-performance businesses. In the next section, we will explore how the masters of finance tailor their finance capabilities to align them with corporate strategy and help deliver enterprise transformation.

ABOUT OUR RESEARCH

Designed to identify distinctive characteristics of leading finance organizations, our study involved in-person interviews with more than 250 chief financial officers from leading companies around the world, as well as an extensive benchmarking study carried out in collaboration with The Hackett Group. For the CFO interviews, Accenture used a shareholder value analysis to identify common traits among companies that have mastered the finance function. Quantitative and qualitative questions were designed to enable us to understand: 1) the relationship, if any, between finance mastery and leading companies; 2) whether a relationship differed across industry, business model, or growth expectation; and 3) common capabilities that finance functions at leading companies share, and how businesses can determine where they should be investing. For the benchmarking study, Accenture used The Hackett Group's global finance database of companies to analyze and compare the finance mastery of leading businesses to non-leading businesses.

To identify finance masters, Accenture evaluated study participants on five key finance capabilities – value-centered culture, enterprise performance management, finance operations, capital stewardship, and enterprise risk management. We gained a more complete picture of their finance capabilities by further evaluating companies' finance performance along 21 related competencies – such as finance governance, transaction processing and shareholder value targeting – and rated them using a scale classification of "basic practice," "progressive practice" or "pioneering practice" on each (see Figure 3.5). Based on this scale, organizations needed to achieve a pioneering ranking in at least 25% of the competency categories that we examined and achieve a combined pioneering or progressive ranking of 65% to be ranked as finance masters.

TAILORING THE FINANCE MASTERY FRAMEWORK TO SUPPORT CORPORATE STRATEGY

Customizing the finance mastery framework is important. How components are prioritized and which are given emphasis will depend on where an enterprise is in its competitive cycle, its readiness for change, and the

Hypothetical Company Status — Basic · Progressive · Pioneering

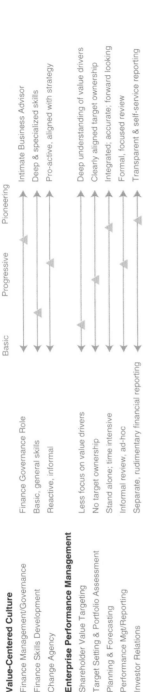

Dimension	Basic	Pioneering
Value-Centered Culture		
Finance Management/Governance	Finance Governance Role	Intimate Business Advisor
Finance Skills Development	Basic, general skills	Deep & specialized skills
Change Agency	Reactive, informal	Pro-active, aligned with strategy
Enterprise Performance Management		
Shareholder Value Targeting	Less focus on value drivers	Deep understanding of value drivers
Target Setting & Portfolio Assessment	No target ownership	Clearly aligned target ownership
Planning & Forecasting	Stand alone; time intensive	Integrated; accurate; forward looking
Performance Mgt/Reporting	Informal review, ad-hoc	Formal, focused review
Investor Relations	Separate, rudimentary financial reporting	Transparent & self-service reporting
Finance Operations		
Transactions Processing	Manual processing; multiple apps	Outsourced and/or workflow mgt & self service capabilities; ERP
Financial/Reg. Reporting	Non-standardized; 15+ days to close	Automated, standardized
Management Reporting	Ad-hoc, non-standardized	End-to-end standardized; single chart of accts
Internal Control	Poor control, high risk	Optimized, low risk
Capital Stewardship		
Capital Investment	Low returns relative to industry returns	High returns, portfolio optimized
Capital Structure	High capital charge	Optimized debt/equity leverage
Working Capital & Balance Sheet	Low liquidity & WC	High liquidity, high asset utilization
Tax Management	Inefficient mgt; high effective tax rate	Sophisticated; low effective tax rate
Off Balance Sheet Items/Intangibles	Poor mgt; focus on P&L	Optimized management
Enterprise Risk Management		
Financial Risk Mgt	No clear RM goals; limited use of tools	Optimized risk throughout company
Business Risk Mgt	Poor understanding; separate risk mgt	Enterprise-wide risk mgt system linked with strategy and operations
Operational Risk Mgt	Separate risk mitigation	Integrated risk mgt system & analyses
Event Risk Mgt	Separate risk analysis & mitigation	Enterprise-wide, integrated risk system

Figure 3.5 *Accenture's Finance & Performance Management Mastery Scale*

stability of its business model. Pursuing finance mastery is a dynamic process. To achieve new levels of performance, a company's finance operating model and deployment of resources must change over time. The CFOs featured in this book have chosen different paths to transform their finance organizations. They also tailor their finance capabilities to support unique finance strategies and operating models.

At a global metals producer, for example, recruiting and developing a top-caliber cadre of talented finance professionals and knitting them together into a strong, cohesive team was central to successfully navigating through tough economic conditions in the aluminum production market. During this period, the company more than doubled its revenues, acquired global scale, disposed of non-core businesses and expanded vertically into new, adjacent markets. This could not have been accomplished without strong financial leadership, discipline, and change management skills. Creating a value-centered culture with top-class capital stewardship and risk management capabilities has also been key to this success story.

In Dell's case, it has experienced dramatic growth over a sustained period. To support the business, Dell's finance team has expanded along with the company, through the continuous hiring of finance talent. Special attention has been given to ensuring that Dell's high-performance culture is not diluted by an influx of a large number of external resources. In recent years, Dell has grown a larger and larger proportion of its executive talent internally. Five years ago, 75% of its positions for vice president and director were filled externally. Today this figure is 30%, due to an increased focus on talent development, coaching and training.

Since the high-tech electronics industry moves at a faster velocity than other business sectors, Dell's development of corporate agility is a critical factor in its success. Dell outmaneuvers the competition by a "plan to act" process that has a short cycle time and enables the company to make major or minor changes of direction in real time. Dell's direct model affects the level of importance that management places on a given finance capability. For example, the need for tight integration of the value chain is critical to ensuring that Dell has adequate inventory to build equipment to order to fulfill customer demand. In contrast, billing, credit and collection operations for Dell are rather simple compared with these functions at other firms.[3]

Verizon, on the other hand, directs significant effort to the order-to-cash process. With millions of customers and billions of transactions, Verizon's efficient use of leading practices targeting timely and accurate billing, credit and collections activities has a positive impact on business performance.

Verizon competes in a capital-intensive industry. The scale and time horizon of capital investment required make the development of strong capital stewardship capabilities mission critical. Efficient capital allocation, authorization and control processes reinforce the governance process to ensure that Verizon's risk/return equation for invested capital is optimized.

WHAT IS THE JOURNEY TO HIGH PERFORMANCE?

As the examples above underscore, the journey to finance mastery is different for each organization. The priority given to specific finance capabilities will be dictated by industry dynamics, business strategy, and, most importantly, agreement by the management team that the specific performance improvements being planned will create better alignment with corporate targets.

Even though each company will prioritize capabilities differently, we have found that achieving excellence in the finance operations arena is typically a prerequisite for making material improvements to the other four pillars of finance mastery (enterprise performance management, capital stewardship, enterprise risk management, and value-centered culture). As noted earlier, there is no single formula for gaining mastery in finance and performance management.

To illustrate the different transformation paths that companies are on – and the different stages that they have reached in improving their finance operations – we briefly explore the approaches taken by three companies: BP; SAP Asia Pacific; and the Corus Group.

BP, one of the leading energy companies in the world, is a pioneer in the outsourcing field. It first outsourced its European accounting services in 1991. By 2002, the outsourcing of finance and accounting (F&A) had been extended to other businesses in the world and BP had negotiated the largest and longest-standing F&A outsourcing arrangement ever. BP currently outsources a broad range of services, from systems, technology, and tax, to HR services and procurement. Its outsourcing strategy continues to deliver powerful cost savings and flexibility. (See Chapter 5, *Enterprise Performance Management*, for more on BP's finance strategy.)

In contrast, SAP Asia Pacific went live with a captive in-house shared service center in 2003. Its award-winning regional center has generated tremendous benefits in supporting SAP's rapid growth in Asia. According to Colin Sampson, COO and CFO of SAP Asia Pacific, its shared services strategy has given SAP "control over its own destiny" in performance management, process design, and other key areas. As a result of this program, the whole region has markedly improved its ability to cope with rapid growth and escalating service demands (for a more detailed discussion, see Colin Sampson's interview, Chapter 6, *Finance Operations*).

In yet another contrast, the Corus Group is just beginning to redefine its financial operations by embracing the shared services model. In the wake of the company's major restructuring effort, according to CFO David Lloyd, the company is moving into a phase in which shared services is seen as a prime vehicle for enhancing efficiency (see the Corus Group case study, Chapter 9, *Managing the Change Journey to High Performance*).

As noted earlier, excellence in finance operations is often the first step toward finance mastery. BP's outsourcing strategy and SAP Asia Pacific's use of shared services in Asia Pacific both represent widely used approaches. Taking another route, Caterpillar and UnitedHealth Group have achieved high levels of finance mastery by extending their capabilities in the other areas of competency *before* moving into shared services. As their abilities in these areas grow stronger, high performers are typically able to focus on contributing greater value to their organizations. These organizations' leaner transaction-processing efforts form the foundation for further improvement.

One misconception many companies fall into is thinking that finance mastery is achieved by driving the total cost of finance as low as possible. In the early 1990s, the average finance cost as a percentage of revenue was more than 2%; it has been cut in half to less than 1% over the past 15 years through the introduction of enterprise resource planning (ERP), process redesign, shared services, and outsourcing; but as we report in Chapter 6, Finance Operations, costs are now on the rise. Most of the value created by finance over this period has been generated by increasing the efficiency of the transaction processing components of the finance organization. However, in many companies, incremental savings through increased efficiencies are reaching the point of diminishing returns. In short, "You can't save your way into prosperity."

WHY DOES FINANCE MASTERY CHANGE OVER TIME?

The constantly changing competitive environment and evolving customer demands present a dynamic set of success criteria over time. Even as an organization is mastering the specific finance capabilities required to compete effectively in the current environment, the mix of capabilities required to compete is highly likely to change due to customer and competitive demands. The following case studies provide insights into changing conditions at two companies and the response of the finance organization as they focused on driving value over time.

CASE STUDY
From finance management to finance leadership

With revenues of over $36 billion, Microsoft is the number one software company in the world. Its global operations span seven major business units supported by 57,000 employees. Over the past three decades, Microsoft has led a technology revolution, taking the personal computer from a toy that amused hobbyists to a key business tool sitting on 600 million desks around the world. Over this same time period, Microsoft has gone through several transformations. In the early 1990s, it implemented a robust shared services program, centralizing key elements of trans-action processing across the company. Standardized processes and systems were introduced to drive efficiencies.

- *Microsoft established a centralized European Operations Center in Dublin, installing a single chart of accounts running on a single instance of SAP.*
- *The company outsourced credit and collections, VAT, accounts payable (AP), and customer care.*
- *Automation of internal processes has resulted in much higher levels of financial control and improved internal audit and reporting capabilities.*

The role of finance at Microsoft has changed from finance management to finance leadership. Over the past two years, its CFO has strengthened the finance team by hiring seven senior finance executives into new positions in the seven Microsoft product businesses. These new business division CFOs are critical in responding to SOX's demands for greater control, consistency, and transparency. They are also driving finance leadership change and are working alongside the division CEOs as business advisors.

Historically, sales and marketing wielded primary influence over the direction of Microsoft's product groups. Today, finance is increasing its influence in the product area. There is a new finance leadership training program targeted at the top 300 finance professionals across the company. A major advance in finance skills development, the program doesn't just focus on technical training. Its goal is to help talented professionals move from finance management to finance leadership.

Keys to finance leadership strategy at Microsoft include:

- *an influx of finance skills and capabilities – increasing finance's bench strength;*
- *strong technology and tools to improve decision makers' access to timely, accurate, and consistent information;*
- *wide distribution of information supporting increased transparency and accelerating the "plan to act" process: and*
- *introduction of a personal competency model for finance that has increased the level of rigor for the finance function in recruiting and skills development, resulting in a stronger team committed to continually raising the bar for finance expertise and contributions.*

Changes in strategies or industry structural shifts can create gaps that require reprioritizing finance capabilities. A good example of this change is Marriott International.

CASE STUDY
Refocusing finance priorities

Marriott is the world's leading hotelier by revenue, with 2700 operated or franchised properties in more than 65 countries. Over the past several years, Marriott's business model has changed from property owner to hotel management company and franchiser. This has unleashed a new level of growth and profitability for the enterprise and precipitated the need to retool its finance capabilities to better match its new business model.

Marriott is not just a lodging company. It is a service company that excels in the finance domain. It is a leader in exploring creative ways to add value to its enterprise, stakeholders, and shareholders. Marriott was the first lodging company to sell its properties and charge others fees for managing them. It was the first lodging com-

pany to expand into timeshares and make it a legitimate business. These capabilities demonstrate how finance supports the business focus on owner and franchisee service and value-delivery excellence.

Marriott has a strong track record for implementing new finance capabilities. Beginning in 2000, it consolidated a large portion of its finance function into a shared services model. The program to create shared services capability was designed to reduce costly, redundant processes in individual hotels and to streamline information systems support and business process integration procedures. "We had a number of obstacles slowing us down," recalls Marriott's President and COO, Bill Shaw, who was the executive sponsor of the shared services program.

"All around us the new economy was taking hold, and the business environment was speeding up. We needed to leverage our operations to provide consistent, cost-effective service, achieve economies of scale, and make our organization quicker and more flexible."

The shared services operating model appealed to Shaw, not just because it provided the opportunity to cut costs dramatically – the typical benefit of shared services – but also because it could reposition Marriott's support organization as a service provider to the core business. For instance, 75% of hotel controllers' time had been spent managing processes like accounts payable and accounts receivable. Marriott wanted to use technology to streamline processes and free up controllers to work more actively with line managers to improve profitability. Bill explains: "We have never thought of ourselves as a hotel company. Anybody can provide a room and a bed. Marriott is a service company. With the capabilities we could gain through this transformation, we would be well positioned to provide our global workforce with the tools and information they needed to better serve our customers. And we would be better able to do business the way our customers, owners, and franchisees want us to."

Based on the success of Marriott's shared services operations, the company underwent a finance organization redesign focused on three key segments of the finance function: finance business partnerships, centers of excellence, and enterprise accounting services. Each group is charged with a unique set of capabilities and objectives that are integrated across the entire finance organization. Even more important, this structure was designed to align tightly with Marriott's busi-

ness strategy to ensure that finance supports key internal and external stakeholders across the enterprise.

Formally developing these three elements of the finance function has better equipped the finance organization to support Marriott's business strategy. Marriott has successfully developed a world-class finance leadership team as well as a mechanism to grow future leaders with strong finance acumen both within finance and elsewhere in the business. In fact, Marriott moves employees across various parts of the organization to spread its value-centered culture. Many employees begin their careers in finance. When they move to hotel operations, or to sales and marketing, they bring an analytic culture along with them. The benefit is a consistent focus on value.[4]

HOW DO YOU KNOW IF YOU HAVE ACHIEVED FINANCE MASTERY?

Finance mastery is not a destination. It is a state of readiness for proactively delivering value. Finance operational excellence is most often, though not always, a prerequisite to reach finance mastery. If an organization struggles with the basics, it is really difficult to focus on higher order finance capabilities.

It is hard to think of a company that has more consistently demonstrated finance mastery spanning decades of accomplishments than General Electric. Being a pioneer in the finance area is not new for General Electric. Its history is rich with examples of how its finance organization broke new ground in areas that today are widely viewed as best practices. More than fifty years ago, GE formed the first investor relations department in an American corporation. GE's financial management program (FMP) has been the training ground for one of the strongest financial executive teams in industry, and GE's senior executives, ranging from the CFO to division CEOs, trace their roots back to FMP. The bench strength of GE's finance organization is the envy of the Global 1000. In fact, many alumni of GE's FMP program have been recruited for the C-suites of some of the most respected companies around the world.

The FMP program at GE is only part of the story. Senior executives devote several weeks a year to teaching at GE's world-renowned training center in Crotonville, New York. GE further builds its finance talent pool through a robust rotation program that typically includes a two- or three-year tour of duty in GE's famous internal audit group (IAD). IAD acts as an internal consulting firm for GE. The 250 professionals in the group are handpicked for this rigorous program, which is designed to test future finance leaders' ability to consistently deliver value in challenging environments across a diverse set of industries and geographies. Most senior finance executives at GE have spent time in IAD, as well as in several multi-year assignments in three or more of GE's diverse portfolio of businesses – from household appliances and jet engines to insurance.

Results speak louder than words. Many companies have "training programs" and "rotation programs." Yet, GE creates more top performers than 10 of its peer companies. GE's Session C is widely known and has been replicated at other high-performance companies like Dell. GE has a very formal process to manage, train, mentor, and test high-potential executives, including those in finance. GE uses both formal and informal processes to ensure leadership remains at the top of its agenda. Each year, top finance officials visit GE's business units as part of the Session C process to identify talent and help it flow up through the pipeline on an enterprise-wide basis.

GE's finance mastery goes beyond hiring and growing the best finance talent. For several decades, GE has been widely recognized as one of the pioneers in implementing shared services. GE started in the 1980s to consolidate finance operations into shared service centers. It has been an early mover in advancements, driving improvements in efficiency and effectiveness across finance and beyond.

In pursuit of high performance, GE seeks best practices from all sources and rejects a "not invented here" philosophy. GE's adoption of Six Sigma is an example of this in action. Six Sigma is a quality initiative and problem-solving methodology that was designed by Motorola in the 1980s to reduce error rates in its plant operations. In the past 25 years, it has been leveraged more broadly by companies such as GE. Six Sigma is a rigorous process that practitioners summarize as define, measure, analyze, improve and control. GE has built this methodology into the fabric of everything it does, including finance. GE "black belts" have long been known for their positive impact, from the shop floor to the C-suite.[5]

In the mid-1980s, former CEO Jack Welch launched the now-famous "Work Out" process. This initiative increased GE's corporate agility through a rigorous, fast-paced business analysis process that cut bureaucracy and increased productivity. At first, many of the target areas for the work out process were in the finance domain, but over its nearly 20-year history the process has expanded into many other areas.

Total Finance Costs as Percentage of Revenue, 2003 and 2005

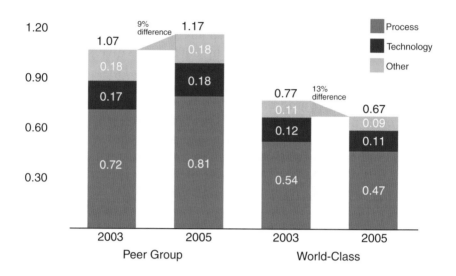

As the GE story shows, finance mastery must be achieved over and over again as new business challenges emerge and different capabilities are required to succeed.

THE HACKETT GROUP ON FINANCE MASTERY

For the first time in 13 years, The Hackett Group has seen a dramatic increase in finance costs as a percentage of revenues, driven by a heightened focus on controls and risk management. The new regulatory requirements of the Sarbanes-Oxley Act, for example, have placed increased demands and cost burdens on CFOs. Hackett has seen a sizeable increase in compliance management and the costs of related activities, including the fees paid to external advisors as well as increased audit fees.

It is worth noting that over this same period of time, total finance costs for world-class performers have actually decreased by 13% to 0.67% finance costs as a percentage of revenues.

Through the utilization of critical best practices, such as standardization and centralization, these leaders have continued to outpace their

**Finance process costs as a percentage of revenue
by process category, 2005**

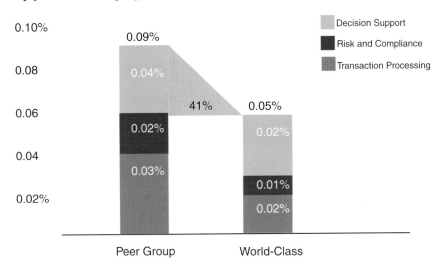

Allocation of analysts' time for standard reports, 2005

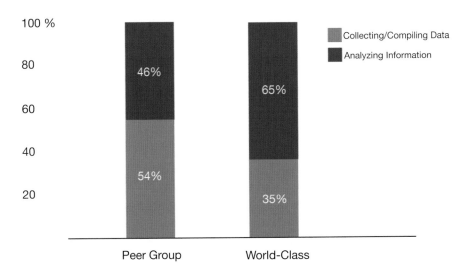

peers. Standardized processes and technologies have given them true economies of scale and more streamlined operations that enable them to respond more efficiently than their peers as regulatory legislation continues to evolve.

Looking ahead, our analysis indicates that leading organizations have achieved most of the efficiencies in transaction processing that can be gained through best practices. They are now looking beyond transactional efficiency for improvement opportunities, including the embedding of best-practice controls and monitoring tools into their processes to meet regulatory requirements and mitigate risk.

CFO INSIGHTS: LESSONS FROM THE MASTERS

- There is a high correlation between high-performance business and the deployment of the five capabilities defined in our high-performance finance framework.

- A large proportion of the companies we studied have implemented the type of comprehensive enterprise performance management system described in this chapter, or intend to do so over the next three years. This is consistent with the universal view that the CFO has a pivotal role in enabling the creation and maintenance of a strong value-centered culture.

- There is no standard textbook answer to the question of which capabilities are most important to your business. However, we did find that mastering finance operations is generally a prerequisite for attaining mastery of the other four capabilities.

- Managing the journey to a high-performance finance organization requires that the finance executives stay in rhythm with the drivers of change at the enterprise level, so they can invest in some capabilities slightly ahead of business need without investing in capabilities that the business is not going to find useful. High-performance CFOs are most successful when they are very focused on understanding the gap between the capabilities that exist today and the capabilities they think the business is going to need tomorrow – and then invest to build them.

REFERENCES

1 Accenture, *Finance and Performance Management Mastery and the High Performance Business*, 2004. http://www.accenture.com

2 Michael R. Sutcliff, Leveraging Innovative Finance and Performance Management Capabilities, *DM Review*, January 2004. http://www.dmreview.com

3 Thomas A. Stewart and Louise O'Brien, Execution Without Excuses, *Harvard Business Review*, March 2005. http://www.hbr.com

4 Carter A. Prescott, Marriott Redefines the Shared Services Model, *Competitive Financial Operations: The CFO Project Volume 1*, October 2002.

5 General Electric. http://www.ge.com

CHAPTER 4

Value-Centered Culture

FINANCE IN THE CENTER OF THE VALUE-CREATION PROCESS

Mitch Blaser, CFO
Swiss Re, Property & Casualty Americas Division

With 70 offices in 30 countries, Swiss Re is one of the world's leading reinsurance companies. Known for its innovative, knowledge-driven finance approach, Swiss Re offers a comprehensive range of capital and risk management products and services tailored to the needs of its clients. For nearly a century, it has been devoted to excellence in the US reinsurance market. Swiss Re's presence in North American property and casualty lines of business covers the spectrum, from niche specialization to global solutions.

Swiss Re is a recognized expert in the field of risk and capital management. While it does not necessarily seek to be number one in terms of volume, it aspires to global leadership in creating value for its clients and shareholders. To determine and manage value, Swiss Re relies on its proprietary Economic Value Model (EVM). Finance is a key player in the EVM process, not just from a numbers and results standpoint, but also from a business planning and decision-making perspective. In addition to its focus on value, Swiss Re is committed to professional development and opportunities for all its employees. Next to its financial strength and resources, the company considers its employees' knowledge and cultural focus on value to be among its primary competitive advantages.

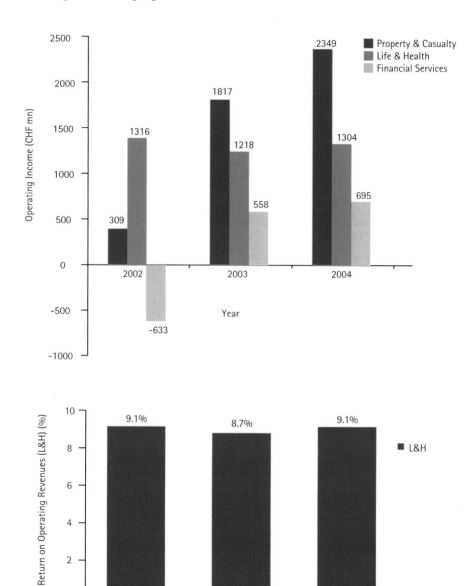

Figure 4.1 *Swiss Re's financial performance*
Source: Accenture analysis

Mitch Blaser, the CFO of Swiss Re's Property & Casualty Americas Division, recognized early in his tenure that finance's role in the company was due for a major change. As he recalls, "The reinsurance markets were just rousing from the tragic events of 9/11 and the outlook for increased demand and competitive pricing for reinsurance (insurance sold to insurers to leverage their risks) looked promising. In this type of environment, a tactical risk can develop if the focus is short-term in nature, such as capitalizing on a new business cycle, and is not balanced with longer-term goals of profitable growth and value creation."

At the time, finance's role was basic: it performed required accounting and reporting functions, provided business units with reports and analysis, and made sure that the right numbers were delivered to the parent organization accurately and on time. Describing finance's transformation, Blaser evaluated his finance team and realized that, "... with the talent at hand, it could be doing much more to better serve the organization by creating value, not just reports. Critical finance services, such as forecasting and receivables management, could be enhanced and new services could be offered, such as client auditing and business-unit based planning and analysis." More important, the CFO recognized that he needed to create a leadership role for finance, and position it at the center of the value-focused management structure that was taking shape at Swiss Re.

By its nature, a reinsurance contract is long term; it usually requires years to determine the ultimate impact on income and capital. Careful risk selection, underwriting, contract design, and pricing must take place before a reinsurance company enters into a contract. Once a contract is signed, the company must keep an unremittingly sharp focus on claims management, cash collection, and liability estimation. While periodic GAAP income statements provide an industry-comparable review of results, reinsurers such as Swiss Re also need to continuously reevaluate the economic value of their underlying contracts. Throughout this cycle, finance's role is vital. Mitch Blaser wanted to make sure that role was clear and customer focused.

Swiss Re's strategic map and mission statement focus on the whys and hows of managing and maximizing economic value. They are intended to center the organization on optimizing operating income and protecting capital at the individual contract level, at all levels in between (line of business, market, channel, legal entity, etc.), and all the way up to consolidated group results. As a reinsurer, Swiss Re issues insurance policies to other insurers to assist them in diversifying and managing their risks. In effect, it shares the strength of its balance sheet and capital with its customers. Applied to day-to-day business, Swiss Re's mission statement is intended to result in writing the highest quality business with the highest quality clients.

To achieve its objectives, Swiss Re relies on its Economic Value Model (EVM), a comprehensive valuation process supported by an automated calculation system that is run and maintained by finance. As described by Blaser, "EVM consistently calculates the economic value of each piece of business all the way down to the individual contract level. Numerous variables are included in our EVM determinations and factored in for the current period as well as expected future renewal periods. Variables include ultimate underwriting profitability, expected claim and expense payout patterns, cash flows, and cost of capital, to name a few. EVM is applied for each individual contract to evaluate pricing and contract structure, determine financial projections, and track individual and business-unit performance goals.

"Finance works cooperatively with our business units to evaluate every contract through the EVM process and then weighs in heavily with its business partners on whether a piece of business is written, how it is priced, how it is managed, and whether it is renewed. On a continuous rolling forecast basis, EVM is applied by finance to analyze and evaluate financial performance, value creation and the achievement of performance targets. Finance is also central to the annual planning and target-setting process. This involves setting pricing benchmarks that impact the nature, volume and quality of every piece of business presented and written."

What has this done for finance's relationship with Swiss Re's business units? Finance is currently rated number one in customer focus across Swiss Re's Property & Casualty Americas Division, up from last place just 12 months before. Blaser and his team have been implementing a transformation centered on finance's mission statement: "Finance provides financial services with a strong commitment to client satisfaction, quality people and increased financial strength of the firm."

Finance has defined its value proposition to include effective partnering with Swiss Re's businesses and improved customer service. Blaser explains: "Finance's value proposition drives not just what gets done in finance, but how efficiently and accurately goals are accomplished." The guiding principle of finance is customer focus through timely value-added services, teamwork and integrity. Another key guiding principle, continuous improvement, has helped finance chart a course that yields ongoing measurable value to its larger organization. Among its accomplishments, this continuous improvement initiative:

- *established a client audit group that has significantly improved client management, collections and cash flow since its inception;*
- *reduced past-due receivables by more than 30% through focused accounts receivable management, process improvement and effective resource allocation;*
- *reduced the accounting and reporting close cycle by one week, even while intentionally building in several business days for quality management and review of results for both EVM and financial projections;*
- *improved customer service by assigning planning analysts to work closely with business units as the official liaisons for all their reporting, analysis and finance needs; and*
- *implemented a new reinsurance accounting application, based on ground-up user feedback, that has significantly reduced account processing cycle time and improved information management, controls, and work flow.*

CFO Blaser and his leadership group energize their finance team on a daily basis around their value proposition and the specific benefits they deliver to the larger organization. Finance is thoroughly focused on the future and ways to achieve continuous improvement. The vision, mission statement and guiding principles that Blaser and his team developed more than three years ago still serve as regular reminders of how finance is supposed to work. Blaser elaborates: "On an annual basis, the entire finance organization engages in a goal-setting process and develops collective and departmental balanced scorecards. Key guiding principles are contributing to the business bottom line, providing maximum value to the larger enterprise, and ensuring the overall productivity and job satisfaction of its people." Bottom-up goals and targets are established at the departmental level and balanced with top-down, cross-departmental direction from Blaser and his leadership group.

Performance objectives and targets are set across the following dimensions: client focus, operational excellence, human capital development, and financial results. At an annual finance organization event, department heads introduce their scorecards and cross-departmental teams evaluate them. The teams provide feedback, generate new ideas, refine goals and targets – and balance current initia-

tives with continuous improvement priorities. The scorecards are revised and then a team-building gallery walk is performed to reevaluate them; ensure that goals and targets are consistent with core values and mission; and identify required initiatives and resources (scope, benefits, timing and deliverables). Key elements in this process are an equal vote on priority items and a process check to ensure that current plans and targets are truly transformational, add value, and are people-focused to help make finance the best place to work within Swiss Re.

Blaser does not stop at the initiatives described above. The CFO and his leadership team encourage finance personnel to think beyond their day-to-day activities to identify strategic, innovative and value-adding opportunities. Periodic meetings are held to check progress, vote on priorities, build consensus and refine courses of action. Scorecards are maintained and shared with the broader group so that the measured value provided by finance is showcased, and employees are recognized and rewarded for their contributions. Through these processes, finance regularly explores opportunities to take its strategic value added to the next level.

On the road ahead, finance needs creative minds to help advance EVM. Blaser says his plans include "... adding increased sophistication to model variables, drilling down to deeper levels of information, and applying outside variables (economic, currency, interest rate movement, etc.) to our existing model. These are some of our organization's future expectations for finance. In addition, linking all of the step-by-step management processes that utilize EVM (underwriting, pricing, planning, reserving, etc.) into a seamless and continuous stream of analysis, planning, and decision making is an important goal for improved control and better client selection and management." The next generation of EVM is already in development, and finance intends to seriously up its stake in contributing added value to Swiss Re.

CFO Mitch Blaser and his leadership team are constantly seeking out new ways to promote continuous improvement and identify innovative value-adding opportunities for contributing to their larger organization. By clearly defining finance's value proposition, Blaser has linked its mission directly to the value-creation objectives of his company as a whole. And by encouraging members of his team to think beyond their day-to-day roles, this creative CFO is fostering an exciting, highly charged environment.

DEVELOPING A VALUE-CENTERED CULTURE

A critical step in positioning the business to create and sustain high performance

One of the consistent features of high-performance businesses is that they have a sense of energy, a special buzz that permeates their atmosphere and the attitude of everyone who works for them. This energy is focused on achieving excellence in those areas that set the business apart from industry peers. It is this intangible but relentless organizational focus on success that lies at the heart of a value-centered culture. Customers see it in well-designed services and processes that make value-centered organizations easy to do business with. Suppliers see it in the seamless connections of processes and information that allow trading partners to rapidly respond to market and geographic opportunities. Employees see it in the organizational processes, policies and management philosophies that are aligned with their value-added contributions on a daily basis. Managers see it in their organizations' capacity for rapidly bridging and repairing broken processes – and for consistently producing superior results. What is it that allows some organizations to capture and nurture this buzz and capability?

At GE, the answer is its Financial Management Program (FMP) – a highly disciplined process for promoting its value-based culture built on a foundation of financial excellence. The program is a critical element in GE's leadership development training. All managers on GE's leadership track complete a business simulation in which they play the role of division CFO for a fictitious GE business. This exercise includes interviews with key members of the business management team, operational reviews and presentations to the division president. It combines computer-based business simulations with in-person management networking sessions. The ultimate objective: to foster a culture of finance excellence within the entire class of managers in the program. This comprehensive program, reinforced by a distinctive management philosophy, has contributed greatly to the laser-like focus on value creation that GE is known for the world over.

Hans-Dieter Scheuermann, SVP and head of SAP's Business Solution Architects Group, considers a value-centered culture and enterprise performance management to be the two most important finance mastery capabilities described in Chapter 3. Hans-Dieter notes that SAP has emphasized "more and more transparency in its leadership approach, which has greatly enhanced understanding among employees" of its value-centered culture. This understanding, regularly monitored via employee surveys, supports measurement and improvement. Even the company's organizational structure has been adapted to bring value to the forefront. As Hans-Dieter notes, "SAP has moved to a performance-based rewards system and alignment is tighter, so that business strategy objectives cascade down to operating entities. Different key performance indicators (KPIs) are set for each business area to maximize returns, performance, and effective interaction across the wider organization. Our rewards structure is not based on building large teams that own huge numbers of people. It is focused on performance and delivery. The key is execution!" In Hans-Dieter's view, a value-centered culture is instilled within an enterprise by having "50% of objectives based on team or organizational performance and 50% based on personal performance."

At Dell Inc., the "Dell Values in Action" program describes in detail what it means to work for and partner with the company. Shareholder value is only one of the elements highlighted. Customer aspirations; what it means to be part of the Dell team; customer relationship management; global citizenship; and what it means to win are all defined. Dell posts newsletters that highlight activities and achievements that exemplify its value-driven approach. Effective communication, backed by appropriate behavioral reinforcements, enables Dell to connect directly with its employees and maintain its strong value-centered culture.

Our research shows that it is this ability to convey a company's core values and mission at a very personal level that differentiates high-performance businesses from their peers. People do not get excited about generating more shareholder wealth unless they understand how it affects them personally. The opportunity to create these linkages between mission and employee – and ignite a passion for outstanding performance – is what building a value-centered culture is all about.

Just as there are wider cultural views in human societies, so there are multiple cultural trends within business and governmental enterprises. Some of these organizational cultures lead to high performance, while others do not. In recent years, we have seen spectacular organizational failures triggered by inappropriate cultures. Consider the rule-bending, "do the deal at any cost" culture that apparently drove Enron's management team. While cultural minefield stories like this make the headlines, there is far less exposure given to companies with healthy cultures. Perhaps this is because such outstanding enterprises form a very select group.

For example, of the companies ranked among the S&P 500 when it was established in 1957, only 125 remain on the current list.[1] Those who have made the list year after year, such as GE and Johnson & Johnson, have thrived through market changes, periodic leadership transitions, good economies and bad. Winning organizations like these have cultures that sustain them through the tumultuous changes that derail peers whose cultural foundations are weaker.

A value-centered culture can endure through changes in leadership,
organization structure, type of work, and people
While there are many contributors to business excellence, research indicates that culture is the most enduring element of success, outlasting leadership, processes, and organization structure.

Johnson and Scholes[2] (1993) suggest the concept of a "cultural web", in which culture is seen as the influential composite of a number of variables, including leadership style, prevailing stories and myths, accepted rituals and symbols, the type of power structure, the form of organizational structure, the decision-making process, functional policies and management systems.

Johnson and Scholes contend that the strength and intensity of each of these cultural variables may vary from person to person and from group to group within an organization and between organizations, *but that the dominant organizational culture will prevail as a common theme.* Linking their argument to performance, they suggest that *the nature and intensity of their cultural recipe determine whether or not one organization develops greater competitive advantage over another,* even though both may have access to similar resources.

Building a value-centered culture is a good investment in the future. It can transcend the following four types of culture defined by Brewerton and Millward (1999).

- *Leaders-based culture*: Strong leaders can shape the culture of their organizations. A leader-centered culture can be very effective if the leader has the right values. However, Enron and WorldCom are examples of this type of culture in its most destructive form. A leader-centered culture is also inherently fragile in the sense that, as leaders change, there is always a risk of cultural crisis. Consider, for example, Apple Computer and its success under Steve Jobs compared with its performance in those periods when Jobs was not at the helm. To ensure sustainable performance, enterprises must seek to develop a culture that transcends the leader of the day.

- *Organization-based culture*: Culture is more fundamental than organization structure and the roles people play. Culture does not fundamentally change as an organization changes. For example, there is no shortage of companies that have outsourced significant portions of their businesses, including manufacturing operations, IT development and customer support. Yet, such major internal changes have not altered these organizations' basic cultural underpinnings.

- *Task-based culture*: Culture is more powerful than any specific task or initiative. If it were not for culture, for example, every project team at Accenture would have a different set of values and this would yield a different level of service to our clients. To overcome this, Accenture has nurtured a common culture around a set of core values that include client value creation, best people, respect for the individual, integrity, one global network and stewardship. This common culture allows Accenture to deliver projects and organizational change consistently around the globe.

- *People-based culture*: An enterprise's employees can largely define its culture. The dot-coms of the 1990s were dominated by young entrepreneurs, many fresh out of MBA or technology programs. For a time, it seemed that these emerging dynamos would redefine all of corporate culture. The energy of this period was intense and infectious. At the end of the day, however, because the dot-com inspired culture supported flawed notions of value, it was not sustainable.

A value-centered culture is deeply rooted in fundamental principles that are aligned with the objectives of the key stakeholders of an organization. When cultural drivers and stakeholders' goals are fully attuned, the culture remains evergreen. Value-centered culture is not just about financial success, though this is a critical and necessary outcome. It is also about understanding how an enterprise creates value for all of its stakeholders – including employees – and consistently delivers mutually beneficial results over time.

The Lockheed Martin Skunk Works®[3] model illustrates how culture can help an organization sustain high performance over long periods. This unit, at the forefront of aviation innovation since 1943, faced one of its greatest challenges in 1960 when Gary Powers' U2 (laden with spy-cameras) was shot down over the USSR. The incident created a diplomatic migraine for the US government. Not only did it sour the relationship between Moscow and Washington, it also forced America to devise a new strategy for meeting its reconnaissance objectives.

US leaders set an ambitious goal: building a plane that could fly at Mach 3, at an altitude of 80,000 feet, with minimal radar cross-section. Designing and constructing such an aircraft posed some daunting challenges. The shortlist included these attributes.

- The plane had to be made from new materials, including titanium.

- The fuel had to be able to withstand the 300+ degree temperature in the plane without igniting.

- New engines had to be designed to withstand the sonic shock waves of Mach 3.

- Tires had to be strong enough to resist exploding at high temperatures.

The rest is history, as they say. The Skunk Works team produced the SR-71 'Blackbird,' a plane that met all the above criteria and has since earned a proud place in aviation history.

But Skunk Works was not just about one plane. Since 1943, the group has created more than 20 magnificent aircraft designs for airplanes that are operated by air force fleets around the globe. The Skunk Works culture was created by its now-legendary leader, Clarence 'Kelly' Johnson. What allowed Kelly to run Skunk Works so effectively and efficiently was his unconventional organizational approach. He broke the accepted rules, challenging a widely accepted bureaucratic system that stifled innovation and hindered progress. Johnson formalized how his unit would operate by creating his own distinctive value-based approach. In fact, the "14 practices and rules" that he devised are still part of Lockheed Martin's ethos today. The Skunk Works model has allowed Lockheed to stay at the forefront of military aviation for more than 60 years.

HOW CAN FINANCE HELP FOSTER A VALUE-CENTERED CULTURE?

Finance plays a critical role in a value-centered culture, both in defining what value means and in helping to embed value-based decision making at every level. Put simply, finance frames how business alternatives should be analyzed with the goal of optimizing value creation. While line management retains ultimate responsibility for strategic decisions, finance sets the economic terms of the debate and is an integral member of the decision-making team. Finance has assumed a new set of responsibilities that position it to help reinforce the "value" in a value-centered culture. How can finance organize in a manner that fosters and nurtures this culture?

Ideally, financial planning and analysis (FP&A) resources are physically deployed in the business units or departments that they work with and support. This organizational model is preferred because it enables a close, day-to-day working relationship between finance and line management. All the benefits of strong partnership accrue: finance professionals understand the enterprises they support – their strengths and weaknesses. Finance is trusted by its customers in the line organization. And equally important, finance is seen as part of the team, rather than an outsider, so it is included more frequently in key decisions.

This kind of decentralized FP&A organization is not always possible, or even optimal. In some cases, the scale of business units or departments does not justify dedicated FP&A support – and a centralized, pooled-resource model is more practical. In other cases, there is a need for deep skills in specialized areas, such as merger and acquisition (M&A) analysis, complex pricing or deal structuring, risk assessment or tax planning. In these and other areas vital to an enterprise's unique needs, it may not be feasible to build the critical mass in each business unit or department that leads to world-class skills and capabilities.

A better answer may be to organize around a center with deeply skilled individuals whose expertise can be tapped as needed by the rest of the organization. Consider the challenge facing Bob Young, the CFO of Teradata. Pricing and contracting decisions around Teradata's software and services were increasing in complexity. In response, Young says he "... built a world-wide community of pricing people. This small pricing group regularly shares its experience and handles the most difficult and important transactions. The group's members have become consultants to the sales organization on how to craft a transaction based on competitive analysis, customer business propositions, and our experience and history with particular customers."

To help promote a consistent way of thinking about value, finance needs a certain amount of organizational cohesion. This is also true when it comes to supporting the business with standard tools and methodologies for applying value concepts. The more decentralized and far-flung a finance organization is, the more challenging it is to achieve a consistent value-centered culture, both within finance and throughout an organization. While a decentralized, "forward deployed" finance model may be preferred, regardless of structure, all finance professionals must be accountable for meeting the imperatives of finance as a whole.

There are a number of ways to achieve this accountability. Many businesses structure their finance organization so that everyone has solid line accountability within a clearly defined hierarchy. In our view, this is not an absolute requirement, but there should be provision for at least dotted-line accountability. Finance should also have input into compensation, performance evaluation, training and career development. Having this input helps ensure that finance keeps the attention of its professionals wherever they are, and that they meet capability standards in supporting the business.

THE JOURNEY TO A VALUE-CENTERED CULTURE

Cultural change is one of the most difficult journeys an organization can embark upon. There is no 12-step program with concrete milestones to confirm your progress. While developing a value-centered culture is an ambitious goal, it *is* achievable. The prerequisites are executive leadership, a willingness to tackle the challenge from many angles at once, and a recognition that it takes time for old patterns of behavior to change.

The starting point is executive leadership. The CFO must be prepared to play the role of chief evangelist for value-centered thinking within his/her organization. This is the role that Mitch Blaser took on at Swiss Re. If the tone is set at the top, then the rest of the organization will pay attention. However, a CFO can play this role only if the necessary foundational work has been completed and a clear understanding has emerged about how his/her enterprise creates value for its stakeholders. So an important step early in the process of creating a value-centered culture is to develop a strong analytical framework for 1) the metrics that will be used to measure value creation, and 2) how each facet of an enterprise contributes to its overall value proposition. At Swiss Re, EVM was the tool used to put value creation on a fact-based foundation.

First and foremost, the CFO must mobilize his/her own organization and get the entire finance leadership on board. Whether at the corporate level or within business units, team members must be aligned with the CFO around the importance of developing a value-centered culture and the strategy for making it happen. Achieving this level of alignment within finance leadership may mean rethinking how finance is organized, and how its activities are measured to ensure the greater accountability required to promote change.

Once value and accountability are clearly defined, the multidimensional "cultural web" described earlier in this chapter provides a useful framework for action. Based on this model, the next step involves assessing whether the attributes of a value-centered culture are in place in terms of rituals and routines, stories, symbols, power structures, and control systems. The speed of cultural change is enhanced by pursuing just this kind of multidimensional strategy.

Finally, it is important to measure progress. Results can be seen on three fronts. First, in the wider use of value concepts in day-to-day business decisions. Second, in finance's growing role in setting business direction. And finally, progress is reflected in the increased perception across the broader enterprise about the importance of finance's contributions. These kinds of results are seen clearly in the customer-focus ratings that finance now receives at Swiss Re.

When a value-centered culture is alive and well, employees at every level have a better grasp of how their enterprise can achieve high performance and how they contribute to its value proposition. We believe the evidence supports the view that this deeper understanding and focus on value brings with it greater success in meeting the expectations of primary stakeholders. In business, that means higher returns to shareholders, and in the public sector, better value for citizens.

THE HACKETT GROUP ON VALUE-CENTERED CULTURE

The Hackett group's research shows that the CFO of a world-class finance organization is in many ways the most powerful executive after the CEO. Although they continue to be custodians of the books and related fiduciary responsibilities, CFOs have seen their responsibilities evolve dramatically. Their newest role: acting as a member of the core teams leading their enterprises. This shift has occurred not only because CFOs are integrally involved in all aspects of the business, but more importantly, because they have unique insight into the economic trade-offs and priorities that will result in achieving greater value creation. The difference between world-class organizations and their peers in this area is striking. While 94% of CFOs in world-class organizations have a seat at the table

Percentage of companies where finance management is involved
in developing business strategies and objectives, 2005

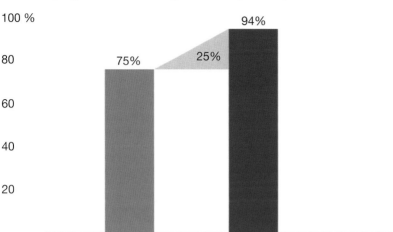

in driving major decisions, their less successful peers participate at this
level only 75% of the time.

Going forward, finance organizations must be involved at the highest and earliest levels of corporate planning and decision making, while
providing the tools and services that senior management needs to steer
the business (such as balanced scorecards). Finance organizations must
finish the work they have started in improving transactional efficiency
so that they, too, can turn their attention to assuming a leadership role in
building a value-centered culture.

CFO INSIGHTS: LESSONS FROM THE MASTERS

- Develop a clear definition of value for your enterprise and an
  understanding of how your business plays in the value chain
  to create it. Put the definition into as concrete a set of terms as
  possible and place it on an analytical footing.

- Ensure that finance is at the table when strategy is being developed and business decisions are being made. Be prepared to

inject insight based both on business acumen and on finance's unique technical expertise in value analysis, tax impacts, risk impacts, GAAP, P&L effects, etc.

- Place a high priority on developing the types of higher-order finance and business skills needed to provide insightful business analysis. Target skills that are more similar to those of business managers rather than those of traditional accountants. The new skills that are most critical include analytical skills, business acumen, industry acumen, change agency and effective communication.

- Educate line management and employees in value concepts and their application to day-to-day decision making. Employ formal and informal strategies, including both structured curriculum as well as the on-the-job learning that occurs when line managers interact with well-versed finance professionals.

- Organize finance to ensure close day-to-day interaction with finance's internal "customers." Balance the customer-facing organization with deeply skilled centers of expertise that can be drawn upon for the most technically challenging issues.

REFERENCES

1 Andrew Bary, Going Strong: The S&P Stocks of '57 Have Aged Nicely, *Barron's*, February 28, 2005. http://www.barrons.com

2 Gerry Johnson and Kevan Scholes, Exploring Corporate Strategy, Sixth Edition, *Financial Times Prentice Hall*, 2002.

3 The Lockheed Martin Skunk Works® http://www.lockheedmartin. com

CHAPTER 5

Enterprise Performance Management

TRANSFORMING FINANCE IN THE JOURNEY TO VALUE-BASED MANAGEMENT

Seck Wai Kwong, CFO and Senior Executive Vice President
Singapore Exchange Limited

Singapore Exchange Limited (SGX) is Asia Pacific's first demutualized and integrated securities and derivatives exchange. SGX was formed in 1999 and became the first exchange in Asia Pacific to be listed via a public offer and a private placement. Home to Singapore's leading listed companies, the securities exchange was the first fully electronic and floorless exchange in Asia. As of September 2005, 648 companies were listed, with a total market capitalization of S$418.6 billion. More than a quarter of the companies listed were foreign, with their principal business outside of Singapore. Most of these companies were from Greater China. In FY2005, SGX's securities market achieved a turnover value of S$168.3 billion, with 148.5 billion shares traded. With its derivatives market offering an extensive range of Asian equity index and interest rate products, SGX is also emerging as Asia's offshore risk management center.

We asked Seck Wai Kwong to discuss his priorities since he became CFO in 2003. "I concentrated on transforming the organization and finance so we can move to a much higher performance level," he said. "We have been working on things like value-

centered culture, performance management, systems and capital stewardship. The market seems to like that. Our stock price has doubled in the last two years.

"One of the first issues we addressed was performance management – we wanted to incorporate a value-based management structure. When I started, we had rudimentary management reports, so we designed a road map taking us to value-based management. We also needed a profitability management system. And part of the journey toward value-based management is segmenting it by product and customer. Now we understand profitability, but we need better information and the ability to automate it. That's what we are working on right now."

We asked Seck if he was setting a goal and working backwards to achieve it. "Yes," he replied. "We want to move towards a value-based management system, so what we build along the way should help us get there. You don't want to establish profitability management systems and then dismantle them because you want to do EVA®. You should have a structural goal in mind, as well as the building blocks required to get there."

Seck went on to tell us about his organization's vision and the challenges he faces. "As an organization, we have 600 people, with annual revenues of about S$300 million. Between S$100 – S$130 million of that is profit, depending on the markets. So it's not too large to get your hands around.

"Profitability management is one of many priorities. Basically we view our key priorities as 'clock-building' efforts, putting in place the necessary infrastructure to build an enduring marketplace. For instance, we're establishing a project portfolio management framework. There are a hundred projects our people want to do and they can't be done at the same time. So you decide which ones to invest in, and then make sure they are delivered on budget and on time, generating the intended business outcome. All of the processes and structures we're creating should contribute to the overall goal of meeting our value targets.

"I'm giving myself three to five years to get there, and we're currently in year two, so we need to get the new structures in place quickly. Here's how I see that journey. The major building blocks will be in place in the next six months. Then the organization gets accustomed to the new ways of working. You could go to value-based management tomorrow, but you could lose your people along the way. So we've got to encourage them to buy in and raise their comfort level with a new approach to managing the business."

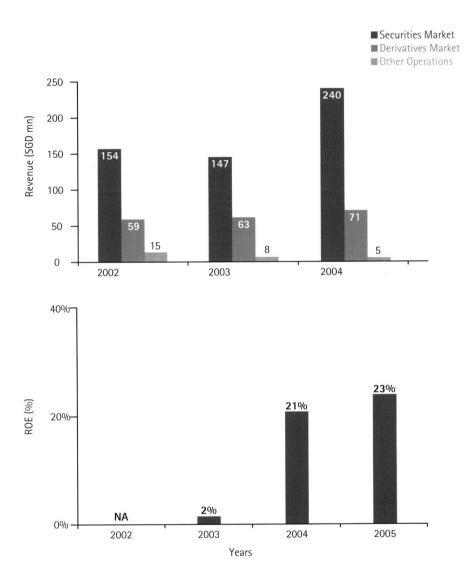

Figure 5.1 *Singapore Exchange performance trends*
Source: Accenture analysis

Intangible assets account for up to 80% of the Russell 3000 Index balance sheet, so financial reporting should be broadened to include these non-financial elements. Despite this, current financial reporting standards do not require the codification of intangible assets and their impact on equity value.

We asked Seck to give us his perspective on the inclusion of intangible assets in a value-based management system. He noted, "We are very aware of brand value. We know that our SGX brand is worth a lot in terms of enterprise value and the financial integrity of Singapore Inc. When we market to China, our reputation there attracts Chinese company listings to SGX. People often ask me why they should list in Singapore; one reason I give is to get a better PE. Another reason is the 'Good Housekeeping Seal' attached to a Singapore listing – that's essential to unlocking our brand value. The SGX brand name has brought us customers who are interested in collaboration agreements. Over time, we think we'll be able to facilitate joint selling efforts by leveraging on the co-branding of our products with other partners.

"Unlocking this asset through things like employee development training programs and focusing on the customer is relatively new to us. When we restructured the organization in 2003, the customer became our central focus. We have four main customer groups: intermediaries through whom our retail and institutional customers trade stocks and derivatives, retail customers who trade for themselves, institutions, and issuers. We've got floor traders here who are a very important constituent when it comes to providing market liquidity. The fund managers and retail customers are also important. We have functional teams that focus on each of these constituents. We also focus on encouraging feedback between our exchange and the final customer.

"We also spend a lot of time on the human capital side – leadership, retention policies and compensation structure – to make sure we get it right. Our bonus pool is directly linked to our firm's profitability."

Commenting on the critical success factors for a CFO in Asia, Seck observed, "Our leadership is clearly focused on the business: managing the costs, increasing revenue, and managing capital. This makes our people and our customers feel secure, and that's important. I think that the quality of our leadership contributes to SGX's value. Hsieh Fu Hua, our CEO, inspires investor confidence. He conveys a very clear vision of where this company is going and how we'll get there.

"As for our people, we have a strategy map that explains our financial objectives and the customer value proposition. Our team understands this and can see where their contributions fit. It's important for everyone to see our line of sight and feel that their contribution makes a difference."

We asked Seck if he thought that finance enables a valued-centered culture. "That's exactly what we do. As the Corporate Services Group, we are a partner who helps to shape the vision and strategic direction of the organization. We partner with different business units to provide an infrastructure that can promote the necessary change.

"We support the different business groups by putting value-based performance management, portfolio management, and other systems in place. When we build a portfolio management system, it's not meant for technology and products only. We are providing the framework and the infrastructure to support the entire organization."

As Seck noted, performance management is important: "Because we are an exchange and clearing house, there are lots of capital needs. We have to ensure that we have the financial resources to withstand unexpected events like the market crash of '87, so we keep a lot of capital in reserve. We've been carefully re-evaluating how much capital we need, what is surplus, and what can be returned to our shareholders. I'm happy to report that we've actually returned capital twice in the last two years."

Without a reliable enterprise performance management system, SGX could not deliver. Asked to share his thoughts on the deployment of finance at SGX, Seck said, "Finance operations are the backbone of what we do, and we always seek faster and better ways of doing things. For example, when I came to the job, the first set of results took about two-and-a-half months to report. Our financial year ends on the last day of this month, and I will report the results within 20 business days. The fact that we are an exchange means that we should lead the way. We report our quarterly results within the first seven business days."

We asked Seck to discuss the risk management capabilities that have been deployed in the last 24 months. "It was critical that we put a new risk management framework in place. We used to have a narrow focus on clearing funds. Now, we've broadened our capabilities to include the different parties we work with and all the exposure we have – operational risk, reputation risk and credit risk – and put them together in a systematic framework. We formed a risk management committee at the board level to reach consensus on the top risks and ensure that these risks are mitigated and managed properly."

Some executives view the new regulatory requirements as a cost; others see them as just good management practice. We asked Seck to comment on this. "As an exchange, we view the regulatory aspects not as a cost, but as part of our success. The Singapore Exchange has regulatory responsibilities, and we are also a listed company. Sometimes there's tension between these two aspects. We handle this through a conflicts committee. This is a group of independent board directors who oversee conflicts of interest, which I'd define as maintaining the proper balance between profit-seeking and regulatory obligations. Occasionally, there may be tensions between these two imperatives. We want 'Company X' to be listed – we'd love to have its fees – but does it meet regulatory requirements? How do you resolve that tension? The conflicts committee also makes sure that SGX is devoting adequate resources to its regulatory responsibilities, because the easiest way to stifle regulation is to deprive it of resources. So the conflicts committee takes an in-depth look at such issues. That's how we balance it right now."

EFFECTIVE PERFORMANCE MANAGEMENT

Better decisions and more disciplined execution

Many businesses view performance management as a "soft science" with few obvious benefits. However, there's clear evidence that a comprehensive enterprise performance management (EPM) approach can make a major difference in the way that companies plan, forecast, monitor and manage business performance.

- EPM improves the execution of organizational strategy. By facilitating better and faster decision-making, it maximizes sustainable shareholder value by consistently promoting optimal resource allocation.

- EPM consistently defines and models the key drivers of both current and future value – financial and non-financial, tangible and intangible – and explains how these drivers interrelate.

- EPM promotes the management and optimization of business performance across a single enterprise or business network.

- EPM enables the identification and evaluation of performance-driving strategies, and facilitates the translation of these strategies into tangible tactics and plans.

- EPM enhances the monitoring of strategy execution across the organization through improved forecasting, reporting and analytics.

Despite these potential benefits of enterprise performance management, the vast majority of EPM systems in place today do not generate great value. While a recent *Harvard Business Review* study reported that best-in-class companies with EPM systems achieved 2.95% higher returns on assets and 5.14% higher returns on equity, these impressive gains were realized by fewer than one in four companies (23%) that utilize EPM.[1]

In addition, many organizations spend significant amounts on developing point solutions that consistently fail to deliver real value. By adopting a more comprehensive EPM approach, these organizations can be more proactive in their delivery of useful management information. They can also save money by focusing their efforts on those processes that maximize financial return.

Focusing on improved EPM capabilities

We live in a world that seems obsessed with performance management. Survey data suggests that in the five years to 2000, between 30% and 60% of companies began to transform their performance measurement systems.[2] A recent AMR survey of 363 companies indicates that 60% will increase EPM budgets, 35% will maintain current spending levels, and only 5% will decrease EPM spending in 2005.[3] Why all this effort to improve performance management systems, when the evidence suggests that many fail to generate significant value? Our research identified both internal and external drivers of companies' efforts to improve performance management.

Regulators and legislators around the globe are demanding that organizations release ever-increasing amounts of information about their performance and practices. Legislation, such as the Sarbanes-Oxley Act in the US, will force organizations to disclose information on a wide variety of performance issues. Even in the absence of such legislation, it is clear that investment analysts are becoming increasingly interested in non-financial information – especially the "intangibles" that can provide insight into an organization's future value creation potential.

From an internal perspective, traditional accounting measures that focus on tangible and past performance indicators tell only part of the story. Non-financial and intangible measures that look at brand equity, people satisfaction and intellectual property, are becoming more critical for many companies. However, when internal reporting systems are examined, many have a predominant focus on financial measures that report what has happened in the past. Many organizations indicate a gap in their ability to adequately manage the full range of elements that drive their business.

The emergence of point solutions

The drivers discussed above resulted in new and improved performance management methods. Frameworks such as the balanced scorecard, activity-based management, and "beyond budgeting" were developed. Organizations spent significant sums of money implementing non-integrated ERP systems, data warehouses, financial reporting packages, budgeting and forecasting systems and scorecard/dashboard tools.

Through the analysis of performance trends and causal relationships, business leaders have tried to generate value by allocating resources more strategically. While they have seen some efficiency improvement, they have realized little in the way of more effective management systems and significant value creation. Sizable gaps remain in companies' abilities to understand the true drivers of value in their business models. As a result, many executives are frustrated and dissatisfied with their EPM systems.

Many EPM efforts have failed to deliver the desired capabilities
Recent research highlights the common factors that explain why most companies continue to struggle with improving performance management.

1 *The wrong metrics*: Only 23% of companies with balanced scorecards had any proven link between the scorecards and growth in shareholder value. Only 12% of companies link their quality measures to stock returns, and at least 70% of companies employ metrics that lack statistical validity. This lack of precise metrics creates confusion and hinders strategy execution.

2 *The cost of data quality*: Estimates of total dollars spent on data warehousing applications exceed $40 billion per annum. Of this amount, more than 60% is spent on cleansing data.[4]

3 *Oceans of data*: Even with these huge investments, many results seem counterproductive: "60% of workers feel overwhelmed by the amount of information they receive,"[5] and "43% of managers believe that important decisions are delayed and the ability to make decisions is affected by too much information."[6]

4 *Islands of systems*: We found many examples of targeted solutions for budgeting and planning, balanced scorecards, EVA® and reporting tools. The lack of integration between these separate initiatives produces additional cost and inconsistent results and conclusions.

5 *Current management systems ignore and under-manage value-creating assets*: In 1980, $100 invested in the S&P 500 Index could be backed by $80 of hard assets on the balance sheet. Today, only 25% of the S&P 500's value can be traced to tangible assets.[7] The balance is largely intangibles (i.e., customer retention, brands, employee productivity, etc.). A study of 300 buy-side investors (including large investors, institutional investors, portfolio managers and research staff) indicated that 50% of their allocation decisions were based on non-financial performance.[8]

6 *The wrong incentives*: Our experience and research show that many organizations have put in place the wrong incentives to drive performance. The incentives tend to be near-term focused and don't strike the right balance between short- and long-term performance. An example is incentives for performance measured by financial metrics that have no clear linkage to the creation of long-term shareholder value.

HOW DO THE MOST SUCCESSFUL ORGANIZATIONS APPROACH EPM?

While there is no single recipe for optimizing performance management, we have found seven attributes that enable many high-performance companies to deliver sustained value creation through EPM.

1 An integrated framework for quick decision-making and action.

2 A firm grounding in driving value, with an external value creation perspective.

3 A deep understanding of the organization's critical value drivers.

4 An external, market-based approach to setting targets that minimize gaming and negotiation.

5 Dynamic evaluation of initiatives, planning and resource allocation.

6 Action driven by focused performance monitoring and analytics, with improved statistical relevance over time.

7 Key people, process and technology enablers to sustain high performance over time.

We believe that many high performance businesses and organizations adopt these leading practices in a holistic framework for EPM (see Figure 5.2). This framework enables them to create the appropriate future vision for EPM in a phased and logically organized manner.

An integrated framework for quick decisions and actions

The integrated nature of EPM management processes has at its core – and is driven by – a focus on the right information.

1 The key result measures of successful strategy execution – for example, Total Economic Profit (see Figure 5.3) and revenue growth.

2 The few but critical performance measures of strategy execution that measure performance against the key drivers of current and future value.

3 Information regarding the key strategic initiatives the company is investing in to improve performance.

4 A governance framework for decision making and driving value that builds on accurate information and empowers people to make the right decisions.

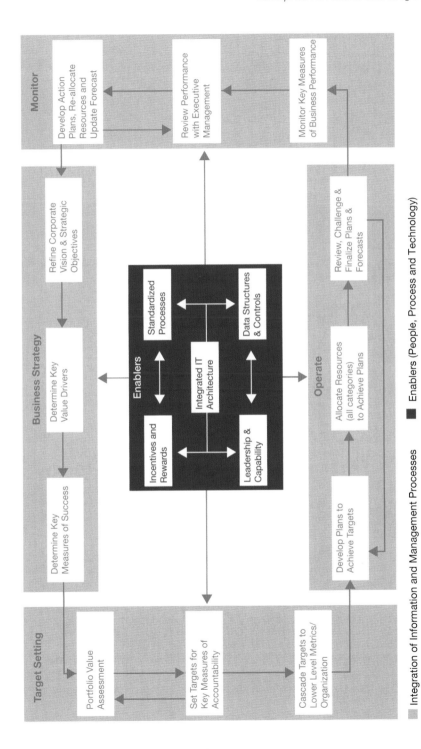

Target Setting

Portfolio Value Assessment

Set Targets for Key Measures of Accountability

Cascade Targets to Lower Level Metrics/ Organization

Business Strategy

Refine Corporate Vision & Strategic Objectives

Determine Key Value Drivers

Determine Key Measures of Success

Monitor

Develop Action Plans, Re-allocate Resources and Update Forecast

Review Performance with Executive Management

Monitor Key Measures of Business Performance

Operate

Review, Challenge & Finalize Plans & Forecasts

Allocate Resources (all categories) to Achieve Plans

Develop Plans to Achieve Targets

Enablers

Standardized Processes

Data Structures & Controls

Integrated IT Architecture

Incentives and Rewards

Leadership & Capability

Integration of Information and Management Processes

Enablers (People, Process and Technology)

Figure 5.2 *Enterprise Performance Management integrated framework*

TRS Mapping Shows a Complete Mapping of Value Creation

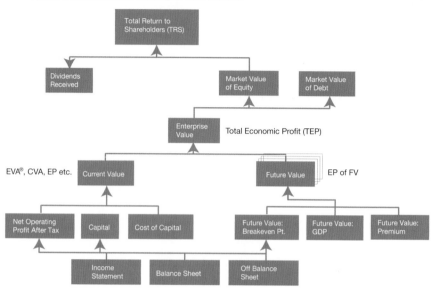

Traditional financial results measures (e.g. EPS, RONA, EVA etc.) purport to be linked to shareholder value by illustrating the correlation of these measures to TRS—anywhere from 0% to 55%. These measures are not more highly correlated because they are current value focused. Most of a company's value is tied to future growth expectations. TRS Mapping comes at this from a different angle by starting from the top and identifying its component parts:

1. TRS consists of dividends received and the change in the market value of equity.
2. Enterprise value is the market value of equity and the market value of debt.
3. Enterprise value is current value (i.e. current profitability into perpetuity) and future value.
4. Current value is determined by traditional measurements such as Economic Profit.
5. We arrive at a periodic performance measure for future value by decapitalizing Future Value into the Economic Profit of Future Value (EP of FV).
6. Adding the current value of Economic Profit to the future value of Economic Profit results in Total Economic Profit—the first performance measure that is directly tied to TRS.

TRS Mapping scorecards fiscal year accounting performance. Just as importantly, it also integrates fiscal year "value" performance. For the first time, this permits the measurement, management and reward of the future value created by intangible capital investments.

The EP of FV also provides direct shareholder feedback on management's strategies and investments. Indexing further separates market movement from management accomplishments. These frameworks—applied to competitive performance and peer benchmarking—provide management with an invaluable view of the future, plus comprehensive competitive intelligence.

Figure 5.3 *Total return to shareholders (TRS) mapping framework*

CASE STUDY
Designing an integrated EPM strategy

Like many companies that have grown quickly, one global retailer faced some key challenges in driving profitable growth and shareholder value within a maturing retail industry. Due to its rapid growth over the past few years, they tended to have a rigid focus on short-term financial performance and a less disciplined focus on its key drivers of value over the longer term. In addition, there was a lack of integration of strategy, capital investment evaluation, resource allocation, budgeting and performance monitoring.

They recognized the need to establish a fully integrated EPM program that focused on improvements in the following key areas:

- *Improving external benchmarking capability to provide a better context for value creation goals and long-range planning processes.*
- *Developing a driver-based planning structure with common definitions and performance language.*
- *Designing consistent and fully integrated management processes to strengthen the linkage between strategic planning and execution.*
- *Facilitating process changes with the Cognos technology platform for planning/performance reporting.*

In less than a year, these capabilities have generated major benefits:

- *Its fact base for strategic and capital investment decisions has been improved.*
- *It is now taking a more dynamic approach to the development of innovative and differentiated business plans that are resourced for execution, and balance short- and long-term returns.*
- *Its performance monitoring debate now focuses on the key performance indicators (KPIs) that are driving tangible results.*

One executuve summed up the benefits of the enhanced EPM program: "Our strategic and business planning process is a competitive advantage. It gives us a better road map, and through this process our organization has a much more robust understanding of what is needed to achieve our goals."

CASE STUDY
Using EPM as a competitive weapon

Dell is a good example of a company that uses EPM as a competitive differentiator to drive sustained high performance. In the summer of 2000, Dell began to see trends indicating a slowdown in demand, and industry weakness ahead of the projected global economic downturn. "As more data came in each day, it was clear to us that demand was really starting to drop," said Jim Schneider, SVP and CFO of Dell.[9]

Armed with this information, Dell's management team quickly used it to cut costs and lower prices. At the same time, Compaq, Hewlett-Packard and Dell's other competitors were not predicting the same trouble. They spoke optimistically about the fourth quarter and alluded to Dell-specific problems. The investment community did not know what to make of Dell's price cutting announcement and downgraded its stock.

Dell's ability to quickly assess overall trends in the external industry, its understanding of the key drivers of demand, and its ability to use its insight to drive decisions at a faster pace than the competition paid off handsomely. Dell saw its value increase by more than 23% in 2001, while Compaq, Gateway and Hewlett-Packard saw theirs decline by 36%, 62% and 32%, respectively. Dell's 2001 sales remained relatively flat (down 2.3%), while sales by its competitors declined 7% to 37%.

CFO Schneider noted, "Our competitors' information pulls are not the same as ours because we work directly with customers. That's why we embarked on this pricing strategy so early – before the other guys missed their numbers in a huge way the following quarter."

High-performance businesses have a very strong value orientation. They firmly ground their strategy in driving value and the key result measures of performance that are linked to total returns to shareholders. They clearly understand their value drivers and have a proven process for the identification and prioritization of the key causal drivers aligned with strategy and value creation. They focus on the few critical drivers of value and causal information necessary and sufficient for managing their business.

CASE STUDY
Understanding critical value drivers

Recently, a European utility faced a number of challenges (i.e., earnings pressure and poor share performance, as well as a new CEO and management model). Internally, there was no single set of measures and no consistent management processes for development or review; these processes were varied, non-transparent and had a heavy financial focus.

The new CEO began by aligning the utility's executive team and its top 200 managers with the company's key value drivers. They first focused on quantifying and identifying the sensitivity of the value drivers and then eliminated critical organizational barriers that were inhibiting improved performance. The company then established performance agreements (contracts) linking targets established for the executive team and the top 200 managers with the key value drivers. Finally, the utility adopted a standardized approach to performance reporting using value-based balanced scorecards across major business lines and functions.

This initiative resulted in a number of benefits:

- *It more effectively aligned the organization with the execution of its strategy.*
- *Board, executive, division and business unit meetings became much more effective and efficient.*
- *The definition and understanding of key value drivers were enhanced.*
- *98% of the top 200 executives were given clear contracts that aligned with business unit scorecards.*
- *Financial performance and total return to shareholders (TRS) were improved.*

An external market-based approach to setting targets can minimize gaming and negotiation.

In most companies, the target-setting process is a sub-optimal, time consuming and non-strategic process that is made worse by game playing. Targets established through this budget negotiation process are inevitably tied to incentive compensation, so they set both a performance ceiling (i.e., "never go over your budget") and a floor (i.e., "always spend your budget").

CASE STUDY

Aligning business targets with strategic goals

Global energy giant BP had a significant internal debate over which targets were most important. This resulted in a misalignment between management's priorities and those of outside stakeholders.

When the consolidated financial plan created by BP's operating units did not align with the financial result required by the board of directors and shareholders, top management decided that gaps in financial performance would be allocated across the businesses in the form of "stretch targets." This simple technique removes argument and negotiation among different layers of management about what is going to be achieved and what the budget should be. Reviews during the year now focus on how successful each business unit is in closing the gaps.

Although BP still spends a significant amount of time on the budget process, the company spends much less time than comparable oil majors. Additionally, this approach is more effective at aligning targets with strategic goals and the expectations of external stakeholders.

Companies can learn a lesson from BP by focusing on a few key improvements:

- Use a top-down approach to target setting that is based on external benchmarks and minimum market expectations of returns (i.e., a cost of capital return on enterprise value over the industry life cycle).

- Targets should be derived from the strategy-planning phase. Clear governance structures should be in place to support the target-setting process.

- Targets are not negotiable based on bottom-up budgets.

Dynamic evaluation of initiatives and resource allocation

Eighty percent of organizations believe that budgeting and planning processes are not value adding because they are very time consuming[10] and not strategic. However, the annual budget is typically the symptom – not the root cause – of the problem because it is used to set targets against which people will be measured and compensated. The annual budget is therefore prone to gaming. There is little or no distinction between the budget and the forecast. The forecast is just an extension of the target created in the budget; it is inaccurate and subject to gaming.

High-performance businesses use planning processes to allocate resources (i.e., capital and people) to highest-value opportunities to achieve the targets against the key drivers of value (i.e., most material and volatile over time) and strategy execution. These companies do not artificially restrict planning to the current fiscal year, nor do they tie incentive compensation to meeting an annual budget. Instead, they use a rolling business planning process that is dynamic and focused on reallocating resources to drive business performance.

Magyar Oil and Gas Company (MOL), an integrated Hungarian oil and gas group, was a typical example of a large company with a strategic objective to improve their planning and reporting processes, as well as reduce the cost of the support organization (finance and IT) providing information access and analysis.

MOL developed a long-term business intelligence strategy that focused on improving decision-making capabilities through logically formatted, high quality information. They achieved this by focusing on improved planning, forecasting and process effectiveness reporting. They also streamlined technology-enabled processes for better information analysis.

This resulted in improved process efficiency and significant planning and headcount reductions. More important, the effectiveness of management decision making improved through better information quality and a closer link between planning and actual performance.

Focused performance analytics and monitoring

Performance monitoring and reporting is a tedious process for most companies: more than 70% of the effort goes into report generation. This typically results in too much data and a lack of keen insight to drive decision making.

High performers focus on enhancing performance monitoring and analytics capabilities to improve the statistical fact base and the relevance of what is being measured. High performers have EPM capabilities with fast reporting cycles and common data models that focus on the decisions and actions required to meet or exceed performance targets.

Peter Rasper, CFO of SAP Corporate Services, comments on the use of EPM at his company: "We use the full capabilities of the SAP toolset. It provides a clear and global single set of measurements. Information is captured and reported consistently for all levels and all parts of the business. Consequently, there is no need for large consolidation efforts and information is always 'on-line' and available. It is very true that when you have deep analytics, leaders can see all. At SAP, our cockpit data is available for our boards to access, review, and react to immediately."

Outokumpu, one of the largest stainless steel producers in the world, is an example of a company that struggled to effectively measure strategy execution in an industry characterized by demand for increased return on investment and a constant squeeze on margins.

Outokumpu focused its initial capability improvements on aligning strategic plans, target setting, value drivers, forward-looking performance indicators, reporting and rewards. This was then operationalized at all business units and management levels by adopting a common performance management process, tools and language to describe all of the elements of the solution.

This led to an increased focus on activities and behavior, creating value as defined by sustainable positive economic profit throughout the organization.

Jouni Grönroos, Outokumpu's Executive Vice President – Finance and Risk Management, commented: "The alignment of strategic plans, short-term targets, action plans, performance measurement and reporting, combined with rewarding and developing people, is the key factor in executing corporate strategies. When this aligned force is directed at creating sustainable shareholder value, you can see the results throughout the organization, as well as in shareholder returns."

SUSTAINING HIGH PERFORMANCE OVER TIME

Over the past 20 years, a large number of companies have been frustrated with the problems discussed above, and many have addressed them through the implementation of point solutions. These solutions have produced some efficiency increases. However, they cannot deliver more effective integrated management systems supported by the key people, process and technology enablers, that will sustain these improvements over time.

Key people enablers

Research into high-performance businesses and organizations shows a number of common leadership and productivity-enhancing characteristics.

1 *Leadership*: Our experience shows that implementing a best-in-class EPM capability requires strong sponsorship and leadership. Conversely, effective leadership in high-performance businesses requires robust EPM capabilities.

2 *Value-focused structure*: Form should always follow function. The structure of the organization should not be an impediment to value creation. Enabling an effective EPM capability requires cross-functional skills organized around how the work gets done.

3 *Skills and capabilities/talent*: To effectively and successfully change its business performance management, the company must have the appropriate training and education programs in place to support the change.

4 *Value mindset and culture*: People at every organizational level must understand how individual actions contribute to the achievement of overall business goals.

5 *Aligned incentives and rewards*: An incentive plan ties total returns to shareholders directly to current and future value performance, with multi-year budget targets driven by investor expectations. This eliminates bottom-up budget negotiations and gaming. Aligned incentives at lower levels of the organization should provide "line of sight" to focus on what really matters.

Key process enablers

From a business process perspective, there are a few important enablers to sustain EPM over time. These enablers include:

1 *Common performance language*: Robust and consistent definitions are used for all key metrics, assets, and decision support information requirements. This performance language "dictionary" should be consistently used to eliminate or minimize endless debate about such straightforward measures as customer, headcount, returns, etc.

2 *Standardized management processes*: EPM is fundamentally about improving decision making in a way that drives sustainable value. Therefore, it is of tremendous value to clearly specify the processes and associated governance frameworks that define how key decisions are made (e.g., prioritization of value drivers, approval of capital investment, change in strategy direction, etc.).

3 *Information quality and integrity*: Before embarking on an expensive technology project or data warehouse implementation, it is wise to consider the quality of information needed for business decision making. Within accounting rulemaking, a tension has traditionally existed between relevant information and reliable numbers. For management decision making, it is more important to get relevant information quickly than perfectly accurate information late.

For most companies, performance trends must be understood and the signal-to-noise ratio must be high if the quality of decision making is to be improved. The key point here is that the company should set specific thresholds for the quality and timeliness of information, based on the decisions that are to be made with this information. This is very different from the traditional accounting paradigm.

Key technology enablers
The search for performance management solutions has been greatly aided by recent technological developments. Many believe that implementing a technology solution (e.g., data warehouse, executive dashboard, budgeting tool, etc.) will solve their problems. However, it is important to recognize that technology is not a panacea; it is a key enabler for a robust EPM capability that includes many of the components discussed above. Technology enablers include the following.

1 *Enterprise data model*: This model specifies how data will be captured, aggregated and reported. This is an important exercise, because the data model must:

- be cross-functional (e.g. marketing, supply chain, etc.);
- cover intangible as well as tangible assets; and
- take into account the company's priorities for non-traditional data (e.g. customer satisfaction surveys, point of sale transactions, etc.).

An enterprise data model for today's organization is analogous to the common chart of accounts and "one version of the truth" that companies have focused on in recent years.

2 *Integrated technical architecture*: Current technology vendors are creating integrated capabilities, either by developing their own tools or purchasing others. At this point, it is unclear who will emerge as the leader, but capabilities to integrate technology should be taken into account when evaluating and selecting software. The potential power of an integrated technical platform is significant, as it eliminates redundancy and provides an effective management tool that enhances decision making and value creation.

3 *Information access and delivery*: The use of a "one stop source" is a technology enabler that facilitates the delivery of information, including self service trends, market projections, customer satisfaction, competitors, suppliers and other data. The standard approach is to deliver this information (tools, processes, standards and timelines) across the organization.

4 *Controls*: Recent regulatory requirements (e.g., SOX in the US and Basel II in Europe) make it increasingly important for companies to ensure that their business processes have adequate internal controls. Some would argue that these controls focus primarily on financial/statutory reporting and do not have a significant impact on non-financial performance reporting. However, SOX requires reporting transparency and faster reporting of significant events (real-time reporting). It is therefore important to have adequate controls across your entire performance reporting infrastructure. We recommend that companies view these new regulatory requirements not as a compliance burden, but as a catalyst for reviewing and improving their controls and information infrastructure across the entire EPM framework.

EPM CAPABILITIES DRIVE VALUE AND ENABLE STRATEGY EXECUTION

There is a compelling value proposition for leveraging the benefits that highly developed EPM capabilities can deliver. Over time, superior EPM resources have a major impact on both organizational effectiveness and efficiency:

Effectiveness:

- focuses and aligns management on the key drivers of value;
- provides fact-based guidance for value-based decision making;
- enables a consistent process and framework for the evaluation of decision trade-offs (current/future) on investments;
- supports driver-based planning and forecasting to enable predictive and dynamic resource allocation;
- focuses strategy/operations around key value drivers; and
- aligns incentives and rewards more closely with shareholder value creation.

Efficiency:

- streamlines planning and reporting processes using consistent key drivers of value;
- streamlines decision making;
- focuses time and effort, eliminates redundant work and minimizes manual intervention and errors;
- integrates processes and controls to improve the integrity of data and quality of outputs;
- provides a strong, value-based foundation for infrastructure improvements; and
- provides a dynamic learning capability and leverages resources/time more efficiently.

Most companies achieve their vision in a phased approach (see Figure 5.4 below). EPM evolves to link strategy and execution – producing strong, sustainable returns over time to achieve high performance.

THE HACKETT GROUP ON ENTERPRISE PERFORMANCE MANAGEMENT

World-class CFOs are actively involved in establishing enterprise performance

Yesterday — Today — Tomorrow

	Traditional	Lay the Foundation	Scale and Improve	Operate World Class
Linkage	Strategy and execution are linked in concept	Strategy and execution are linked explicitly at corporate	Strategy and execution are linked in Business Units and function plans with improved trends, drivers and actionable levers	Strategy and execution linked in practice at Business Unit and function level
Business Units	Business Units focus on detailed P&L data	Business Units start to include KPIs in plans and analysis	Business Units start to include causal drivers in plans, measure capital efficiency, and prioritize and track initiatives	Business Units have more autonomy on strategy and execution to achieve required return within guidance
Corporate	Few below top executives see big picture of how business generates economic return	Corporate broadens performance discussion guidelines in Business Reviews	Corporate starts to improve guidance to Business Unit portfolio with differing fact bases for growth objectives and return expectations	Corporate provides funding, performance expectations, and stewards EPM structure
Enablers	Minimal automation; performance management is done through laborious manual processes	Foundational technology and tools are deployed; consolidations and statements are more automated	Enhanced technology provides more "rhyme and reason" to management data, information, and applications Automation shifts time to improving plans and analytics	Technology leveraged highly to scale Broad organizational thinking as to success of strategy and plans to deliver

Figure 5.4 *Moving towards tomorrow: the journey to high performance*

targets. This is typically accomplished through the annual budgeting process. The difference between the average CFO and the world-class performer is that the leader develops processes and people that will actually enable enhanced performance of the organization. This is accomplished through a variety of key skills and tactics.

One critical tactic in achieving enterprise performance targets is to ensure alignment between the organization's established targets and its enterprise-wide priorities. The balanced scorecard is a widely recognized tool to help achieve and measure this alignment. Balanced scorecards are not simple to create or maintain. Nevertheless, when properly constructed, they offer management a useful way to look at financial results and operational drivers, leading and lagging indicators, and metrics that track a wide range of activities. According to The Hackett Group, world-class companies are almost twice as likely as the average company to use balanced scorecards. They are also faster at generating ad hoc business performance reports and reports from general ledger, providing faster access to critical information.

A recent rise in the number of CFO-to-CEO transitions at major corporations indicates a swing back to seeking leaders from inside the organization, particularly in finance. For companies to retain their

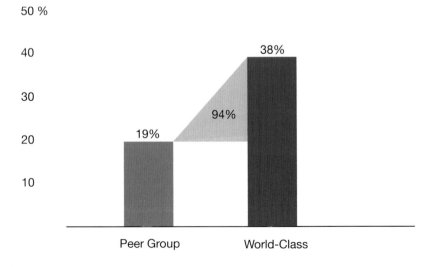

Percentage of companies utilizing mature balanced scorecards with both operational and financial measures, 2005

best and brightest finance minds, they will need to do more to develop these people as future leaders of business, not just finance. An increased emphasis on developing processes, professional skills and business experience focused on enterprise performance management is crucial in order to help finance executives adopt a broader, operational perspective.

The context in which businesses look at performance has changed, but significant gaps remain. Traditional performance management systems tend to focus on current value and tangible assets. Recent enhancements have often produced fragmented systems that add some value but conflict with other systems. In addition, incentive plans for managers are usually rooted in traditional measures of current financial performance, which account for only a small percentage of a company's total value.

Going forward, future enterprise performance management will require an integrated solution that focuses on proactively managing current and future value from all assets.

CFO INSIGHTS: LESSONS FROM THE MASTERS

- Value creation is the overarching goal and there is a bias towards external benchmarking and competitive intelligence to inform strategic direction, tactical course changes and performance evaluation.

- Focus on developing a deep understanding of the organization's critical few value drivers (current and future) upon which a competitive advantage will be built.

- Develop an integrated framework for establishing strategic direction, setting targets and timeframes for measuring success, developing plans and allocating resources to achieve targets, monitoring progress towards objectives continuously and putting proactive course corrections in place when needed.

- Instill a capital markets discipline into internal planning processes, by utilizing a market-based approach to establish minimum performance thresholds/targets and dynamic evaluation of the allocation of capital and resources to the best value creating opportunities.

- Focus on improving the speed and efficacy of performance monitoring and statistical analysis so that the decision makers closest to the customer have the information and tools to make decisions and take actions on a faster cycle than competitors.

- Sustain high performance over time by embedding a performance and value management mindset deep within the organization in terms of the skills, capabilities and incentives for the people and the integrated nature of the processes that utilize information to drive decision making and action.

REFERENCES

1 Christopher D. Ittner and David F. Larcker, Coming Up Short on Non-Financial Performance Measurement, *Harvard Business Review*, November 2003. http://www.hbr.com

2 L. Frigo and K.R. Krumwiede, Balanced Scorecards: A Rising Trend in Strategic Performance Measurement, *Journal of Strategic Performance Measurement*, 1999.

3 Jacqueline Coolidge and Eric Klein, EPM Spending, 2004–2005: Enterprise Performance Management Grows Up, *AMR Research*, December 13, 2004. http://www.amrresearch.com

4 Thomas H. Davenport, Dave De Long, Jeanne G. Harris, and Al Jacobson, Data to Knowledge to Results: Building an Analytic Capability, *Accenture*, June 1, 2000.

5 Thomas H. Davenport and J.C. Beck, The Attention Economy – Understanding the New Currency of Business, *Harvard Business School Press*, Boston, 2001.

6 P. Waddington, Dying for Information: an Investigation of Information Overload in the UK and Worldwide, *Reuters Business Information*, London, 1996.

7 John J. Ballow and Robert J. Thomas, Future Value: The $7 Trillion Dollar Challenge, *Journal of Applied Corporate Finance*, Winter 2004.

8 Tony Siesfeld, Valuing Intangibles: Putting a Price on Brand, *Knowledge Directions*, Fall/Winter 2001.

9 Eric Krell, All the Right Moves, *Business Finance*, May 2002. http://www.businessfinancemag.com

10 Andy Neely, Mike Bourne, and Chris Adams, *Better Budgeting and Beyond, Competitive Financial Operations: The CFO Project, Volume ll*, October 2003.

CHAPTER 6

Finance Operations

DRIVING CORPORATE-WIDE BENEFITS THROUGH HIGH-PERFORMANCE FINANCE OPERATIONS

Colin Sampson, COO and CFO
SAP Asia Pacific

As one would expect, SAP is a leader in finance operations. While SAP has helped thousands of organizations achieve finance operations excellence, it has also achieved superb finance performance internally. As Colin Sampson explains, SAP's high-performance finance operations and success with its shared service center have brought tremendous benefits to the organization.

SAP is a successful global business – and is experiencing exceptionally rapid growth in Asia. In 2005, SAP Asia Pacific won two regional awards for its shared services center – the International Quality Improvement Productivity Award (Most Advanced Automation of a Shared Service Organization) and MIS IT Excellence Award (Best Bottom Line IT). Operating in China and other parts of Asia is an exciting challenge. Colin Sampson, COO and CFO for SAP Asia Pacific, shares his experience in developing SAP's high-performance finance operating unit. He also explains the central role that shared services has played in this development.

Colin takes up the story: "We have a tremendous culture in this organization, one which is very much driven towards success. I think that every person in SAP has a passion about the company and a thirst to contribute. There is a lot of excitement in

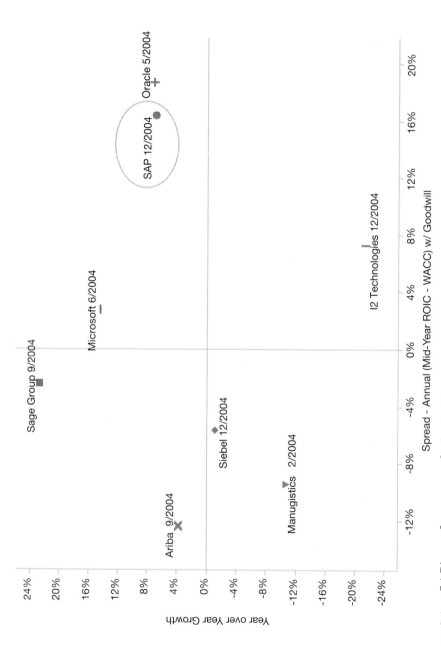

Figure 6.1 *SAP's performance relative to its peers*
Source: Accenture analysis

SAP Asia Pacific because of the growth phenomenon in Asia generally. Specific parts of Asia are the growth engine of SAP worldwide, and I think that adds an element of excitement for a lot of people. It's the place to be, if you like.

"In Asia, you need maximum transparency and governance because of the unique requirements of doing business here. That was one of the main reasons we decided to deploy shared services – so that we had better control over our own destiny in terms of our performance management capability, improving the design of our processes, deploying our finance resources more effectively, and better positioning our local finance teams to engage more effectively in front-line commercial operations.

"Because our processes are consistent across the region, we now have more robust controls and hence less exposure to risk. Shared services, in particular, has created focus for me as the CFO and has helped me rethink how we develop the finance organization going forward. I think that high performance is about looking to the future rather than worrying about what revenues and costs were booked in the past. And, if you have shared services, you can develop very efficient and effective structures in place with well-defined processes. This enables the finance people both here in the Regional HQ and out in the countries to concentrate on decision making. They now spend most of their time with the managing director, they sit with the line of business, with the consulting manager, with the account executives, with the education guys, and they say, 'How do we grow this business? How can I as a finance person out in the middle of Thailand, provide better support to help you in making your decisions?'

"From a managing director's perspective, we say to them, 'What keeps you up at night? What are you worried about? Are you worrying about whether your payrolls are being met, or your billing is done on time? What you should worry about is where your next dollar is coming from, whether your customers are happy, whether the implementation is going successfully, whether your alliance partner is doing the job – all this is what's important. You need to focus on the drivers of performance at the enterprise level and let the shared services organization worry about everything else.' This lets the in-country finance people focus on what's important: closing business, looking at growth opportunities, executing according to our business plan and managing risk.

"The high levels of enterprise performance that we're now seeing in the region only began since 2003, when we really felt the full force of shared services and cen-

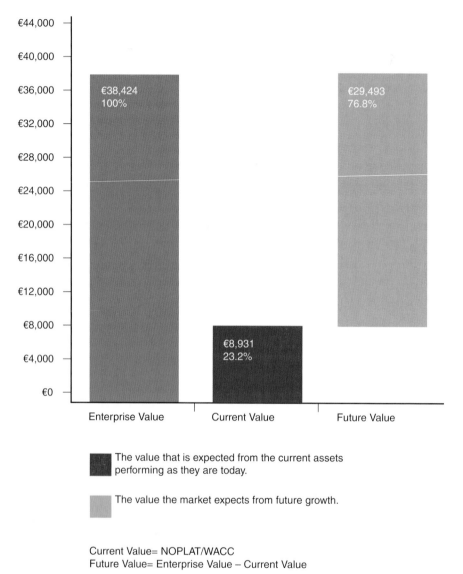

Figure 6.2 *SAP's future value*
Source: Accenture analysis

tralized finance and administrative operations. We're seeing better performance from subsidiary SAP companies, and an improved ability to cope with fast regional growth."

Colin goes on to explain the various functional areas that are included in the shared services operation. "Our regional shared service operations cover all our finance, accounting and administration activities, starting with the general ledger, and all the transactions and closing processes, all software and maintenance billing and contract management, the intercompany transactions, and the banking and cash management activities. They also encompass all the administrative functions that relate to the consulting and education businesses. These include all the time recording and billing for consulting, all the education and course arrangement, and registering and billing customers. It involves payroll and master data maintenance, and procurement, accounts payable, travel management and expenses. Lately, we have also started moving into some service areas, such as administrative processes, that support our alliance relationships. This is the first time we've embarked on services as opposed to transactions – partner relationship management."

While service quality and extended finance capability above and beyond basic transaction processing and administrative support are the centerpiece of the SAP story, Colin also reports significant economies-of-scale benefits. "We have delivered cost savings in excess of forty percent since we started our journey. Not only that, but we have increased our focus on providing high value-added decision support to the business. I think these are the critical components in a high-performance finance organization. You also get the benefit of being able to showcase the operation to customers and prospects, and talk about this at a CFO-to-CFO peer level. This is a very powerful message for an organization like SAP."

A central theme of this book is the extended capabilities that high-performance finance organizations demonstrate. SAP is a prime example of this, so we asked Colin about the role of the finance professionals who are not part of the shared service operation in Singapore. Colin noted: "They are now very much more customer focused and commercial in their orientation, focusing on things like closing new business. Years ago, it would be surprising to hear a group of finance people on a conference call talking about the detailed specifics of software sales, or the consulting business and alliance activity that make up the bulk of our revenue forecasts. Most of them were too busy closing the books, doing retrospective analysis, and dealing with control issues.

"Now, when we have those calls, we get finance and business people asking the same questions from a fairly common starting point. The result is a much more bal-

anced view of the robustness of our forward planning, and greater confidence that our plans can be reliably met. Our finance people (and myself, for that matter) now spend the vast majority of our time on helping close business and being part of commercial deal shaping. When we put a deal together, we know how it is going to work, understand the US GAAP implications, and can explain to the account executive the implications for both our customers and SAP. We help them construct an implementation agreement that makes commercial sense for our customers and SAP.

"Our finance people now work on growth acceleration plans. We have acceleration plans in place for China, for India, for Korea, for Australia. These are formalized, so we now use the same template and planning process. As we go forward and focus on the future, we look at all the different industries – focus where we are now, where we need to accelerate, etc. Then we look at what kind of resources we need. What sort of partners should we work with to make the plan happen? The finance people play a central role in this process. In the past, they weren't involved in these areas for two reasons. First, they weren't trained; these issues simply weren't their focus. Second, they were involved in other activities that are now performed by the shared services organization. So it's a different focus.

"The finance team at SAP in Asia continues to leverage the baseline capability put in place since shared services went live. We are continuing to expand the scope of shared services. One of shared services' most redeeming features is that the management teams in the field, including the finance people, are constantly looking to leverage central finance and shared service operations capability. That's a key indication that they've accepted shared services and feel that there's value in adding to it."

As the SAP story illustrates, high performance in basic finance operations releases management bandwidth to focus on the higher, value-added areas of decision support. This implies a fundamental change in the leadership posture for finance professionals. The senior finance team at SAP has gone from being reactive and passive to being proactive influencers.

We asked Colin to elaborate. "I agree with your research conclusions, but I also think there are some prerequisites. I think that as a finance person, as a CFO, you have to have a 'seat at the table.' If you're not at the table and you haven't won that seat – or you don't continue to earn that seat, then I think you lose credibility. You have to sit side by side with the management team, with the managing director in *our case, and act like a business person, knowing when to take your finance hat off and when to put it on. I think you have to play that role very carefully, because I think as a finance person you're the driver and the communicator, a kind of linchpin in the middle. You have all the information – nothing that the rest of the organization isn't privy to – but you bring it all together and then step up to the role of change agent.*

"The board may make all the decisions, and the CEO plays a critical role. But I think the finance person, more so than ever before, can actually help lead and be a very strong communicator. In the past, finance people were not necessarily the best communicators. I also think this is no longer true. That, in itself, is a huge change."

Accenture research conclusively shows that the focus for finance is all about service, the customer, driving growth, maximizing profitability, delivering the required investment returns, and developing capabilities that perhaps were not in existence before the advent of high-performance finance operations. As Colin observes, "All these changes have enabled finance people to get involved in a whole host of different things. If you looked at the portfolio of activities that a finance person was involved in maybe five, six or seven years ago – and the expectations for a high-performance finance person today – they're incredibly different.

"If I look at all this from the perspective of my own role and daily activities today, I'm much more actively involved in decision making related to strategy, tactics, and operational execution and risk management at the enterprise level. A few years ago, these were not areas that I would have been as actively involved with as I am now.

"I now get more involved with customers in site visits, helping to close business in peer-to-peer meetings with other CFOs in thought leadership, and in governing the delivery of key relationship obligations – much more than I used to do before. So you can see that the role of a senior finance professional at SAP is very customer focused. It's very much about trying to partner with the business on an intimate basis and making sure we execute efficiently and effectively. If we continue to do this and live by these values, then I am confident that we will be even more successful in the future."

FINANCE: BUILDING AN EFFICIENT ENGINE

Finance operations generate the power in the engine room. Without an effective finance operations group, the other more advanced capabilities that all CFOs strive to obtain are difficult to achieve. To generate high performance, finance organizations must achieve excellence within their basic accounting and administrative operations because these activities are prerequisites for the development of other more advanced capabilities.

Bringing your finance operations up to the level achieved by SAP and other industry leaders – as reflected in their superior performance, standardization, and consistency across multiple geographies – is often the first step in the fundamental upgrade of the five finance capabilities discussed in Chapter 3 and elsewhere in this book. We have also discovered that in some parts of the world, risk management, enterprise performance management, and capital stewardship are sometimes the first disciplines to be put in place before the job of tackling the efficiency and effectiveness of finance operations is undertaken. A small number of companies have achieved high performance by tackling these other capabilities first. However, our research shows conclusively that it is just too difficult to create the infrastructure necessary to achieve the other more advanced capabilities without first achieving absolute command and control of the basics. At a minimum, a "solid foundation" for finance operations is mandatory before other more advanced finance services can be deployed effectively. Simply put, to earn their seat at the table, CFOs need to get their house in order.

The scope of these finance operations is depicted in Figure 6.3, which shows the range of activities typically aggregated and delivered on a scaled basis across business units, geographies, and regions.

Historically, finance operations have made due with disjointed processes that were focused on financial record keeping. For international organizations, often the primary focus was local bookkeeping, based on local Generally Accepted Accounting Principles (GAAP). Information was not readily available, nor did the finance groups have direct access to the upstream processes. In today's high-performance organizations, finance operations are an extension of the enterprise. These groups understand the value chain, both internally and in the broader external networks, so they can translate economic events into financial code. They begin to optimize processes by implementing end-to-end connectivity, eliminating redundant steps across departments, and then including customers and suppliers to drive out additional process inefficiencies. These high-performance organizations are far from complacent; they are constantly looking for areas where they can eliminate redundant or non-

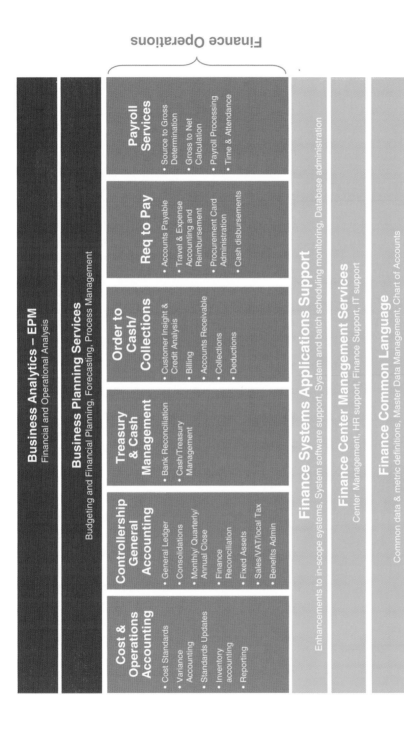

Finance Operations

Business Analytics – EPM
Financial and Operational Analysis

Business Planning Services
Budgeting and Financial Planning, Forecasting, Process Management

Cost & Operations Accounting
• Cost Standards
• Variance Accounting
• Standards Updates
• Inventory accounting
• Reporting

Controllership General Accounting
• General Ledger
• Consolidations
• Monthly/ Quarterly/ Annual Close
• Finance Reconciliation
• Fixed Assets
• Sales/VAT/local Tax
• Benefits Admin

Treasury & Cash Management
• Bank Reconciliation
• Cash/Treasury Management

Order to Cash/ Collections
• Customer Insight & Credit Analysis
• Billing
• Accounts Receivable
• Collections
• Deductions

Req to Pay
• Accounts Payable
• Travel & Expense Accounting and Reimbursement
• Procurement Card Administration
• Cash disbursements

Payroll Services
• Source to Gross Determination
• Gross to Net Calculation
• Payroll Processing
• Time & Attendance

Finance Systems Applications Support
Enhancements to in-scope systems, System software support, System and batch scheduling monitoring, Database administration

Finance Center Management Services
Center Management, HR support, Finance Support, IT support

Finance Common Language
Common data & metric definitions, Master Data Management, Chart of Accounts

Figure 6.3 *Finance operations services*

value-added steps by simplifying and standardizing processes.

For example, by capturing data earlier, creating consistent data definitions, and standardized processes, high performers have accelerated the close cycle and made non-value-added tasks, such as account reconciliation, an accounting activity of the past.

Achieving end-to-end process connectivity

As business models become more complex, the role of finance operations must evolve and expand. Successful finance operations groups do a lot more than simply processing financial transactions faster and more cheaply, and taking their shared services operation offshore to do it. They have internalized the notion that process elimination is more effective than simply doing something faster and less expensively. Eliminating *noise* from the end-to-end transaction processes also helps speed up cycle times. Finance plays an active role in driving value into the whole organization by creating extended end-to-end process connectivity, and then using this to capture both financial and non-financial data – real-time, active data which is used to deliver high value-added business analytics.

We asked Nick Rose, the CFO of Diageo, to comment on this subject: "We certainly have to do more for less, but we do also have to get smarter at some of the basics. Technology has an important role to play in helping us achieve better standardization across the enterprise, and I agree with your assertion that we need to establish greater end-to-end process connectivity so that our systems, SAP in our case, can extract transactional data at speed. We can then use this data to drive our business analytical tools – providing high-impact decision support information to management teams at the front end of our business.

"The extended enterprise that you talk about is something we buy into as well. Going forward, it is important that all our core processes – whether they sit inside the company or reside in an extended ecosystem of trading partners – connect seamlessly. Technology gives us the basis to do this. We are not there yet, but this is where we are heading: towards greater automation of the provision of intelligence. Insight into how our business is performing and understanding why that's the case, is more important than ever."

Figure 6.4 provides an illustration of what we mean by this end-to-end process connectivity. Historically, the vast majority of organizations have focused primarily on white-collar productivity. The problem with this limited focus on processing efficiency is that it creates an artificial boundary, with cost reduction as the main benefit that can be delivered to the business.

Our research has uncovered a much greater ambition for value creation among many companies. Phelps Dodge Corporation, for example, experienced difficulty in analyzing global supplier expenditures, and needed a better data platform for supplier negotiations. By expanding the process scope of accounts payable to include procurement and strategic sourcing, the company was able to use its data processing engine to capture transactional data about daily spending on goods and services consumed by business operations. Phelps Dodge is now able to delve deeply into day-to-day operations and monitor contract compliance by supplier, which has resulted in many benefits. For example, staff can now track qualifications for additional discounts because they understand what the company is consuming and when. The result: a $2.2m. return on investment in one year, achieved through negotiating better terms with suppliers and taking advantage of existing discount terms.

Bob Young, the CFO of Teradata, a division of NCR, describes his company's approach to creating value through end-to-end process improvement: "When you extract online data from your operational systems – the transaction data in your enterprise data warehouse – and then use it to work on projects or programs that help you identify problems, you give management action-oriented data it can use to make better business decisions much more rapidly. Our procurement example is a very good one. In our case, we already had all the accounts payable data in our data warehouse and we've got all the purchase order data. So now we know worldwide who we buy from and what we bought. We know when we bought it and what we paid for it. Then we put that data in the hands of the procurement organization and give them some targets for vendor consolidation and cost reduction – and then measure the results. Technically this is not a very difficult thing to do, but it's very important in terms of empowering people to do something that they naturally should want to do anyway. Then, as part of the governance process, you measure it so you know whether you've made progress."

Our research finding that high-performance finance operations drive higher enterprise-wide performance becomes especially significant when we examine its impact on the revenue generation cycle. We examined hundreds of shared service operations and discovered that most had erected unnecessary boundaries, defined by either simple accounts receivable processing or by the "order-to-cash" cycle. On the other hand, we also found examples where these unnecessary boundaries had been

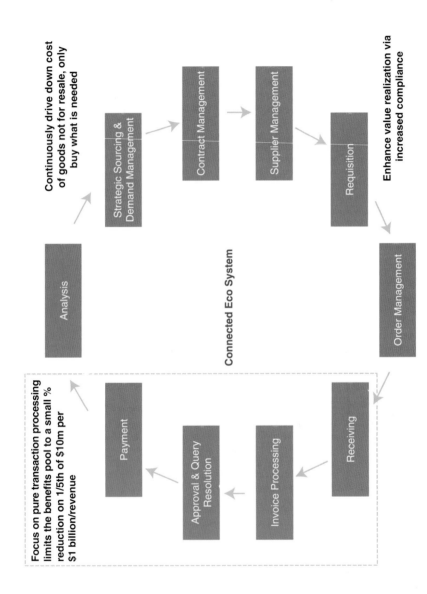

Figure 6.4   *Procurement value chain: end-to-end process connectivity*

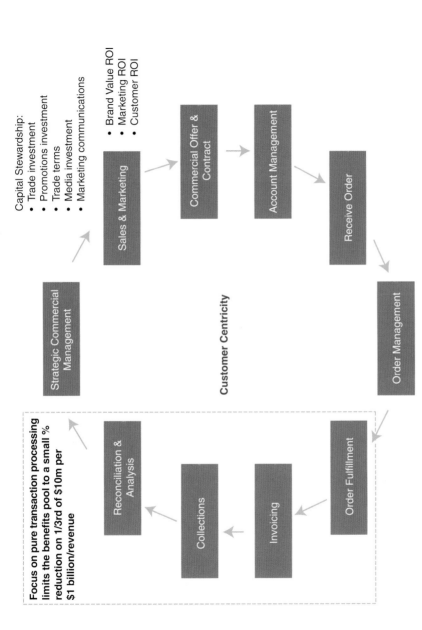

Figure 6.5 *Process connectivity*

replaced by what we call "extended enterprise end-to-end processing." In these cases, commercial processes like trade investment and sales promotions management are connected directly to the conventional order-to-cash processing that takes place in the finance back-office.

By creating this extended end-to-end process connectivity, organizations are equipping their marketing and sales teams in front-line field operations with powerful business analytics that provide deep insights into consumer buying patterns and shifts in supply and demand, as well as a profound understanding of the relative competitiveness of their product and service offerings. As a result, marketing and sales are armed with up-to-the minute information on brand value return on investment, marketing return on investment, and customer return on investment. Figure 6.4 illustrates extended enterprise end-to-end process connectivity.

3M is a case in point. It suffered from the inability of its various business units to share sales data. This problem manifested itself in highly fragmented data spread across 40 business units and 60 independent international subsidiaries. This caused inefficiency in the deployment of 3M's sales force – a problem that was compounded by a lack of global product visibility, which in turn led to high levels of inventory. Worst of all, inaccurate customer data was creating costly delivery problems.

Today, 3M is in a completely different position, with single line-of-sight visibility to the customer at the SKU (stock keeping unit) level. After five years of achieving end-to-end process connectivity across a range of demand generation and customer management operations, the accrued net benefit is more than $100m. This benefit results from the enhanced timeliness and accuracy of decisions taken "at the coal face in the field," increased cross-selling and improved asset management. Sales force productivity has increased by 10%, and 3M has added $437 million to cash flow through a one-month reduction in inventory.

Companies like 3M are leading examples of our end-to-end process connectivity story. They have progressed beyond the premise that finance operations should simply improve white-collar productivity via better invoice processing. They have a more ambitious agenda: using high-performing finance operations to drive growth, profitability, and capital efficiency, with a relentless focus on what we call "consumer centricity."

Process digitization

The shared service revolution has been under way for 15 years or more, and much progress has been made. However, we are beginning to see the next stage of evolution. In this stage, process digitization will improve the efficiency and effectiveness of cross-company transaction processing platforms. Until now, there was a limit on the degree of industrialization of basic transaction processing that could be achieved by shared service operations. Figure 6.6 reveals that manual labor is still used extensively in the processing cycle.

From the buyer's point of view, this is a procure-to-pay conversation. However, the very same process is viewed as an order-to-cash issue from the supplier side. Between the boundaries of these two perspectives lie considerable pain and inefficiency.

Electronic trade settlement exchanges are emerging as a potential solution to this problem. Early results by some pioneering companies have shown promising results. Take Sprint, a global communications company serving over a million business and residential customers in more than 70 countries.

Sprint embarked on a program to reduce its accounts payable operating cost. The organization wanted to replace paper invoices and payments with electronic processes to lower processing costs and target savings opportunities through early payment discounts. The results of deploying Xign speak for themselves. Over 90% of invoices at Sprint are now received electronically. Furthermore, Sprint has been able to discount yields by 90%. Between 2004 and 2005, discounts at Sprint increased by more than 400%. In addition, Xign's software-as-service approach has lowered Sprint's total cost of ownership by 40%. As a Sprint corporate finance executive explained, "Payment is a key building block of the supply chain strategy to e-enable procure-through-pay. An electronic invoicing and payment platform, such as Xign's, delivers a compelling value proposition. It helps us eliminate paper, achieve our electronic payment targets, and brings us closer to our goal of building the perfect payables experience."

The efficiency provided by electronic invoicing and payment networks completes the digitization of the end-to-end source to settlement process that we discussed earlier in this chapter. This functionality is illustrated in Figure 6.7. In return for guaranteed cash flow, we have found examples of suppliers willing to provide additional pricing discounts as an incentive to others in the supply chain to help them achieve desired efficiencies. Xign customers are capturing supplier discounts that range from less than 1% to 5%. When you annualize the return on investment from these discounts, they easily fall into the double digit range. For example, a 1% discount for early payment translates to an 18% annual return; a 2%

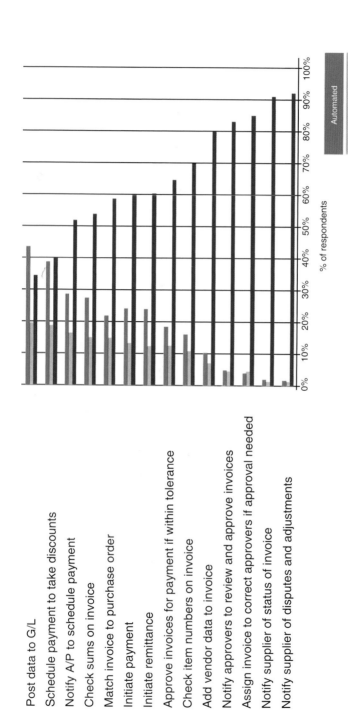

Figure 6.6 *Process automation levels for key finance functions*

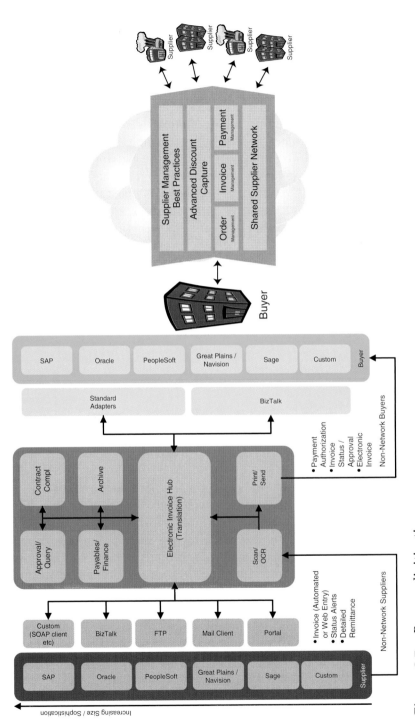

Figure 6.7 *Process digitization*

discount equates to a 36% annualized return. According to Xign surveys of Fortune 500 companies, several million dollars of annual savings can be realized for every billion dollars of spend by capturing discounts on less than 20% of total spend. In addition, Xign's shared supplier network enables customers to accelerate the transition to e-payments as well as discount ramp-up programs. In the communications industry, one Fortune 500 Xign customer found that more than 55% of its total spend was with suppliers already enrolled in Xign networks. Because these suppliers would not have to be recruited to join the network, this proved to be a strong incentive to become a Xign customer and reap immediate benefits.

Our research indicates that rapid growth in this area will follow as more and more companies move to the next level of process digitization.

Governance and internal controls

The accounting and controllership functions are the de facto custodians of the financial data management and internal controls that form the basis of modern day governance and risk management. Most important, for high-performance organizations they are the *only source* for both internal and external financial reporting. In other words, the single source of data capture is the basis for reporting "one version of the truth" for the entire enterprise. In this environment, personal spreadsheets and special ad hoc reports that purportedly provide different reporting views and interpretations do not exist. Everyone works from the same data set and the same reports and bases decisions on consistent, uniform interpretation.

For the first time in many years, The Hackett Group reported a year-over-year increase in the cost of finance in 2005 of 18%[1], and forecast that this rise will continue as the intensity of basic controllership and governance requirements increases in response to changes in regulation and compliance requirements. In this new era of heightened control awareness, the finance function's duties are expanding to include: acting as a watchdog, ensuring that all transactions are compliant with accounting policy, maintaining audit trails, testing documentation, and rigorously applying internal controls across all business processes.

In the 1990s, due to well-publicized corporate governance failures, many companies believed that the pressure to reduce costs outweighed the need for tight controls. In many organizations, the processes defined or updated during this period had only one objective: cost efficiency. Now, as organizations revisit those processes with the internal-control lens, additional steps are being added. Since those steps are not an integral part of the original design, they are by nature an additional layer and cost. In today's environment, general concerns and visibility controls have led many companies to add controls everywhere, without understanding the inherent risks. Since controls are being added as an afterthought and implemented without consideration for risks, the resulting finance function cost increases are predictable.

Graham Skeates, Asia Pacific regional finance director at Prudential, notes that, "This could be a blip because there will be two developments going forward. First, when the additional control processes are all in place the costs will be stabilized, and second, the regulators are saying, 'Hang on, we didn't quite mean you to go this far, you're spending more money on this than you are on running your business.' So they are starting to take note of the cost of compliance, and the damage to business and the people they are trying to protect. In terms of finance's scope, that will increase because more and more financial information and interpretation is required in running a business. That's a progression that has been going on for some time. and I think it will continue."

As Stephen Ferraby, CFO for Exel in Asia Pacific, comments, "If you look at requirements related to corporate responsibility and environmental reporting, there is a whole raft of governance that falls on the shoulders of the finance team to implement that was not there even two years ago. Even in Exel's environmental report, we are estimating our contribution to worldwide CO_2 (carbon dioxide) emissions. I believe that finance has the basic disciplines in terms of getting the data right and reporting consistently and reliably. So it does tend to fall on us to handle this. I wish I had a 20% budget increase to cope with it. We need to find a way of doing it and it comes down to the system solution that we put in place. It is a real challenge. It's not just how you implement the governance requirements, which you 'have' to do, it's also making sure that you extract the maximum value out of the process for the business. This is another reason that all this tends to fall on finance's desk."

There is much debate about who owns internal controls. While finance and the CFO are best positioned to be the champions for those controls, high-performance organizations make internal controls a corporate-wide responsibility, and embed them within their mainstream business processes. Like Caterpillar, UnitedHealth Group, and Motorola, they design good quality in rather than inspecting bad quality out – using robust techniques such as Six Sigma. One finding of our finance executive interviews is that the deployment of Six Sigma supports high-performance finance. For example, it is common knowledge that a good requisitioning process – regardless of whether purchase orders are necessary – provides more effective and efficient controls than the practice of sending vendor invoices across various departments for approval. The latter process simply adds time, cost, and increased internal control risk.

Controls can be categorized as automated versus manual, mandatory versus discretionary, and preventive versus detective. The automated versus manual decision is a function of the labor effort needed to effect the control. For all organizations, it is critical to define key controls properly, since these will become the mandatory controls that cannot be bypassed. While detective controls represent after-the-fact actions to determine if any errors or omissions are present, preventive controls are designed to preclude any problems from occurring. New technologies (e.g., automation), which incorporate preventive controls, are usually more cost effective.

Finance operations groups need to sensitize and educate the entire organization on the importance of controls. Then they need to work with other functions to determine the most appropriate method for implementing preventive controls. To do this, they need an in-depth understanding of upstream processes: where data is captured, quality of data and data sources, and the audit trail. Once finance has this understanding, it can incorporate and document the appropriate controls within those upstream processes.

Capturing data from these upstream processes not only reduces work within finance operations, it also reduces the need for secondary detective controls within finance. This, along with standardizing processes throughout the enterprise, significantly reduces the compliance burden. This built-in quality mindset can help stem the increasing cost of finance operations. As a global beverage company's CFO notes: "It's almost like defaulting to audit trails, documenting your internal control processes and all that kind of stuff. Corporations used to do this all the time, but with the advent of computers everything started getting hidden in little gray boxes and the whole thing got a little fuzzy. And perhaps people stopped thinking about these issues as they should have. I think all Sarbanes-Oxley is suggesting, in a certain way, is that we go back to the basics."

SAP's finance and reporting processes reflect its proactive approach to finance operations. As Peter David, CFO of SAP Germany explains, "By complying with US GAAP, we ensure that revenue recognition is accurate for the business. Given all the sources of revenue within the

SAP environment, this is very complex. As well as accurately including all the figures on the balance sheet and profit and loss statement, we are developing and implementing integrated financial processes to enable us to give precise forecasts for all revenue drivers in a single model." With regard to the Sarbanes Oxley Act, SAP has adopted an aggressive approach. Peter David observes, "Our process has already gained recognition. We see this as a great opportunity for the finance department to implement a legal requirement and improve processes in the company at the same time."

It's all about converting data into insight

The idea of achieving the elusive "single version of the truth" was introduced earlier in this chapter. As we have seen, the challenge for finance organizations is that much of the data needed for financial reporting purposes and business analytics originates outside the traditional finance department. Traditionally, finance operations create their own financial data from documents received from upstream business processes. Best practice is for finance to be involved in the upstream process and system design to ensure that the complete business DNA is captured. Many groups within an enterprise require data such as customer profiles, orders, inventory availability, production and purchasing requirements, etc. High performers have put in place a collaborative process to share such data elements.

A word of caution is needed, however. Prior to deeming that data needs to be common and consistent throughout an enterprise, you need to understand whether it will truly be useful and used. For example, many companies have tried to create common vendor or customer master files. While this sharing is valuable, the pain of creating such an infrastructure will not be worth the effort unless multiple business units purchase or sell to the same entities. A major global retailer concluded that very few of its vendors were truly managed on a global scale. It also concluded that the number of vendors it wanted to aggregate globally was limited. In total, fewer than 50 suppliers fell into this group. As a result, the retailer determined that there was no need for a common global vendor master: The cost of sustaining this capability over time did not justify the benefits. Instead, it created common data definition structures and then put in place a basic process to gather the data for the 50 or so vendors it wanted to manage globally.

Figure 6.8 illustrates how the rewired information architecture that we discussed in Chapter 5 is powered by the capture of "active transactional data" from the entire enterprise. High-powered business analytics and decision support move managers from a passive, retrospective way of looking at things to a more forward-looking, predictive stance – which may even lead to customer interactions being triggered in real time.

For WESCO, this type of forward-thinking, predictive finance approach means better product discount and margin analysis. At Victoria's Secret, it means making decisions about product placement in quarterly catalogs based on margin capture and sales throughput analysis. For SBC, it means moving to real-time selling and improved call center productivity.

FINANCE OPERATIONS: SERVICE CAPABILITY, NOT SIMPLY EFFICIENCY

A lot has been written about shared services – the precursor to the broader operational capability illustrated by the examples discussed so far. Even so, misconceptions remain about what truly constitutes a shared service. Many companies claim to have shared services in place, yet they have centralized only their disparate back-office functions. To truly create a scaled shared service capability, an enterprise needs to balance both:

- the economies of scale and synergies that come from consolidating disparate processes and systems that are distributed across locations; and

- a service culture that delivers higher levels of quality and effectiveness.

A shared financial operations center must be continuously relevant to the businesses it serves. Service is its core function, and only if this objective is embraced can the center deliver sustained high quality and low cost. High-performing centers have created continuous improvement teams to ensure that costs and processes are always optimized. They look beyond the center and analyze current processes from a holistic perspective. This vantage point gives them the opportunity to incorporate evolving business requirements into process designs. Finance operations are at the back end of many core business processes, and without a holistic view of these processes, the overall impact of a center's service offerings will be sub-optimized.

By listening to customers and routinely challenging their centers' performance, high performers have been able to create a customer-centric culture within their service centers. This culture is critical to ongoing

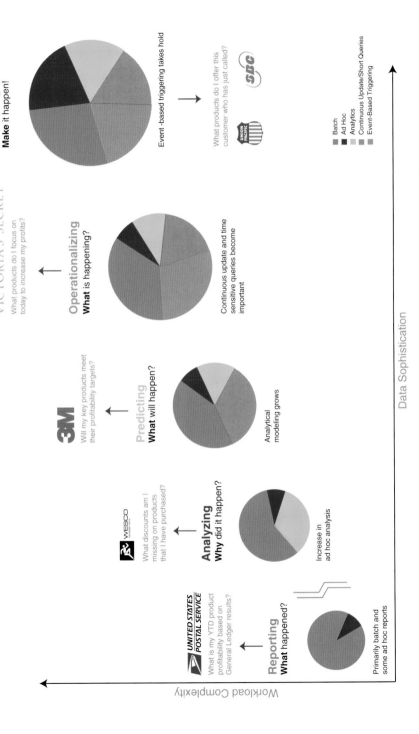

Figure 6.8 *Converting data to value*

success because it ensures relevance and proximity to business needs and challenges.

Strengthened internal control processes are an additional benefit that many companies gain from shared services. As Graham Skeates of Prudential describes his company's rationale for shared services: "… we are not centralizing finance for cost efficiency. The finance section in a life assurance company is not driven by cost; as it is relatively small in the first place, but it is driven by integrity and reliability of data, which is being affected by new controls such as the Sarbanes-Oxley Act (SOX) and changes to international standards along with other external factors. You need to develop reliable controls and processes so that you can sleep at night. Cost savings in the finance area per se do not keep me awake."

The finance organization has seen significant cost reductions in the last decade, as it has evolved from a decentralized model to a shared services environment. Our research conclusively demonstrates that this is a transitional stage on the journey to high performance.

As shown in Figure 6.9, the operating model for finance operations has many dimensions, and consistency across them is important. The model's dimensions are meant to guide the enterprise in formulating its vision for finance operations. No enterprise is on either the right or the left extreme for each value dimension. The left-to-right axis for each lever does not imply that one side is better than the other. It is simply a statement of management's position on the role it has assigned finance operations.

While many talk about becoming a "business partner" and a "service culture," these terms should be clearly defined. A good starting point for finance operations executives is a discussion of the issue with their stakeholders. Jointly, they should debate the left to right spectrum for each dimension and lever to determine the role that finance operations should play within their enterprise. Based on the role given to finance operations, cost-effectiveness can take on several meanings. High performers are less concerned about achieving lowest absolute cost than they are about the efficiency and cost-effectiveness of the services they provide their stakeholders. Achieving high service levels cost-effectively allows them to be credible business partners and take on additional value-added services.

Scope of services – extended functionality

Many early shared service adopters are now in the second or third generation of their programs. As Colin Sampson of SAP observed in the

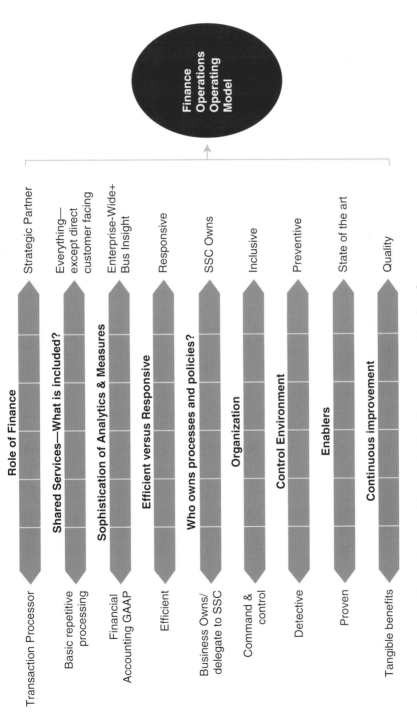

Figure 6.9 *Key dimensions and levers in the finance operation's role*

beginning of this chapter, today the functional scope of shared services has expanded to include pricing support, alliance management, and customer relationship management. There are processes, such as credit and collections that are either overlooked or, more often, deferred in initial implementations. By moving such processes into a shared service operation, an enterprise can bring focus and added professionalism to working capital and customer management. Achieving these same results can be difficult using alternative operating models.

CASE STUDY
Going global with the help of an outsource provider

The European division of a global pharmaceutical company had a diverse and far-flung customer base. One of the company's strategies was to globalize its operating model. Key to this process was establishing a regional outsourced accounting center in Prague. The European finance director tells the story: "One of the challenges we face is that demographically our customer base is very dispersed. For example, in Italy, we sell our product through more than 18,000 retail outlets, and having aged receivables of over 100 days is not uncommon if you don't stay on top of the issue.

"We were making progress in getting our DSO (days sales outstanding) down to a reasonable level, but we wanted to improve this further and make sure we could sustain the lower levels over the long term. Working with our outsourcing provider, we implemented a business analytics tool that enabled the people doing the receivables processing in Prague (who, by the way, are supporting many countries and languages) to move from chasing in late payments to proactively examining the key causes of those late payments in the first place. Over time, we have learned a lot about our customer base, as well as achieving our working capital objectives."

These insights are collected at the point of customer interaction. The data is then analyzed to enable individualized action plans to be put in place appropriate to the type of collection treatment that should be used. The result is maximum collection impact, plus new data to refresh the closed-loop decision support engine that feeds sales, marketing, and supply-chain operations with real-time data. This enables the company to refresh strategy and improve the velocity of product supply. Figure 6.10 illustrates how this works.

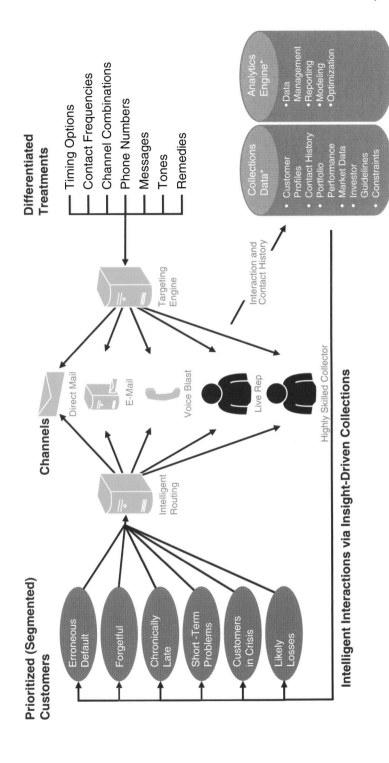

Figure 6.10 *Insight-driven collections*

We observed several examples of different finance operations extending their capabilities at the interface of customer relationship management (CRM) in the way that Colin Sampson described. Connecting CRM digitally with cash collection processes provides a deep and insightful understanding of customers, mined from the operational data that is collected and analyzed. Action plans can then be implemented based on the principle of mass customization. In these cases, unique customer profiles are created using ongoing transactional data along with history, product, and demographic attributes – all brought together in a single place.

In the management of receivables, the profile of each customer segment is categorized/coded to support the most effective collection outcome. One profile, for example, is the "erroneous default" – a customer with a positive payment history or a multifaceted relationship whose delinquency appears to be a first payment default. Another profile is the "forgetful" customer who periodically exceeds the grace period and requires contact only to note the reason code and explain the implication of late payments. Cash flow optimization is one of the most overlooked opportunities in finance operations, yet the payback is often substantial and rapid.

Shared services vs outsourcing

Outsourcing provides additional performance levers to an enterprise. Whereas some organizations begin with an internal shared service center and move to outsourcing as a second step, many choose to leapfrog their peers and competitors by moving towards this model directly. These organizations view outsourcing as a capability make-versus-buy decision. Outsourcing enables them to quickly achieve the desired end state. Partnering with someone whose core competency is finance and accounting operations gives instant access to scale and resources, and also provides risk mitigation.

Effective finance operations need to be supported by a strong corporate commitment to investing in innovative solutions – and this is not always easy to maintain. Through previous Accenture research[2] we discovered that the decision to enter into outsourcing arrangements rather than adopting the in-house shared service option is motivated by six factors:

1 *Efficiency*: Multiple business units operating with independent support organizations and systems are closely scrutinized for cost-effectiveness.

2 *Growth*: Intent on growing through acquisitions/joint ventures, companies are concerned about efficiently absorbing acquisitions.

3 *Scale*: Large transaction volumes and/or above-average processing costs are pressuring large companies to improve operating performance, while small- and medium-sized businesses want access to economies of scale.

4 *Location*: Companies are seeking new geographic opportunities to cut costs without compromising skills.

5 *Capability*: Outdated legacy processes/systems and the need for change are tempered by concern over previous failures to build new capabilities.

6 *Reputation*: Internal and external pressures are mounting to increase the finance function's service and value while improving controls and transparency.

CASE STUDY

Moving from an in-house shared service center to an outsourced model

Stuart Young, European finance director for Exel PLC, explains his experience in initially deploying a captive in-house shared service operation and then moving it to an outsourcing model. "The company first outsourced the finance functions supporting our contract logistics business in the UK in 1996, as part of a transformational change program that we had embarked upon. In so doing, Exel consolidated 13 administration centers and six different accounting systems. We did this because, at the time, our business challenge was to deal with fragmented support operations characterized by non-standardized systems, ineffective processes and high costs, a lack of customer focus and value, and the absence of any formal improvement program. Between 1996 and 1997, we transitioned our Bedford delivery center to our outsourcing partner and implemented a standard, Oracle-based ERP platform to support the UK contract logistics business – as well as enhanced business processes, such as purchase ordering. This enabled us to reduce the cost of accounting by 40%, create a flexible, scaleable service and establish a strong platform to grow the business, both organically and through acquisition.

"Over the years of the outsourcing contract, our finance processes and systems have continued to improve. We are on a collaborative journey with our outsourcing partner, and since 1997, we have been able to efficiently integrate several major acquisitions in a way that would have been far more difficult had we had to do it on our own. The results have improved business performance and streamlined information flows, making it easier for Exel to track customer profitability and credit issues – and gain a better understanding of our cost base. These new capabilities have enabled our line managers to make more informed decisions that benefit both Exel and its customers through more efficient and cost-effective supply chains."

The improvements have not stopped there. Even today, a further step change is being introduced into the UK contract logistics business through leveraging global capabilities. As Young points out: "Cost-cutting wasn't the main objective, though cost reduction was welcome. Customers are much more important than individual countries: thanks in large part to Exel's outsourcing initiatives, the company went from being a country-driven organization to being a customer-driven one."

Many finance executives are realizing the opportunities available through externally-based service operations. Business process outsourcing (BPO) service providers have an operating scale that allows them to buy more competitively and pass on these savings to their clients. Service providers can offer access to global capabilities that companies other than large multinationals may find difficult to develop in house. As a consequence, in-house shared services options are often much more limited. Specialist providers can leverage scale, specialization, and reuse to provide a strong value proposition. Moreover, they can bypass and overcome entrenched processes and resistance to change – factors that can undermine even the most earnest of in-house efforts.

In addition, outsourcing can provide greater accountability than in-house programs. Performance guarantees can be provided through service level agreements along with incentives for improvements and penalties for performance shortfalls. Outsourcing also offers the advantage of continuous improvement. As outsourcing matures, providers recognize that sustaining an outsourcing relationship is dependent on far more than simply doing what the contract requires. Ongoing investments are needed to continually innovate. To keep the spark alive, performance indicators for innovation are often included as KPIs in an outsourcing deal.

For many organizations, it is not a case of whether to outsource, it is a case of when. An aspiring high-performance finance function needs to take the first step towards superior performance: embracing finance and accounting outsourcing and freeing itself from extraneous detail in order to strive for its desired strategic goal. Once it has freed up time and management attention, it can focus on working with the business side to add value, acting as a strategic partner and helping it arrive at better decisions.

Creating a service culture

A key differentiator between a centralized operation and shared services, whether in-sourced or outsourced, is that the former is driven by cost and headcount whereas the latter are focused on service capability and business relevance. A shared service center demands a *contracting approach* that is normally not addressed via centralization. *Service level agreements (SLAs) and operating level agreements (OLAs)* introduce *transparency* within organizational relationships. This transparency clarifies and simplifies credit-debit rationales and approval processes. When contract-based, these simplified processes support the negotiation of performance issues, pricing, and delivery timing. The relationship will be that of a *customer (business service) and a supplier (service center)*.

As depicted in Figure 6.11, the shared service center, through SLAs and OLAs, forces the enterprise to manage the services in a way that centralization does not traditionally require or imply. *Service becomes the product* "sold" by the shared service center and "bought" by the enterprise.

Service can take the form of a single process or a pool of processes. In order to define the right service pricing, a center will require a *bill of materials*, which may, at a minimum, include the following:

- human resources (number of full-time equivalents), allocated by service-process;
- key performance indicators (KPIs), by service-process;
- timing, by service-process;
- application system functionality tightly related to process flows and performance required, by service-process; and
- infrastructure requirements (space, PCs, etc.), by service-process.

The model is based on a formal agreement signed off between the service provider and each key internal client to define responsibilities and to motivate both parts to a continuous focus on end-to-end process improvement

Service Level Agreement (SLA) – Output
Contractual agreement that defines in detail each single service (output) that the Shared Services unit has to deliver to customer companies/units, and the related level of service (quality and time)

Operating Level Agreement (OLA) – Input
Contractual agreement that defines in detail each single input that Shared Services unit need to receive from served companies/units to deliver the service according to SLA agreed levels

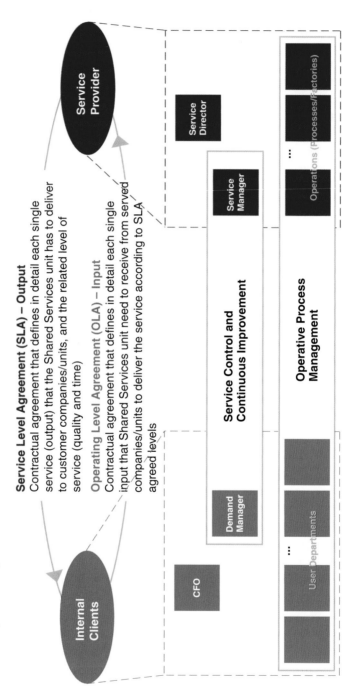

Figure 6.11   *SLA/OLA model*

Including these elements in a *bill of materials* will lead to a fully measurable and executable service-level agreement, as illustrated in Figure 6.12.

The contract approach supports high performance by requiring an enterprise to identify volume targets, performance KPIs, process improvement KPIs, efficiency targets, and measurable benefits. Equally important, a service-oriented organization can act as a professional development engine. Once trained, service center staff can move into business unit finance or elsewhere within the enterprise, bringing qualified skills and business operations knowledge with them. Again, when compared with centralization, the shared service center model can explicitly provide training and motivation to skilled professionals.

HIGH PERFORMERS EMBRACE BEST PRACTICES SELECTIVELY

The finance cost gap between average companies and high-performance businesses is substantial – high performers spend significantly less to run their finance operations. How do you achieve and maintain this level of excellence in finance? According to The Hackett Group's benchmarking research, world-class companies excel at contributing business value in the form of efficiency (cost and productivity) and effectiveness (value and quality) to the organization as a whole. They are also sharply focused.

Countless corporate initiatives and mandates have sunk under the weight of trying to be world-class in everything all at once. The Hackett Group's data demonstrates that there is no single path to world-class finance operations. However, managing improvements in a way that provides the right balance of efficiency and effectiveness – while keeping up with the pace of change – is of critical importance. A phased approach often proves successful. This involves prioritizing finance areas with the greatest impact on the business and then identifying best practices that will support improved performance. For instance, one goal may be to reduce costs, another may target improving cycle time. Best practices need to be used selectively, based on the desired outcome and also with an eye toward the cultural context of the organization.

One key attribute of a high-performance business is the executive team's vocal and unwavering commitment to infusing best practices throughout their organizations. Those promising maximum impact are identified and deployed in areas where they will provide the greatest business benefit.

To ensure highest impact and value, most high performers deliberately balance the two major contributors to value: cost-efficiency and effective-

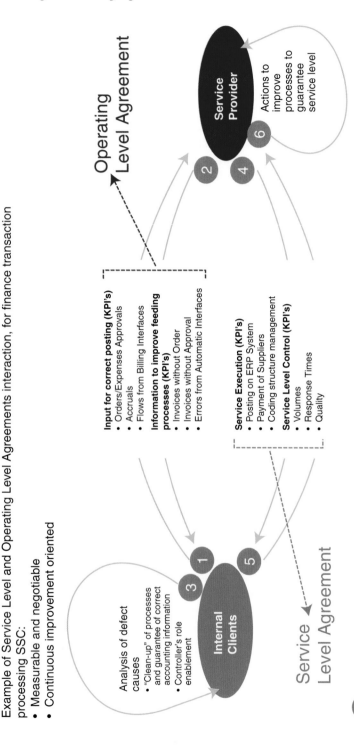

Example of Service Level and Operating Level Agreements interaction, for finance transaction processing SSC:

- Measurable and negotiable
- Continuous improvement oriented

Operating Level Agreement

Service Provider

6 Actions to improve processes to guarantee service level

Input for correct posting (KPI's)
- Orders/Expenses Approvals
- Accruals
- Flows from Billing Interfaces

Information to improve feeding processes (KPI's)
- Invoices without Order
- Invoices without Approval
- Errors from Automatic Interfaces

Service Execution (KPI's)
- Posting on ERP System
- Payment of Suppliers
- Coding structure management

Service Level Control (KPI's)
- Volumes
- Response Times
- Quality

Analysis of defect causes
- "Clean-up" of processes and guarantee of correct accounting information
- Controller's role enablement

Internal Clients

Service Level Agreement

n Operation sequence in service delivery

Figure 6.12 *SLA/OLA: representative examples*

ness. This balance is adjusted based on operational strategy. Take retail, for example: The business strategy of discount retailers like Wal-Mart is to keep costs low, and therefore, their support functions should typically be aligned to the same objectives. On the other hand, luxury department stores like Nordstrom, Inc. gain competitive advantage by "knowing the customer" and are oriented towards high service levels. Improvement activities for companies of this genre should be aimed at adding even greater customer service value.

Our research suggests that effectiveness-oriented organizations make investment decisions based primarily on quality and value, and only secondarily on how those decisions may affect cost or productivity. Efficiency-oriented organizations typically make decisions based on whether and how soon they will receive a payback in the form of reduced cost. In reality, few companies maintain an "either/or" focus on efficiency and effectiveness. By and large, executives will find that their company's business goals require them to improve both. Their major challenge is to establish the correct balance between the two.

In one real-life example, a major international hotel company has prospered by dividing its back-office processes into three categories and designating them as key to:

- competitive advantage
- strategic support
- business necessity.

Activities that affect the quality of the hotel guest's experience can make or break any effort to gain competitive advantage. Processes in this category must be performed at world-class levels of effectiveness. Training for customer-facing positions and interpreting market research to better understand the customer base is considered strategic support – they must be performed better than competitors, but do not have to be world-class. Finally, activities such as processing payroll – areas where the goal is to relentlessly drive down the cost of providing acceptable service – have been designated as business necessities. Here, best practices are selected based on their ability to reduce cost, rather than achieve overall world-class performance. The company reports that, since implementing this approach, each area has been able to create a strategy that aligns with that of the business, and people are able to stay focused on guest satisfaction and profitable growth.

The leadership capacity of today's executives is being challenged as never before. Mergers, acquisitions, and corporate restructurings; government and shareholder demands for transparency; and interest in globalization as an avenue for growth – all demand specialized skills and better access to information. It is important not to become fixated on efficiency – on reducing cost under all circumstances to the minimum sustainable level. Consider that while functional or process costs at high-performance organizations compare with those of more typical companies, there is a significant difference in how world-class organizations invest their budget dollars.

World-class finance organizations are not reducing costs equally across the four major finance categories. For example, while they spend 42% less overall than the typical company, they spend only 38.8% less on technology (Figure 6.13). Successfully balancing best practices to achieve levels of both efficiency and effectiveness that are appropriate for your business can be the catalyst for moving your organization away from "business as usual" and toward replicating the successes of the best companies in the world.

Research by The Hackett Group indicates that the key questions concerning best practices are what to focus on and where to start. World-class finance organizations do not implement a best practice, or a change for the sake of change, or solely to keep up with the competition. A change needs to be closely linked to a desired business outcome.

For example, a global manufacturing company invested a significant sum in a state-of-the-art credit and collections process in order to screen potential customers' credit worthiness and track collections. While this may be a worthwhile best practice for many organizations, it did not prove to be one for this company. The project generated no benefits. Worse yet, extra documentation created frustration, both internally and with paying customers. In reality, this company did not have a bad debt issue. They already were world class in this area. The specialized products they sell are critical to their customers' success, and their customers are all blue chips and pay their bills on time. High performance businesses will often refer to managing their portfolio of risks. This concept is critical to finance operations. If your enterprise is in a higher risk industry, adding additional risk to the overall corporate profile by adopting pioneering best practices in finance operations may not be ideal. A simple reason is executive management bandwidth.

Pioneering best practices can generate superior cost or quality improvements. Implementing such practices can help an enterprise leapfrog

Total Finance Costs as Percentage of Revenue, 2005

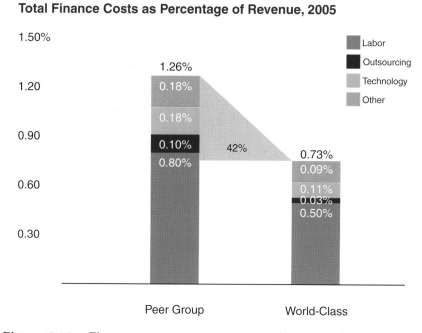

Figure 6.13 *Finance costs as a percentage of revenue, 2005*
©The Hackett Group. All Rights Reserved

its competition. However, they are, by definition, new and potentially unproven. The very nature of pioneering changes also creates organizational disruption, similar to the new release of an ERP package. If the amount of change in the new version is significant and the current platform meets business needs, then what incentive is there to be first?

That said, high-performance finance operations are among the early adopters of best practices, though they are not necessarily the first. They constantly monitor their environments to find new ways to add value, increase cost efficiency, and seek to better understand the underlying drivers of business performance. They are relentless in their pursuit for improvement. There are a number of levers these organizations use to drive mastery, as depicted in Figure 6.14. For example, they embed continuous improvement in their daily activities.

As finance operations transform themselves from their historic basic bookkeeping and controllership role by embracing progressive and pioneering capabilities, their enterprises will realize many benefits. Those with mastery of finance operations have significantly greater capabilities in their arsenal to assist their organizations. As a result, their value to these organizations increases.

Basic	Progressive	Pioneering
• Total finance cost (% of revenue) – more than 1.20%	• Total finance cost (% of revenue)– more than .80% and less than 1.20%	• Total finance cost (% of revenue) – less than 0.80%
• Total cost of transactions as % revenue – more than 0.40% (includes accounting, external reporting, revenue cycle and cash disbursements)	• Total cost of transactions as % revenue – more than .25% and less than 0.40%	• Total cost of transactions as % revenue – less than 0.25%
• Common applications and single ERP systems are rare	• Common ERP system using key functionality, less manual work,	• Taking advantage of advanced ERP functionality to better serve internal and external customers and suppliers (e.g. customers and suppliers have access to their accounts online; better integration between order entry and sales; billing)
• Back-office mentality – Stand alone operation focused on transaction processing	• Focus on process simplification, standardization and improved communication	• Front-office mentality – Focus on continuous improvement and better service at lower costs
• F&A operations organized by function within division	• F&A operations organized by function within region	• F&A operations organized by end-to-end, global processes
• Cost of operations is measured to maintain predictable results	• Cost of operations is benchmarked to help close performance gaps	• Focus on new value levers – working capital optimization, effective tax management, etc.
• Finance function level performance management program in place	• Team level performance management program in place	• Individual performance management program in place
• Focus on closing the books – 15+ days to close and report	• Focus on better information – 10-12 days to to close and report	• Focus on true decision support – 4–6 days to close and report
• Distributed processes and fragmented, interfaced systems	• Centralized process, common Chart of Accounts – moving to Shared Services	• Leverages full benefit of Shared Services and outsourcing
• F&A operations staffed to support peak period-end requirements	• Workload planned and balanced throughout the accounting period	• Work eliminated through workflow and self-service capabilities
• No common standard chart of accounts	• Standardization of chart of accounts and basic use of data warehousing	• Use of single, standard chart of accounts and data warehousing is common
• Much processing remains manual (reconciliations, adjustments, etc.)		
• Internal controls meet basic expectations but are not extensive or well documented; internal controls put organization at risk	• Internal controls exceed expectations and are well documented; some risk still exists	• Highly optimized internal controls with well-integrated and seamless process; no risk to organization

Figure 6.14 *Finance operations – mastery scale*

CFO INSIGHTS: LESSONS FROM THE MASTERS

- Most high-performance finance organizations begin their journeys by creating an efficient engine to capture and process data. This efficiency achieves superior cost performance and gives the CFO needed organizational credibility to tackle the other challenges the enterprise faces.

- Target end-to-end enterprise-wide process connectivity and standardization by eliminating artificial barriers created by functional silos. Begin by understanding the process and information needs across the enterprise. Ensure that decisions and information flows are transparent, consistent and shared. Leaders also internalize the notion that process elimination is more effective than doing something faster and cheaper. Eliminating *noise* from the end-to-end transaction processes helps accelerate cycle times.

- Information and insights are critical elements of an enterprise's success. The business benefits of information-driven analytics and insights that result from process connectivity are significantly greater than the productivity gains. Leading organizations use these insights for competitive advantage.

- Finance needs to play a key role in establishing data standards and governance to achieve the elusive "single version of the truth." To effectively convert data into insight, it must be timely, action-oriented, and in a format easily understood by decision makers.

- High-performing organizations make internal control a corporate-wide responsibility and embed controls in their mainstream business processes. Embedding appropriate controls in these upstream processes and directly capturing data not only reduce work within finance operations; they also reduce the need for secondary detective controls within finance. This, along with standardizing processes throughout the enterprise, significantly reduces the compliance burden.

- Once the internal value chain is optimized, address process efficiency across the entire supplier/customer ecosystem.

This will drive further productivity benefits. Technological advances in process digitization are effectively removing the cross-company boundaries and complexities of transactions. While this revolution helps drive out costs and increase information transparency, it also poses a risk to the laggards – to be part of this next-generation ecosystem, one must have the needed capability or perish.

- While the notion of shared services has been around for many years, leading finance organizations are in their second or third generation of change. In addition to basic transaction processing, they are adding extra capabilities to further serve and continue to be relevant to their customers. Finance leaders view their operations as a service business and constantly seek feedback on both cost and quality. High performers use the capabilities within their shared service functions as weapons to quickly absorb new markets or acquisitions.

- Outsourcing provides additional performance levers to an enterprise. While some organizations begin with an internal shared service center and move to outsourcing as a second step, many choose to leapfrog their peers and competitors by moving toward this model directly. These organizations view outsourcing as a capability make-versus-buy decision. This allows them to quickly achieve the desired end state. It also provides risk mitigation by partnering with someone whose core competency is finance and accounting operations. This gives instant access to scale and resources.

REFERENCES

1 Richard T Roth, Chief Research Officer, The Hackett Group, Accenture Global Shared Services Conference, June 22, 2005.

2 Stewart Clements, Michael Donnellan, in association with Cedric Read, *CFO Insights: Achieving High Performance Through Finance Business Process Outsourcing*, Wiley, 2004.

CHAPTER 7

Capital Stewardship

CONVERTING FUTURE INITIATIVES INTO VALUE

Darren Jackson, CFO & EVP – Finance and Treasury
Best Buy

Best Buy is the number one consumer electronics retailer in the world and is known in its industry as a value creator. This Fortune 100 company, with over 900 retail stores in the US and Canada, has a relentless focus on managing capital effectively and maximizing shareholder value. As Darren Jackson explains, the finance organization has been a key driver in focusing the company on the right strategies, programs, and investments – all with an eye on superb capital stewardship.

Best Buy has emerged as an industry leader and high performer by demonstrating obsessive customer focus, operational excellence, innovation and commercialization, alliance and collaboration capabilities, and differentiated talent management. As it has grown, its industry has become 1) more complex, with multiple channels and formats, higher service level expectations, and globalization; 2) more competitive, with intense price competition, enhanced customer loyalty programs and increased promotions; and 3) more sophisticated, with the uptake of advanced analytics and technologies, and enhanced customer insights.

Best Buy is a high-octane, finance-driven story and we began by asking Darren for an overview. "Our success is derived from: 1) the imperative to maintain strong growth, and 2) the need to constantly innovate in developing our business model.

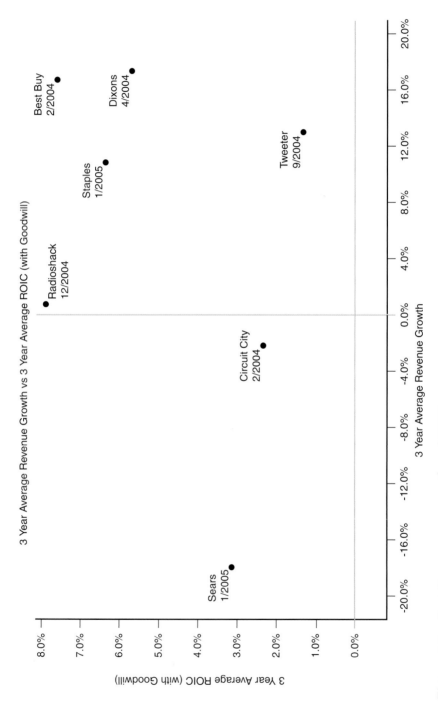

Figure 7.1 *Best Buy revenue growth and ROIC.*
Source: Accenture analysis

We continually strive to find new sources and places for growth."

Delivering this type of growth is integral to Best Buy's finance agenda. We asked Darren how he characterized this challenge. "I think about the challenge on three dimensions. The biggest issue we face is: 'Do we have the pipeline of growth ideas, including stores, products and services that will fulfill the future value expectation for this company?' In my organization, I own the new business development group, treasury, and finance – and they are spending nearly all their time working with the businesses to sort out the agenda for future growth. Challenge number two is my decision-support team, which is embedded within the organization. How do I strip out of that all the arduous activities of planning and forecasting and allow them to focus on their primary goal of moving from insight to outcome – and driving that within the context of the business? Challenge three is managing financial operations for growth, and thinking not about how I optimize those businesses, but what are the constraints in those businesses for future growth? Am I ensuring that I can drive the growth agenda and understand where the future can take us in terms of the pipeline?"

When we asked about scaling Best Buy's current finance operating model to support future value targets, the conversation turned to capital stewardship. Darren noted: "The biggest changes will come in the resources that we apply to converting future value initiatives into operating initiatives. Today, too many of the initiatives we work on fall through the cracks because we don't dedicate enough resources to them. I think that in the future, we will have more resources in that space than we have today."

Brand is critical to Best Buy's growth engine. We asked Darren to describe his approach to capital stewardship with respect to brand. His response focused on two factors: the here and now, as well as future value. As he put it: "I think about intangibles on two dimensions; the company's ability to grow in the future and its ability to deliver excess returns. The key health indicators of those intangibles include everything from the vitality of the brand to growth potential. For instance, Dell has a way of thinking about the robustness of its business model as it affects success in the future. That is partly strength of the brand. It includes ROIC, sustainable productivity, quality management, value, customer pools, and efficiency of operating model."

Darren's response implies that Best Buy looks at the company's market potential versus its returns on capital across different dimensions. He continued, "Yes. You identify the value in that gap and it's in the intangibles. They are in the brand, the management teams, and the customer pools."

In examining effective capital stewardship, Darren asks a series of questions. "What are your strategies to leverage assets to fill that value void? When I look at that part of our stock price that is based on future, I see that it is worth more today than it was 90 days ago. What do I think is happening? The marketplace sees a lot of growth potential. They see the value in Best Buy's customer pools; the service dimension has to get access to these customers. Then your growth potential is going up. Your ability to go into China and be successful is going up, although in a different way. The questions you ask have to focus on deal with the return potential: Can you make money? Is the value of your flow through your business model going up? How efficient is your operating model? What is the ROIC? Are those things improving in the future?

"I look across all these areas and ask myself, 'What is the efficiency level of our operating model? Do we have enough value in the customer pools and strategies that we are pursuing? And how long does a retail brand last? It has to have a beginning, middle, and an end. What does that curve look like?' If you ask 10 people, you would get 20 answers, because we do not actually know the asset productivity."

Darren's comments indicate that timing and entry strategy are critical to investments and the allocation of assets. For instance, Dell was very careful in deciding when to enter the printer business. Darren shared his perspective on Dell's success: "If you stay with that example and do the math on the current and future value, you would probably find that 85% of Dell's value is projected into the future and 15% exists today. Why? Because the marketplace sees the growth and return potential of that business model. Now, you know what the limitation of that business model is? It is predicated on the known needs of a customer and simply out-competing the investment model. It is not dependent on innovating around unmet customer needs." When asked about the future, Darren talked about building a value-centered culture throughout the organization, followed by capital stewardship, which he sees becoming more important in three years' time. He explained, "It will go up because we will try to figure out how to fund China's growth." Darren added that his finance organization is poised for growth as well. "At our last board meeting, the board *accepted my proposal to change our finance committee to 'the strategic growth in finance committee.' We need to devote more time to our pipeline of ideas and to fill that future value void. We need to have much more energy, focus, and capacity to identify future value initiatives and strategies – along with the resources that they demand, so that there are real platforms for growth.*

"When I think about where value will come from in the future, three or five years from now we will be discussing in detail customer markets – not product markets or geographic markets. Geographic and product markets will be the backdrop to customer markets in driving our growth potential. And we will be talking about value propositions, extensions from customer needs, and the capabilities required to deliver to those needs. We will see a future based on a platform of converting customer needs and insights by directly accessing sourcing capabilities, as opposed to just traditional vendor networks. That is what we will be spending time on: seeing the pipeline, understanding it, and dedicating the resources to convert on pipeline ideas. Those pipeline ideas will be principally driven by customer markets. Best Buy will be building the capabilities to realize customer-market opportunities identified through the pipeline process to fill the value void. That is what I think about the future."

Best Buy is a high-growth company and capital stewardship in particular, looking at the future value creation and the ideas in the pipeline that will require assets, is integral to its success. This strong focus on growth potential and future value creation is a defining attribute of high performers.

Generating returns above the risk-adjusted cost of capital is a basic criterion for a high-performance business. Our research demonstrated a strong correlation between a high-performance business and mastery of a new suite of finance capabilities that includes capital stewardship. More than two-thirds of the finance masters studied scored as pioneers in the area of capital stewardship using the Accenture finance mastery scale. By comparison, less than a quarter of non-high-performance businesses had differentiating capital stewardship capabilities. High-performance companies embed the capital management capability within their approach to performance management to create a value-centered culture capable of making the tough decisions about where and when capital is invested.

CAPITAL STEWARDSHIP IS A CRITICAL SKILL IN CREATING HIGH PERFORMANCE

Capital stewardship is the process by which business executives manage capital already deployed in an enterprise and capital deployed to new investments to drive growth in total returns to shareholders. The management processes created to determine where capital will be invested and to maximize the returns generated often involves making choices between competing business segments, types of investment, and time horizons for return. It is a politically charged process in most companies. No single answer will satisfy all the interested stakeholders.

Creating and sustaining a high-performance business requires close attention to the consumption of capital and the ability to consistently generate acceptable levels of risk-adjusted returns on the capital invested. Pioneering companies have mastered the range of activities involved in capital management. They start with a long-term view of when and how to raise capital, often acting in cycles that seem counter to the activity of their competitors. These companies dedicate substantial discipline to linking capital project investments across the organization with expected returns on their income statements. They are disciplined about learning from prior mistakes to improve the success rates on new projects. They also understand how to redesign core operating models to minimize the need for working capital and shed unnecessary risks to other players in the value chain.

Finance executives interested in developing leading capabilities in the area of capital management should start by focusing on the calculation of how much capital is really required to compete effectively. A combination of small changes in the assumptions built into common operating models can frequently redefine which players in a given value chain must invest capital and how much capital must be consumed within a specific company. Finance literature is filled with stories of companies that have introduced capital management programs and reduced the volume of capital required to operate the business. A clear understanding of industry economics, value drivers associated with current strategies, and leverage points across the value chain can substantially reduce the capital required.

A second area of focus is appropriate capital structure and the mix of capital from available sources. The answers to both capital structure and cost-of-capital questions differ significantly by industry and also by phase of development in the enterprise lifecycle. As a result, the wide range of decision factors required to answer these questions is beyond the scope of this chapter.

The next area of focus in developing leading capabilities in capital management is an understanding of the risks associated with capital investments in each segment of the business. Once separate risk profiles and experience curves are documented and understood, different return rates can be assigned to individual capital investments to create a risk-adjusted capital investment plan. This approach can eliminate the common error of assigning a single hurdle rate for investment decisions across individual opportunities and sub-optimizing the potential returns to the business.

Managing the portfolio of capital investments to accelerate investments in some projects while stopping investments in others is one of the capabilities which finance executives find most difficult to develop. The discipline required to conduct post-investment audits and actively learn from prior mistakes is not evident in many of the finance organizations involved in the high-performance business research. Respondents to the research indicated that filling this gap in capability is high on their priority list because it offers room to increase the success rates for future capital investments and the returns on those already made.

Successful capital management requires constant trade-offs and tough decisions between competing options. This challenge is well recognized by the finance executives at world-class companies. United HealthGroup, for example, has grown dramatically while increasing its stock price tenfold since 1998. Pat Erlandson, the CFO of UnitedHealth Group (see also Chapter 2, High-Performance Leadership), makes the connection between value creation and capital stewardship: "We have a capital management process that helps us figure out how best to deploy scarce resources. Capital management is critical in this business. Deploying investment across five businesses in an efficient and effective way is central to making sure that we get good returns across each one of these businesses. These are the decisive factors that have enabled us to continue to experience strong, sustained growth from $400 million of revenues in '89 to $17 billion of revenues in '98 to $45 billion today. Today, we're much better stewards of our capital, which I think has driven the value that you see coming through in our TRS numbers ... Capital management ... is where I spend most of my time."

The basic steps of minimizing funding costs, optimizing the capital structure, and creating effective capital allocation and management techniques provide a solid platform for generating acceptable returns on capital invested in the business. Unfortunately, these steps alone do not help with a larger problem of explaining how capital investments are going to drive future value to the business.

FOCUS ON EXPLAINING HOW CAPITAL INVESTMENTS WILL GENERATE FUTURE VALUE

The standard analysis of capital investment focuses on the movement of capital on the balance sheet, and the expenses and returns related to the investment of that capital as it flows through to the income statement. Financial analysts and investors frequently struggle to understand the potential returns to be earned when capital is invested inside the business to build brands, customer relationships, increased manufacturing or distribution flexibility, intellectual property or other intangible assets. Our research confirms that this problem can be addressed through analysis of both the 'current value' and the 'future value' components of a company's enterprise value. "Current value" is the present value of the total earnings potential of the existing enterprise in the current year and into the future. "Future value" is the incremental value creation potential of the enterprise beyond the current value – usually due to increased margins, volumes, or new revenue streams. A common trait of high-performance management teams is the ability to clearly communicate to external stakeholders how capital investments will impact both current and future value.

Generally accepted accounting standards define income statement and balance sheet reporting requirements, which no longer provide external stakeholders with a transparent understanding of the potential value creation capacity of assets developed through many of the investments required to compete effectively and grow the business. As noted in Figure 7.2, the composition of market value has changed over time.

In fact, as shown in Figure 7.2, assets listed on traditional financial statements accounted for only 35% of an enterprise's value as of March 2005. The remaining 65% of total market value is not derived from tangible assets. External stakeholders must look beyond the balance sheet to understand the true nature of the capital sources that are driving value in most businesses today. Helping external stakeholders understand this gap is an important step in the capital stewardship process. Because enterprise value cannot be explained by assets recorded on the balance sheet, financial executives must be prepared to explain the intangible assets and how they are expected to drive future returns to the business.

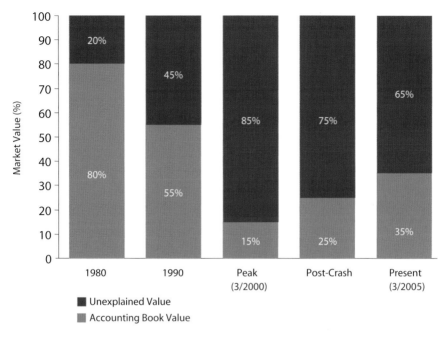

Figure 7.2 *S&P 500: book value as a percentage of market value.*
Source: Accenture analysis

Current value and future value

The difference between accounting book value and market value has
been increasing over time. As this gap continues to widen, stakeholders
are beginning to focus on the unexplained market value by analyzing
the nature of intangible assets. At the same time, stakeholders are also
noticing that the percentage of enterprise value that can be explained by
calculating the present value of future cash flows from the existing business ("current value") is decreasing. Finance executives have a key role
in helping explain the difference ("future value").

An analysis of the broad Russell 3000 stock index is illustrated in
Figure 7.3. As the figure demonstrates, approximately 49% of the aggregate market value of Russell 3000 companies is represented by traditionally defined current value: operating-year earnings capitalized by a
weighted average cost of capital, based on the assumption that firms will
generate those earnings into perpetuity. The remaining 51% of the total
value of the Russell 3000 index cannot be explained by current earnings
stretching into perpetuity. The unexplained portion is based on inves-

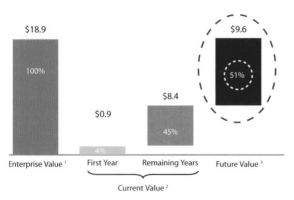

Figure 7.3 *Current vs future value as a percentage of market value*

tor expectations of future growth and encompasses intangibles, such as intellectual capital, market sentiment, and other extrinsic factors over which a company has no direct control.

A small percentage of the total enterprise value is explained by the current year earnings. Figure 7.3 shows that the current year annual earnings account for 4% of total enterprise value (current value, first-year earnings). The remaining 96% of enterprise value is represented by both the current year's earnings capitalized into perpetuity and unexplained market value. A staggering result is that of $18.9 trillion of aggregate equity value in the Russell 3000, the current year P&L accounts for only $0.9 trillion.

The analysis of current and future value is conservative in that it assumes that these enterprises can maintain current earnings forever with no improvement or decline. Assuming that is possible, the analysis illustrates that the Russell 3000 market has an astonishing $9.6 trillion of growth premiums priced into the market. This future value premium is distributed unevenly through the economy. As illustrated in Figure 7.4, it is largely created by and concentrated in industries and companies investing huge amounts of capital to develop intangible assets.

As noted earlier, we believe that finance executives should be prepared to explain how and when investments in intangible assets are expected to convert to future value. The risks associated with these investments and the probability of conversion to positive net income results are not often addressed in internal or external financial statements or in management discussions.

Sector	Current Value ($M)	Future Value ($M)	FV as a % of MV	Market Value
Automobiles & Components	251,689	207,923	45.2%	459,612
Banks	1,002,637	475,518	32.2%	1,478,155
Capital Goods	644,999	821,963	56.0%	1,466,962
Commercial Services & Supplies	118,047	133,477	53.1%	251,524
Consumer Durables & Apparel	211,781	121,365	36.4%	333,146
Consumer Services	182,314	269,858	59.7%	452,172
Diversified Financials	682,333	539,474	44.2%	1,221,807
Energy	1,222,588	483,998	28.4%	1,706,586
Food & Staples Retailing	259,981	250,600	49.1%	510,581
Food, Beverage, & Tobacco	500,015	268,387	34.9%	768,401
Health Care Equipment & Services	344,966	487,660	58.6%	832,626
Household & Personal Products	169,565	185,407	52.2%	354,972
Insurance	641,367	262,328	29.0%	903,695
Materials	534,739	334,336	38.5%	869,076
Media	242,902	623,995	72.0%	866,897
Pharmaceuticals & Biotechnology	468,395	637,680	57.7%	1,106,074
Real Estate	90,119	209,364	69.9%	299,483
Retailing	366,876	456,430	55.4%	823,306
Semiconductors & Equipment	47,412	347,997	88.0%	395,409
Software & Services	163,846	565,597	77.5%	729,443
Technology Hardware & Equipment	156,976	772,210	83.1%	929,187
Telecommunication Services	297,956	440,766	59.7%	738,721
Transportation	172,487	304,103	63.8%	476,589
Utilities	572,563	416,359	42.1%	988,922
Totals	**9,346,552**	**9,616,794**	**50.7%**	**18,963,346**

Figure **7.4**   *Russell 3000 future value by industry, December 2004*

In Chapter 9, Nick Rose, CFO of Diageo, talks about the role finance plays in managing the investments required to build brands in the global alcoholic drinks business. As he notes in that chapter:

"Economic profit and returns on invested capital are something that we pay particular attention to as well as segmented profitability analysis ... Our strategic plans start with setting a total return to shareholders target analytically derived from where we want the share price to be going out into the future. We then disaggregate this into our various businesses on a multidimensional basis either by geography, brand, or some other segmented basis ... We rigorously assess how much investment we need to make to deliver that plan. In fact, as a brand-led com-

pany, the investments we make are all around our brand portfolio and our intangible assets ... When we look at any change
proposal, potential investment, or proposed expenditure on a
promotional campaign, you always see a thorough evaluation of
the economic profit flows, the risk-adjusted returns and the cash
flow we expected to see. This runs through the company at all
levels, and our compensation system links performance-related
bonus payments to this as well."

The focus at Diageo on evaluating investments with a view to risk-adjusted
returns and cash flow demonstrates that traditional finance skills can
add value to both tangible and intangible asset investments. While brand
value is one example of an asset that does not always appear in financial
statements, there are others that can be key determinants of future success in generating free cash flow or increasing profitability.

A framework for evaluating the assets required to generate future profitability
Working with AssetEconomics, a strategy advisory firm, we have classified the different types of assets within an enterprise. As noted in the
shaded boxes in the top left quadrant of Figure 7.5, standard financial
statements only present information about the tangible monetary and
physical assets required to execute the business model. The mix of relational,
organizational, and human assets and the wide range of intangible assets
identified in Figure 7.5 are often key drivers of future value.

Finance executives must focus on helping their management teams
make the best decisions about investing in those assets that are critical
to future value creation – even as they balance the adverse short-term
accounting impact to metrics such as Return on Capital Employed (ROCE)
and EVA™. One of the biggest practical difficulties in establishing a capital management process for intangibles is determining how they can
actually be measured within an enterprise, since it is notoriously difficult,
if not impossible, to manage what you cannot measure.

The requirement to make good decisions on where to invest in both
tangible and intangible assets and then monitor results over time often
means that the finance team must get involved in establishing performance
management systems that extend well beyond the traditional financial
metrics. As an example, finance executives in a retail business may find
that customer loyalty is a powerful asset and a significant barrier to entry
for competitors. It may be recognized as a key pricing lever and a consistent predictor in generating future value. Finance executives may find
that investments in programs that measure customer loyalty (for example,

Asset Type

	Traditional Accounting Assets		Intellectual Capital Assets		
Asset Recognition	**Monetary**	**Physical**	**Relational**	**Organizational**	**Human**

Tangible	• Cash
	• Investments
	• Receivables/debtors
	• Payables/creditors
		• Property
		• Plant
		• Equipment
		• Inventory
		  - Finished goods
		  - WIP
		  - Parts/raw materials
			• Customer contracts
			• Formal alliances, JVs, supply agreements
				• Systems
				• Formalized processes
				• Codified knowledge
				• Patents
				• Brands
				• Mastheads
					• Management contracts
					• Documented accessible skills inventories

Intangible	• Credit ratings
	• Undrawn facilities
	• Borrowing capacity (relative to like companies, based on character)
	• Borrowing covenant slack
	• Receivables certainty
	• Accruals convertibility
		• Plant flexibility
		• Plant modernity
		• Infastructure surrounding plants
		• Stranded assets?
		• Tradability of assets?
		• Access rights
		• Balance sheet strength
		• Inventory (good and usable, obsolete, redundant)
			• Customer loyalty
			  - Behavioral
			  - Attitudinal
			• Quality of supply contracts
			• Right to tender, right to compete, right to design
			• Strength of stakeholder support (including opinion leaders)
			• Networks
			• Regulatory imposts
				• Structural appropriateness
				• Informal processes
				• Organizational reputation
				• Brand meaning (strength, stature)
				• Productivity of R&D process
				• Quality of corporate governance
				• Know how, show how
				• Tacit knowledge
					• Top management quality
					• Top management experience
					• Ability to execute on strategy
					• Leadership Capabilities
					• Problem-solving ability
					• Employee loyalty
					  - Behavioral
					  - Attitudinal
					• Personnel reputation
					• Workforce adaptability
					• Employee engagement

Figure 7.5   *Identifying tangible and intangible assets*

through rigorous and meaningful customer feedback processes and customer attrition analysis, including interviews with former customers), are worthwhile as part of the management reporting system.

CASE STUDY
Outperforming competitors through strong capital management

E. Follin Smith, CFO and chief administrative officer of the Constellation Energy Group, believes that one of the keys to Constellation's success is its ability to constantly renew itself and improve performance through relentless innovation with a keen focus on the right priorities. "We focus on bringing the right people together, who are best in class in every area that's important to the company, eliminating distractions, setting aside the things that don't matter, deciding what your priorities are, and putting the best resources on the things that are priorities."

Capital stewardship is one of several finance and performance management areas that Constellation Energy gets right. Follin Smith says: "Capital stewardship is one of the most important finance and performance management capabilities for outperforming others in our industry. Because our business is capital intensive and we have competing interests, we need to ensure we have capital available for the right revenue-producing opportunities. We are pioneering in capital investment. We have a very rigorous process of review and approval for material commodities deals, which involves committee reviews and challenges at the business unit level and then reviews at the CFO and CEO levels. These reviews focus on analyzing the key value drivers of the investments, sensitivities, and inherent risks so that we can develop a risk-adjusted hurdle rate. In addition to these thorough finance reviews, we have a risk department that ensures our capital appraisal and follow-up processes are robustly adhered to; it continually monitors value at risk and assesses the different risks on all significant deals that we have in play. The performance indicators we monitor include return on invested capital in different business unit segments, internal rate of return (IRR), and risk adjusted RR."

Managing the risk in capital projects and learning from the past is one of the toughest disciplines to master. Follin Smith goes on to say: "We've definitely institutionalized one thing: we go back and analyze big capital investments. We have a large project-tracking process. Every six months Andrew Good (senior VP of finance) sits down with the management committee, reviews several large capital invest-

ments that we have made or are making, and asks where we are versus the return on investment that we originally committed ourselves to. If we're not within a narrow band of what was committed, we ask why, what the lessons learned are, how and why something went wrong, and what can we do better. We reevaluate the basis of how we allocated the capital, and we look at what we need to change about our processes for evaluating capital. We're rigorously managing the risk in capital projects, and some aspects become institutionalized so that we don't make the same mistakes next time around."

Determining where capital will be deployed is often a contentious process. Constellation Energy starts with a broad perspective on where value can be generated, and balances investment between current year return and future value creation. "There are several ways that capital is allocated in Constellation Energy Group (CEG). During the business planning process, the business units submit 5-year capital plans delineating capital for revenue generation, regulatory purposes, environmental spend, and infrastructure spend. CEG ensures that capital is prudently allocated to revenue-producing spend based on expected returns as well as the risks associated with those returns. When reviewing our capital investments, we look to total expected value and the allocation between current-year and future-year value, since one of the metrics we share with the street is total gross margin created in a given year and not just the current gross margin created. An interesting challenge is allocating contingent capital to the business units. We explicitly address this with our risk-adjusted return on capital, but we continue to analyze how to be more explicit in the method we use to determine how to more efficiently allocate capital."

Making balanced investment decisions is an important priority. "I think we're pretty good in the skill sets we bring to the table in general to run the business, and in making every decision such that we weigh the intangible aspects of every decision. It's not a pure financial decision. With capital investment we start with the financials, what the pure numbers say. Then we talk about the intangibles. We often make decisions that can't be justified on the financials alone."

Constellation Energy considers its most significant intangible asset to be its knowledge of the industry and its ability to understand the various components of the energy value chain. In the merchant energy business – and especially in a fully-integrated energy company – a complex interaction of factors, ranging from migration of population centers to trends in energy efficiency patterns, combined with *long-term contracts and the transient nature of electricity, has resulted in a formula for financial performance which is more intricate than in many other industries. Compounding the problem is the relative newness of the industry, making statistically reliable data rare. Considering the impact knowledge-based transactions could have on the company, management attributed the bulk of Constellation Energy's future value to its institutionalized knowledge.*

Constellation Energy used teams of highly educated and deeply skilled professionals to manage and develop proprietary knowledge assets that drive future profitability, chiefly through measuring and modeling activities. "That resource has enabled us to better manage our knowledge assets by ensuring that our bids for service offerings are not driven by gut instinct," said Andrew Good, senior vice president of finance. Using a data-driven approach to determine sales tactics was unusual in the capital-intensive energy industry where measuring and modeling activities were often left in the hands of a sales force or traders. Constellation Energy's differentiation in mindset evolved from the trading operations partnership the company had with Goldman Sachs during the late 1990s. Over the course of the relationship, Constellation Energy acquired the investment bank's cultural orientation to intangible asset management.

Calculating the return on investments is not always possible. Follin Smith says: "With brand we are already tracking unaided awareness. No matter how you track investments in these types of assets, there will never be a tangible ROI that you can hang your hat on. It just takes good business judgment to know that it's there because it's so difficult to quantify."

Constellation Energy will continue to improve its capital stewardship capabilities. Follin Smith explains, "The key capital stewardship areas of focus for CEG for the next two years are working capital, the efficiency of the balance sheet, and tax management. From a working capital/balance sheet perspective, we are looking at driving metrics throughout the company that would charge for net working capital balances. The goal is to make the company more efficient in the use of cash. In addition, we are looking at different deal structures that may reduce our cost of capital. Our business model requires us to perform significant amounts of energy trading. Consequently we must have a strong investment-grade credit rating, and we engage in frequent conversations with the rating agencies and bankers to hone our capital structure and strategy. In the area of tax efficiency/tax effectiveness – the goals are to decrease the number of legal entities and the time it takes to process tax returns, and by solid tax planning to decrease the effective tax rate. Tax effectiveness will have a direct impact on the bottom line."

DEVELOPING A RIGOROUS CAPITAL ALLOCATION PROCESS

High-performance organizations require a rigorous capital allocation process. Strong capital stewardship programs share a common set of attitudes and approaches on capital allocation and management. The most successful companies make their assessments within a broad context while focusing on the risks associated with individual investments.

- Start with an understanding of the drivers of both current and future value. This requires a complete analysis of the competitive landscape, industry trends, new threats and emerging business models, and requirements of both tangible and intangible assets. Understand the total capital already employed in the business and how it is performing in generating expected returns.

- Identify the key capabilities required to deliver both current and future value, and assess gaps with existing capabilities to prioritize where investments are required across the business. Understand the appropriate cost of capital for specific capabilities based on their risk profiles. Time investments to create required capabilities in front of market movements while protecting against the risk of making investments too far ahead of the market.

- Make the tough sourcing and divestment decisions required to minimize required investments – and shed unprofitable assets or stop investments that are not performing as expected. Sourcing decisions focus on building the portfolio of required capabilities with optimal trade-off between cost and probability of success in the desired time frame. Divestment decisions focus on exiting businesses that are not expected to drive future value in order to free up unproductive capital.

- Set measurable, specific, and prioritized high-level targets to balance current and future value delivery. Articulate enterprise strategy clearly and communicate its impact on investment decisions. Integrate capital and operating budgets – and highlight the relationship between changes in operating budgets and specific capital investments approved. This is critical, since operating and capital budgets are often looked at separately because a capital budget is not seen as having an impact on short-term metrics. Integrating the capital and operational budgets will force managers to think about the operational assumptions used in project evaluation and encourage a focus on value realization. Integrating the capital and operational budgets will also encourage managers to view capital deployments holistically. For example, spending for new projects does not have to come from new funds if it can be released from the current capital fund through improved working capital deployment. Set targets for each business, align them with capital deployment plans, and then measure outcomes transparently.

- Eliminate much of the gaming commonly found in the capital decision process by improving the consistency and quality of the business cases for each investment. Develop the skills of future leaders in the business by allowing management teams to finalize capital investment decisions and manage delivery within the boundaries set forth in the corporate strategy and high-level capital allocation process. Involve the corporate center in individual capital management reviews only if investments breach a certain risk or financial threshold. Develop skills across the organization to create disciplined financial models with common assumptions on key factors (such as market growth rates, demand patterns, price points, development time lines) and offer multiple scenarios to develop new capabilities. Multiple options should be considered if they are available, including "make versus buy", "do nothing", and "wait for more information."

- Establish multiple gates (phases of work with specific expected outcomes) for major investments and schedule future investment approvals around completion of each major gate. These gates should be formally recognized when a project receives preliminary approval, and future investment approvals should be treated as rigorously as the initial approval.

- Include a risk and sensitivity analysis with a common framework and measurement approach. The project evaluation process should be designed so that all relevant risks – including implementation and forecast risks – are assessed and a risk mitigation plan is developed to address them. The formal inclusion of risk analysis within the capital allocation framework will negate the tendency to deal with risk in an arbitrary way by increasing discount rates or hurdle rates. It is essential that risk and sensitivity analysis be dynamic. The process should include updates as the quality of information available improves over time. Risk mitigation plans should also cover non-financial risks such as health and safety considerations. The effectiveness of the risk mitigation plan can be judged in post-implementation reviews, which can also provide feedback to improve risk mitigation in the future.

- Adopt a cross-functional approach to capital allocation instead of limiting the effort to the finance organization. Although capital allocation is inherently a cross-functional process, many companies tend to allow base-case financials and other key capital allocation requirements to be completed by finance in isolation. The accuracy of base-case financials can be improved by the including operating executives with direct responsibility for projects in the process of delivering against individual capital investments. Adopting a cross-functional approach to capital allocation also improves buy-in from across the business.

- Link business unit and individual performance contracts and compensation plans to the delivery of a balanced set of operational metrics. Reward delivery of both short-term profitability and development of long-term capabilities as defined by the capital investment program. Limit gaming of the performance management system by using consistent metrics that measure performance on multiple time horizons. Using multi-year metrics ensures accountability for managers' decisions over time. Ensure that lines of responsibility are clearly defined so individuals cannot step away from the capital allocation decisions they have made.

- Create a consistent approach to post-investment reviews. Encourage learning across the organization to improve the accuracy of future investment forecasts and business cases. Identify the most common causes of investment failures and the leading indicators that existing investments are not going to achieve the desired returns.

These best practices associated with capital management processes illustrate the techniques employed by leading companies. Developing the most effective process within a specific company requires finance executives to consider an array of factors, including culture, decision-making processes, and financial acumen across the organization. Although it takes substantial effect to develop the capital management practices discussed here, the impact on future profitability makes it well worth the effort.

THE HACKETT GROUP ON CAPITAL STEWARDSHIP

World-class finance executives do not focus primarily on costs and related efficiency metrics, such as productivity and number of cycles. Because the leaders of finance organizations that have achieved performance excellence believe they have the transactional side of things under control, they have turned their attention to increasing business value.

The major driver of business value in finance is working capital or cash flow. By this yardstick, world-class finance leaders do an exemplary job of increasing cash flow through a variety of channels. One of these is tax management, as measured by effective tax rate. The leaders manage an effective tax rate of 28%. For the peer group, the average is 32%. A one-percent tax on every hundred million dollars of pretax earnings equals $1 million in taxes. Assuming that a company had pretax earnings of 15%, every 1% reduction in effective tax rate would equate to 0.15% of revenue, or $1.5 million per billion of revenue.

Similarly, days sales outstanding (DSO) is another fertile area where the finance function can add significant value. The average organization comes in at 48 days; world-class organizations collect what is owed in less than half that time, at 22 days. Assuming a 10% cost of capital, every day outstanding on a billion dollars of sales represents roughly $275,000 in capital costs.

Accelerating the collection of accounts receivable is another way to improve an organization's cash flow. In fact, there is a sizeable difference between the peer group and world-class performers. It is interesting that the key factor in accelerating cash payments is the use of electronic invoicing.

With the growing availability of outsourcing options to handle the purely transactional aspects of finance, we believe that finance organizations that do not increase their ability to increase working capital and positively affect economic return will see their influence with senior management decline.

CFO INSIGHTS: LESSONS FROM THE MASTERS

- Focus on minimizing the capital required to compete effectively by leveraging investments made across the value chain, modifying operating practices to minimize working capital requirements, and shedding unproductive assets.

- Constantly optimize capital structure and mix of sources to lower total cost of capital while providing adequate capital flexibility to capture emerging value opportunities and weather unexpected competitive challenges.

- Develop a risk-adjusted capital management program that is integrated with the strategic priorities of the business and optimizes both short-term and future value growth. Design capital allocation and management processes using a cross-functional approach to create accountability for delivery of expected results across the business.

- Implement rigorous processes to stage gate approvals for individual investments and systematically stop investments that are not generating expected results.

- Integrate operating and capital budgeting processes and link specific changes to operating results with approved investments. Create performance management programs with multi-year views to balance delivery against both operating results and investment programs.

- Prepare to explain how and when investments in intangible assets will convert to income statement results. Adjust investment criteria to balance strategic and pure finance hurdles to ensure that the portfolio of investments selected will generate the mix of capabilities needed to grow the business, and capture new opportunities as the competitive space continues to change.

CHAPTER 8

Enterprise Risk Management

MANAGING RISK IN A VOLATILE INDUSTRY ENVIRONMENT

E. Follin Smith, Executive Vice President, CFO and Chief Administrative Officer
Constellation Energy

International companies are operating in a globally complex, highly competitive environment. The world in which they do business is fraught with risk, tension and unanticipated events that frequently create discontinuity and disrupt business plans. More than any other, the energy industry is exposed to a volatile and high-risk environment. Commodity prices are subject to rapid changes and energy companies are arguably in one of the industry sectors most directly exposed to geopolitical events and rapid regulatory changes. In the face of all these challenges, Constellation Energy was named "Most Admired Energy Company in America" by Fortune magazine after jumping from 352 to 203 on Fortune's annual rating of America's 500 leading companies – the greatest advance of any company on the 2004 list.

Constellation Energy was chosen for the feature interview of this chapter not only because of its outstanding economic performance (see Figures 8.1 & 8.2) but also because of the distinctive features of its business model and its mastery of enterprise risk management. We asked Follin Smith, the company's Executive Vice President, CFO and Chief Administrative Officer, to comment on risk management as a success factor in the deregulated energy markets.

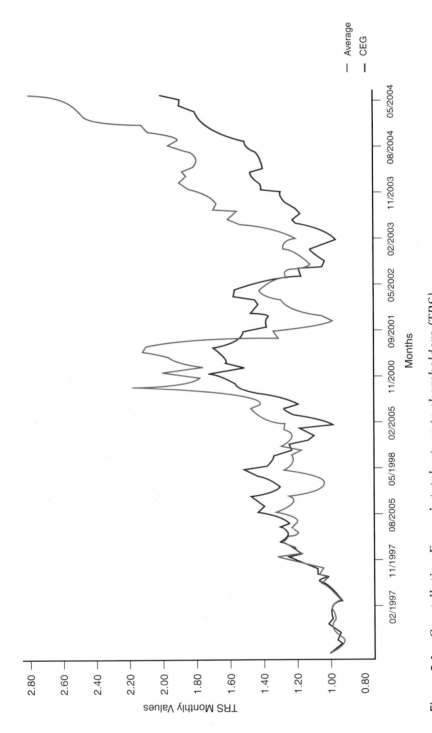

Figure 8.1 *Constellation Energy's total return to shareholders (TRS).*
Source: Accenture analysis

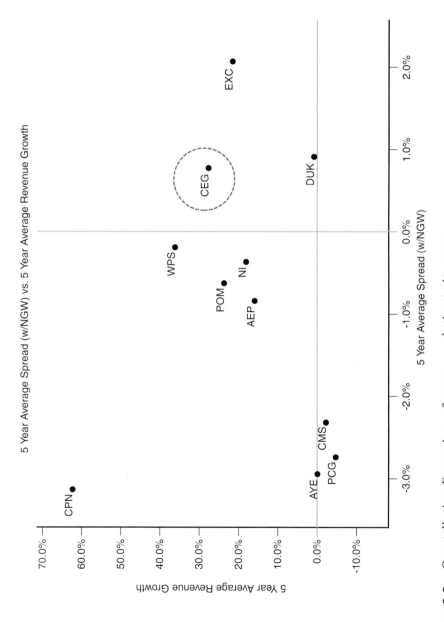

5 Year Average Spread (w/NGW) vs. 5 Year Average Revenue Growth

Figure 8.2 *Constellation Energy's performance relative to its peers.*
Source: Accenture analysis

"The reason deregulated energy failed is analogous to what happened in the savings and loan (S&L) industry. You had people operating in it who were quasi-government skilled, because that is what a regulated utility is like. When the shackles were taken off and they began participating in competitive businesses, they failed because they did not have the basic skill sets to manage them. You can run through a litany of the skills they lacked which are needed to run a business in a competitive field: how to evaluate capital, how to hedge away risk in capital, knowing how to communicate results and cash flows to investors, on and on. Also, the ratings agencies that focused on this industry had focused only on regulated utilities. They didn't even understand the concept that moving into commercial businesses was riskier and that this risk meant lower leverage. Instead, the ratings agencies let these companies with unskilled managements pile on leverage – not only on-balance sheet leverage, but also phenomenal off-balance sheet leverage.

"Everyone was looking at the energy industry as if it was going to grow to the sky. They were saying, 'Let's put power plants everywhere and make these plants produce this undifferentiated commodity and sell it out into the grid.' It was this trading market 'yahoo' attitude: 'Let's go build these home-grown trading operations in Texas.' The result: huge amounts of risk that company managements didn't understand they were taking on.

"We said, 'There's this huge class of customer needs that's been created by virtue of deregulation.' In 22 states and provinces, utilities currently don't have the ability to generate all the power they need. Utilities in those places operate like a distributor who pumps the commodity into your house over their wires and infrastructure, but doesn't have the wherewithal to make the electricity. They've got to procure it somewhere. There's a big procurement process that's wildly complicated and is all about managing lots of risk. What the utility wants to buy is fundamentally different from what a power generation plant generates. Someone has to step in and manage this complicated procurement risk management process for utilities in these 22 states and provinces.

"Commercial and industrial customers have the ability to shop away from their local utility. But it's a very complicated commodity to procure, and it's very unfriendly to a company. I was in charge of hedging GM's commodities for a period of time. Hedging electricity, compared with copper or aluminum, is so much more complicated, because it's a commodity whose price fluctuates from day to day, hour *to hour. You can't just stockpile some to use when you need it. You've got to be a very capable forecaster of what you'll consume, when you'll consume it, and be able to hedge away the risk if you're wrong."*

The failure of Enron had a seismic impact on the energy industry. Not only did it shake investor confidence, but it gave rise to the Sarbanes-Oxley Act (SOX), which reached far beyond the industry. Follin Smith comments on the impact of Enron's collapse at Constellation: "It was very clear that the world was thinking that deregulated energy was going to implode. We had to decide very quickly what we were going to do and how we were going to get there. We had to recapitalize the company. The industry in general had been financed like a deck of cards. It had very short-term financing, inadequate liquidity, and was over-leveraged. We had to recapitalize very quickly. Not only did we have to decide what we were going to go after from a business perspective, we also had to tell the story to the investment community with enough granularity and detail about the path forward to persuade that community to believe us and give us an opportunity to run the company.

"In January of 2002, Mayo Shattuck had been Constellation's CEO for just 90 days. We went to the investment community with a presentation that had projections on where we were going to take the business, how we were going to make money, and what we were going to do – all in more detail than I've ever seen in any investor presentation. It was the complete 'open kimono.' Given the climate around Enron, I think this was the only way we could have convinced the investment community to say, 'OK, we'll give these guys a chance to run this company.' All January, every night at 10, I'd sit in my office and listen to a replay of another big deregulated energy company's calls to Wall Street. They were just getting slaughtered. People were furious. When we finished making our pitch, we opened it up for a Q&A session. Because we had spoken in such great detail, I'll never forget when it dawned on me after five minutes or so, 'They're not hostile. They're curious.'

"We adopted a full-disclosure policy before SOX because this was the way to show investors what we were doing. Prior to this, business accounting had been viewed as a dark art that led only to evil. This was the view at the time that Enron fell apart. Another thing we did, very early on, may seem awfully arcane. The industry had shown ever-upward spiralling profits because Enron had convinced the accounting standards board to treat long-term energy contracts as if they were bonds. They were marking to market profits on a 10-year contract, when there weren't even* *liquid marks to mark yourselves against. This was not the treasury market. It's like they were marking themselves against sunspots on Venus out past the first year – showing triple digit million profits on single deals. I remember, after being at Constellation a month, I understood what we were doing – it complied with all the standards, but I thought our earnings needed to look more like our cash flow. Ultimately, we prevailed and the Accounting Standards have evolved to reflect the economic realities. Our earnings now look more like cash flow.*

"Take the example of Johnson Controls. If they enter into a long-term seat contract with GM, over 5 years they're going to sell them all their seat assemblies. They don't know how much profit they're going to make. They have an agreed-upon purchase price, but they don't know what's going to happen to American automotive sales. There is such a huge range of variables around their profitability that there's no way they should recognize profit other than as they go and sell seats. It's that way with a long-term energy supply contract. If we're selling power to a utility in Massachusetts, we don't know if their customers will be taken away by competitive suppliers like NewEnergy, or what will happen if there's a switch to gas from electricity. It's a long-term supply contract, and we were taking all the profit on day one.

"So that was another thing that helped us get back to a good performance measurement. Getting back to cash flow and accounting – and looking more evenly at how much earnings we are generating relative to our capitalization and how much leverage we can have in a particular business – all this was being obfuscated by the mark-to-market accounting that had been going on in the industry. We moved to accrual before the FASB changed the rules. We were on the Emerging Issues Task Force (EITF) that changed the rules for the industry back to accrual accounting.

"The crisis we faced was that the investment community did not want to give deregulated energy a chance. How did the company's values help resolve that crisis? Through full disclosure and by confronting the realities of the market and the business. It was very important to quickly say, 'Guess what, mark-to-market accounting, spiraling earnings – that's not a strong foundation. Here are certain plants without a strong foundation, their businesses are not real, and we need to get out of them.' Confronting the realities of the situation in a very frank way was the path we chose. Full disclosure to investors was our strategy. We were willing to take a step back to be able to march forward. These were all good cultural underpinnings for building our business."

THE CHANGING DEFINITION OF ENTERPRISE RISK MANAGEMENT

Risk management has a very broad context. It encompasses everything from using financial instruments to managing specific financial exposures, to effectively responding to rapid changes in the business environment, to reacting to natural disasters and political instability.

Later chapters in this book will look at Latin America, Asia, China, and Eastern Europe including Russia – and explore the different forms that risk in these regions can take. In Latin America, for example, CFOs must regularly deal with major economic and political instability, currency crises, and chronic indebtedness. Asia and China present a different set of challenges associated with hypergrowth. In Russia, companies must cope with the constant risk of unexpected government intervention, as demonstrated by the renationalization of Yukos Oil.

Along with the macro-economic factors at work in developing regions around the world, companies must contend with the standard challenges that threaten business: new competitors that constantly change the rules of the game (e.g., Dell's direct business model); technology advances that can offer competitive advantage, but also disrupt (e.g., radio frequency identification (RFID), web service and wireless technologies); and globalization (e.g., Air China's intent to expand from its domestic market and become a true international player across Asia).

These are just a few of the realities that continue to drive increasing business complexity. They require business executives to be more agile, intuitive and rigorous in their approach to the issues raised in this chapter. Beyond these typical business challenges, publicly traded companies face a wave of new regulations in the form of SOX, International Accounting Standards, International Finance Reporting Standards, and Basel II. In this environment, stakeholders mandate that executive management not only excel in business, but also provide surety that they will actively and transparently manage the risk of generating promised results. CFOs worry about sustaining corporate performance and returns to shareholders on the one hand while also bearing the burden of stewardship imposed by new compliance requirements. Regardless of whether finance executives sit in Seattle, Beijing, Kuala Lumpur, Bangalore, Prague, London or New York, they all live and work in a wired, interconnected world where the pace of change is unprecedented and continues to accelerate.

As regulatory constraints become increasingly stringent, they place large and growing demands on an organization's resources (e.g., people, finances and capital), while consuming management bandwidth and capacity. Our research reveals fundamental shifts in the CFO's response, from simply tinkering with the role of the audit committee to implementing new organization models that embrace what Nick Rose, CFO of Diageo, calls "business risk assurance." This involves providing a holistic response to regulatory requirements together through extended capabilities that include new processes, systems, tools and an enterprise-wide governance model. This governance model is anchored independently at the board level on the one hand, yet drills down through levels of management to formally institutionalize notions of controllership. Virtually all the CFOs interviewed discussed their new emphasis on managing risk and validated the view that we have truly moved into the era of enterprise risk management (ERM).

Lauralee Martin, Chief Operating Officer and Chief Financial Officer of Jones Lang LaSalle, was asked to comment on the hypothesis that regulatory change and the associated requirements for compliance have pushed organizations to embrace broader approaches to risk management. Her response: "It's already happened. We've implemented a Global Operating Committee that I chair. It includes members from the broader business community globally, such as our regional COOs, legal, internal audit and risk. This committee meets monthly, reviews identified risks, and determines whether the risk is isolated or whether we need to specifically address it in a broader way."

A RISK MANAGEMENT FRAMEWORK

Enterprise risk management is a strategic, tactical and operational instrument. It assists organizations in enhancing and protecting shareholder value while fulfilling regulatory obligations and leading the business. Risk management as a function has existed for many years. However, significant variations exist among industries in both their definition and management of risk. Consequently, any comprehensive discussion of enterprise risk management must establish a common framework for defining the different risks to which a business is exposed.

Risk is the degree of probability of a loss or peril. That is to say, risk is the relative likelihood of an unfavorable outcome due to an event or a series of events that may result in negative earnings, an adverse impact on the future prospects or growth potential of an organization, or, in the worst case, corporate insolvency. From a business perspective, risk is most often viewed in the context of financial instruments. However, as discussed earlier, in today's business environment, risk has a much broader scope and impact.

The financial services industry (i.e., banking, insurance, capital markets) is unique with respect to risk management. It proactively accepts and manages risks to generate shareholder returns. Efficient management of risk can be a distinct competitive advantage for banking and insurance enterprises. For a banking organization, enterprise risk management is a core component of business strategy rather than a mere enabler. Consequently, some companies may have a comparative advantage in bearing certain financial market risks – an advantage that is derived from the information acquired through normal business activities.

Types of risk

Risks can be primarily classified as financial and non-financial. Financial risks are defined as events that have a potential for adverse impacts on earnings or financial performance, i.e., an actual loss. Financial risks (apart from liquidity risk) are measurable and exhibit a direct relationship between the loss event and the actual loss. Key categories of financial risks are these.

1 *Credit risk*: the possibility of loss due to default by a counterparty or a customer, or an increase in potential loss or deterioration in the credit quality of a counterparty or customer (risk migration).

2 *Market risk*: the possibility of loss due to adverse movement in market prices, e.g., foreign exchange, interest rates and commodity prices.

3 *Liquidity risk*: the possibility of failure to meet cash commitments, particularly those of a short-term nature.

Non-financial risks are more difficult to quantify but have a significant impact on an enterprise's business health and its growth. Though not comprehensive, the following represents key risks recognized by various organizations across a broad range of industries.

1 *Operational risk* is defined as the exposure to loss from inadequate or failed internal processes, people, and systems. It is the risk of direct or indirect loss or damaged reputation due to deficiencies or errors in a company's internal operations, which may be attributable to employees, the organization, control routines, processes or technology. Operational risk is a focus for most organizations, due to large

losses such as those experienced by Barings Bank and to the many forms that operational failure can take. In addition, The Basel Committee on Banking Supervision has added operational risk as a new risk category for which banks need to maintain capital.

2 *Business risk* is a prime indicator of business volatility and is defined as the risk of adverse outcomes due to competitive pressures and/or poor decisions concerning strategy, products, markets and structures. Business risk is determined not only by type of business activity but by factors within each business sector, including growth rate, competition, market share, and the experience and reputation of senior management. An example of the implications of business risk is General Motors' decision not to go into production of the hybrid car following government-sponsored R&D support. Toyota, Honda and Ford all decided to pursue hybrid car development and are now the market leaders, having established a six-year competitive lead.

3 *Compliance risk* arises when a failure to meet certain compliance and regulatory requirements subjects an organization to financial penalties or reputation damage – or both. Understandably, this risk has received increased attention due to mounting regulatory requirements. The spate of settlements between Wall Street investment banks and Eliot Spitzer, the attorney general of New York, is an example of the implications of compliance risk. Other examples are the damage suffered by Nortel due to restatements and the damage suffered by Shell due to the under-reporting of its oil reserves.

4 *Pension risk* is a specific form of liquidity risk that arises if the projected cash outflows (i.e., liabilities) exceed the projected cash inflows (i.e., assets) of a defined benefit or defined contribution pension scheme, and the organization is responsible for funding the gap. Pension deficits can be material and damage the competitiveness of an organization, as demonstrated in the airline and automobile sectors. The collapse of the Maxwell publishing empire was partly attributable to a pension plan "black hole."

5 *Legal risk* arises when an organization becomes subject to financial loss or reputation damage as a result of legal actions brought against the company, whether warranted or not. A class action lawsuit against a tobacco company is an example.

Risk can be classified and evaluated based on the time horizon involved, i.e., long-term or strategic risks and short-term or tactical risks. The impact of strategic risks extends beyond the immediate financial year. Strategic risks arise as a result of decisions in a range of areas, including management reorganization, mergers and acquisitions, research and development, transformation projects, and growth strategy. Management of strategic risk is a responsibility of a company's executive management committee and board of directors. Dell's decision to let its competitors fund the development of the personal digital assistant (PDA) market before it entered the market is an example of a strategic risk. Tactical risks arise from the day-to-day operations of a business and are generally short term, high in frequency, and usually, but not always, low in impact.

Some risks are not directly measurable because a direct relationship between the risk event and actual loss or impact on shareholder value is often difficult to establish. Some of the most serious losses are measured by a proxy variable – enterprise value. A share price can collapse when there is a profit or earnings warning. This was the case with Morrison's supermarkets in the UK, which issued five successive warnings in the 12 months following their take-over of Safeway.

While some risks can be insured against, effective management of business risk is a core function of all organizations. Business risk cannot be managed through outsourcing or insurance. Understanding business risk is critical for effective portfolio optimization and capital allocation: returns from all business units should be commensurate with risk profiles. As an example, working capital allocated to a unit with stable sales should be subject to a hurdle rate that is lower than the hurdle rate of a unit with relatively volatile sales.

THE COMPONENTS OF GOOD RISK MANAGEMENT

Good risk management is a fundamental requirement for a high-performance business. There are four main pillars for good risk management practice.

1 Identification of material risks

2 Clear definition of risk appetite

3 Robust control processes and mitigation techniques

4 Well-structured governance at multiple levels in the organization

Identification of material risks

All material risks should be identified to determine the risk profile of the business unit, and a risk-adjusted return framework should be used to make strategic decisions, such as portfolio optimization and capital allocation. As described above, these risks are financial as well as non-financial. Organizations also need to assess the potential impact and probability of each risk type so they can focus on the ones most likely to have major impact.

Companies often ignore material risks, particularly when risk management is not a core function of the business. Risks that are material for certain organizations may not be material to others. Successful organizations do not rely on a predefined set of standards in defining material risk, but use tailored risk evaluation techniques to assess their own circumstances. For example, a company under government scrutiny because of certain behavior or losses will have a risk of reputation loss that is higher than its peers in the same industry or sector.

The CFO of a global metals producer provides some insight on the economic impact and importance of risk assessment: "I can't think of too many companies that are as exposed to financial risk as ours. What makes us unique is that not only are we very exposed, but we're in a business where, in fact, you can mitigate that exposure through robust risk management. In our case, you've got the metals exposure, you've got energy exposure in terms of electricity, raw materials, oil, gas, etc. Then you have currencies.

"Until five or six years ago, insurance companies used to come visit us and end up correlating all these different risks into a single number, which we then bought a policy for. I think that was nonsense. You'll never get there. So for me, enterprise risk is about financial risk. Then you've got event risk and business risk. In the context of the economic cycle, you've got the risk of timing: when you invest capital, which has a huge, huge impact – I mean it's monstrous. The cash payback period is influenced so dramatically. If you can't fix that, if you can't get it right, then you are sunk ..."

CASE STUDY
Exel PLC

We asked Stephen Ferraby, Chief Financial Officer Asia Pacific, for Exel PLC, a global logistics company, to comment on how he viewed the risk of doing business in Asia.

He responded: *"There are individual emerging markets that are riskier than others. We have been operating in Pakistan for two or three years. It is risky because it is hard to get good quality, experienced people to manage the business. Growth in China brings a whole set of potential concerns that are different from those in more mature markets. Beyond this, I would say that it is no riskier operating in Singapore or Hong Kong than it is operating in the US or the UK. It is broadly comparable.*

"We have a challenge operating in a lot of countries that are fairly low cost and low margin. Indonesia is a classic example. If we work for a consumer goods company in Indonesia, our turnover and our margin, which tends to be pegged to the turnover, will be about a fifth of the European one for the equivalent size. However, that consumer goods company is going to expect us to take on the same sort of liabilities as we have in Europe and the US. One of the more difficult messages to get across to our customers is that their corporate risk management approach is pushing down a standard set of contract terms. That is quite a tough debate, because risk management is, at the moment, in a privileged position. A lot of 'corporates' have powerful risk management teams, but they do not have to deal with their suppliers or have responsibility for execution and the operational consequence.

"We then have conversations with our customers and operators that they have to relay back to their risk departments and back to me again. That can be quite a challenge. My colleagues in Europe go to UK retailers and have a very sophisticated conversation about how you price risk into a contract. There are significant execution challenges in Asia. One of the hardest, particularly for US companies, is trying to impose US contract terms on an Asian market environment."

We asked Stephen if that implied that Asian companies are trying to transfer their risk to Exel, a practice that is then embedded in a series of fairly aggressive terms and conditions of business.

He replied, *"Yes, and that pressure gets stronger every year. A lot has been written about the margin pressures in this industry, but relatively little about the risk transfer. There was a period of time when it was undercover; now it is out in the open. It is still a difficult area, both with our customers and with our people. For instance, when you are bidding for a piece of domestic trucking business in China, big terms will come out; they will want fifty thousand dollars per truck of liability, but they want Chinese trucker prices. Yet they do not want to go to the Chinese trucker because he is not going to sign. He will sign for the terms, but he is never going to pay the fifty thousand dollars if something happens. They are trying to squeeze our commercial guys into a corner. I have certainly come across instances of outsourcing in emerging markets, where the whole strategy is about risk management. It is about getting an international player on board who is effectively going to take on your risk for you, and the actual transaction is almost incidental."*

Clear definition of risk appetite

Organizations need to take and manage a calculated amount of risk in their business. Offloading or mitigation of all risks, i.e., finding a risk-free option, is not plausible since risk is an inherent component of any business. Some extreme risk events may be managed more cost efficiently within the business. Further, risk taking may be required to optimize profitability and the bottom line of the business performance. Therefore, the senior management of any business defines the risk appetite and determines tolerance levels for the business as a whole and its different components.

A risk appetite statement articulates the nature and level of risk that a business is willing to take to achieve its core strategic objectives as communicated to all its stakeholders. Through established policies and procedures, risk appetite should be embedded in business planning, capital allocation, performance measurement and management reporting. Quantifiable risks, such as credit and market risk, are often translated into specific risk limits or mandates for monitoring and control. The chief risk officer is responsible for framing the risk appetite statement on behalf of the CEO. The statement is then submitted to the board of directors for approval. Risk appetite and risk measurement should be reviewed periodically to ensure their relevance and alignment with organization objectives. Although it can be perceived as a hindrance to growth, a defined risk appetite is, in fact, a prerequisite for managed growth.

Nick Rose, CFO of Diageo, comments on the requirement for risk to be well understood at all levels of the company: "When we look at any change proposal, potential acquisition or proposed advertising or promotional expenditure, you see a thorough evaluation of the economic profit flows, the risk adjusted returns, and the cash flow we expect to see. This runs through the company at all levels, and our compensation system has the performance-related bonus payments linked to this as well."

CASE STUDY
Singapore Airlines

We interviewed Goh Choon Phong, SVP Finance of Singapore Airlines, and asked him how a company's ability to respond to events impacts the approach to risk management.

"The airline business is very sensitive to economic sentiment and to external events, be it 9/11, natural disasters or relations between governments. I think all of these can have an impact on our business. For instance, 9/11 affected confidence in air travel, and that fear may linger as new cases of terrorism occur. This also adds to our costs, because we have to put in place security measures to manage the risk and to instill confidence among travelers. If you look at the past five years, the airline industry has experienced so many external shocks, that we have now taken such possibilities into consideration in our planning process. We cannot assume that everything is going to be plain sailing. It requires a nimble mentality. The challenge for any successful company is to react quickly to changes."

We asked the SVP Finance how his company views risk appetite in the context of continued large capital investment, such as fleet expansion or the decision to purchase the new Airbus A380 aircraft. He responded: "The airline business has a long planning horizon. If you want to significantly increase capacity in the next 12 months, you can't do it just like that. You have to go through a comprehensive planning process, including lead time required for pilot training and putting in place necessary technical support, in addition to actually acquiring the aircraft. This increases the risk of error, because you cannot predict an event such as 9/11, the Bali bombing or a tsunami. Again, you have to be nimble in responding to such events, shocks or major changes. But that does not diminish the importance of forward planning. You still need to have a rolling plan to make projections of what you believe will be the growth profile for the company. We believe in achieving sustainable growth, and having a fleet renewal plan to capitalize on new aircraft technologies. This is an ongoing process.

"We have a framework to guide in our analysis; to consider multiple scenarios in our planning and evaluation processes. There are many challenges facing airlines, including that of high and volatile fuel prices. In the short term, you can defray some of the price hike through fuel surcharges and manage some of the volatility through fuel hedging. But fuel prices are now at a historical high level. How do we manage that? In making those projections, you have to make assumptions. Do you assume prices will remain at this level, or do you assume that they will return to lower levels? Whichever assumption you use, unexpected external events could throw the assumption completely off. Hence, while it's important to plan ahead, it's equally important to be nimble in making adjustments to respond to changes."

It is commonly accepted that the main objective of a business is to maximize its shareholders' wealth. Concurrently, the overall return on investment must be commensurate with the risk profile of the business. Different organizations have different levels of risk, and it is this that determines the required returns on investments and the variability of the returns shareholders will demand as the cost of capital. As a result, the role of risk management in business strategy should be articulated in the risk appetite definition. This is part of the charter of enterprise risk management. The linkage of risk management to shareholder value can be measured reactively as projects are evaluated.

Alternatively, finance can take a proactive approach as described here by Goh Choon Phong: "To some extent, even in investment decisions, finance works closely with the rest of the company. For example, when the IT department is reviewing a new initiative, such as an outsourcing model, we work closely with them. But that process can be improved to move from just cost control to the planning and decision-making process. At the moment, the link with other divisions in the company is made principally by getting them to look at delivering investment returns in excess of the WACC (Weighted Average Cost of Capital). It is very clear to all divisions what our WACC is and that in deciding whether to invest in something or to engage in a certain contract, they will have to meet our requirements for risk adjusted returns. In that respect, we work closely with the divisions in making financial assessments. Yet, it is not enough, because it is at a stage of the decision-making process that is already quite advanced. I am trying to move up the value chain. Finance should be involved from the beginning as a business partner to the divisions, rather than only in assessing the financial returns of initiatives."

Robust control processes and mitigation techniques
Effective risk management practices require a process control environ-

ment and risk mitigation techniques that work within the boundaries of the risk appetite defined by senior management. It must be remembered that a foreign exchange market trader's perception of currency volatility differs from that of a commercial user of the market. The trader has an interest in high volumes and big fluctuations in exchange rates; these increase the opportunity for making profits. For the commercial user, volatility only increases business risk, since the actual conversion in the foreign exchange markets from one currency to another has a direct effect on cash. To reduce this risk exposure, the commercial user undertakes hedging activities, i.e., transactions designed to produce a profit that correlates reasonably with a potential loss on the exposure that arises naturally within the business.

A survey of chief financial officers in the US reports that when companies involved in the foreign exchange markets were asked if they hedge exchange risk, 22% of these companies answered "yes." According to the survey, public companies are more likely to hedge foreign currency risk (39%) than are private companies (16%)[1]. Companies within the European Union (EU) act differently from companies in the US. In a similar survey, the majority of EU organizations responding hedged their foreign exchange exposure (transaction and translation exposure), as well as their interest rate risk. In general, the companies described their policy and hedge strategy as influenced by the materiality of the exposure, management's level of aversion to risk (risk appetite), the degree of centralization, and their competitive situation.

While currency and interest rate fluctuations are expected, risk is defined by the probability of unexpected losses occurring due to rare events, characterized as high-value and low-frequency events. One of the main challenges in risk management is the quantification of the frequency and impact of such events. The inherent lack of credible historical data makes any kind of statistical analysis extremely difficult. As a result, conclusions are questionable. Capital is maintained as a cushion to protect the organization from the financial impact of unexpected loss events. However, it should be noted that capital does not reduce the likelihood or impact of such an event, but merely ensures solvency of a business if such an event occurs. Furthermore, the amount of capital required as a cushion depends on the target credit rating of the organization. An AAA rating requires a higher capital cushion than a BBB rating. Since capital is an expensive resource and accurate measurement of required capital is difficult, a focus on risk management as opposed to measurement is considered optimal. In some industries, the critical issue of inadequate data is being addressed through industry consortiums that allow companies to contribute loss/incident data to be used for risk modeling.

REGULATORY REQUIREMENTS AND COMPLIANCE

In the last few years, organizations in all industries have seen dramatic changes in the regulatory and compliance environment globally. Risk management is the area that is most affected and targeted by the new requirements and changes to the current rules.

Sarbanes-Oxley

The Sarbanes-Oxley Act (SOX) was accelerated into law in the aftermath of the Enron collapse. It mandates an annual assessment of internal controls over financial reporting and certification by the CEO and CFO that financial statements and accounting practices are accurate. These requirements are proving to be onerous. In simple terms, the rules demand more explicit management of controls and more involvement from senior management. Similar rules are being enacted in Canada and in the EU – and are due for implementation by 2006. These directives will require all listed companies to implement a complex package similar to SOX. Here again, the documentation of risks and controls will require the extensive involvement of senior management in risk management activities.

Noncompliance with these requirements can have a direct financial impact, creating significant risk to corporate reputation, and negatively affecting the future value of an organization. An initial review of the first 120 companies to have failed the Section 404 audit on their 10-K filing shows that they may experience negative impact on share price. Indexing of the companies' average share price versus the Dow Jones Industrial Average (DJIA) for the year preceding the filing date and the initial weeks following the date showed that the group of stocks went from generally outperforming to generally underperforming the DJIA. Furthermore, in the four weeks following the filings in mid-March 2005, the average share price for the group of companies that failed was off 7.5% while the DJIA was down 4%.

Certainly this is very preliminary data, and the population is too small to draw broad conclusions, but the implications cannot be discounted. Failure to meet compliance requirements will have an adverse impact on share price and a company's ability to raise capital. The most significant impact will likely be felt in the future. Companies that fail a second time can be expected to be significantly penalized by the market. Analogies can be drawn with companies that issue earning warnings. The first offence carries a 10% to 15% impact on share price, but a second offence can have a devastating 40+% impact from which it can take years to recover.

Accounting for financial instruments

Changes in accounting standards continue to increase companies' compliance risk exposure as they deal with increased complexity within US Generally Accepted Accounting Principles (GAAP), or with the adoption of International Accounting Standards (IAS) in the place of traditional local GAAP. The regulatory requirements continue to become increasingly complex, as demonstrated in Federal Accounting Standard 133 (FAS 133), Accounting for Financial Instruments; International Accounting Standard 39 (IAS 39) Financial Instruments: Recognition and Measurement; and FASB Interpretation Number 46 (FIN 46), Accounting for Variable Interest Entities. These pronouncements introduce the notions of current value accounts through such measures as mark-to-market adjustments and hedge accounting restrictions. They also increase the level of disclosure while increasing the level of complexity and compliance risk.

IAS 39 and FAS 133 impact the recording of financial instruments on the balance sheet of an organization. Going forward, financial instruments will need to be recorded at their fair value unless a company elects to use, and qualifies for, the application of hedge accounting, where the exposure will need to be linked to the underlying transaction. Where the financial instruments do not qualify for hedge accounting treatment, the mark-to-market adjustments create major volatility in the profit and loss (P&L) accounts; for example, a UK bank predicted that the impact of this volatility on their retail book will exceed £250m every year.

In reaction to the requirements of IAS 39 and FAS 133, financial management could limit itself to the recording and reporting of assets and liabilities using the new rules. However, risk management can be proactive. It can decide on the appropriate hedging strategy to reduce volatility, apply best practice to maintain good documentation, and enhance capabilities to link different financial instruments and the underlying hedge to qualify for hedge accounting treatment.

Basel II

The new proposals for risk management and capital adequacy in the banking industry are based on three complementary pillars: 1) minimum capital requirements, 2) the supervisory review process, and 3) the enhancement of market discipline through detailed public disclosure. The three pillars work together to encourage banks to invest in effective risk monitoring and management practices. They also set up a framework to calculate capital charges for risk.

For most banks, operational risk (i.e., internal or external fraud cases) is the least developed risk area. Basel II, which defines operational risk as "loss resulting from inadequate or failed internal processes, people and systems or from external events," requires banks to invest in sound operational risk management and introduces a capital charge to cover unexpected operational losses. The latest proposed estimate for an average bank to cushion itself against unexpected operational losses is 12% of the current minimum regulatory capital, reducible to 9% if a bank can demonstrate to the regulator that it has advanced management and measurement structures in place.

Credit risk lies at the heart of a banking business. Most transactions in financial services involve the risk that the obligor will default on its financial obligations when due. Recent history has shown that this can be the case for governments, banks, corporate and retail customers alike. Though credit risk was a major focus of Basel I, minimum capital requirements were linked only in broad terms to the obligor's credit quality. In Basel II, the required capital levels are much more sensitive to credit quality, captured in the internal/external credit rating models.

Banks that can deliver these new rigorous and sophisticated internal risk management capabilities first, will reap the benefits. The implementation of the standards requires senior executives to spur action in all key areas (e.g., risk methodology, governance framework, data history and risk mitigation). Ensuring the coordination of all relevant activities across all portfolios and businesses will be a major challenge for management throughout the entire implementation effort.

According to an academic study, the net private cost of SOX (cost minus benefits as perceived by the stock market as the new regulations are enacted) amounts to $1.4 trillion. This is based on an econometric estimate of "the loss in total market value around the most significant legislative events"[2]. A working group estimates that "for multi-billion dollar companies, the cost may run at approximately 0.05% of revenue, but for small companies with revenues below $20 million, the costs can rapidly approach 3% of revenue"[3]. These estimates represent the costs of sustaining compliance on an ongoing annual basis. First-year compliance costs can run significantly higher. On the other hand, a recent survey of the cost of implementing Basel II projected that banks will spend between $100-$400m each (depending on the size and complexity of the bank operations).

A recent study[4] has identified 25 separate regulatory initiatives that will continue to impact the financial services industry over the next three years, such as Basel II, International Financial Reporting Standards (IFRS), Anti-Money Laundering, Sarbanes-Oxley and the Markets in Financial Instruments Directive (MiFID). Key objectives driving these initiatives include proactive risk management, enhanced corporate governance, harmonization of global accounting practices, prevention of terrorism and money laundering, and promoting transparency. Organizations are addressing these compliance requirements by forming project teams, sponsored by senior management.

Scope and impact

The scope and impact of each of these rules is profound in any organization. The rules have changed the way companies are organized and do business, and increased the need for senior management to be involved in risk management activities. The new regulations are also pushing for strong alignment and integration of the risk and finance functions. Traditionally, the two functions have run in parallel in most organizations (banks in particular). Now IAS, Basel and SOX are all pushing toward integration of some processes and the reliance on a single instance of data, i.e., "one-version of the truth."

Regulatory requirements are also having a significant impact on the strategic direction and planning of organizations. For example, certain companies have considered delisting from the US market as a result of issues associated with implementing SOX. In other cases, new regulations have been a barrier to entering new overseas markets.

In the past, most companies considered a 100% hedge of their foreign exchange, interest rate, and commodity price risks as the optimal hedging strategy. Based on emerging regulatory requirements, this type of strategy has been reassessed. Organizations are being forced to evaluate risk and hedging strategies based on the rigid hedging criteria in IAS 39 or FAS 133. The probability of future cash flows has to be documented, the relationship between risk exposure and hedging instrument has to be identified, and hedge effectiveness has to be measured during the hedging period. These requirements steer for selective hedging and strive for a clear and documented definition of the organization's degree of aversion to risk (i.e., its risk appetite). Since hedge accounting is applicable only when the requirements of documented management intention are met, an established and approved policy is essential. Moreover, as a good corporate governance practice, selective hedging activities and internalizing risk management strategies should be disclosed to relevant stakeholders. These issues are covered by the requirements of IAS 32, Financial Instruments; Disclosures and Presentation; and IAS 21, Effects of Changes in Foreign Exchange Rates.

Compliance projects are not subject to stringent return on investment (ROI) assessment, usually a core aspect of the project planning process. The cost of compliance is now at excessive levels and is forcing management to rethink its attitude toward compliance projects. However, returns can be derived from compliance investments by incorporating them within the broader enterprise risk management framework. ERM can assist in identifying overlaps and synergies across regulatory initiatives.

The senior executive team is under increasing pressure to meet regulatory and compliance requirements. Having gone through a number of major acquisitions, the CFO of a global metals producer comments on the challenge of reaping value from compliance initiatives: "In our case, the whole compliance issue is a lot more acute. We decided to change our accounting practice to US GAAP – not because the US GAAP is any better – but because US investors don't trust anything else. It's as simple as that. We've converted everybody to US GAAP – and then you had SOX! We opted not, like many foreign registrants, to wait a year. We said, 'No, we're going to behave like an American company and we're going to meet the deadline as of the end of 2004.' So on the one hand, as CFO I can sleep better with SOX – but maybe only two minutes longer, not much more, because 190 sites and 600 to 700 reporting entities is a lot to deal with.

"In recent years we've experienced a huge increase in complexity – the value of our assets has increased and debt has risen. But the biggest change was the increase in the number of reporting units from 100 to 700, and of course, that's why SOX compliance is so complex. All these things happened at once."

Regulatory changes – impact on enhancement of ERM

Regulatory changes imposed by the Sarbanes-Oxley Act for companies registered in the United States, and similar legislation such as the Ontario Securities Act for public companies registered in Canada, will push organizations to enhance their enterprise risk management frameworks. In particular, companies are being forced to make their compliance risk processes part of their ongoing operations rather than dealing with compliance and disclosure issues on a periodic or ad hoc basis.

As a result of increased exposure and complexity, companies have made substantial investments in their compliance risk initiatives. The current estimate of the cost for annual certification under Section 404 of the Sarbanes-Oxley Act is up to $1 million per $1 billion of revenue.[5] The first-year certification costs are substantially higher as companies deal with first-time documentation and assessment. Given this level of investment, firms are starting to ask two questions:

1 How can we make our compliance processes more effective and efficient?

2 How can we maximize the return on our investment in compliance processes and systems?

A critical first step to addressing each of these questions is to evaluate compliance risk in the context of an enterprise risk framework. This is an undertaking that many companies were historically reluctant to do, due to a lack of perceived need or objections to the total cost. Outside of financial services or commodity-driven businesses such as energy and utilities, risk management has traditionally received very little attention. Changes in the marketplace, however, have brought risk management to the fore. The cost of these programs has become a secondary consideration as companies look to do all they can to comply with the new requirements and avoid unnecessary surprises for their shareholders.

As companies scramble to respond to new developments and interpret new standards, the lines are beginning to blur between the finance and risk functions. In addition to the new compliance risk exposures, CFOs must assess risk relative to their capital plans, and organizations are being asked to create and capture the information needed to calculate value for reporting. High-performance businesses with strong finance functions and a clear understanding of value management will find it easier to respond to these needs and will be less affected by the developing requirements. In particular, good risk management practices and a strong information architecture will allow an organization to capture and respond to the information needed to address a variety of requirements.

The way forward
For most organizations, risk is a by-product of operations, strategies,

investments, or asset holdings; risk management is not a core competency. If an organization cannot avoid a risk, it should share it with other corporations through hedging, outsourcing or insurance. This argument is based on the logic of core competencies; i.e., the focus should be on activities in which the business has a distinct competitive advantage. If a risk cannot be shared or avoided, then an organization must accept and manage it, assuming the risk is an enabler to the broader corporate strategy. To effectively respond to the events arising from risk and to manage that risk accordingly, organizations must embrace change management as a core competency.

Though the economic capital framework provides an objective approach for assessing risk-adjusted returns, management must use discretion when making risk assessments. Risk management metrics are tools to facilitate management judgment and decision making, not to replace them. Deviations of risk-adjusted returns from absolute returns should be investigated, thoroughly dissected, and communicated to all relevant stakeholders. Analytical effort should focus on understanding risk metrics and drivers in order to ensure effective monitoring and control. The economic capital framework is dependent on assumptions. This should be challenged and tested by the board of directors on an ongoing basis.

In evaluating the return on a company's investment in risk management, a key consideration is the cost of failure. In the case of compliance risk, the ultimate cost of failure is evident in the share price collapse or business failures associated with Enron, WorldCom, and Andersen.

The effect of failing to pass a Sarbanes-Oxley Section 404 audit, however, is still subject to debate. Unlike a traditional financial statement audit, where statements are almost always adjusted to accommodate the auditors, and a qualified or adverse audit opinion is so rare as to be considered theoretical, a Section 404 audit leaves no room for correction of errors. Qualified opinions are far from rare, with more than 7.5% of the first 1500 filers failing their first-year audits. Such a high failure rate makes it difficult for the market to respond. In addition to the market costs, failure has a substantial internal cost, since resources must be devoted to remediate the processes and systems. Furthermore, failure to institute strong compliance processes will result in increased audit fees, in addition to the 15% to 20% premium already being charged by auditors to accommodate the new requirements.

In view of the cost of failure, developing systematic ways of dealing with risk and creating risk management capabilities within the finance function have become the responsibility of the entire finance team.

While leading practices from the financial services industry or commodity-based businesses would indicate that ERM should be an embedded capability, many organizations have not devoted time and resources to planning their response. Consequently, they are creating parallel or ad hoc ERM functions. While this approach addresses the immediate, first-year requirements, it is not likely to be sustainable as a special project and fails to accommodate changes in the business model, processes or systems going forward.

In recent years, the desire to focus on long-term value creation has led to the use of a variety of models for measuring economic value and the effective use of capital. At the same time, businesses have begun to take action to understand how the processes of the business create or destroy value, and how these processes support strategies, goals and objectives. The outcome of these exercises can be quite powerful. As a result of these projects, many companies have robust enterprise performance management frameworks and a wealth of information on their business processes, cost drivers and performance measures.

Unfortunately, in many organizations, despite the investment in comprehensive EPM frameworks, risk seems to be a key requirement that is not included. The response of many businesses to the changing regulatory and reporting standards has been to adapt and work with outdated tools developed for other needs. Companies have been documenting processes and applying audit standards that were developed in the 1970s to assess and report on the effectiveness of their internal control environments. At the same time, the management information needs of the business have been given a lower priority as companies struggle to meet their reporting deadlines.

Ironically, the process models developed to support internal control requirements are similar in many aspects to the process models driving the organization performance scorecards and costing models. In the latter cases, the processes are tied to key measures or cost drivers. In the former case, the process is linked to key financial statement accounts and associated internal controls. If a company truly takes an enterprise-wide view of its key risks, these models can and should be directly integrated into existing performance management processes.

This linkage of the processes to key risks, financial exposures and controls actually allows a company to manage risks in a more comprehensive environment. Furthermore, by building this into a structure that demonstrates the interdependencies among the processes and controls with drill-down and analytical capability, the company can get a better view of its overall control environment. This is not only key to meeting the requirements of Sarbanes-Oxley related to the overall control environment, but it also facilitates the sign-off as to the effectiveness of the controls at any point in time.

To meet the changing needs of the business, risk management functions must be developed at the enterprise level and deployed throughout the business in a manner that is scaleable and flexible. By focusing on the critical processes and data requirements at each level of the organization, risk management can be embedded into routine performance management processes. This can support compliance requirements while also driving business performance. We believe that ERM is not a big-bang project, but rather an iterative process in which a company improvises risk management capabilities through experience. Whatever approach companies embrace, the need for enterprise risk management has never been greater.

THE HACKETT GROUP ON ENTERPRISE RISK MANAGEMENT

With the recent trend toward increased regulatory controls and reporting, it should come as no surprise that compliance management costs have increased for all companies. The intricacies of complying with the Sarbanes-Oxley Act (SOX) have created an enormous burden for all publicly held corporations, compounded by an across-the-board increase in external audit fees.

However, CFOs at world-class organizations have been able to, if not stem the tide, at least slow the growth of this cost area. Peer group companies have seen compliance management costs go up over the past two years from 0.074 as a percentage of revenue to 0.094%. World-class organizations, on the other hand, experienced an increase of just 0.043% to 0.060% – a lower proportional cost today than peer groups managed to achieve two years ago. The difference is the use of best practices at world-class corporations.

Looking ahead, the control and corporate governance issues of SOX are forcing CFOs to face up to one of the most strategic decisions in over a decade. The Hackett Group believes that, depending on their position relative to world-class performance, finance organizations will either choose to remain on course in their goal to be a strategic business partner with a seat at the table, or they will readopt the "corporate cop" role so common in the early 1990s. Finance organizations that choose the governance role could see a two-to-three-year setback in their ability to deliver greater business value. Analysis indicates that, based on decisions in this arena, the existing gap between world-class finance organizations and others will widen even more.

CFO INSIGHTS: LESSONS FROM THE MASTERS

- Compliance initiatives and programs are opportunities to improve enterprise risk management and create high-performance businesses. They are not just a cost to the business.

- Regulatory compliance should be met as part of an overall enterprise risk management framework, and not implemented in small silos without an overall framework.

- Risk management and capital planning need to be linked to optimize shareholders' value and enhance the future value of the organization.

- Risk-adjusted investment is an approach that maximizes the value of the organization. It should also be linked to performance and compensation of management.

REFERENCES

1 Bank of America Corporation, *2005 CFO Outlook: A Survey of Manufacturing Companies Chief Financial Officers*, December 2004. http://www.bofabusinesscapital.com

2 A Price Worth Paying?, *The Economist*, May 21, 2005. http://www.economist.com

3 American Electronics Association, *Sarbanes-Oxley Section 404: The "Section" of Unintended Consequences and its Impact on Small Business*, February 2005.

4 CBI, *UK as a Place to do Business: Financial Services – Promoting a Global Champion*, October 2004.

5 Section 404 Costs Exceed Estimates, *Finance Executives International*, December 2004. http://www.fei.org

CHAPTER 9

Managing the Change Journey to High Performance

PACING CHANGE IN FINANCE TO THE RATE OF BUSINESS CHANGE

Nick Rose, CFO
Diageo

In recent years, Diageo PLC has transformed itself from a global consumer products conglomerate to the world leader in its industry. The company has strong spread performance, driven by improved return on invested capital (ROIC) over the past few years (see Figures 9.1 and 9.2). We feature Diageo because it is a master at managing change and continually recalibrating finance capabilities to maintain competitive rigor. As CFO Nick Rose explained: "The company has experienced a radical overhaul as it exited the food business (Pillsbury) and the fast food business (Burger King). We have transitioned to a highly focused brand-led premium drinks business with a truly global footprint. This presents a new set of challenges for our finance professionals in a highly competitive market. We need to be constantly in tune with the consumer's changing tastes, preferences, and buying behavior in the mature markets of Europe and the US – and the faster growing markets in Asia, especially India

PreTax ROIC

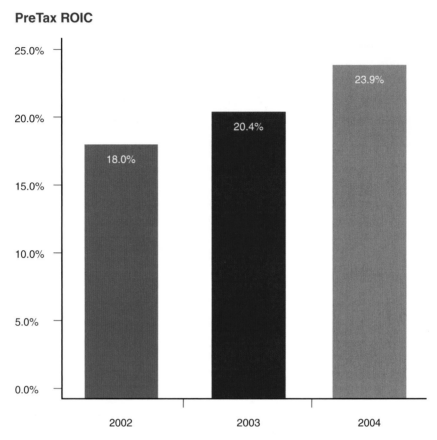

Figure 9.1 *Diageo return on invested capital (ROIC)*
Source: Accenture analysis

and China. We also need to understand better and enhance relationships with our key customers, who work with us to drive performance in each marketplace.

"Our finance professionals are business partners working closely with sales and marketing in front-line commercial operations. Our suite of business analytical tools allows us to provide our management groups with multidimensional profitability reporting by geography, brand, and segment. Economic profit and returns on invested capital are measures that we have always paid particular attention to, along with a segmented profitability analysis captured in our dashboard reporting."

PreTax ROIC

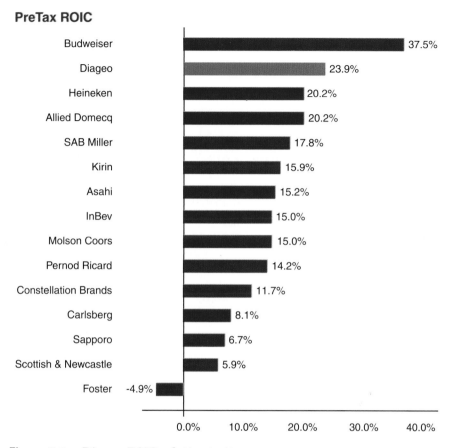

Figure 9.2 *Diageo ROIC relative to its peers.*
Source: Accenture analysis

We asked Nick to provide his perspective on our research finding that a value-centered culture lies at the heart of a high-performance business. He responded: "Every single one of our managers, wherever he or she is, understands the importance of value. As a brand-led business, this is the essence of what we are all about. Our strategic plans start with a total return to shareholders target derived from where we want the share price to go out into the future. We then disaggregate this into our various businesses by geography, brand, or some other relevant segmented basis. Next, we rigorously assess how much we need to invest to deliver that plan. With *a commitment of £1 billion per year in brand, we treat this category of expenditure with as much analytical rigor as we do our capital investment plans.*

"In fact, as a brand-led company, the investments we make are all around our brand portfolio and intangible assets. Interestingly, when we first introduced more discipline into our marketing planning programs, we discovered many long-held beliefs about promotional spend in long-favored areas that simply did not stack up. Now, there is far more rigor in what we do to ensure that we are maximizing the economic returns and value that we are creating. Our finance professionals in this area are called 'value architects.' We equip them with the best leading-edge tools at the interface of marketing and finance. We have partnerships with a number of academic institutions to keep our thinking fresh and up to date in this field.

"At Diageo, we fervently believe that enterprise performance management goes hand in hand with a value-centered culture. The best way to institutionalize this is to instill a 'managing to value' set of behaviors. When we look at any change proposal, potential acquisition or proposed advertising or promotional expenditure on a promotional campaign, we always do a thorough evaluation of the economic profit flows, risk-adjusted returns, and cash flow we expect to see. This runs right through the company at all levels, and our compensation system has performance-related bonus payments linked to this as well.

"I agree with your assertion about greater end-to-end process connectivity. We need this so that our systems – SAP in our case – can extract transactional data at speed. We can then use the data to drive our analytical tools which, in turn, can supply high-impact decision support at the front end of our business. The 'extended enterprise' concept that you talk about is something we buy into as well. Going forward, our core processes – whether internal or part of an extended ecosystem of trading partners – all have to connect seamlessly. Technology gives us the basis for this by providing intelligence and insight on how our business is performing. Understanding 'why' is more important now, as the intensity of competition grows."

A number of years ago, Diageo established a global shared service center in Budapest. "The value it brings has been well proven," Nick commented. "At first, there was some resistance to a perceived loss of control, but as we gradually expanded the center's geographic footprint, and as its capabilities evolved, people began to change their views. They began to see that more management time and resources were available for decision analysis. The information that finance was providing was becoming more relevant, focused, and useful.

"We are well down the road to fully adopting shared services. In fact, we recently rolled Australia into the service provision from Budapest. We are looking to transfer more business analytics into the center as well as statutory financial reporting. Our vision is to use outsourcing for some basic transaction processing while we focus our captive in-house center on delivering stronger decision-support capabilities on a shared basis to multiple geographies."

We asked Nick to comment on his priorities for further capability development. "Given the intensity of competition, value-centered culture and performance management will remain at the very top of our agenda well into the future. I simply do not envisage this diminishing. Finance operations will stay on my radar screen, but its importance will diminish as we move to greater levels of efficiency in the shared service organization. The same is true of capital stewardship and enterprise risk management. Our approach to managing investment in intangible assets is quite advanced, and I am quite happy with our capabilities. But that's not to say we cannot get better. We can.

"A couple of years back we put quite a lot of effort into creating what we now call our business risk assurance group. Managing risk is something that we take very seriously. We decided to considerably strengthen this area, so we took our internal audit group and added new skills and resources. Every major proposal now has to be evaluated using the new processes and disciplines that this team has developed. Its approach is really quite robust and gives us a lot of confidence when we make a decision and then start to execute."

Diageo's finance journey reveals a pronounced focus on managing for shareholder value. Creating end-to-end process connectivity for the extended enterprise will enable Diageo to "re-wire its information architecture" and move beyond basic accounting and reporting. The harmonization of supporting systems and technology has produced a highly efficient and effective transaction engine that supports the delivery of high-impact business analytics using real-time data captured at the source. This ensures that Nick and his finance team are able to support the business with up-to-the-minute relevant business and environmental insight.

Diageo's CFO, Nick Rose, acknowledges that this is a multi-year journey but one that is essential if finance is to remain a great business partner supporting an ultra-competitive business that is performing at the top of its game. His experience highlights one of many successful paths to finance transformation that are open to companies committed to achieving finance mastery.

CHANGE MANAGEMENT: A FINANCE IMPERATIVE

Managing change effectively has been critical to Diageo's success, not only in transforming the finance function, but in integrating acquisitions and bringing about a value-centered culture. As Diageo's CFO emphasized, change is a continuous process. It must be championed at the top and embedded deeply within an enterprise.

Among the leadership traits shared by the CFOs of high-performance businesses is their ability to infuse their organizations with a commitment to outstanding results. These CFOs display a rare talent for finding numerous ways to embed the objective of delivering superior shareholder returns within the DNA of their companies. They make this objective explicit by setting strategic and operational performance targets consistent with their goal of generating superior economic value. Then they reinforce this approach by deploying comprehensive, robust performance management systems, such as those developed by Motorola and the Singapore Exchange.

These sharply focused CFOs continually refine their strategies so that managers can implement actions flexibly and at pace. They stay alert to new value-creating opportunities while quickly and incisively tackling any value-destroying factors that threaten their businesses. CFOs sharing these qualities also tend to be quite ruthless when it comes to underachievement. Another key leadership trait is their obsession with execution and their understanding that their success is rooted in – and sustained by – operating models that must be continually realigned with their businesses' goals.

As our discussions of developing markets emphasize, the competitive field of play is more dynamic today than ever before. Change is a constant and its pace will only intensify in the future, whether you are a CFO facing the challenge of hypergrowth in China, accelerated innovation in Asia, global outreach in continental Europe, or cut throat competition in North America. All the CFOs we interviewed for this book unanimously agreed that change management is the biggest challenge facing today's cadre of senior finance executives. The CFOs we spoke with see change management as a core competence of the finance professional. Beyond this, they view it as a critical success factor in the journey to high performance. Figure 9.3 highlights a sampling of the dozens of companies we have studied to evaluate how the finance operating model is evolving in response to accelerated change.

Regardless of geography or whether they are in manufacturing, aviation, retail or consumer electronics, we have found that leading companies like these are radically revising their old ways of thinking about what makes conventional business models succeed. In Asia, companies like Air China and Starbucks are expanding at extraordinary double digit rates. In retailing and consumer electronics, industry leaders like Best Buy and Dell are driven by repeated waves of fast-moving innovation. Even at companies that are successfully weathering turnaround situations, such as the Corus Group or NCR/Teradata, CFOs must manage change on multiple fronts. We have identified three principal drivers behind the change situations that these companies face.

1 An expectation that corporate performance will increase significantly beyond the level currently being delivered, resulting in a superior valuation of the company, e.g., Google, SAP, and Singapore Exchange.

2 Globalization and hypergrowth, e.g., Air China, UnitedHealth Group, and Starbucks.

3 Innovation and business turnaround, e.g., Dell, Best Buy, Corus Group, and NCR/Teradata.

It might seem odd that we group innovation and business turnaround in the same category. The reason is simple. Both these forces drive extensive change through the operating model of the businesses that are exposed to them. With few exceptions, the degree of business change the companies highlighted in Figure 9.3 face is high. It is not surprising that intense competition is forcing CFOs to prioritize EPM as a "must do" in the next three years. In fact, there wasn't a single company that rated EPM as a priority lower than 4 (1 being low, 5 being high). Virtually all of the CFOs we spoke with see rolling out extended EPM competencies as a finance imperative.

It might not be obvious, but the pace and extent of the finance transformation journey must be consistent with the evolution of an enterprise's operating model. Finance transformation has to be managed

Company	Competitive Driver	Finance Objective	Priority Capability	Degree of Business Change
Constellation Energy	Capture future value	Managing to value	EPM	Low
Diageo	Capture future value	New finance operating model	EPM	Low
Singapore Stock Exchange	Capture future value	Standardization to get to VBM	EPM	Med
Corus Group	Globalization	Standardization & Internationalization	Shared services/VCC	High
Cadbury Schweppes	Growth & delivery of shareholder value	New finance operating model	ERM/CS	High
Exel (Asia)	Hyper Growth	Standardization	ERM/CS	High
Caterpillar	Hyper Growth	New finance operating model	EPM	High
SAP	Hyper Growth	Extended finance capabilities	EPM	Med
Starbucks	Hyper Growth	Scale	VCC	High
UHG	Hyper Growth	New finance operating model	EPM	High
Air China	Hyper Growth & technology	Standardization, extended capabilities	EPM	High
Dell	Innovation	Sustaining managing to value	EPM	High
Best Buy	Innovation, change in business model	New finance operating model	EPM	High
Prudential	Managing risk off the back of growth	Standardization	EPM	Low
NCR/Teradata	Refocused business, deliver new strategy	New finance operating model	Advanced EPM	High

Figure 9.3 *Evolving finance agendas of leading companies*

proactively and in rhythm with the rate of change within the business. We cannot stress this strongly enough. In Chapter 2, we describe how staying in rhythm with the business begins with the CFO's deep understanding of how, where, and why the business creates or loses value.

The CFOs of high-performance finance functions and their teams understand the competitive dynamics of their value chains and are able to articulate the distinctive capabilities that provide their companies with a cutting edge in the marketplace. This type of "hands on" knowledge allows you – as the CFO – to anticipate the needs of your business, build capabilities in time to support those needs, and avoid wasting precious time and resources. As noted earlier, building capabilities in a timely fashion implies that the CFO matches changes in finance in synch with the pace of business. This can be challenging. In managing its own change process, finance must not get too far ahead of the business side of its enterprise. But it also cannot wait until business change occurs, because it will not be able to respond quickly enough.

The competitive dynamics of the marketplace are the ultimate determinant of how radical and fast-paced your transformation journey needs to be, whether your company is a high performer or not. Take the Corus Group, the eighth largest steel producer in the world.

CASE STUDY
Finance supports a turnaround program

We asked CFO David Lloyd about the role of finance in the Corus Group's turnaround over the past three years. As David recalls: "The turnaround was first launched in 2001. At that point, the short-term objective was survival. It was nothing more glamorous than that. It was recognized that we were embarking on a project that would take us to the end of 2006. Although we had a definitive end point, we had to start mobilizing a new way of working in the company so that we didn't get to the end of 2006 and then have to refocus to decide where we would go next. We had to maintain our momentum consistent with the performance milestones that we had set and committed to reaching for our investors. To support this momentum, we had to embed a culture and way of working that was very different from anything we had experienced before. If I go back to 2001, we were undertaking a very, very significant restructuring of the business: closing unprofitable sites and optimizing our operational configuration.

"The role of our finance team in this restructuring process was pretty fundamental. This is a capital-intensive industry, and we have to live with investment decisions that have a 30- to 40-year life span. So undertaking this degree of transformation was like changing the direction of a supertanker. Initially, finance played a role in shaping the vision of the Corus Group. We also played a major part in communicating that vision to the market and our shareholders. And finally, in executing the turnaround, finance was key in supporting operations management.

"There were huge challenges along the way, of course. The finance function was working at the side of operational management much more closely than ever before. We were providing both governance and leadership as we worked the business into competitive shape. At one level, the change program actually helped to solidify and enhance the role of the finance function. During this time, finance's role was recognized as being critical. The restructuring process called for fairly strong leadership – and multidisciplinary teamwork – at all levels within the function."

David Lloyd is a strong believer that change management is now a core competency for all finance executives. The period from 2001 to 2005 that he spent helping to orchestrate a turnaround at the Corus Group emphasized the need for flexibility and the ability to drive change consistently and at a fast pace. Not only did David's team need to communicate effectively; it also had to assume wide-ranging responsibilities for the restructuring process. Throughout that process, the Corus organization looked to its finance professionals to provide greater direction and support for operational management than would normally be expected.

The finance transformation journeys of companies in turnaround situations, such as the Corus Group, often prove far-reaching in their impact. All these companies experienced broad and deep structural change that had to be managed and executed at the fastest speed possible. The competitive market drivers in all these cases were globalization, innovation, and commoditization. For David Lloyd, his initial priority was to establish process consistency: his finance team needed to become more efficient and effective at the basic blocking and tackling of finance and accounting. Beyond this, he needed to build new, extended capabilities firmly grounded in a robust, industrial-strength IT platform that had to be installed quickly and efficiently. In common with nearly all the CFOs we spoke with, his next priority is institutionalizing a value-centered culture using EPM as a backbone. We have illustrated a typical finance transformation journey in Figure 9.4.

When asked to describe the characteristics of the end state of this journey, David said, "I would like to see a company that, first of all, is recognized as having real manufacturing process excellence within the steel industry. What do I mean by this? Today, there isn't a Toyota of steel. It doesn't exist. I think that within the process industry there is a real opportunity for a player to emerge that is recognized as really being at the forefront. Secondly, we would have a geographic footprint that's very different from the one we have today. It would complement our European asset base if we had vertically integrated facilities that allowed us to leverage our low-cost manufacturing base. It would also give us exposure to growth, which, fundamentally, Europe and North America are not generating in the steel industry.

"As an organization, Corus would have a broader mix of international management resources. Within finance, the journey would be to a shared services organization, to one common SAP implementation across our group. We would have the ability to break off strategic parts of the group with ease, to integrate new acquisitions with relative ease. What I'm

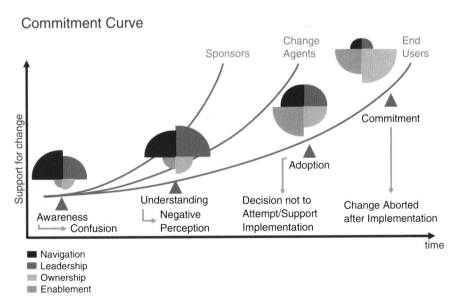

Figure 9.4   *Typical finance transformation process – Commitment Curve*

describing is actually a core capability that allows us to be responsive to opportunities and to have a reputation for being an acquisitive company that knows how to extract value."

CONTINUOUS RENEWAL: MANAGING FOR THE UPSIDE

An organization's ability to learn, grow, and refresh itself is critical to high performance.[1]

Why are some organizations so much better at renewing themselves than others? How can some companies face the same set of external conditions as their competitor – changing customer patterns, new competitive threats, and disruptive technological developments – but still produce superior performance? What enables them to identify breakthrough, market-making innovations – and manage all the streams of activity successfully to achieve their desired outcomes?

In Chapter 1, we discussed *performance anatomy,* one of the three building blocks of a high-performance business. In this chapter, we look at *continuous renewal* as a distinctive attribute of the most successful companies. Fundamental to these success stories is a focus on managing projects with the upside in mind rather than on managing only with an eye to avoiding failure. These organizations inspire people to make the commitment, develop the passion, and summon the energy necessary to achieve and sustain excellence. This ability to renew continuously reflects high-performance anatomy at the enterprise level. But it is most visible at the project or initiative level. This is where the actions that drive change occur.

Listen to effective project managers, and you will frequently hear phrases like "pulling the right levers" or "putting the right pieces in place," as if an organization is a machine or a puzzle to be solved. By raising the expectation level a few critical notches to effectively pursue initiatives, highly successful companies can break new ground or deliver truly innovative outcomes. Executives leading such programs are likely to be "bilingual": Along with "pulling the right levers," they also talk about "orchestrating" initiatives or "unleashing" energies to get everyone focused on extraordinary achievements. In other words, although these leaders are skilled at the mechanics of project management, where they really stand out is in the dynamics of mobilizing people and their diverse energies. To lead highly successful initiatives, traditional project management is not enough. High-performance businesses embrace sev-

1. Reach beyond your grasp
   - Pursue a cause, not an objective.
   - Aim high, even if you are not sure how to get there.
   - Take the initiative personally.

2. Blaze your own trail
   - Open up possibilities; explore broadly.
   - Step outside well-worn organizational pathways.
   - Carve out your space; try unusual approaches.

3. Create a strong emotional field
   - Leverage emotion as your initiative's powerful "silent partner".
   - Ask people to do things they never have before.
   - Use opposition and scarce resources as foils to magnify your team's strength.

4. Spiral up
   - Proceed holistically, not serially.
   - Use success in one area to fuel momentum in others.
   - Evaluate progress based on the value you aspire to create.

5. Use luck as an accelerator
   - Welcome uncertainty; recognize that risk drives value.
   - Turn unexpected events to your advantage.
   - Use setbacks to improve solutions.

Figure 9.5   *Counterintuitive management delivers extraordinary results*

eral seemingly counterintuitive principles that enable them to achieve extraordinary results. These principles are summarized in Figure 9.5.

CASE STUDY
Fostering a continuous improvement culture

Darren Jackson, CFO of Best Buy, describes success in terms of "the imperative to maintain strong growth and to constantly innovate the development of its business model. Best Buy continually strives to find new sources and places for growth, and we are constantly looking for ways to improve our business model."

Even though Best Buy is one of the highest-performing retailers in North America, it relentlessly pushes its execution and outcomes to higher levels, striving to become fitter and stronger. Darren describes this journey using the masters of finance capability framework: "For us, value-centered culture from an organizational perspective is about our responsibility, not only to fulfill the expectations of our investors about the future value of the company, but also to build a pipeline of quantifiable business opportunities that will support this growth. This is our highest priority, both today and into the future. Strengthening our enterprise performance management system is high on our agenda right now, even though we feel quite satisfied with our capabilities in this area. The next stage of development for us is to establish direct line of sight between enterprise value and what we call 'customer centricity'. This is because the marketplace changes so much and the services that Best Buy creates constantly take on new dimensions.

"Building new capabilities such as capital stewardship is an emerging priority for us just now, and my sense is that it will increase in importance in three years' time. We will need to put in place new processes and disciplines to fund our growth plans as we penetrate new international markets such as China.

"In terms of upgrading our finance operations, I would say that we are already reasonably efficient. Since our retail footprint has exclusively been in North America and Canada, we have progressively developed a shared service 'accounting factory' here in Minneapolis. Due to our rapid rate of growth, however, we are at an inflection point where this whole area will have to transform. Three years from now, finance operations will be reinvented to support our transformed business model.

"If I look across the dimensions of the capability model, the one area that requires constant attention is enterprise risk management. Many retailers, by and large, have defined risk very conventionally and attacked the issue through internal audit and loss-prevention programs. Intuitively or instinctively, they also thought about brand risk, employee risk, and market dynamic risk, but they didn't proactively manage these.

"They reacted to these risks as opposed to planning for them. We need new skills to cope with the new challenges that are just around the corner and to navigate the inevitable risks that we will face. As we enter China, for example, we will be developing and acquiring additional competence around managing partnerships and alliances. What we call audit committees today will become enterprise risk management committees, and they will take on a more holistic shape. Out of this governance structure, you will see us outsourcing more of our internal audit functions and adopting an enterprise risk management operating model to focus on larger enterprise risk and integration issues."

Susan Grafton, senior vice president for finance at Best Buy, describes how the leadership posture of the senior finance team has evolved during her company's transformation journey. "There has been a drastic change in the way we support the development of the company during the last four to five years. What we see now is finance being very much a partner. We have a very different seat at the table than we had several years ago and are relied on in a very different sort of way. A number of years ago, we weren't invited to the table often and we often weren't involved in major decisions. Now, finance is always involved in decisions. In fact, we're not just playing a financial role, or just a business role, we're playing a partner role. We're challenging ourselves to become activators and help push our business forward and break through the status quo. So we're not always in a financial role, although we are much respected from that perspective. Again, we're more of a general business partner who can help the business to move forward. Today, we're all about change.

"Finance professionals have to be good change agents. We look for good business acumen, not just good financial acumen, in our finance leaders so that they can partner with the business in front-line commercial operations. They must also be able to teach financial acumen to others. One of our top goals this year is to teach our business partners to look at things from a more holistic standpoint and under-stand the financial aspects of our operations. So we are activating change, helping our business partners to understand finance, and driving change.

"Our leadership model is quite distinct. We want people who can innovate and bring entrepreneurial thinking to breaking down the status quo. We also look for people who can motivate. When you think about leading, you have to be able to motivate. We use a Gallup Corporation tool, which measures employee engage-ment. We are all paid as leaders according to the level of employee engagement we achieve. We understand that having the right talent and engaging that talent fully is what produces the results we need to propel our business forward."

Darren Jackson describes the future of finance transformation at Best Buy. He says: "There are two parts to this. The first is that our pipeline of ideas to fill the future economic value void is not strong enough. We have to bring much more energy, focus, and capacity to identifying future value initiatives and strategies, but we also have to have the full set of skills and resources needed to create real platforms for growth. Second, when I think about where value will come from three or five years from now, I think we will be discussing the detailed make-up of customer markets and not product markets or geographic markets.

"Geographic markets will be the backdrop for customer markets in tapping our growth potential, and we will be talking about value propositions and extensions of customer needs and capabilities in order to deliver against those value propositions. I see a future based on a new growth platform: converting customer needs and insights into action – and going directly to sourcing capabilities rather than relying on traditional vendor networks. This is what we will be spending time on: positioning ourselves to understand changing needs, strengthening our pipeline, and dedicating resources to converting pipeline ideas into growth and value."

The Best Buy finance transformation journey is not unique. All the companies profiled in this book face one inescapable fact: change programs are growing increasingly complex. Equally important, they must address more diverse stakeholders – including employees. As Pat Erlandson, CFO of UnitedHealth Group, noted in Chapter 2, CFOs are ideally positioned to lead, align, and prepare their companies' workforces in change readiness training and in steadily expanding their program management capabilities.

Typically, in large transformational projects, a dedicated governance structure is put in place to manage the initiative and ensure that it meets strategic objectives. Governance activities are not simply about establishing steering and project committees, monitoring progress and milestones, and designing reporting and metrics requirements. The very nature of business transformation demands much more from a governance perspective. This is particularly true as CFOs become more dependent on the performance and commitment of strategic partners in navigating their way through multiyear change programs.

Rodger Hill, a partner in the Accenture's Finance & Performance Management service line, has worked with many CFOs around the world. He comments on governance: "The CFO of a high-performance business has to be absolutely integrated with the CEO, the COO, and the business as a whole. I believe there are not enough CFOs taking this strategic approach to finance.

"The CFO of a high-performance finance function normally is embedded in the leadership team as a key member of its decision-making process. His/her leadership team within the finance function must also be focused on supporting the business, rather than inwardly focused on pure numbers. In my experience, too many finance leadership teams take a numbers approach – simply because they did it that way last week, last month or last year, rather than looking forward to directing the business and assisting their company's leadership in driving strategy. I've also seen some exceptional finance executives in action. Some of the CFOs I have worked with are truly embedded in the business and truly direct their business leadership – the CEO and COO – towards high performance."

MEASUREMENT: DEVELOPING YOUR TALENT POOL

In Chapter 1, we described how high-performance businesses achieve remarkable levels of employee effectiveness and productivity through the creation of a "talent multiplier." We have identified this as one of the elements of high performance[2]. An early task for the CFO in developing its talent pool is deciding how to measure new roles/jobs/teams in order to reach desired performance goals – and to do this using a structured framework for increasing workforce capabilities. As illustrated in Figure 9.6, to measure the return on their human capital investments, many CFOs deploy a human capital development assessment tool.

This framework is a four-tier model that links business results to key performance drivers to human capital development, and the underlying management processes that underpin operational effectiveness. As described in the case study below, American Standard credits its strong performance to its investment in people.

CASE STUDY
Linking investments in people and financial results

American Standard, a US $9 billion global, diversified manufacturer of bathroom and kitchen fixtures, air conditioning, and vehicle control system products, began using the framework presented in Figure 9.6 in 2002 to assess its human capital processes and capabilities. Larry Costello, the vice president of human resources, is a firm believer in the links between investments in people and financial results. He explains, "When we looked at the results of the analysis, I could almost guess the financial performance of a particular business by seeing the assessment of our

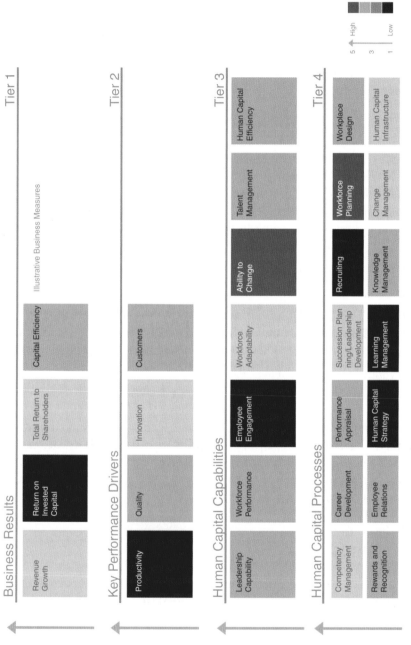

Figure 9.6 *Accenture's Human Capital Development Framework*

people programs and processes. The more the color red (indicating poor performance) showed up in a business unit, the worse the financial performance of that business unit was."

Based on recommendations resulting from using this framework at American Standard, Costello has worked on improving performance management, career development, employee relations, human capital strategy, succession planning, knowledge management, and learning management processes. For example, he implemented a 360-degree performance feedback process, started measuring employee satisfaction, and designed methods to improve and encourage collaboration among employees.

Since American Standard adopted this framework and the initiatives it indicated, its stock price has risen about 50% and its revenues have risen by 9%. There is no way to definitively know if the investments that American Standard has made in people are the root cause of these improved business results. This would require multiple implementations of the framework over time in the same company. However, Costello and his executive management team do credit American Standard's superior financial performance in large part to their continued focus on people. As Costello points out, "We have changed our company's performance because of our emphasis on human capital. Many business-unit executives have made compelling changes based on the framework. Without this analysis, we would probably never have obtained the additional support and investments needed to transform the way we work and maximize our human capital."

Other companies, such as SAP North America; Harley-Davidson Motor Company, the American motorcycle producer; Briggs & Stratton, the American industrial equipment company; and Sinclair Knight Merz, an Australian engineering and construction professional services company, are using this framework with impressive results. It is enabling them to rigorously analyze human capital investments that have, until now, largely been unmeasured.

For the first time, executives have a comprehensive tool to assess human performance, align HR and learning strategy with business strategy, and make human capital investments that generate real business value and move an organization further down the path to high performance. The framework enables an organization to diagnose its strengths and weak-

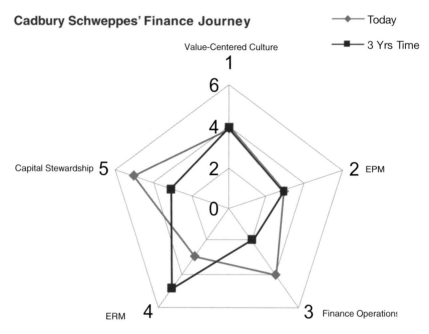

Figure 9.7 *Finance transformation priorities at Cadbury Schweppes*

nesses in key human capital practices, prioritize investments and track performance. Ultimately, it empirically establishes the links between human capital investments, business practices, and overall business performance. In many ways this represents the fusion of finance and human performance capabilities.

FINANCE AND THE TRANSFORMATION JOURNEY

The high-performance finance framework lies at the heart of the transformation journeys described throughout this chapter. Companies are developing and implementing the capabilities it identifies at different speeds, and are focusing on different areas of the framework depending on their competitive circumstances. We asked Ken Hanna, CFO of Cadbury Schweppes, the global confectionery and soft drinks company, to reflect on the finance transformation that he began in 2003.

CASE STUDY
Evolving finance priorities

"Leadership of the finance function is about agreeing on a vision and agreeing on our priorities. I want the function to feel as though it has got a strong voice, strong leadership and we are all pulling in the same direction," Ken explained. " In Cadbury Schweppes we are realigning the function to that of a commercial advisor and business partner and our priorities will evolve as our business and function evolve."

Ken fully expects, indeed plans, that the level of focus on the different elements of the high-performance finance framework will evolve.

"A value-centered culture was first introduced into the company in 1997 and I am continuing to build on this legacy at Cadbury Schweppes," Ken Hanna explained. "The fact that our people are compensated based on their contributions to promoting that culture indicates that our focus on it is not going to be reduced any time soon. Value-centered culture is a four out of five in terms of focus and attention, and will remain so."

Managing for value requires absolute alignment of the performance management system at multiple levels in the organization. Like many CFOs, Ken is currently streamlining the problem of information overload. Companies across the board have made limited attempts at implementing scorecards or using analytical techniques based on economic profit or return on invested capital to support their value-centered approach. However, few have succeeded at integrating and scaling these across the full span of the business.

At Cadbury Schweppes, Ken has been trying to cut down the amount of data finance reviews, but he has a very information-hungry board. He commented, "We are improving. I have put in some new software, which is working. We've got KPI reports. The pictures and diagrams are online, and I can get the reports very quickly. I would rate this area as a three, and I think it will stay there, going forward."

Capital stewardship is another area where he is spending a lot of time. Ken explains: "Approximately half my presentation to the board is about capital allocation: where we should be investing our money and resource allocation. Based on previous experience, instead of just spreading our resources like peanut butter, we've focused on growth and where we have the ability to win. We have to become more sophisticated in our capital stewardship. I would assess this priority as a five at this moment in time. In three years' time, it will be a two or a three because we will have institutionalized how we manage this, and our people will be living with it day-to-day as a matter of routine."

In Chapter 6, we explored the scope of finance operations and concluded that mastering this area involved a lot more than simply performing the basic mechanics of transaction processing faster and cheaper. A strong finance operations capability is a source of competitive advantage in its own right.

We asked Ken to share his views on this. He observed: "In terms of my priorities, I see this moving down the list as I get SBS – shared business services – more automated and more broadly implemented around the group. We are working harder, and in three years' time we'll pretty much have achieved enterprise-wide adoption. We have intense activity taking place at the moment, so I would assess this as a four at the moment, moving down to a two.

"However, in the area of enterprise risk management I see an increase in focus. The whole risk arena is becoming higher profile. I'm reporting to our board next week about the impact of Hurricane Katrina on our business. The bigger you get, the more likely the shocks from cataclysmic events will affect your business and how you manage it. This area is probably a three going to a five."

Linking this discussion back to Chapter 1, we can see how the three key characteristics shared by high-performance businesses form the basis for a successful transformation journey. First, high performers really understand the sources of value in their industries and explicitly identify the value drivers that can propel their businesses to new levels of growth. As a result, they function more quickly as a management team in mastering new value creation opportunities as they occur and in thinking strategically about how to pursue them.

Second, high performers focus on a few core capabilities that differentiate them from their competitors – and strive to master them. They are very flexible about whether they source these capabilities from their own workforce or from strategic partners. This flexibility enables them to move forward quickly to develop the third attribute shared by exceptional companies: high-performance anatomy – the predisposition to excel and out-execute competitors.

In finance, agility and flexibility are equally vital attributes. The finance organization has to flex and adapt to the business pace of its organization as it moves into new markets, adopts new competitive strategies, or pursues new capabilities that will enable it to compete differently in the future. At the same time, finance must exercise fiscal discipline to control and monitor the core activities that support value creation. Masters of the change process are experts at balancing flexibility and control with aplomb.

CFO INSIGHTS: LESSONS FROM THE MASTERS

- Whether you are the CFO of a company at the top of its game or in a turnaround situation, you can benefit from using the high-performance finance framework to help guide the change management process within your enterprise.

- The competitive dynamics of the marketplace are the ultimate determinant of how radical and fast paced your transformation journey must be, whether your company is currently a high performer or aspiring to be one.

- With few exceptions, business change is occurring globally at an unprecedented pace. Cut throat competition is forcing CFOs to prioritize enterprise performance management as a "must do" in the next three years as a way of institutionalizing a value-centered culture.

- CFOs of high-performance businesses have a unique ability to infuse a commitment to outstanding results. They display a rare talent for finding numerous ways to embed the objective of delivering superior shareholder returns within the DNA of their companies. They make this objective explicit by setting strategic and operational performance targets consistent with their goal of generating superior economic value. Then they reinforce this approach by deploying comprehensive, robust performance management systems.

REFERENCES

1 Jane C. Linder, Continuous Renewal: Managing for the Upside, *Outlook Journal*, June 2005. http://www.accenture.com

2 Susan Cantrell, James M. Benton, Robert J. Thomas, Meredith Vey and Linda Kerzel, The Accenture Human Capital Development Framework: Assessing, Measuring and Guiding Investments in Human Capital to Achieve High Performance, *Accenture,* July 1, 2005. http://www.accenture.com

CHAPTER 10

High Performance in the Public Sector

IMPLEMENTING A FINANCE TRANSFORMATION PROGRAM

Kathleen Turco, CFO
US General Services Administration

The General Services Administration (GSA) was established in 1949 when the United States Congress mandated the consolidation of the federal government's real estate and administrative services. For more than half a century, GSA has carried out its mission to help federal agencies better serve the public by offering, at its best, superior workplaces, expert solutions, acquisition services, and management policies. Few organizations face the magnitude of challenges that the GSA does in ensuring productive work environments for millions of employees.

Kathleen Turco has been the CFO of the General Services Administration since 2003. As she explains its transformation story: "Finance transformation at GSA is centered on changing the role of the CFO from a predominant focus on transaction processing and financial reporting to serving as a strategic advisor to the agency's executive leadership. There were three drivers that placed finance transformation squarely on my radar screen when I became GSA's CFO.

"First, the US President's Management Agenda (2002) required that federal agencies become more citizen centered, results oriented, and market based by implement-

ing reform initiatives in a number of areas: (1) the strategic management of human capital, (2) competitive sourcing, (3) improved financial performance, (4) expanded electronic government, and (5) budget and performance integration.

"Second, federal agencies were also required to improve accountability and performance by complying with legislation such as the Federal Managers' Financial Integrity Act (FMFIA) of 1982; Chief Financial Officers' Act of 1990; Government Performance Results Act (GPRA) of 1993; and the Government Management Reform Act (GMRA) of 1994.

"Third, GSA's internal strategic goals were a major driver and we decided to include the following objectives as part of our transformation plan:

- *provide the best value for customers and taxpayers;*
- *become better stewards of the assets that we were responsible for managing;*
- *operate efficiently and effectively;*
- *ensure financial accountability;*
- *maintain a world-class workforce and workplace; and*
- *diligently carry out social, environmental, and other responsibilities as a federal agency.*

"One of the unique characteristics of GSA compared with other federal agencies is that our funding is based on transactions related to goods and services provided to specific customers, or as rent for space in GSA-owned and leased buildings. In FY 2005, 99% of GSA's $23.5 billion budget relies on revenues from customer transactions. In contrast, most federal agencies receive annual lump sum appropriations from Congress, and their operations are not expected to be self-sustaining. Because of the nature of GSA's funding, we operate much more like a business than most government agencies. As a result, we face the same pressures associated with delivering services efficiently and being responsive to changing customer needs.

"Our finance transformation began as the by-product of an agency-wide human capital strategy. As we examined our long-term goals and business strategies, the initial program scope, its intended outcomes, and the business processes used to deliver value to our customers became clearer and more focused. We decided that we had to go further and deeper with the changes that we originally envisaged. So, we began to build out from this assessment and identify the core organizational

capabilities that my functional areas of responsibility (e.g., Budget Office, Controller's Office, Financial Systems, Transaction Centers) needed in order to accomplish their missions. Once the demand for human capital was identified, human capital requirements were evaluated to identify gaps. We then developed strategies and action plans to close those gaps and formulated an implementation blueprint.

"Although GSA's finance transformation program is in the early stages of a multi-year process, some benefits have already been realized. Among them are clearly defined objectives across the office of the CFO (which have reduced duplication and overlap), alignment of staff recruitment with skills required to execute the agency's strategic plan, and implementation of best practices in transaction-processing units. The ultimate impact of our finance transformation work will become clearer as the federal government expands its use of cross-agency shared service centers or expands competitive sourcing. Today we feel that GSA's CFO operations are better prepared to deliver administrative services to other federal agencies and/or compete against the private sector (where appropriate). This is a direct result of the finance transformation strategy that we are pursuing."

The GSA has one of the most ambitious finance transformation agendas among large and complex public agencies in the United States. However, it is not alone in striving to improve operations and customer service. Governments around the world are facing intense pressures to change the way they deliver services, raise revenue, and transact business with citizens. In fact, finance is often the principal launching pad for government transformation efforts in countries as diverse as Australia, Canada, Ireland, Singapore, and the United Kingdom.

The recent downturn in the global economy has increased near-term fiscal pressure on public agencies, especially in the area of burgeoning long-term deficits. Along with strong resistance to higher taxes, there is widespread public sentiment that government agencies must start operating with greater efficiency, accountability, and responsiveness – especially by embracing technology. As governments attempt to do more for less they are often hampered by aging workforces, and difficulties in retaining skilled professionals who feel constrained by inflexibility, and value the agility offered by private-sector enterprises. As these long-term factors accelerate and deepen, we have concluded that the era of governments as dominant direct service providers to all citizens has come to an end.

THE CASE FOR GOVERNMENT TRANSFORMATION

In some respects, there is nothing new about the quest to improve public-sector performance. After all, government reform has been a consistent theme around the globe for the past century. Historically, reform has focused on eliminating waste, fraud, and abuse by professionalizing public administration. To earn a reputation for "good government" in the past, it was sufficient to demonstrate competence in managing public money. Today, the bar has been raised: there is a widespread call for public managers, especially chief financial officers (CFOs), to be entrepreneurial and take the helm in guiding transformation programs.[1]

The CFO's shift in focus from accounting and transaction processing to strategy and policy planning may seem like old news in the corporate world. However, many public-sector CFOs are only now beginning to make this transition. Like their corporate counterparts, these CFOs are expected to foster transparency, integrate budgeting and performance management, provide timely business intelligence, offer competitive services, adopt integrated systems, and implement applicable best practices.

While focusing outwardly on users of financial information, CFOs and their senior finance executives are also focusing inwardly. They are setting performance measures for finance operations, benchmarking against peers, and treating the various users of financial information as customers. In short, the public-sector CFO is in the eye of the storm, leading initiatives and programs intended not only to transform the finance function, but also to shape strategy and execution for the government enterprise as a whole.

Transformation in this context can be viewed as a multi-faceted journey in which governments evolve from high-cost, transaction-processing bureaucracies into lower cost, high-performance service providers, driven to relentlessly pursue public sector value through customer service and continuous improvement. In taking this path, the public sector is mimicking the private sector by focusing on front-line customer operations and extending service support capabilities far beyond the basic blocking and tackling of accounting, administration, and financial management.

This chapter examines the role of the public sector CFO in finance transformation. It highlights how CFOs view their role, the challenges they face, and the new levels of customer service they are pursuing. We also discuss the characteristics of high performance in government and apply our high-performance finance operating model to the public sector.

THE CHALLENGE

While the goal of many reform efforts is to have government agencies operate like businesses, public-sector CFOs face constraints that are not typically seen in the private sector. Perhaps the most important is a fundamental difference in mission: government organizations have a service orientation that is not necessarily related to a customer's ability to pay. They face different process issues as well. Government decision making is built around risk aversion, minimization of political conflict, and expenditure control rather than the pure value creation that drives publicly listed companies. Legislative bodies charged with oversight often protect ineffective programs that serve narrowly defined interest groups. The public budgeting process has a short-term, fiscal-year orientation detrimental to long-term planning. Bureaus frequently operate as service monopolies, with agency executives focused on maintaining program stability and service continuity rather than on improving outcomes.

Here are the findings of a recent survey of US federal government CFOs and their customers, the Association of Government Accountants (AGA). [2]

- Leadership from the US CEO certainly counts! Federal CFOs felt that the US President's Management Agenda (PMA) was having a positive impact on government efficiency, implying that transformation efforts can be strengthened by presidential mandate.

- While an aging workforce poses a challenge to most agencies, an even bigger challenge is their lack of critical financial management and analytical skills. CFOs are increasingly moving to a "blended workforce model" in which government staff is supplemented with contractors to bridge skill gaps.

- CFOs are interested in methods such as activity-based costing and performance-based budgeting. Yet program managers and legislators seldom use these tools in budgetary decision making, presumably because politicians and agency heads are pressured to balance demands for transparency with the need to placate interest groups.

- Many federal agencies have made significant progress in modernizing financial systems. However, the CFOs surveyed are concerned that new systems are designed primarily to satisfy government-wide financial reporting requirements and will not meet the needs of individual agencies and program managers.

- Customers of finance organizations are not convinced that new financial systems are worth the added cost. This is not surprising, given that most financial system replacements have not achieved their business process improvement goals.

- CFOs are concerned that the performance measures they use to assess financial operations are not in line with customer needs.

- Overall, CFOs are optimistic about impending changes, are pleased with their own successes, and see financial management reform as inevitable.

The AGA survey also found that many US government CFOs do not measure the performance of their own operations. Among the agencies that do so, the measures they use do not adequately capture what their customers want most. The AGA survey proved especially revealing in its findings concerning two questions.

What do CFOs measure?

- Speed with which they give feedback to program officials.

- How long it takes to process payments, including paying bills and collecting payments.

- Late penalties and discounts.

- How quickly and accurately necessary reports are provided to management.

- Customer evaluation on CFO-related training, policy, and procedures.

- Administrative expenses as a percentage of all expenses.

- A 360-degree review process with bureaus, in which they evaluate the CFO.

How do customers judge a CFO's value?

- How well CFOs prepare budget packages, including timeliness, frugality, budget management, and making sure that the submission does not break the budget.
- Getting a clean audit opinion.
- CFO's knowledge of where the money goes and how to move it around.
- Improving cost and performance management.
- Ability to act as a broker in presenting and promoting budgets.
- Ability to keep fiscal issues at the forefront of resource allocation.

Measuring the performance of the finance function

The AGA's survey findings show that steady progress is being made in improving financial management, even in organizations as large and complex as the US government. The tools of transformation include technology, performance management, outsourcing, customer-focused processes, and leadership. The new breed of CFOs recognize that their roles are changing. Susan Grant, CFO of the US Department of Energy, exemplifies this view:

"As I see it, the role of the government CFO has evolved from a chief accounting officer to a chief advisory officer. To be truly successful, the CFO must be sought after and recognized as a strategic partner and an integral member of the organization's senior leadership team. The CFO must be at the table when the real decisions are being contemplated, not brought in afterwards to figure out how to pay for them."[3]

These comments very accurately reflect the sea change we discovered during our research for this book: the transformation of the government CFO from "chief accounting officer" to "chief advisory officer" and "strategic partner." Today, there are more and more examples of public agencies in which CFOs and their senior finance teams are central to decision making – strategic, tactical and operational.

WHAT IS HIGH-PERFORMANCE GOVERNMENT?

The AGA survey raises several interesting questions. Is the drive toward high performance in the US federal government an exception or a trend among governments around the globe? Given the constraints and challenges facing public managers, is there even such a thing as high-performance government? We believe the answer to both these questions is a clear yes. Research by Accenture's Institute for High Performance Business has indeed identified examples of governments and public agencies worldwide that are high performers. In general, they are guided by six key principles.[4]

1 Customer-centered service
High-performance governments routinely scan their environments to better understand public needs. They recognize that citizens and businesses can "vote with their feet" if their jurisdiction's bundle of taxes and services does not match the public's policy preferences. Citizen participation in the budget process is also of considerable importance if financial plans are to have legitimacy.

Kingston upon Hull, a municipality with approximately 250,000 residents in the United Kingdom, became one of the first local governments in the world to implement a customer relationship management (CRM) initiative when it launched a call center. The municipality's efforts offer a prime example of the type of customer-focused government that the Pathfinder project, a national initiative to spread e-government best practices, seeks to recognize and disseminate.

2 A focus on outcomes
Government agencies are notorious for focusing on inputs and spending down annual appropriations. By focusing on results, high-performance governments "create a virtuous cycle that encourages policy makers to set more precise and far-reaching objectives for government programs and services."[5]

The city of Baltimore, Maryland, tackled its frustration with its existing budgeting and planning processes by transforming itself into a metrics-driven organization. CitiStat is a technology-enabled management system under which department heads meet personally with the mayor periodically to review key "real-time" indicators of department performance. The indicators are taken seriously by the mayor's office to the point where department heads have been replaced due to poor performance.

Baltimore has realized immense benefits from CitiStat. The city estimates that the program has resulted in more than $40 million in cost savings and revenue enhancements over a three-year period. CitiStat is also responsible for important service improvements.

3 Accountability

High-performance governments strive for transparency by establishing systems that track public spending and assess the effectiveness of programs and services. To bring greater accountability to internal customers and stakeholders, managers of back-office functions are increasingly adopting service management principles.

For example, the shared services program of the Government of Ontario in Canada benefited significantly by applying service management principles at a time when it faced a budgetary crisis and cutting administrative costs was viewed as a target of opportunity. Ontario's response was to transform performance by reorganizing itself around customer-focused "clusters." Under this approach, Ontario's ministries (i.e., business units) are organized into clusters that monitor a specific strategic issue, such as business and economic development, justice, or human services. The results are impressive – in addition to reducing the budget by $300 million (a 33% decrease in costs), Ontario's shared services initiative has improved customer service.[6]

4 Innovation and flexibility

High-performance governments are often "first movers" in adopting or experimenting with the latest thinking in management practice. Flexibility – the capacity to challenge existing ways of doing things – is almost a necessary condition for innovation in government. Innovation may be driven by a sense of urgency; a budget crisis, for example, may force a CFO to think out of the box. In other instances, success breeds innovation – that is, governments with "slack resources" are in a much better position to undertake the risks that innovation entails.

5 Openness and collaboration

Governments have significant opportunities to collaborate with business or other government agencies. Business partnering through outsourcing, for example, allows public agencies access to private sector expertise in areas that are not core government competencies. As a result, collaborative business process outsourcing (BPO) is a strategic option that governments are closely examining.

Singapore's Ministry of Defense is an especially interesting case. One goal of transforming the country's public services was to provide the private sector with an example of the need for greater competitiveness. "Because the government is encouraging innovation, it has to set the example itself," explained Colonel Png, director, D'eXecutive Services for Singapore's Ministry of Defense. "So this is the current political climate and the spirit that I believe has caught on across all ministries: the need to focus on core business, outsourcing what is non-core, cost cutting continually, being more effective, being more efficient and always doing more with less."[7]

6 A passion for excellence

Enthusiasm and dedication among both employees and leaders is a common characteristic among high-performance governments. Due to the "power of the purse," CFOs hold a prominent place in the hierarchy of government leaders and must often rally support for transformational change.

One way that governments demonstrate passion is in the level of leadership they bring to change efforts. Consistent executive support of employees proved critical to success for the State of Queensland, Australia's shared services organization. As Mike Burnheim, executive director of the Shared Service Implementation Office for Queensland noted, "If you haven't got powerful sponsorship for the initiative, it won't get up. They [executive management] needed to have the commitment and the stamina to back the initiative and follow through on it – and by and large we have had that all the way through."[8]

THE HIGH-PERFORMANCE BUSINESS FRAMEWORK: WHAT DOES IT MEAN FOR GOVERNMENT?

As described in Chapter 1, Accenture embarked on an intensive research program in an effort to understand mastery of the business functions that drive leadership and success. One of our findings is that the finance organizations of high-performance businesses are stronger, better equipped, and more skilled than those of their peers.[9] "Stronger" refers to achieving mastery in the capabilities discussed in Chapter 3. In the course of our research into high performance, we also examined the progress that governments have made in the key areas of mastery. Specifically, we looked at how well the public sector is doing in developing three of the high-performance capabilities that our research has identified: value-centered culture, enterprise performance management, and finance operations.

A value-centered culture

A value-centered culture requires that the finance function act as a true business partner to help public-sector bureaus accomplish their service delivery objectives. Building a value-centered culture starts with a human capital strategy focused on attracting and retaining people with the skills and expertise to help the finance organization meet its objectives. When a value-centered culture is all-pervasive, public sector decision making embeds financial analytics and value-oriented metrics throughout an organization. Finally, as our interview with the GSA's CFO illustrates, a finance function that is value-centered structures itself so that it balances traditional expenditure control and transaction processing with a "center of expertise" function that enables it to act as an internal consultant to the rest of the organization.

Despite these obvious benefits, most government finance departments have yet to adopt programs that promote and sustain a value-centered culture. Why is this the case? One of the biggest reasons for this lack of progress can be traced to public sector budgetary processes.

First, these budgetary processes use expenditures as a proxy for value creation. For example, legislators often direct greater budgetary allocations to public safety – as if this alone will automatically improve crime fighting. While interest in performance measurement is growing, most governments have yet to integrate this tool into their resource allocation process. Instead, "staying within budget" continues to be the main indicator of sound management. In contrast, a value-centered budgetary system's mantra would be service outcomes, as measured by the well-being of individual citizens and positive changes in the health and quality of life of society at large.

Second, the dominant behavior in public budgeting is *incrementalism*: the previous year's appropriation (i.e., the "base" budget) is the starting point for the current year. The same is true for many private sector companies, although the difference between underspend or overspend versus budget is measured by the impact on profitability for that year. Under the deadening influence of incrementalism, bureau negotiations with central finance focus on a narrow range of increments or decrements to the base budget. In essence, bureaus regard the base as an annuity to be granted each year. It is difficult for a value-centered culture to take root if resources cannot be reallocated to priority programs. If there is one strategic policy change that can lead to a step change in performance, it is this one.

Public budgeting practices promote bureaucratic silos and erode natural incentives for collaboration across departments and boundaries. Central finance is often viewed suspiciously by operating units as the "money police." Operating units, in turn, are suspected of single-mindedly focusing on maximizing budget spend. Given the prevalence of such practices, is value-centered culture just a theoretical construct when applied to the public sector? Our research indicates otherwise. As described in the case study below, some governments are making real progress in developing value-centered strategies and initiatives.

CASE STUDY

National Institute of Science and Technology: Developing a value-centered culture

Key characteristics of a value-centered culture are the finance organization's customer focus and capacity to serve as a business partner to operating units.

The National Institute of Science and Technology (NIST) is an agency within the US Department of Commerce. Its mission is to develop and promote measurement, standards, and technology to enhance productivity, facilitate trade, and improve the quality of life. NIST's finance organization provides services to nine bureaus within the Department of Commerce.

One of the ways that NIST's CFO sought to position the finance organization as a business partner to its customers was creating a Service Management Group with responsibility for:

- *identifying opportunities to provide additional decision-support services and financial analysis to customers;*
- *working with group managers to track and analyze performance metrics at both the organization and group levels;*
- *developing and maintaining service level agreements that define the expectations and requirements of both the customer and the NIST finance organization;*
- *meeting with customers to solicit feedback and communicate the status of continuous improvement initiatives;*

- *identifying continuous process improvement initiatives and working collaboratively with group managers to implement appropriate changes;*
- *communicating policy and process changes throughout the NIST finance organization;*
- *developing and maintaining knowledge management tools; and*
- *conducting proactive internal audits, and monitoring policy compliance and financial report quality.*

NIST customers are each assigned a relationship manager drawn from the Service Management Group. Like account executives in the private sector, these individuals monitor the services provided by the NIST finance organization and perform diagnostics to improve customer responsiveness. The Service Management Group has been one of the key drivers in transforming the finance function at NIST.

Enterprise performance management

Especially in times of fiscal strain, elected officials seek ways to generate value from a shrinking resource pool in three ways: raising taxes, increasing borrowing or curtailing selective programs and initiatives. Excessive reliance on traditional strategies for reducing spending (e.g., cutting programs 2% across the board, reducing staff through layoffs and attrition, freezing purchases) often proves counterproductive and is viewed by operating units as "cutting into the bone." Rational resource allocation requires trade-offs between cost and value. As a result, public-sector interest in enterprise performance management (EPM) has been on the rise in recent years.

EPM is a critical capability for high-performance governments because it enables government executives to understand how changes to their resource allocation mix affect value creation. In addition, EPM helps organizations plan, execute, and monitor the effectiveness of activities and programs that drive public-sector value.

Although many governments have EPM implementation efforts under way, most have yet to achieve the promised benefits due to several factors that frustrate comprehensive adoption and execution. Accenture's Institute of High Performance Business recently conducted a survey of American state governments and discovered several widespread roadblocks to progress.[10]

- Government executives have not found a clear, comprehensive way to measure the value of agency services.

- The technologies needed to power EPM in government are not deemed to be in place. Many governments are focusing on putting enterprise resource planning (ERP) systems in place first and seeking EPM and business intelligence solutions afterwards – rather than undertaking both business change efforts simultaneously.

- Governments have faced challenges in gaining legislative support for performance management primarily because of the condensed time frames of public-sector budgeting processes. In other cases, executives have overwhelmed legislators with too many performance management metrics, leading to conflicting indicators and information overload as government executives and policy makers drown in seemingly meaningless statistics.

- There is a fundamental lack of understanding about performance management concepts. Equally critical, inadequate skills in this area continue to impede progress.

- When performance measurement information is developed, political realities can often prevent executives from using it.

These roadblocks notwithstanding, governments around the world are taking the EPM plunge. One of the by-products of our research on high performance is the development of the Public Sector Value (PSV) framework. The purpose of this framework is to address the most challenging of these roadblocks – and find convincing metrics that demonstrate value creation in public services.[11] PSV uses a disciplined methodology to define outcomes: an agency's intended results based on a combination of strategic goals and stakeholder expectations. The framework also uses a structured and balanced approach to quantify results by linking outcomes to costs. This allows agencies to compare results from year to year to assess "value creating" or "value destroying" events, as well as plan for the future. The case study below describes the application of this PSV framework to a revenue administration agency.

CASE STUDY
Indiana Department of Revenue: Applying the Public Sector Value
(PSV) framework

The Indiana Department of Revenue (IDOR) enforces the tax laws of the State of Indiana in an equitable and courteous manner. It also seeks the highest degree of public trust and voluntary compliance in administering these tax laws. Wanting to reconnect with the taxpayers of Indiana and reinvent itself, IDOR recently adopted far-reaching technological and operational changes. The agency's transformation resulted in improved service for the taxpayers of Indiana, and critical acclaim, including the Center for Digital Government's #1 ranking in 2001 and 2002 surveys of leaders in the revenue industry, awarded in recognition of IDOR's outstanding return on investment in government.

Despite progress, IDOR was facing increasing pressure to institute further performance improvements. Taxpayers were beginning to demand levels of electronic service comparable to those they were receiving from private sector companies. IDOR needed to find a way to respond to its constituents' needs and confirm the value it was creating. Accenture's Public Sector Value (PSV) model provided a solution for IDOR's dilemma. By using the PSV tool to measure historical performance, IDOR was able to demonstrate its cost effectiveness while validating its success in delivering service outcomes for Indiana taxpayers.

The model, which has been validated by several government agencies and the US Federation of Tax Administrators (FTA), focuses on the four key outcomes for state revenue agencies: 1) maximizing tax revenue, 2) maximizing compliance rates, 3) minimizing taxpayer burden, and 4) maximizing responsiveness to taxpayers. These four outcomes represent a successful balancing of a revenue agency's statutory responsibilities and public expectations for service delivery.

Analysis validated what the Indiana Department of Revenue expected to find – its performance has improved significantly in recent years. More specifically, since 1998, IDOR generated increasing public-sector value for Indiana taxpayers. Findings from the analysis aligned with the activities of IDOR's recent transformation. The department's performance improved steadily from 1998 through 2001 according to the analysis, as it gradually implemented its new integrated revenue process-

ing system (RPS). RPS was the focal point of the agency's transformation, making interactions with the department convenient, efficient, and comprehensive.

As IDOR implemented the core components of the revenue processing system – individual income tax, trust tax, corporate tax, and accounts receivable – it improved both cost-effectiveness and the outcomes delivered to Indiana taxpayers. The RPS was fully implemented in FY02. As Figure 10.1 reveals, the agency experienced its most significant PSV performance improvement between FY01 and FY02.

Since the PSV project was completed, IDOR received the 2003 Value in Technology Achievement Award from the National Electronic Commerce Coordinating Council. Indiana earned first place among more than 70 nominations from across the country. The award recognized the outstanding return on investment within government that the IDOR had achieved.

IDOR views PSV as only one component of the tools it has to guide agency decision making. In concert with the agency's other planning processes and decision making tools, PSV has helped the IDOR understand its performance history. The department is already linking current projects to the four PSV outcomes to determine where specific initiatives will drive future value. By aligning projects with key outcomes, IDOR is able to focus on activities that coincide with the Governor of Indiana's agenda.

Finance operations

Our research shows that the quality and cost-effectiveness of finance operations directly affect an organization's ability to achieve high performance. This statement is especially relevant in the public sector, because budgeting and financial control considerations permeate most policies and programs. High-performance governments are working to improve finance operations through three main strategies: 1) benchmarking and leading practices reviews, 2) adoption of ERP systems, and 3) sourcing through shared services or business process outsourcing (BPO).

Benchmarking and leading practices

Governments are increasingly interested in comparing their performance both with that of their peers and with leading private-sector organizations. Benchmarking involves measuring and comparing activities, functions, and processes against the highest performing organizations within

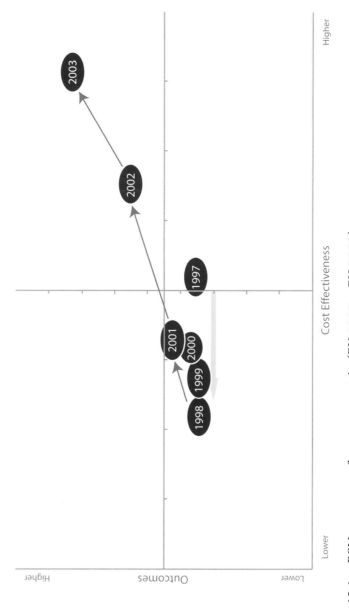

Figure 10.1 *PSV agency performance matrix (FY 1997 – FY 2003)*

or across industries. Leading practices are breakthroughs in management practice – emerging or proven "best" ways of doing business – that reduce costs, raise quality or improve customer service. One of the most valuable uses of benchmarking is to support the business case for various transformation initiatives, such as investing in a new financial system or assessing the benefits to be gained from shared services. Leading practices can serve as strategies that can potentially close performance gaps identified through benchmarking analysis.

Adoption of ERP systems

The implementation of ERP systems has served as a major foundation for transformation efforts in government. Early ERP projects were driven by technical objectives, such as the ability to complete a project "on-time/on-budget" or to address the millennium bug. The parochial focus of these implementations did not allow governments to meet the business process reengineering and cost-reduction goals in the ERP business case. Today, governments that have already implemented ERP are pursuing follow-on projects that take maximum advantage of ERP software capabilities. Examples of such ERP optimization projects include business process redesign (e.g., deploying workflows that were not originally implemented), EPM and business intelligence, and shared services.[12]

Shared services and business process outsourcing

Even with the most modern systems, an organization's business processes can be suboptimal due to high cost, lack of standardization, excessive approval requirements, or ineffective execution. ERP technology is capable of reducing many of these inefficiencies through basic automation, but substantially higher performance is achievable only by adopting new service models. Two potential avenues for improving finance operations are shared services and BPO.

Shared services involve reorganizing administrative functions to achieve scale, cost reduction, and service improvement. Accenture's study, *Maximizing the Value of Public-Sector Shared Services* (2005), surveyed the public-sector landscape and found that many governments are embarking on shared services programs.

The US Office of Management and Budget has a "lines of business" initiative that seeks cross-agency consolidation and integration for financial, human resources, grants, health and case management. In the UK, a blue-ribbon commission has targeted 2.5% annual efficiency gains, £21.5

billion in annual savings by 2008 and a significant reduction in the size of its civil service. Shared service centers are considered one means of addressing these challenges. In Singapore, the government has targeted a 3% per year manpower reduction and is currently examining alternative sourcing approaches including shared services.

Although shared services are in a nascent stage in the public sector, several governments have already implemented this model. Ireland's Eastern Health Shared Services decreased operating costs by about 15%, the United States Postal Service reduced its finance costs by about 17%, and the Queensland Government, Australia, saved A\$10 million in its first year.[13] Shared services is more than a means for cutting costs. It also brings a customer-service culture to bureau monopolies. The implementation of shared services in the state of Hesse, Germany, demonstrates the powerful benefits that this approach can offer public agencies.

CASE STUDY
State of Hesse: Transformation through shared services

Hesse is the fifth largest state in Germany and has a population that exceeds 16 million. It is Germany's leading business center and among Europe's most dynamic regions. Hesse embarked on a major government transformation project in 1995, motivated by budget pressures, an excess of accounting systems and the desire to promote transparency and efficiency in public-service delivery. The project itself attracted widespread attention due to its potential as a service model.

The "Hessisches Competence Center" (F-HCC) project, which combined the implementation of a new ERP system with a shared services model, is widely regarded in Germany as one of the most revolutionary projects in public administration ever undertaken. Hesse F-HCC developed an operating model and processes, along with a performance management system, to establish unified revenue management systems for F-HCC services that solved the problems of low transparency, process and system complexity, and inefficiency.

Prior to the project, finance processes had been mostly decentralized. Hesse's ministries wanted to redirect their focus to improving their core competencies and reducing their role in administrative processes, such as invoice processing and accounting. Hesse decided to build a finance shared service center – the first of its kind in any state agency in the world – with the goal of consolidating activities that were scattered across its ministries. The F-HCC was to use statewide standardized administrative processes and rely on SAP as its financial management system.

Today, ministries compensate F-HCC through a chargeback system specified in service-level agreements. A balanced scorecard is used as the primary performance management tool to ensure the delivery of high standards of service. In addition to more efficient process quality, F-HCC has enabled ministries and departments to reallocate much-needed resources to their main service delivery targets.

BPO is an avenue for reducing costs even more dramatically than shared services models permit. Barriers to outsourcing in the public sector are far higher than in the private sector due to factors such as unionization, concerns about offshoring, and risk aversion regarding service disruption. Nevertheless, the public sector's appetite for BPO will continue to grow, especially as it wins acceptance as a stable model with manageable risk levels. A key to expanding the use of BPO in government is the development of creative workforce transition strategies.

BPO presents a number of advantages for government. First, it can reduce total cost due to the benefits of competition. Outsourcing firms can also be more cost-effective because of the labor savings and scale economies they can leverage in serving multiple clients. Second, in some BPO arrangements, governments contract for outcomes and consequently do not have to invest in infrastructure and applications such as ERP. Finally, outsourced services can be contracted for on a per-transaction basis, which eliminates excessive investment risk.

As the public sector begins to accept and adapt the capabilities associated with high-performance businesses, its approach to customer service and value creation will evolve. Consumer demand is likely to play a major role in accelerating this process, as the public pushes for the adoption of private-sector leading-edge practices and technology in the government agencies they turn to for support and service.

CFO INSIGHTS: LESSONS FROM THE MASTERS

- Public-sector CFOs are leading the way in transforming public-sector finance capabilities through a variety of tools, such as service management principles, EPM, benchmarking and leading practices, and ERP systems.

- Although there is growing interest in establishing value-centered cultures, finance organizations are hampered by public budgeting processes that use expenditures as a proxy for value. Furthermore, incrementalism in budgeting erodes opportunities for collaboration and limits reallocation of resources to better meet customer needs.

- CFOs are examining ways to better measure the performance of finance operations and are starting to treat "users" of financial information or transaction processing services as "customers."

- Although measuring value has always been challenging to public managers, breakthroughs such as Accenture's Public Sector Value (PSV) framework are now enabling governments to track their program outcomes in relation to cost-effectiveness.

- Public-sector finance units are increasingly relying on shared services to reduce costs and improve service. BPO arrangements, while not as widespread in government as they are in business, hold the promise of providing new levels of performance – if governments can be convinced that the risks are manageable and that the existing labor force will be accommodated in the transition.

REFERENCES

1 David Osborne and Ted Gaebler, *Reinventing Government: How the Entrepreneurial Spirit is Transforming the Public Sector.* Reading, MA: Addison Wesley, 1992.

2 Adapted from: *Financial Management Challenges 2004: Meeting the Challenges Facing CFOs*, Association of Government Accountants (AGA), Washington, DC, 2004.

3 Susan Grant, Moving Beyond the Numbers: Today's CFO Must Inform, Advise and Strategize, *Federal Times*, June 13, 2005, p. 21.

4 Adapted from: Jane C. Linder and Jeffrey D. Brooks, Transforming the Public Sector, *Outlook Journal*, 2004. http://www.accenture.com

5 Ibid.

6 Government of Ontario, *Innovation in Governance: Working Together in a Connected Organization*, CAPAM International Innovation Awards 2002.

7 Accenture, *Driving High Performance in Government: Maximizing the Value of Public-Sector Shared Services*, 2005. http://www.accenture.com

8 Accenture, *Shared Services and Workforce Transformation in the Public Sector*, 2005. http://www.accenture.com

9 Accenture, *Finance and Performance Management Mastery and the High Performance Business*, October 2004. http://www.accenture.com

10 Jane C. Linder, Christine Dawson, and Jeffrey Brooks, *The Road to High Performance in the Public Sector: Insights into Statewide Performance Management*, Accenture Institute for High Performance Business, 2005. http://www.accenture.com

11 Vivenne Jupp and Mark P. Younger, A Value Model for the Public Sector, *Outlook Journal*, 2004. http://www.accenture.com

12 Rowan A. Miranda and Shayne C. Kavanagh, Transforming Government through ERP Systems, *Government Finance Review*, June 2005.

13 Accenture, *Driving High Performance in Government: Maximizing the Value of Public-Sector Shared Services*, 2005. http://www.accenture.com

CHAPTER 11

High-Performance Finance in Latin America

When one thinks of Latin America, the images that often come to mind are the beaches of Copacabana, the wine regions of Argentina, the mountain ranges of Chile, and Incan homelands such as Machu Picchu. From a business perspective, Latin America is a region rich not only in beauty and history, but also in unfulfilled economic promise. The sheer abundance of the continent, with its enormous natural resources, diverse cultures and markets, and proximity to North America, has repeatedly enticed business leaders from around the world to attempt to harness its potential and realize the rewards seemingly on offer. However, the reality of doing business in this region has demonstrated that there have always been – and will continue to be – significant challenges to conquer on the road to success.

Since addressing all the aspects of such a large and diverse region is virtually impossible, where appropriate we have chosen to highlight specific economic issues related to Mexico, Brazil, Argentina, and Chile to provide a baseline of comparison for Latin America as a whole. Their combined labor forces compare in size to that of the US, offering the prospect of a large and diverse market. However, there is a significant difference in levels of productivity and a 10-to-1 disparity between the comparative disposable incomes of these four countries and America. Unlike Asia, Latin America is not currently enjoying dramatically accelerated rates of economic development. Income inequality[1] remains a major problem in most Latin American economies, making it difficult to compare average gross domestic product (GDP) per capita numbers (against other regions) and to define specific market segments with confidence.

LATIN AMERICA THROUGH THE LENS OF THE CFO

The challenges faced by CFOs in this region include chronic problems such as high inflation, successive currency crises, high levels of indebtedness, poor comparative infrastructures, and a weak legal system. Risk management and capital stewardship figure high on the list of priorities for CFOs across the region.

There is a saying that *"Brazil is a promising market and will always be."* This sense of unfulfilled potential is symptomatic of many Latin American economies. They go through boom-and-bust cycles probably unmatched by those in any other region of the world. Fundamental shifts in economic development strategy have been common. From the 1950s through the 1970s, the region was dominated by the so-called "import substitution" industrialization approach. Tariff barriers were almost prohibitive to trade, and foreign direct investment (FDI) was highly regulated. This strategy proved unsustainable and culminated in the "lost" decade of the 1980s. Ultimately, oil price shocks, debt, high inflation, and default led to the complete reversal of the "import substitution" policy.[2]

In the 1990s, a much more liberal approach, the so-called "Washington Consensus," was adopted. This development program focused on deregulation, open economies, sound fiscal policies, and growing privatization. It triggered an ambitious transformation as regional economies embraced market-oriented principles, becoming outward-looking, open, and integrated. This created real excitement about regional prospects. Early successes made investors feel optimistic about the future. However, various economic crises hitting the region highlighted persistent economic weaknesses. Like previous attempts, the liberal reforms of the 1990s did not deliver expected results. Long-term growth rates were not as stable as predicted – a situation that ruined many business cases made by multinationals during the 1990s when they had invested in the region with enthusiasm.

Nevertheless, the reforms instituted in the 1990s did ultimately produce some beneficial effects. Today, inflation is lower than the hyperinflation historically evident in Latin America – although inflation rates remain high compared with those of developed markets. Across the region, economies remain relatively open, although foreign investment and capital-transfer regulation have moderated from the levels experienced in the go-go years.

Current situation and outlook

Since the mid-1990s, the opening up of national economies has led to greater integration both within and outside Latin America,[3] creating new business opportunities for companies across the region. It has also introduced new challenges for CFOs charged with ensuring that risks are appropriately evaluated and aligned with business decisions – and that investment returns realize their potential.

Opportunities continue to vary by country across the region and are influenced by a number of factors. At present, Chile provides the most vibrant example of a successful, outward-oriented development model. It opened its economy unilaterally much earlier than the rest of Latin America and has many trade agreements in place, notably those with the US, Canada, the European Union, and South Korea.[4] At 17%, Chile's tax burden is also considerably lower than the tax burdens of other countries in the region.

Relative to the tax rates in other emerging markets, with the exception of Chile, corporate top tax rates in Latin American countries remain high; the tax burden in Brazil is *37% of GDP*. Tax laws are complex and subject to frequent changes. An easing of tax rates is made difficult by persistent structural budget deficits.

Despite long-standing structural challenges, 2004 proved to be a splendid year for most Latin American economies. Brazilian GDP grew at 5.2% – a 10-year record high for the country. Risk premiums on Brazilian bonds fell considerably, helping to control interest rates. Brazil's economic outlook was further strengthened by a considerable primary surplus (before interest payment) at about 4% of GDP.[5] In Argentina, growth rates are high (for 2005, GDP rose 6.0%, household goods sales rose 72%), suggesting that severely depressed economic indicators are rebounding – and that the crises of recent years may finally be receding. Mexico's and Chile's fourth quarter GDP respective growth rates of 4.9% and 7.3% year on year are also very promising.

Following the devaluations in Brazil and Argentina, real exchange rates remain low and the whole region – very unusual in historic terms – has realized export surpluses. Currencies across the region are aligned and are all based on free-floating systems. This has eliminated an important source of regional dispute and trade distortion, a positive development that offers certain advantages to the CFO evaluating investment decisions in this part of the world.

So once again, the region's outlook seems bright. However, history has taught business executives to be cautious in their optimism and there are some clouds on the horizon. Inflation has emerged again as a latent threat in some countries as it forces real interest rates to remain near or at record heights. In another red-flag development, regional GDP growth is being driven primarily by current high commodity prices, such as those for steel or copper. This surge in commodity prices is being fueled largely by the booming economies of China and India. A slight cooling of the world economy or, more specifically, a hard landing of the Chinese economy, might have a direct impact on Latin America's mid-term prospects.

Latin America also faces increased competition for foreign direct investment. Currently, multinationals appear to be finding Central Europe, China, and Russia more attractive as investment opportunities, making it likely that the region's share of global direct investment will decline further.[6] In particular, the recent debt restructuring deal enforced in Argentina is likely to influence foreign direct investment levels, though it remains unclear whether this will affect Argentina alone or its neighbors as well. In Argentina, continued local resentment against foreign direct investments may prevail. If so, then its potential must be carefully evaluated by corporations, particularly because price controls and political efforts to influence corporate strategies within the country are on the rise once again. These political actions range from a call for a boycott of Shell's gas stations (resulting in an across-the-board price reduction by Shell) to strict price controls in the utilities industries.[7]

Today, as in the past, opportunity in Latin America lies in striking the right balance between tapping into its huge growth potential and minimizing risk exposure. Predictably, most organizations are looking to their finance leadership to detect early warning signals. In the discussion that follows, we explore how CFOs can provide the information and influence needed to help companies achieve high performance.

Consequences for the CFO

Our research and experience have shown that there are two main themes to succeeding in Latin America. The first is speed, the second is agility. In Asia, these are precisely the two capabilities that India and China are already deploying with aplomb as they acquire and build significant competitive advantage within their region and globally.

As a whole, Latin America is far more stable than it has been in the past. Equally important, companies have learned to adapt to the region's economic uncertainty. In particular, Latin America's historic "boom and bust" cycles and extended periods of high or hyperinflation have required finance executives to develop regional-specific capabilities for coping with recurring instability. Organizations that have survived and prospered in Latin America have done so by developing some of the most sophisticated and up-to-date finance strategies available.

For example, the region's turbulent economic history has led the banking sector to develop highly sophisticated operational capabilities. Due to the speed of economic change in the region, banks have had to invest in creating management solutions that can be implemented at a pace faster than is required almost anywhere else in the world. Today, these approaches are being applied outside the banking sector by companies like Votorantim, one of Brazil's largest private-sector business conglomerates.

One specific focus for CFOs in Latin America has been their approach to hedging. With large movements in currency valuations a given, and local interest rates of 20% still fresh in the memory of most finance executives, hedging strategies can make or break the year-end profitability of almost any organization in the region. As noted earlier, yet another regional-specific challenge is the complexity of its tax laws. These laws, particularly in Brazil, demand constant attention and are a source of irritation for the finance head of major companies. In other parts of the world, CFOs can expect reasonable periods of stability with respect to the tax code. In Latin America, however, the high frequency and severity of national tax-code changes, combined with complexity, often force the finance function to play a game of "catch-up." The prevalence and size of local shadow markets is another area with enormous implications for finance that must be factored into operations across Latin America.

These challenges must be balanced with positive aspects of Latin America's economic outlook. One regional lever that CFOs have to their advantage is low labor costs. Affordable labor is a powerful unexploited asset, along with the huge, largely untapped captive consumer market that Latin America represents. State interventionism is a relic of the past and there is more opportunity today in Latin America than in any other period in its recent history due to the greater economic freedom that countries in the region now enjoy.

Latin America is seen as an excellent training ground for international finance managers within multinational organizations. The skills and capabilities learned in this environment provide a strong foundation for operating in other geographic regions. In some instances, this can actually become a problem. Too much turnover in key finance leadership positions (via appointments from other countries) can introduce unnecessary complexity into both the finance organizations and local operations of Latin American companies. If not managed carefully, such turnover can add to the other chaotic elements in the region that finance executives must deal with. Unilever has addressed this issue by establishing two shared service centers to provide a full suite of finance-and-accounting operations across 18 countries in Latin America. These centers have reduced Unilever's dependence on local resources while creating shared capabilities for the region.

HIGH-PERFORMANCE FINANCE IN LATIN AMERICA

Our research has proven that the high-performance finance model is as applicable in Latin America as it is in any other part of the world, although the capability framework does need to be tailored to meet the unique requirements for doing business in this region. Some of the approaches that successful CFOs are using are exemplified in this case study on AmBev.

CASE STUDY

Creating value and managing risk in a volatile region

In 2000, AmBev was created through a merger – and immediately become the number one brewing company in Latin America and the sixth largest in the world. Recently, it formed an alliance called InBev with Interbrew, a Belgian company. CFO Joao Castro Neves has overseen the introduction of economic value added (EVA®) at AmBev and its use of increasingly sophisticated risk management techniques.

AmBev developed its finance program in two phases. In the first phase, Neves recalls, "We were very focused on profit and loss (P&L) and earnings before interest, tax, depreciation and amortization (EBITDA) – the development of a simple performance management tool that could accurately track sales. In 1996, we launched our second phase and began to implement EVA®. A year later, we had systems in place and EVA® had cascaded down into our organization. From then on, we really managed the value drivers within our company and linked them to our management systems. We also focused closely on having an optimal capital structure.

"We started using share buybacks and dividends to give cash back to shareholders, although it is true that we had to take being in Latin America into consideration. For a long time, we maintained a high level of cash. This is much more important in our volatile region than elsewhere, as markets are not always accessible for external financing."

AmBev has experienced significant changes in its culture, finance processes, and systems in the last 15 years. According to Neves, "The next wave will be a more rigorous centralization of activities in our shared service center. We have completely centralized back-office functions at the plant level in Brazil, but we have not done the same yet with our non-plant centers. Brazil probably represents 65% of our business, but we have not reaped the full benefits of centralizing the back office in the other countries where we operate. We want local operations to focus on the sales and the cost side – and leave the back office, the transaction piece, to the shared service center."

Under the guidance of Neves, the finance function has played a key part in the supporting AmBev's internationalization process. As he notes, "We have a specific area within the finance department that takes care of mergers and acquisitions. Our first acquisition was a very large Pepsi bottler and we realized synergies beyond those originally envisaged. We are already in our fourth large acquisition. We map out synergies very thoroughly and execute rigorously to realize them."

Is AmBev advantaged or disadvantaged regionally in terms of cost of capital or economic volatility? When asked this question, Neves responded, "More and more of our peers are the global brewery companies, especially when it comes to acquisitions. Of course, the cost of capital is a disadvantage that we have been able to overcome only through financial discipline – by establishing the right operations in the right place, developing our execution skills, and really understanding the region better than companies from other parts of the world."

We wanted to know how AmBev hedges against risks specific to the region, and which risks his company considers most important. Neves commented, "I think we see a couple of risks. If you think back about 10 years ago, the development bank of Brazil provided credit at very good rates for Brazilian companies engaged in remodeling or growth programs. Later on, we saw the opportunity to access the US capital market. We took advantage of it and issued dollar-denominated debt. Though we made this move, we did not want to take the resulting currency risk or have a mis-

match between our operation and our outstanding debt – especially as the volatility of the currency in Brazil is high. So we financially hedged our dollar-denominated debt. In addition, we try to manage risks for our variable cost structure for both beer and soft drinks, in particular, the commodity risk of aluminum, sugar, and wheat prices. We use derivatives, risk-modeling approaches such as Value at Risk, and a trading desk to make sure that the positions we take minimize overall risk exposure.

"What makes us different from other areas of the world is that there is more volatility here, which makes planning more difficult. But the approach we use can be the same. Risks exist, but no matter what happens in the marketplace, we cannot use that as an excuse for not achieving our targets. We have a three-year cycle. We believe that forecasting for more than two years becomes a meaningless exercise. For our area, it is very hard to go beyond the third year. We go into a great level of detail in terms of commodities, currencies, pricing model, GDP, inflation, interest rates, and market share for the coming year on a country-by-country basis. We have a yearly rolling forecast and then we open that yearly forecast on a quarter-by-quarter basis." When we asked whether he does scenario planning, Neves answered quickly, "Sometimes too much!"

We asked this insightful, strategically positioned CFO to step back and take a broader look at his region. Specifically, we sought his view on changes in Latin America over the past decade and its opening up to the rest of the world. He responded candidly, "What helped us more than the opening of the marketplace was having controlling shareholders that have stakes in other businesses and that have very good friends in other countries. We dealt for a long time with Budweiser and we had good access to Wal-Mart, because one of the controlling shareholders was a good friend of Sam Walton. We received good ideas from people who really traveled. Even before the market was open, we could benchmark a lot with companies, either in the US or in Europe, and share ideas with organizations such as Gillette and Wal-Mart. Our management always tried to bring ideas here, so that we could be ahead of the market. The implementation of EVA® is a good example. In Latin America, no one had ever implemented that metric before we did."

Value-centered culture

Foreign investment, competition from other developing regions, and social responsibility are hot issues for CFOs in Latin America today. Deeper integration among Latin American and global economies as well as globally has triggered fundamental changes. Opening up the region's economies has put them in direct competition with rapidly developing nations in other regions. These regions have become a battleground for foreign direct investment, as investors move their capital in and out of the best-performing countries and companies. A deep understanding of how to acquire competitive advantage – a precondition for global integration – must be supported by a pervasive belief in the creation of economic value that supersedes socially driven factors.

Value-creation strategies are being pursued by a growing number of Latin American companies. Take the Techint Group, for example – an Italian and Argentinean conglomerate with holdings in steel, oil, and gas. One of the region's rare international giants, the Techint Group has expanded internationally from its core operations by leveraging its own managerial strengths as well as Argentina's comparative advantage in natural resources. Building on these assets, the Techint Group has successfully acquired and turned around businesses in Venezuela, Bolivia, Brazil, Ecuador, and Peru – and beyond Latin America as well, from Canada to Japan and Romania.

Increasing mergers and acquisitions (M&A) activity, escalating competition, and the importance of foreign direct investment, have all put value-centered culture at the heart of Latin America's transformation agenda – whether a company is a multinational subsidiary or a local enterprise embarking on internationalization for the first time. AmBev, for example, has grown quickly in size and scope via M&A over the past 10 years. In planning its M&A strategy, AmBev has put value creation center stage, resisting the temptation to buy just to gain market share. In each M&A deal, the company carefully assessed its position and strengths – and then meticulously evaluated the synergy potential offered. In each M&A situation, AmBev's finance organization identified the real costs of the proposed deal, including the higher cost of capital required compared with that of European-based competitors typically pursuing the same M&A opportunity.

Another successful example of a value-centered culture is provided by Gerdau Group, a steel conglomerate that expanded from Latin America into the US market by acquiring Ameristeel. Gerdau invests in targets that are in financial distress, relying on its ability to transform failing businesses in relatively short time frames. It bases acquisition decisions on sound analysis and extensive due diligence – and then closely monitors the realization of value over the long term. It also manages the entire deal process, from pre-deal assessment to post-merger integration, using only internal resources. Gerdau Group has internationalized successfully by cultivating deep M&A capabilities and building a core competence within its finance function around such transactions. By giving finance a central role right from the pre-deal phase, the company has flourished.

Other companies, such as Volkswagen and Fiat, have not been as rigorous in consistently applying value-based principles in their Latin American transactions. Both these automotive giants still suffer from the lingering impact of large investments they made in hard European currencies without appropriate structural protection from devaluations of notoriously volatile currencies in the region. Even the largest and most fiscally disciplined multinationals continue to be vulnerable to regional economic challenges. Across Latin America, distressed balance sheets remain a source of major concern in many industries and capital management skills are in much demand.

What can the finance function do to mitigate these ongoing challenges? Consider the case of Volkswagen's rigorous vendor specifications. Potential suppliers must guarantee that they are able to export, have the necessary economies of scale, and can meet quality levels required for cars being sold abroad. Finance played a key role in helping to formulate and execute Volkswagen's supplier program. During the launch of the Fox car model, finance specialists worked with other business functions to establish supplier criteria, define joint incentives to induce suppliers to participate, and monitor their performance. The Bosch Group, a leading global supplier of automotive and industrial technology, goes a step further by helping suppliers become globally competitive. It creates a win-win situation:[8] deepening local product content while creating risk mitigation strategies that use both operational and financial risk management instruments. To support sales and marketing, finance provides decision support to help analyze market segmentation so that the right mix of products and service offerings are brought to market using financing instruments that appeal to specific customer markets.

Petrobras Distribuidora has involved its finance function in building the company's distribution network. Across the vast expanses of Brazil, small service stations need financing support in the absence of major investors. In response, Petrobras Distribuidora's finance function provides guidance and collaborates with banks to screen potential service station operators. Assuming this role allows its finance function to have impact beyond narrowly defined boundaries – and bring on board more and more people who understand the business.

Capital stewardship

Should capital allocation decisions be made using rigorously applied value-oriented principles? Or should longer term criteria be applied in Latin America's developing economies as they are in India, Asia and China? This is a critical issue for CFOs today. The current structure of corporate ownership and control in Latin America makes the long-term nature of investment decisions a dominant concern. Latin America's publicly traded companies are characterized by a high degree of concentration of ownership. Even among the largest public companies, families more often than not hold controlling stakes.

In other regions, this type of control is seen primarily in small- and mid-sized enterprises. Among Latin American companies, however, one or a handful of investors own the majority of capital in most companies and most board members are related in some way through family ties, friendship, business relationships or labor contracts. In a sample of 1000 companies in Argentina, Brazil, Chile, Colombia, Mexico, and Peru, the largest shareholders of each company owned, on average, some 53%.[9]

This ownership structure constitutes a strategic challenge to managing capital. As enterprises increasingly seek external capital market funding for expansion, the region's corporate family ties are being diluted. This growing trend away from family-owned businesses has several consequences for the CFO. For instance, from about 1994 to date, over 250 depository receipts (DR) have been issued by Latin American entities in the US (around one third of them by Brazilian issuers) – and 93 Latin American companies are now listed on the NYSE (with 37 domiciled in Brazil, including Petrobras, Embraer, and several financial institutions). To compete globally, local domestic players have to adopt internationally accepted corporate management structures and processes – and large corporations tapping global capital markets must meet prevailing regulations and transparency requirements for corporate governance, capital stewardship, controls and reporting.

Sarbanes-Oxley Act (SOX), International Accounting Standards (IAS), and Basel II are all having the same impact in the Latin American region as they are in New York, London and Paris. What effect is this having on finance? In the case of both Unilever and Votorantim, these control-related issues were key drivers in their decision to move towards shared services solutions for their local operations.

As Latin American economies develop, self-interested decision making and the opacity that typically characterizes intra-group transactions are increasingly seen as obstacles to cost-effective financing. Recently, a number of groups have begun to unbundle their operations – separating the operating activities, financing, and governance of their member companies. For instance, Votorantim, one of Brazil's largest conglomerates, separates its financial operations and industrial operations in accordance with its internal governance rules, not only for regulatory reasons, but also to promote greater efficiency. While the unbundling of conglomerates serves the requirements of many classes of institutional investors – including those of emerging professional pension fund management companies – it also provides the basis for a more professional approach to capital stewardship.

Until less-restricted access to financial resources is the norm, corporations in the region will continue to focus most of their time on ensuring the financial liquidity necessity for survival. With the introduction of more open and efficient financial markets and governance structures, companies operating in Latin America will no longer be forced to constantly adapt their finance processes. Region-specific approaches still common today, such as cash pre-payment, hedging risk through high interest rates on outstanding balances, and other sub-optimal finance strategies, will slowly recede.

When this is a reality in Latin America, finance professionals, like their counterparts in other regions, will be able to focus on traditional functional priorities such as integrated financial reporting, planning and forecasting, revenue assurance, and rigorous credit and collection processes. For instance, one large consumer goods organization has significantly increased the efficiency of its customer finance area by developing a regional accounts receivables model. The model defines clusters (traditional market, key accounts, etc.) in each of the six Latin American countries in which it operates – and rules, operations and processes are tailored to the specific needs of these clusters.

Financial institutions and industrial enterprises active within – or interested in – Latin America must still take into account the concentration of ownership in the hands of a limited number of families. Experienced CFOs continue to accept this as a regional reality and apply appropriate levels of risk adjustment when making investment decisions.

Enterprise performance management

In Latin America, enterprise performance management (EPM) was dominated for many years by the need to capture and report information in an environment of hyperinflation. Without adjusting to this inflationary climate, no organization could undertake any major corporate or entrepreneurial activity – or even ensure its basic survival. With greater macroeconomic stability, this has ceased to be a major concern. Regional inflation has recently eased to annualized rates of around 5%.

While inflation is no longer a major problem, other volatile factors, such as political upheaval and disruptive economic shocks, still call for fast, accurate, and consistent management information. Superior capabilities in scenario planning and forecasting are decisive advantages in this environment. Groups such as Votorantim have in place the tools and infrastructure to provide relevant information for timely decision making, regular management follow-ups, and reports to shareholders.

Our research shows that, in this part of the world, budgets take more time to produce than anywhere else, cost too much, divert people from addressing more important issues, and fail to deliver value to organizations. This is a critical finance issue; in a fast-moving, volatile environment, it is especially important that budgeting and forecasting processes be highly efficient. While companies in China and elsewhere in Asia must also cope with fast-moving economies, their prime planning challenge has to do with the upside risks of coping with hyper-growth, not with macroeconomic or political volatility.

In an uncertain business environment still punctuated by hyperinflation, deep experience with multi-currency accounting only intensifies the need for sound management. Integrated planning and forecasting systems are essential tools. We have found examples where the deployment of robust management information systems has made a compelling difference to the effectiveness of the finance function. Independent of the developments in corporate governance that we discussed earlier, privately owned companies are finding that they need a proper understanding of the core sources of value creation, especially as they often face higher hurdles for attracting financing due to their greater reliance on retaining earnings within the business.

Not surprisingly, we have seen a shift toward value-based metrics among many Latin American companies such as Petrobras Distribuidora, AmBev, and Votorantim. This is a logical consequence of the high cost of capital and increasing integration in global financial markets. Petrobras Distribuidora, for example, moved from its focus on market share to a more holistic view and began using EVA ®. Votorantim employs a similar metric called GVA in accounting for operating profit and cost of capital

– and has embedded it into the organization. Today, investment proposals are evaluated against these metrics. At Petrobras, for example, clients are evaluated against their value added to the corporation; if it is negative, they are not blindly marketed to merely for market share purposes, but are "allowed to go to the competition."

Finance operations

The business case for shared services, as discussed elsewhere in this book, has often been predicated on cost reduction and labor arbitrage. This is not the case in Latin America, simply because the opportunity to deliver cost improvement by setting up centralized shared service operations is not present in this geography. This does not mean that shared service operations are not relevant – far from it. As discussed in Chapter 6, there are major advantages to the shared services approach. These are related not simply to efficiency and effectiveness, but also to the development of extended finance capabilities that go to the heart of how risk and volatility are managed.

CASE STUDY
Building a regional shared services program

Across Latin America, many companies have already taken advantage of the opportunities that shared service centers offer. Unilever is one of the leaders in this area. As noted earlier, its two-center strategy has enabled this multinational to serve the finance and accounting needs for 18 countries across Latin America. By centralizing a broad spectrum of activities – such as accounts receivable, accounts payable, fixed assets, taxes, general accounting, and cash management – Unilever has realized major synergies. Shared services is one of the pillars of the Unilever finance strategy. Using this approach has freed up finance resources by simplifying processes so that the function can focus on business partnering. Unilever's specific objectives for shared services in Latin America include:

- *centralize and harmonize processes among its businesses;*
- *improve performance and promote continuous improvement;*
- *improve control and leverage SOX compliance; and*
- *cost reduction.*

This comprehensive approach to shared services has put Latin America in the forefront of financial innovation within Unilever. The company's program in this region is serving as a rollout model for other regions.

Votorantim is another company that decided to move to a shared service center. In the past, each of its seven business units provided shareholders with different reports; the shared service center will set a common standard and provide a more reliable basis for ensuring compliance with regulatory requirements; even adhering to SOX on a voluntary basis will be evaluated. In Votorantim's view, its shared service center will provide a kind of "cushion for control" and offer benefits beyond those of cost-effectiveness.

Taking a different approach to leveraging its financial resources, Gol, a Brazilian low-cost airline, has increased its market share (revenue passenger kilometers or RPK) from 4% in 2001 to 22% in 2004. At the same time, its operating margins have increased from 1% to 29%.[10] To manage this explosive growth and maximize profitability, Gol has turned to an industry-based solution, Navitaire, to handle a large portion of its transaction processing. This has allowed Gol to focus on the customer and market development. By deploying Navitaire's advanced systems, Gol can remain lean and focused in a highly competitive and complex market.

In all these examples, the driver is not simply efficiency, but standardized processes, robust controls, and consistent, focused management information. The finance operations agenda mapped out in this book is as relevant in Latin America as it is in Singapore and Shanghai. This is why a growing number of companies are moving toward shared services to provide more robust, consistent service levels more cost-effectively.

The increasingly close working relationship between political and business leaders across this region has led us to conclude that we will see more pan-regional shared services solutions in the near future. We expect this to lead to specialized hubs of data, information, and business processing for larger local organizations consistent with what we are seeing in other parts of the developing world. Of course, there are challenges to this emerging model. The Portuguese language requirements of Brazil, the political positioning of Argentina "against" the global investment community, and the regional history of instability could all converge to slow the development of this pan-regional shared services model. However, we expect this approach to take root firmly as trading becomes more open across the region.

For multinationals with operations in the region, the strategy for finance operations is to take advantage of their Latin American market position within the context of the global economy. Today, a wide array of corporations such as Unilever, AmBev, Votorantim, Exxon, Coca-Cola, Kellogg, Procter & Gamble, PDVSA, and Camargo Correa are already demonstrating that this is not only possible, but also beneficial. Today, the question to focus on is "how" not "if".

Enterprise risk management

Risk management is an especially challenging critical success factor in Latin America. "Getting it right" is essential, but how do you systematically manage your exposure – and what part does finance play in the process? Our research has revealed several trends in Latin America that can help guide finance towards mastery in the risk management arena.

Currency movements and changes in currency regimes make financial hedging instruments in Latin America expensive and often impossible to deploy. As a result, getting operative hedging right has become key to regional risk mitigation. This is especially true for local companies that embark on intensive internationalization and for multinationals pushing to integrate Latin American operations into their global networks. Hedging capabilities are even more important for companies that depend on relatively rigid network configurations, such as those found in the automotive industry.

Most multinationals today try to balance their import and export material flows to and from the region as well as within it. As an example, Votorantim uses wide-ranging data to determine the most appropriate hedging strategy. This is not as simple as calculating the cost of a currency hedge against the anticipated capital exposure for a given business transaction. Instead, Votorantim must also look at imports and exports across its entire organization, balancing these against one another for like currencies – and leveraging internal banking operations to further reduce the remaining outstanding positions once consolidated.

This is a core competency for companies such as Votorantim as they continue to move toward institutionalizing these capabilities in their ERP systems. At present, Votorantim has one of the most comprehensive ongoing SAP installations in the region. When completed, it will capture all relevant aspects of import and export transactions – including currency data and the timing of payment flows – across multiple business operations. This will remove a huge burden from the finance organization freeing it to undertake more analysis of trade and currency positions with the goal of helping business make more proactive decisions earlier in its planning cycle.

Some companies go one step further. They use simulation to test the impact of potential events on operating hedges; explore the effects of sudden currency shifts; and create scenarios around changes in free trade agreements, such as the imposition of tariffs or non-trade barriers. By simulating such external events using economic models, companies can evaluate new investment opportunities and gain an edge on their competition when crises occur.

Flexibility is the centerpiece of risk management; its value is derived from volatility and increases with it. Along with hedging, we found that operational flexibility is a key factor in controlling the specific risks associated with Latin America. True flexibility requires explicit planning.[11] Mitigating risk depends on identifying and managing a host of intangible assets and ensuring their flexibility, including crisis management expertise, plant and network resources, and workforce capabilities. Risk management can also encompass the design of supplier contracts and data integrity, relevance and timeliness.[12]

Finance organizations need to provide leadership in the areas of risk and flexibility. For example, take the automotive industry. How can you systematically identify options for switching production rapidly between one country and another? Identifying the decision criteria for making a switch or proactively shifting product focus to other export markets are examples of situations where finance can play an active role in managing risk.

Accepting the view that crisis is part of the territory in Latin America induces finance executives to ask the right questions. Coming up with the appropriate answers depends on having the right data and models – and performing the right analysis quickly. This has become a much more complex task as local production sites are increasingly globally integrated. In addition, due to the more fluid movement of capital and more open financial markets, crises can spread more rapidly – giving companies less time to respond.

Financial models must factor in specific risks to cash flow and deliver insights on sensitivities in this area. Beyond increasing investment premiums, it is finance's task to monitor, communicate, and mitigate risks to cash flow. In our experience, high-performance businesses develop their own internal capabilities for evaluating likely policy changes and macroeconomic developments. Why take this approach? Mainly because external forecasts about Latin America have consistently proven wrong during the fast-moving cycles so typical of the region. In the early 1990s, for example, automotive companies forecasted demand of 3 to 3.5 million cars for 2000; by 2003, companies were still selling a meager 1.9 million units. These overly optimistic projections were driven mainly by external data, but few automakers were aware of the underlying assumptions behind them. As a result, they neglected to minimize their risk exposure and were unable to adjust for major shortfalls in actual sales.[14]

Ultimately, though it is often forgotten, risk not only has a downside – it also creates opportunity. Understanding risks and having a robust long-term strategy in place will become more and more important as Latin American economies evolve. Here, as elsewhere, choosing not to blindly "buy into" the predominant market outlook is important. It is also probably truer in Latin America than elsewhere that "finance, corporate strategy and economics continue to converge."[13] Along with major challenges, Latin America provides rich opportunities for finance to develop the high-performance capabilities needed to support their organizations.

REFERENCES

1 Antonio Ortiz Mena, Los Indicadores Económicos y el Beinestar Social, in: América Latina, Democracia, Neoliberalismo, Populismo, Vanguardia, Dossier, Número 4, March 2003.

2 A. O. Krueger, *Trade Policies and Developing Nations*, The Brookings Institution, Washington, D.C., 1995.

3 Heinz Gert Preusse, *The New American Regionalism*, Edward Elgar, 2004.

4 *The Economist*, Chile, Writing the Next Section in a Latin American Success Story, April 2, 2005.

5 *The Economist*, Brazil, The Dangers of Tax and Spend, March 5, 2005.

6 Naned Pacek and Daniel Thorniley, Emerging Markets, Lessons for Business Success and the Outlook for Different Markets, *The Economist*, 2004.

7   Argentina, Taking on Foreigners Again, *The Economist*, March 19, 2005. http://www.economist.com

8   Karsten M. Schlageter, *Strategien der Automobilindustrie in Südamerika*, Josef Eul Verlag, Germany, November 2005.

9   Fernando Lefort, *Ownership Structure and Corporate Governance in Latin America – an Empirical Overview*, OECD, 2003.

10 Gol. http://www.mz-ir.com/gol/eng/

11 Subramanian Rangan, Do Multinationals Operate Flexibly? Theory and Evidence, *Journal of International Business Studies*, 1998.

12 B. Kogut and N. Kulatilaka, Operating Flexibility, Global Manufacturing, and the Option Value of a Multinational Network, *Management Science*, January 1994.

13 Accenture, *Finance and Performance Management Mastery and the High Performance Business*, 2004. http://www.accenture.com

14 Same as reference #8.

CHAPTER 12

High-Performance Finance in Eastern Europe

Eastern Europe is a diverse region encompassing 16 countries that vary widely in population, resources, and economic growth – as well as members of the Commonwealth of Independent States (CIS). Viewed as a whole, Eastern Europe is becoming increasingly attractive to multinationals eager to benefit from its highly educated scientific and technical talent pools, competitive labor costs, and rapidly growing consumer markets. From a business perspective, the growing stability of governments and improved economic performance across the region are also generally seen as encouraging signs. The Czech Republic and Poland, in particular, are being selected by growing numbers of multinational companies as the sites for their shared service centers. It has also become an attractive locale for outsourcing centers.

Since the early 1990s, Eastern European enterprises have been exposed to escalating global competition. The most forward-thinking among them have committed to aligning their strategies, in terms of market focus and positioning, with those of US and Western European corporations. CFOs are playing an increasingly important role in driving change within their enterprises. In Russian companies, for example, they have focused their attention on finance sourcing and working capital management. In contrast, Czech Republic companies have given high priority to finance and accounting, cost reduction, standardizing systems and processes, and performance management.

In general, Eastern European companies face major challenges in achieving mastery in finance and performance management. Their late entry into the global marketplace places a premium on the aggressive acquisition of core skills, forcing them to focus on the fundamentals of finance operations. Eastern European countries are investing substantially in basic business tools with the goal of rapidly becoming competitive with their international peers. The push to upgrade operational efficiency can be observed in virtually every industry. For example, one Russian oil company has established a special department to forecast prices using special mathematical software and advanced statistical modeling. The company has also implemented a derivatives program for selling crude oil. Deploying these sophisticated finance tools has enabled it to successfully weather significant changes in oil prices.

The business landscape in Eastern European countries differs dramatically in many dimensions from that of Western economies. Domestic companies in this region are only now beginning to deal with finance operations concerns that were addressed in the 1980s by their Western competitors. Collectively, Eastern European countries are currently confronting some high-stakes issues, including the following.

- *Explosive consumer demand across industries*: for the last four years, each percentage point in Russian gross domestic product (GDP) growth has produced on average a 1.75% increase in real disposable income. It is projected that, over the next five years, each percentage point in GDP growth will produce, on average, a 2% increase in real disposable income. As their disposable income steadily rises, Eastern European consumers are fueling an explosion in demand for a wide range of products and services. This is transforming a host of industries, all of which are projecting double-digit growth. These industries include consumer goods and services, travel and transportation, fixed and mobile communications, banking services, fashion, industrial equipment, and automotive.

- *Accelerating business expansion*: easier access to the European Union (EU) market is expected to fuel fundamental economic changes and fast-paced expansion. Multinationals like Toyota-Peugeot-Citroën Automotive (TPCA) are coming to the Czech Republic, for example, with plans to use it as a base for servicing EU markets. Local companies in Russia are launching ambitious regional expansion programs. One drug store chain, named 36,6, has expanded from 24 shops in 2000 to

253 at the end of 2004 and opened 192 new stores in 2005. This type of rapid expansion places a premium on speed to market, finance operations, and enterprise performance management – all areas in which Eastern European companies are playing catch-up with both Western and Asian competitors.

- *Growing competition for skilled labor*: growing demand for skilled, well-educated workers is resulting in a new focus on cultural transformation, process and system training, and career development. Local companies currently enjoy a competitive advantage in their ready access to a relatively low-cost, highly educated workforce. However, this advantage may erode rapidly, as more multinationals enter the region. In many leading companies, CFOs are already establishing reward/incentives/benefits programs and offering advanced training to talented, highly educated workers they hope to attract. In fact, the Czech Republic is currently facing a shortage of qualified people, as the demand for its skilled workers outstrips supply.

- *Serious infrastructural problems and investment requirements*: this situation does not materially affect the Czech Republic, since its infrastructure is more sophisticated than those of other Central and Eastern European (CEE) countries. However, the problem of attracting investment to develop its transportation infrastructure is one of Russia's most pressing concerns. Based on government estimates, upgrading this infrastructure will require $100 billion or more, through 2010. The Russian government does not have an infrastructure development strategy or clear regulations for investments in state infrastructure. It is attempting to improve this situation, in part, by transferring its railway assets to a state-owned enterprise. This company's management intends to attract about $600 million in 2005 – and has already gained confirmation from 11 established foreign banks on the provision of syndicated credit in the amount of $540 million.

As the factors cited above begin to reshape Eastern Europe's economic outlook, the finance function is poised to play a central role in improving core operations and developing the capabilities that lead to finance mastery. In light of this region's enormous diversity, we have chosen to focus the rest of this chapter primarily on the Czech Republic and Russia – two countries in which the commitment to high-performance finance appears to be gaining a growing foothold. These two countries are also being spotlighted because they face an array of challenges and opportunities that are representative of new members of the EU. Excellent experiences developed in other countries – for example in Poland – will also be included in the case studies section in order to provide a comprehensive picture.

CZECH REPUBLIC

The Czech Republic is one of the most stable and prosperous of the post-Communist states of Central and Eastern Europe. In the 1990s, its economic growth was dominated by the so-called "Czech miracle," which combined a rapid transfer of ownership to the private sector, low unemployment, and no hyperinflation. Since 2000, growth has been fueled largely by exports to the EU, primarily to Germany, and by strongly rebounding foreign and domestic investment. Domestic market demand is surging, as interest rates drop and the availability of credit cards and mortgages increases.

Among the most advanced transition economies, the Czech Republic was the first CEE country to be admitted into the Organization for Economic Co-operation and Development (OECD) and was 1 of 10 new members admitted to the European Union in 2004. Its economic policy is consistent and predictable. Government influence over the economy is currently very limited. Most industries are privatized and legislation is generally compatible with EU standards. Accession to the EU has given further impetus and direction to structural reform. In early 2004, the government passed increases in the Value Added Tax (VAT) and tightened eligibility for social benefits. Current account deficits of around 5% of GDP are beginning to decline as demand increases for Czech products in the European Union.

An annual report, issued by Moody's Investors Service, notes that the Czech Republic's A1 rating and stable outlook benefit from a decreased debt burden and the reduction of foreign-currency transfer risk, a direct result of economic and financial integration with the European Union. The country's economy is very stable, buoyed by limited inflation and a positive trade balance. Moody's vice president, Jonathan Schiffer, adds, "The burden of external debt remains modest, but in recent years the country's fiscal stance has increased local debt substantially. Nevertheless, the Czech Republic should have no difficulty servicing its debt burden."[1]

Measured on a per-capita basis, in recent years, the Czech Republic has become by far the most successful country in attracting foreign direct investment (FDI) in Central Europe – with $3 to $5 billion flowing into the country annually. It has signed a number of bilateral international treaties that support and protect foreign investments. The protection of property rights is a priority and its policy concerning the repatriation of profit is attractive.

There are currently no limitations on the distribution and expatriation of profits by Czech subsidiaries to their foreign parent companies. Commercial, accounting and bankruptcy laws are compatible with Western standards. The Czech Republic has treaties to prevent double taxation with many countries, including all EU countries, Switzerland, USA, Canada, Japan and Australia. All international money transfers (e.g., profits distribution and royalties) can be carried out freely and without delay. A strong, independent central bank, the Czech National Bank, has maintained an extraordinary degree of currency stability since 1991.

The Czech Republic truly serves as a hub between developed EU countries and its regional neighbors. Its central European location offers excellent access to both established Western and emerging Eastern markets. Its highway network, already the densest in Central and Eastern Europe, is slated to double in size by 2007 and several rail modernization projects are currently under way to link it more efficiently to the heart of Europe.

Among Eastern European countries, the Czech Republic is well known for its skilled, inexpensive labor force and as a friendly environment for expatriates. Its excellent business climate has attracted not only traditional manufacturing, but also knowledge-based services that include software development, research & development (R&D), customer contact centers, and finance shared service centers. These resources are being tapped by major multinationals to establish centers in medical research and other technical disciplines.

Given its feature-rich telecommunications infrastructure, excellent language skills, and an investment climate conducive to growth, the Czech Republic continues to be an ideal option for shared services. As noted earlier, a growing number of multinationals are taking advantage of the Czech Republic's robust economy, government incentives, and low-cost labor to establish their shared service centers in various cities across the country: for example, SAP, DHL, Tesco (Prague), and ACER (Brno).

The Czech Republic is also regarded as a desirable locale for outsourcing, and a considerable number of outsourcing centers have been established there in the last couple of years. Accenture's centers, located in Prague and Bratislava, for example, recently received an award from CzechInvest as the major foreign investment in the Czech Republic. These centers are known for their leading-edge finance and accounting (F&A) operations designed to serve multi-company needs. Rhodia, Delphi, Delta Air Lines, Volvo, Johnson Controls, Jones Lang Lasalle, Nestlé, Outokumpu, Bristol-Myers Squibb all make use of the centers' resources. They support a range of countries, from the United Kingdom (UK), France, Spain, and Italy to Slovakia, Germany, Switzerland, and Belgium. Their multilingual staff of more than 1000 employees speaks more than a dozen languages.

As the Czech Republic's economy evolves, the cost of labor is steadily increasing – a fact that could have major impact on future growth. Some multinationals are already investigating the potential of other Eastern European countries, such as Poland (e.g., Ahold, Philip Morris and Lufthansa in Cracow; Philips in Lodz; Thomson in Warszawa and Citigroup in Olsztyn); Hungary (e.g., GE, Alcoa, Diageo, Oracle in Budapest); and Rumania (e.g., HP). In terms of infrastructure, workforce capabilities, and economic stability, however, the Czech Republic remains well ahead of other countries in its region.

RUSSIA

Since weathering a financial crisis in the late 1990s, Russia has enjoyed six straight years of growth, averaging 6.5% annually. While high oil prices and a relatively cheap ruble are important drivers of this economic rebound, investment and consumer demand have also played a noticeably increasing role. Real fixed capital investments have averaged gains greater than 10% over the last five years and real personal incomes have realized average increases exceeding 12%. Russia has also improved its international financial position. Since the late 1990s, its foreign debt has fallen from 90% of GDP to below 30%. Currently, foreign reserve is in the amount of more than $149 billion. Strong oil export earnings have allowed it to increase foreign reserves from only $12 billion to some $120 billion by year-end 2004. These achievements, along with a renewed government effort to advance structural reforms, have raised general business confidence in Russia's economic prospects.

Nevertheless, serious problems persist. Economic growth slowed in the second half of 2004 and the Russian government forecasts near-term growth of only 4.5% to 6.2%. Oil, natural gas, metals, and timber account for more than 80% of exports, leaving the country vulnerable to swings in global pricing. Russia's manufacturing base is obsolete and must be replaced or modernized if it is to achieve broad-based economic growth.

Other problems include a weak banking system, a poor business climate that discourages both domestic and foreign investors, corruption, and widespread lack of trust in institutions.

The Russian government is relatively stable, unlike other Commonwealth of Independent States (CIS) members, notably Ukraine, Georgia, and Kyrghyzstan – which pose significant political risks and are generally viewed as economically volatile. In Russia, the high-risk profile of the CIS as a whole is likely to slow investment and intensify the impact of historical barriers such as bureaucracy, corruption, and complicated legislation. Offsetting these problems, black markets have definitely shrunk, as supermarkets and retail chains extend their reach and offer more affordable merchandise.

Accessibility remains a major concern for those seeking to penetrate Russian markets. Distances are great and the transportation of goods can take from two to three weeks. As mentioned earlier, its infrastructure is poor and underdeveloped. Regional transit warehouses are required for national market coverage and a shortage of properly equipped and secured storage facilities poses a potential obstacle for fast-growing players.

Other economic challenges include fiscal risks resulting from tax and accounting legislation, which is complicated, unclear, and sometimes contradictory. Companies, for example, can be sued for actions that were considered legal in the past, but are subsequently reinterpreted and subjected to legislative oversight. Courts often act as extensions of government prosecutors' offices, and certain penalties can be imposed even before a court judgment is given.

The need for more effective human resource development is growing in urgency for Russian companies. Before the 1990s financial crisis, human resources management was not an important factor for most local businesses. Over the past seven years, this has changed significantly, due to a number of factors, including:

- increased competition among domestic players;

- an influx of international companies offering attractive salaries and professional growth;

- growing customer demands for higher quality goods and services; and

- more accessible information on employment options.

These factors have contributed to a very high attrition rate and a lack of qualified staff in many companies. Companies are slowly beginning to address this issue. For example, one leading Russian company in the petrochemical industry has experienced a persistent problem in recruiting and retaining talent over last four years. In response, the company has revamped its HR policy and taken serious steps to improve its corporate culture. It has increased salaries, linked bonuses to business performance, and offered credits on housing purchases.

CZECH REPUBLIC AND RUSSIA THROUGH THE LENS OF THE CFO

The CFOs of companies in the Czech Republic are mainly focused on F&A cost savings, and streamlining and standardizing processes and systems. This focus is reflected in the numerous shared service centers located in the country.

The Czech Republic provides companies with attractive opportunities to leverage an abundant pool of highly skilled labor coupled with high levels of productivity. In 2003/2004, there were approximately 68,000 technical graduates available at a fraction of Western labor costs, creating an outstanding environment for both manufacturing and R&D companies. The Czech workforce is well motivated, responds to training, and has an interest in professional development.

There is an uptrend in investments in the fields of research, developments and shared services. New investors, as well as companies with a well-established presence in the Czech Republic, are now transferring their higher value-added development activities – technology centers or business support services centers – to the country. The country's commercial property market is dynamic, with well-developed industrial zones and readily available business properties. The Czech Republic also has proven R&D capabilities. Many multinationals are running Czech R&D or design centers, including Panasonic, Honeywell, Mercedes-Benz, Motorola, and Rockwell Automation.

The robust telecommunications market in the Czech Republic offers many advantages to companies requiring sophisticated infrastructure. Leading domestic telecommunications providers are able to provide a wide range of innovative services and technologies at low cost, including voice, data, radio network, cable, fixed and leased lines.

Compared with other Eastern European countries, the Czech Republic still ranks exceptionally high in both the quality and the level of its university education. Language proficiency, primarily in English, German,

Italian and Spanish, is vital to the interconnected knowledge economy of the twenty-first century, and Czech workers tend to be well trained in this area. In general, lower labor costs contribute significantly to the considerable cost efficiencies enjoyed by companies doing business in the Czech Republic. As shown in Figure 12.1, the Czech Republic benefits from a powerful array of economic assets.

In contrast to the Czech Republic, Russia's economic outlook presents a more ambiguous picture for the CFO. On the positive front, Russia expects to join the World Trade Organization – indicating willingness to observe local customs regulations with the international standards. Low corporate and personal income tax rates are a distinct competitive advantage, especially when compared with Western Europe. The ruble is a stable currency and contracts tend to be denominated in rubles to avoid Euro/US dollar rate fluctuation. On the downside, the ruble's current exchange rate limits export opportunities. As a whole, the country faces a serious risk of commodity price dependency (the so-called "Dutch disease"). The energy sector tends to attract the majority of investments, while other industries remain relatively undercapitalized. Underdeveloped supply

Criteria	Russia	C.Rep.	Hungary	Romania	Ireland
Fiscal Advantage	Low	Low	Low	Low	High
Skilled Labor Availability	Low	High	Medium	Medium	Low
Infrastructure	Low	High	Medium	Medium	High
Educational System	High	High	High	High	High
Cost Advantage	Medium	Medium	High	High	Low
Service Quality	Low	High	Medium	Medium	High
Cultural Capability	Low	High	Medium	Medium	High
Time/Distance Advantage	Medium	High	High	High	High
Language Proficiency	Low	High	Medium	Medium	High

Low ● Medium ● High ●

Figure 12.1 *Comparative assets in selected Eastern European countries.*
Source: Accenture

chain capabilities and information technology (IT) infrastructure may seriously impede corporate expansion.

Russian business practices have tended to be complex and insular. Today, companies are taking steps to align those practices with International Finance Reporting Standards (IFRS). This is an ongoing process and significant differences remain. These are outlined in Figure 12.2.

Russia has begun to establish its credentials as a niche player in the global IT services market. Many IT departments are pondering whether offshoring is a viable option for business-specific, mission-critical development, and are deciding which location to select when securing a reliable offshore partner. The Russian government is considering the creation of a special economic zone to support offshore programming initiatives. Today's Russia may have the right combination of talent, expertise, and cost to be the location of choice for the development of financial technology capabilities, specifically for complex software engineering and R&D projects. Figure 12.3 captures some of the key factors affecting Russia's outlook in the outsourcing arena.

Russia's impressive track record in producing highly trained employees is definitely an asset in competing for outsourcing opportunities. More than two million people – half of them researchers and scientists – currently work in more than 4,500 R&D centers throughout Russia. This skilled workforce is larger than that of any other nation in the world. The vast majority of Russian software engineers and computer programmers hold MS or Ph.D. degrees in mathematics or physics. With a significant R&D heritage, one of the world's best educational systems, and a tremendous pool of software engineers, Russia has become a key location for R&D work for many leading American and European companies. This list includes Bechtel, Boeing, Intel, Microsoft, Motorola, and Sun Microsystems.

As the Russian economy builds momentum, financial sourcing is becoming a critical issue. As a result, many Russian CFOs are increasingly involved in evaluating instruments to fund expansion. While CFOs initially worked mainly with domestic banks, they have begun to approach Western markets and leading foreign investment companies. They are also using wider range of instruments to generate expansion funds, from initial public offerings (IPOs) to fixed-rate instruments, to selling shares to strategic investors. For example, Lukoil Group recently negotiated a credit arrangement in the amount of $500 million from leading Western banks at a significantly lower rate than it would have received domestically.

Accounting Practice	Description of Difference
• Legal form prevails over economic content	Russian accounting is based on fulfillment of Russian legislative acts
• Special requirements for accounts numbering	All accounts in Russian chart of accounts have dedicated numbers
• Special requirements for the format of reports and primary documents	It is necessary to create these reports in Western enterprise resource planning (ERP) systems
• Different financial years	In Russian Accounting Principles (RAP): Starts January 1 In International Financial Reporting Standards (IFRS): It is defined by the company
• In Russia tax and financial accounting principles differ significantly	Requires maintaining parallel financial and tax accounting
• Russian language	It is required by Russian legislation that all primary documents should be in Russian
• Different approach to the definition of useful period for fixed assets	In IFRS: it is defined by the company In RAP: It should be defined by the company but in practice it is defined by legislative acts
• Different classifications of intangible assets	In RAP there is a time factor for the classification, existence of properly prepared legal documents
• Different approach to stock valuation	In RAP: based on actual costs and corrected at the end of the year on provision (if market value of goods has decreased over the period) In IFRS: the lowest from costs and Net Realizable Value (NRV)
• Different approach to the valuation of materials and finished goods issued from stock	In IFRS: First-in-first-out (FIFO) and moving average In RAP: FIFO, moving average, Last-in-last-out (LIFO), based on the total costs of each unit
• Different approach to the creation of provisions	In RAP it is not specified separately In IFRS it is specified
• Different approach to recognition of income	In RAP it is required that sales must be confirmed with primary documents. As alternative there is an opportunity to use cash method
• Different approach to the recognition of expenses	In RAP it is required that expenses must be confirmed with primary documents. Alternative: opportunity to use cash method
• Minor differences in the principles of preparing consolidated reporting	e.g., in RAP the financial data of a daughter company is not included in consolidated reporting if its activities are significantly different from main activities of the holding company In IFRS it is not allowed

Figure 12.2 *Russian accounting practices compared with international standards*
Source: Accenture

Strengths	Weaknesses/Challenges
• Elite university system • Skilled, ample workforce • Cost of labor advantage compared with United States and Western Europe • Geographic and cultural proximity to Western Europe and the United States	• Underdeveloped market. Russian outsourcing market is just at its start–number of companies, leaders–earned effect from this model is not critical yet • Main focus of outsourcing market in Russia is IT outsourcing. Very weak business process outsourcing (BPO) market
Opportunities	Threats/Risks
• Expansion of foreign companies to Russia • Limited range of services • No global players, potentially big market • High growing market	• Negative perception of Russia's political, economic and legal risk • Psychological reasons impede development of outsourcing. Few companies are ready to share part of their business with unknown • Possible tough competition from local companies on IT-outsourcing market

Figure 12.3   *The outsourcing market in Russia*

Across Russia, the effective management of working capital is becoming a higher priority for CFOs, as companies seek to free up additional money to support their growth. Cost management is another hot topic for Russian CFOs, as the competition in the domestic market grows. Wimm-Bill-Dann, for example, has recently put this at the top of its CFO's agenda because of net profit decreases resulting from escalating competition.

What does all this mean for the finance function? In Eastern Europe, companies must operate according to multiple accounting standards (e.g., IAS, US GAAP, RAP, RAS), making integration of capabilities a core challenge. In general, operational efficiency and organizational effectiveness have not been given the priority that they receive in the rest of the world. As a result, internal or external business processes are often unable to operate seamlessly across business entities and/or geographies. However, the extensive use of ERP solutions does contribute to compliance, discipline, and transparency in finance and accounting operations.

HIGH-PERFORMANCE FINANCE IN EASTERN EUROPE

There is a strong need in the finance organizations of Eastern European enterprises for globally integrated information to support internal processes and/or management reporting requirements (e.g., consistent performance data or customer/product profitability analysis). This is especially true when stakeholders operate on a global basis (e.g., European-owned multinationals), when state-owned enterprises are being integrated into private industrial groups, and when significant M&A activity is under way, creating a compelling need to realize the value of synergy.

In Eastern Europe, enterprise solution integration is often considered a simple system replacement or IT integration project, rather than a large-scale effort that affects the execution of strategy and companywide operations (especially finance and accounting). While ERP implementation can enable IT-related benefits via data center consolidation (i.e., upgrade hardware components), and reduce application management complexity (i.e., fewer software packages or legacy systems), its broader impact is far more crucial. Above all, it can profoundly impact business execution by providing the ability to perform generic functions or processes at scale, supporting new capabilities, and enhancing the value of consolidated information. In reality, it is unlikely that ERP implementations will be viable in the absence of such far-reaching business benefits. Adopting this broader mind set concerning ERP poses a major challenge for many Eastern European companies.

Compared with businesses in other regions of the world, Eastern European companies may suffer from structural constraints and the need to play catch-up in mastering logistical basics. However, they have the advantage of being able to capitalize on the hard-won experience of seasoned competitors. In this section, we provide an overview of the progress that Eastern European companies are making in satisfying our key criteria for high-performance finance functions. It is important to note that the market factors and CFO issues outlined here are supported by general trends and may not be indicative of every situation.

Value-centered culture

The most progressive organizations exhibit sophisticated capabilities in building and sustaining a value-centered culture. In such companies, fundamental finance skills and basic analytical resources are firmly established, then upgraded and reinforced over time. Once this occurs, a finance organization's resources are steadily enriched and expanded. As this process matures, a value-centered mind set is identified as a critical priority for the finance organization.

As noted earlier in this chapter, our research and experience suggest that many Eastern European companies are under increasing pressure to master the basic finance systems and processes. As a consequence, many of these enterprises are in the early stages of upgrading their finance resources and capabilities. This reality constrains the extent and pace of their ability to embed value-centered principles within their finance organizations. However, as the following case study illustrates, some Eastern European companies have developed a sophisticated approach to investor relations and corporate governance, both hallmarks of a value-centered culture.

CASE STUDY
Effective investor relations and corporate governance

One Russian company in the Consumer Goods and Services (CG&S) sector has fully embraced the Corporate Governance Code developed jointly by the World Economic Forum and the Russian Union of Industrialists and Entrepreneurs. Beyond adopting these governance principles, it has created a self-service reporting system to facilitate communication with its shareholders. The company also publishes its governance guidelines on its corporate website. These are included.

- *Principle of effective management: the company's long-term commitment to increasing shareholder value.*
- *Principle of financial discipline: describes how the company manages its consolidated and unconsolidated financial accounts, and in particular, the standards it has adopted.*
- *Principle of transparency of the ownership structure: discloses information on the degree of control of its main group of shareholders and its shareholding capital base.*
- *Principle of legality and ethical conduct: explains how the company acts with respect to the laws of the jurisdictions in which it conducts activities.*
- *Principle of corporate social responsibility: explains how the company follows principles of social responsibility and contributes to Russia's economic development.*

This company's publicly available governance information also outlines the roles and responsibilities of its board of directors; how internal audits are conducted; its code of ethics; and its financial disclosure policy. Very few Russian companies adopt and broadcast such detailed governance guidelines. This company's approach clearly indicates its commitment to a value-centered culture.

Enterprise performance management (EPM)

Overall, Eastern European companies attach high importance to EPM, especially for business strategy evaluation and as a financial market perception tool. Nevertheless, this advanced capability is still in the early stages of development in this region. In general, a major upgrading of finance operations must be undertaken before Eastern European enterprises can invest effectively in EPM. However, as the following case study demonstrates, some companies have made exceptional progress in this area.

CASE STUDY

An innovative strategy for performance management

Wimm-Bill-Dann Foods OJSC is an established household name in Russia. Known for its high quality and range of products, the company is the market leader in the Russian dairy and juice sectors. Having been founded by five entrepreneurs, Wimm-Bill-Dann grew from a leased production line at the Lianozovsky Dairy Plant in 1992 to a publicly listed food conglomerate, employing more than 18,000 people.

Today, Wimm-Bill-Dann has an overall turnover of more than $1 billion and owns 25 manufacturing facilities in 21 locations in Russia and throughout the CIS. It also has distribution centers in 26 cities in Russia and abroad. In 2002, Wimm-Bill-Dann became the first Russian consumer company to list Level 3 ADRs on the New York Stock Exchange (NYSE), and only the third Russian company ever to have floated on the NYSE.

The strength of Wimm-Bill-Dann lies in its ability to accurately forecast market fluctuations. Through its shrewd analysis of data, the company has been able to predict changes in market trends, giving it a competitive edge in price negotiations and the adjustment of supply and demand. This ability to "look ahead" can be traced to

Mr. Vladimir V. Preobrazhensky, the CFO of the company. As he points out: "The cost of labor is very low in the Russian market and cost cutting may not have the same priority it does in Western European countries. So, we strongly believe that the key success factors in increasing shareholder value, at least at this stage, are enterprise performance management capabilities."

With the strategic intent of becoming a best-practice leader, Wimm-Bill-Dann recently launched an EPM transformation program focused on a new Tableau de Board, a new automated consolidation system, and enhancements of its financial control and performance reporting. The objectives of this program revolve around improving information delivery in order to drive real insight into enterprise performance. In particular, new solutions have been defined to create more structured planning, budgeting, and forecasting processes – and, perhaps more important, a deeper link to strategy which can be effectively managed through performance-focused metrics.

For Wimm-Bill-Dann, accurate, forward-looking projections drive better business decision-making. The systems it now has in place enable the company's CFO organization to devote two-thirds of its analysts' time to what-if scenarios and goal-seeking analyses, rather on historic results.

Finance operations

In Eastern Europe, inexpensive labor and the low total cost of finance (as a percentage of revenue) enable finance organizations to focus on operational effectiveness rather than cost reduction. Cultivating front office, and service-oriented attitudes for the finance function are viewed as major issues. They are also major challenges, given the non-competitive corporate mind set that prevailed among Eastern European companies until recently.

For such companies, key issues include creating synergies in process and procedures, and taking advantage of ERP-enhanced functionalities. ERP and single accounting codification within the enterprise are perceived as critical success factors, not only for data quality and transparency constraints, but also for cut-off speed enhancement purposes. As indicated in Figure 12.4, the approach and factors influencing an ERP implementation can vary, depending on whether a company is domestic or an overseas firm with access to Western capital.

In general, when it comes to ERP implementation, domestic companies are driven by the search for low-cost solutions; as a result, vendor and software selection focus on developing local solutions and maximizing the use of internal resources. In contrast, Western companies tend to rely more on the solutions adopted by their corporate headquarters; major importance is also attached to the system usability and the reliability of services provided by external vendors.

Implementing an ERP solution at a Russian affiliate of a Western company, for example, offers major challenges due to the comprehensive legislative requirements imposed by the Russian Federation. These requirements fall into two categories: accounting and logistics. Accounting requirements stipulate that:

- statutory annual financial statements must be prepared by all organizations operating in Russia. The format of these statements is prescribed by current regulations;

- bookkeeping entries must be made in local currency (Russian rubles), which is also the reporting currency for statutory purposes;

- all statements must be prepared in the Russian language; and

- organizations in Russia must store original primary documents.

Logistics requirements stipulate that:

- predefined forms be printed for the movement of goods and related operations;

	Domestic Companies	Companies with Western Capital (HQ Abroad)
Coverage of functionality of software selected	2	2
Credential and experience of system integrator	3	1
Implementation costs	1	3

Figure 12.4 *Ranking of factors involved in an ERP implementation by corporate location*

- import/export laws be followed in the preparation of documents and that transparency is ensured for all operations involving imported or exported product;

- tracking certificates be maintained for hazardous, food or pharmaceutical products;

- distribution and transportation chains provide detailed tracking, from vendors to customers; and

- each product has a Russian label with a description of the product and ingredients.

As the case study below illustrates, one Western enterprise operating in Russia has successfully developed finance capabilities that meet local requirements while supporting growth targets.

 ## CASE STUDY
Strengthening finance capabilities

This consumer goods company expects a dramatic expansion of its Russian business in coming years, including the introduction of a new joint venture company, launching new division operations, and opening subsidiaries in other CIS countries. The company found it was strategically important to pursue its growth targets well supported by both an integrated and scalable business information environment. Operationally, it focused on the organic integration of logistics and financial processes within a one-system environment and on business process harmonization at the group level. Key goals included streamlining the following processes:

- *supply chain (integration of sales forecasting, long-term procurement planning, allocation of purchase orders to intra-group factories, logistical execution, and electronic invoicing);*
- *order to cash (electronic order placement, outbound delivery, customer credit management, commercial statistics);*
- *decentralized procurement integrated with budget control;*
- *market segment-oriented profitability analysis; and*
- *sales forecast and procurement planning.*

To develop an integrated system that provided single-source reliable information across business functions, the company adopted the following solutions:

- *Customs clearance tracking, certificate management, relabeling process;*
- *import and export shipments tracking;*
- *Electronic data interchange (EDI) – integration with suppliers to facilitate electronic transfer of purchase orders, delivery confirmations, and invoices – and integration with customers;*
- *integration with banks for incoming and outgoing payments;*
- *Value-added tax (VAT) functionality and reporting;*
- *profit tax accounting; and*
- *enhanced reporting capabilities.*

While the shared service concept is not yet highly developed domestically in Eastern Europe, overseas companies are setting the stage for its wider adoption in the region. As this case study shows, a carefully planned scoping and implementation program can reap substantial benefits:

CASE STUDY

Implementing a shared service center

Ahold is an international food retail and food service company operating mainly in Europe and the United States. After a long history of business success, it faced major competitive challenges. In response, the company launched its "vital transformation program" focused on enhancing customer offerings and boosting competitiveness by improving sales growth, decreasing its cost base, and building a sustainable platform for the future. The program was intended to restore financial health, reengineer the food retail business, and strengthen accountability, controls, and corporate governance.

Ahold Central Europe (ACE) is responsible for operating the business in the Czech Republic, Poland, and Slovakia. As part of the company's "vital transformation program," it decided to launch a business reorganization. This effort included establishing an accounting shared service center (ASSC). Building efficient back-office operations was not the only initiative identified, but it was of fundamental impor-

tance in supporting ACE's overall business transformation strategy. Without the lever of cost arbitrage, creating a sustainable business case was not easy. In the end, a way was found to meet both qualitative objectives and targeted cost reductions. Supported strongly by the reengineered process and advanced technology, the new organizational model substantially boosted efficiency.

The scope of the shared service center was wide ranging. Processes included account payables, account receivables, asset accounting, project accounting, bank accounting, general ledger, stock accounting, cash sale reporting, tax and VAT reporting, and local statutory reporting. From the applications perspective, Ahold's priorities were:

- building a cross-country ERP strongly integrated with the other business systems; and
- realizing a paperless solution that supported the new centralized organizational model while minimizing the disruption of business operations.

A two-month feasibility study ended with a detailed definition of scope. A phased approach was chosen to mitigate project risks. The entire accounting organization of ACE was redesigned. High-transactional, low-value activities were fully consolidated in the ASSC, while a limited accounting team was maintained at the country level to ensure business proximity and on-field management of local fiscal and legal matters.

A significant reengineering effort focused on standardizing processes and procedures across the three countries, improving of the quality and timeliness of reporting, and increasing control and effectiveness of the analysis over business results.

Technology also played an important role. A new scanning and workflow solution fully integrated with the ERP, and an invoice matching tool was included in the scope to enable remote payable invoice processing and matching without impact on business operations.

With payback expected within 27 months, ACE's overall initiative should improve the efficiency of its accounting functions by up to 30%, compared with the current baseline (including process efficiency and consolidation). In addition to quantitative benefits, the new organizational and operating model also offers substantial qualitative improvements:

- increased control over some key processes (e.g. invoice matching, payments);

- *improved quality and consistency of the accounting and controlling reporting;*
- *streamlined closing process thanks to uniformed processes and applications; and*
- *more effective governance of the accounting function.*

Capital stewardship and enterprise risk management

In general, capital stewardship and risk management are two areas that are underdeveloped in the finance organizations of Eastern European companies. Here, once again, concentration on the basics has diverted attention from these more sophisticated finance issues. As more Eastern European enterprises find themselves competing on a global scale, these concerns will rise to the forefront for progressive CFOs.

Capital stewardship, in particular, is an area of growing focus for the top managers of Russian companies. Companies recognize that they must develop this finance capability if they are to attract investment for significant business expansion, and compete both domestically and internationally.

Enterprise risk management is a relatively new discipline across Eastern Europe. In Russia, for example, one of the country's leading banks has developed and implemented its own methodology for credit risk management. The bank has moved aggressively to adopt modern Western practices in credit risk management, and to make use of Western software applications.

In this broad discussion, we have touched on some of the central concerns facing the finance organizations of both domestic Eastern European companies and their overseas competitors. The high-performance finance landscape in this dynamic region is likely to change dramatically in next five to ten years. A powerful mix of assets will fuel this transformation. Chief among them are burgeoning consumer demand, a highly educated workforce, surging productivity, greater economic stability – and growing awareness that the price of entry into the global marketplace is an ever-more sophisticated array of finance tools and capabilities.

REFERENCES

1 Ratings: C & E Europe, *gtnews.com* http://www.gtnews.com

CHAPTER 13

High-
Performance
Finance in Asia

Anchored by China and India, two of the world's largest and fastest-growing economies, the Asian markets are on the march. With 60% of the world's population, the booming markets in this dynamic region offer unprecedented opportunities to companies around the world, and many are arriving with great expectations about the region's buoyant growth. They anticipate rapid market expansion for many years to come. Beneath the dazzling surface, however, lie enormous uncertainty and complexity – a reality that players in Asia must plan for and adapt to. This region is vast and endlessly diverse. Operating successfully in this multi-language, multi-currency, and multi-tax environment demands great flexibility and coordination.

Asia's ways of doing business, evolving finance model, war for talent, and increasing appetite for raw materials, are unique. They add an aura of excitement and volatility to strategic planning and decision making. For multi nationals, building a presence in this region often requires tremendous adaptability in designing and controlling business development programs. Operations may vary in structure from franchises to joint ventures to wholly owned subsidiaries. Some companies may pursue all these approaches within one or more Asian markets in order to hedge their risks regionally.

United States coffee house retailer Starbucks, for example, has different ownership percentages throughout its portfolio of Asian operations. "We have markets where we are the 100% owner, markets where we have 50/50 joint ventures, and others where we are a pure licensor," says Jim Eschweiler, Starbucks' vice president of finance for Asia/Pacific. "One challenging aspect of operating here is balancing how much direct control we have versus how much we can influence results as a licensor."

At global software giant SAP, Colin Sampson, COO and CFO for Asia Pacific, agrees that adaptability is a key factor in doing business in the region. Says Sampson: "You have to partner in a different way with organizations. Working together here is a lot about relationship building. It's not about doing business on an absolutely objective products-and-benefits basis." Sampson adds that, although this makes Asia a riskier business environment, the region is also full of opportunity. Asia is the growth engine for SAP world-wide. This adds an element of excitement for a lot of people working here. It's the place to be, if you like.

ASIA THROUGH THE LENS OF THE CFO

In this region of opportunities, challenges and threats, how should the CFO respond? In conducting the research for this book, we traveled extensively throughout Asia and spoke with CFOs from a wide range of companies. We discussed both the outlook for Asia and business issues within the context of the high-performance finance operating model. While we encountered some unique and varied viewpoints, our team concluded that this model is both relevant and central to CFOs in the region, and that it provides them with a robust way to manage their finance transformation journey.

CFOs across Asia agreed that the finance function is a leading force for change within their organizations and that its importance in driving high performance will increase in the coming years. The CFOs we interviewed felt they differed from their Western counterparts only in their starting point on the road to building high-performance finance capabilities.

For example, Seck Wai Kwong, Senior Executive Vice President and CFO of the Singapore Exchange (SGX), told us that his organization was on a multi-year journey to becoming an enterprise with value-based management at its core. He also told us that SGX has doubled its enterprise value in the 18 months since it started on this path. Starbucks' Jim Eschweiler spoke of his company's growth targets of 20% to 25% over the next three to five years, and the critical role that he expects finance to play in that growth; while SAP's Colin Sampson described the benefits his company's shared service center is already delivering to its Asia Pacific operations.

At a fast-moving global consumer goods company, the CFO for Asia Pacific told us that his organization expects to double the size of its Asian business in the next three years. He also expects that strengthening his company's finance capabilities will be pivotal to this growth strategy. Finance's ambitious program will involve investing in both IT and people. "The first stage, from an enabling perspective, will be associated with what I call the capability game," he explained. "We are talking about explosive growth. So some of the capabilities we have to build will play an enabling role and others will be involved in catching up – keeping pace with demand. I think that these two roles will overlap in part of the finance function, so we'll need enough good people with good skills to do both."

The insights of these and other CFOs explored in this chapter reinforce the importance of high-performance finance functions in the region. The implications of finance's role in two powerful Asian economies, Japan and China, are discussed in greater detail in Chapters 14 and 15 respectively.

Diversity in economic maturity

Asia is not only the world's most economically dynamic region, it is also remarkably diverse. The region encompasses different stages of economic development; varied governments, from monarchies to one-party states; and a myriad of cultures, languages, and religions. The complex interplay of these factors must be addressed in any strategic vision for the region. Consider, for example, the varying levels of economic maturity across the broader Asia Pacific region. While Japan, Australia, South Korea, Hong Kong, and Singapore are viewed globally as highly industrialized countries, nations like Cambodia, China, India, and Vietnam are regarded as emerging/developing countries.

"Each country is in a different evolutionary cycle of growth and demands a different type of thinking, whether you're in a mature economy, a large economy that's growing rapidly or a large economy that's growing more slowly," notes SAP's Colin Sampson. "Responding to each of these varying economic growth levels demands different skills and resources. There's no 'one size fits all' approach."

Figure 13.1 captures the diversity of countries in the greater Asia Pacific region, with their greatly varying market size (total GDP on the x-axis) and economic maturity (GDP per capita on the y-axis). As illustrated, nations across the region can be broadly classified into four categories. At one end of the spectrum is Japan, sophisticated and economically mature. At the other end are China and India, the two emerging giants characterized by rapid growth and vast market potential. The stunning pace of

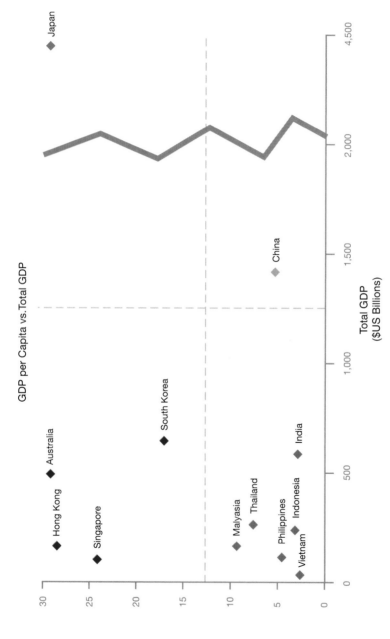

Figure 13.1 *GDP per capita vs total GDP in the greater Asia Pacific region*

their development is reshaping the economic landscape on every level – domestic, regional, and international. The largest group represented in Figure 13.1 comprises the emerging economies of Southeast Asia – such as Malaysia, Thailand, Indonesia, and Vietnam – all of which are resource rich and on strong growth trajectories.

In a fourth category are Hong Kong, Singapore, and Korea – the newly industrialized economies (NIEs). Their growth, which accelerated markedly in the 1980s, has elevated them to developed country status. Also in this group is Australia, one of the Pacific region's anchor economies. A mature, but resource-rich market, Australia is experiencing a powerful surge of growth as it supplies resources to the emerging Chinese and Indian juggernauts.

The economic diversity captured in Figure 13.1 is also reflected in the varying maturity of the financial systems in this part of the world. These different levels of maturity require different responses from finance organizations.

Diversity in cost structure

Across Asia, the cost of living also differs dramatically by country. Based on the Big Mac Index used to compare the real purchasing power of currencies around the world, the cheapest price of a Big Mac hamburger is $1.23 in Beijing and Shanghai (China) while the most expensive is $2.80 in Seoul (South Korea). Wages across the region show wide variation, with the Philippines having the lowest wage index of 5.4 and Japan the highest at 68.3. In a survey conducted by UBS,[1] which measures well-being by estimating how many minutes workers in various countries must work to buy a Big Mac, Indonesians in Jakarta need to work for 67 minutes to afford one of McDonald's burgers, while Japanese in Tokyo must work for only 10 minutes. Such differences reflect variations in productivity as well as disparities in the local cost of ingredients.

At Starbucks, Jim Eschweiler says that differences in labor costs between high-cost countries like Korea and Japan and low-cost countries in Southeast Asia are a major factor in his planning. "You have markets where you need to drive two times or three times the number of transactions than in the lowest-cost structure models to make them work," he says. "There are big differences along that scale, and you need to get into the shoes of those markets to truly understand the opportunities and set the right strategies."

Diversity in culture and language

Asia is home to over half the world's people who speak a staggering combined total of more than 2000 languages. Mandarin (or Putonghua), spoken by more than 1 billion residents, is the standard language in mainland China and Taiwan. As part of its colonial legacy, English and Cantonese remain the official languages of the Hong Kong Special Administrative Region (SAR) of China. Within the Chinese written language, the traditional characters are used in Hong Kong and Taiwan, while mainland China uses simplified characters. Across the rest of Asia, people speak languages ranging from Japanese, Korean, Thai, Bahasa Malaysia, Bahasa Indonesia, and Vietnamese in Southeast Asia to Hindi and Tamil in South Asia. In Singapore, there are four official languages: English, Mandarin, Malay and Tamil.

Inevitably, these cultural differences affect finance activities. Prudential's Regional Finance Director, Graham Skeates, talks of three different and largely hidden, cultural divides in Malaysia alone. At SAP, Colin Sampson says he has worked hard to encourage his in-country finance executives to "... express their opinions independently as much as they can. In the Korean culture, possibly in Japan and China to a lesser extent, the finance person will generally say whatever the managing director says. Even if the plane is going down, they stay committed to his decision: 'We're all going down together, that's great.' So if you want someone who's going to say, 'Whoa, I don't want to go down with that plane, hang on!' to us here in the regional center, then we need firsthand information on their views. I feel that over time we have tremendously increased the transparency in those particular countries."

Exel's CFO for Asia Pacific, Stephen Ferraby, is also aware that negotiating cultural differences in Asia is a necessary part of regional growth. "We are trying to grow like crazy, but in a reasonably disciplined fashion so we are not falling into too many traps," he says. "Culturally, this is difficult. Despite the willingness to get behind senior executives' objectives, people in a number of Asian countries do not like you questioning their business decisions. There is the issue of face and the commitments that they may have made to their customers. Asian executives, in general, do not want to change or undo these commitments."

Across the region, standards of governance and transparency vary widely. For example, some advanced Asian economies have business cultures with strong traditions based on leadership. Singapore Exchange CFO Seck Wai Kwong sees the respect that the market has for his organization's chief executive as a key factor in its success. "I think that part of the increase in value of our organization can be attributed or linked to the leadership factor," he comments. "We have a very clear strategy map in place that explains what our financial perspectives are and our customer value proposition – and all our people can understand this. We share this strategy, so that all of our people can see where they fit in the map and where they are contributing."

Diversity in distances

Asia is also a geographically dispersed region. On average, it takes about 4 hours 45 minutes to travel between major cities in the region. On the near end, it may take less than an hour traveling from Singapore to Kuala Lumpur (Malaysia). On the far end, it can take more than 13 hours to travel from Melbourne (Australia) to Beijing (China). Apart from its superior communication and logistics infrastructure, robust legal system, and high quality workforce, Hong Kong's status as a selected regional "hub" is due largely to the short traveling time required to reach it from numerous locations in different countries.

Diversity in accounting and tax requirements

There are also significant differences in accounting and disclosure standards and practices across businesses in Asia. In particular, while most countries accept accounting records prepared overseas, China, Japan, and Korea require that locally prepared records be kept. Some countries like Singapore and Korea accept digital copies, allowing original accounting records to be maintained in a foreign country. Others require original paper documents for business transactions.

While most countries in Asia allow tax records and returns to be prepared overseas, there are considerable differences in tax policy across the region. In countries like Hong Kong, Indonesia, the Philippines, Singapore, and Korea, tax records can be stored and maintained in a foreign country. However, certain countries, including Japan, Malaysia, and Korea require that tax payments be made from a local bank account instead of a foreign bank account. Some countries like Malaysia, the Philippines, and Singapore offer tax incentives for shared service center activities.

ECONOMIC TRENDS: GROWTH AND MORE GROWTH

According to the April 2005 International Monetary Fund (IMF) World Economic Outlook, regional GDP growth for 2005 is projected at a robust 7% (see Figure 13.2), with a moderate slowdown in China. Continued

	Real GDP				Consumer Prices[1]				Current Account Balance[2]			
	2003	2004	2005	2006	2003	2004	2005	2006	2003	2004	2005	2006
Emerging Asia[3]	**7.4**	**7.8**	**7.0**	**6.9**	**2.4**	**4.0**	**3.7**	**3.2**	**4.4**	**4.4**	**3.9**	**3.5**
China	9.3	9.5	8.5	8.0	1.2	3.9	3.0	2.5	3.2	4.2	4.2	4.0
South Asia[4]	7.1	7.1	6.5	6.3	3.9	4.3	4.6	4.0	1.4	0.1	-0.7	-0.6
India	7.5	7.3	6.7	6.4	3.8	3.8	4.0	3.6	1.2	0.3	-0.3	-0.3
Pakistan	5.6	6.5	6.7	6.3	2.9	6.7	7.9	6.5	4.1	0.3	-1.2	-0.8
Bangladesh	5.4	5.4	5.5	5.9	5.4	6.1	5.7	4.5	0.1	-1.2	-2.4	-2.5
ASEAN-4	5.4	5.8	5.4	5.8	4.0	4.4	5.3	4.5	5.7	5.5	4.4	3.3
Indonesia	4.9	5.1	5.5	6.0	6.8	6.1	7.0	6.5	3.0	2.8	2.2	0.9
Thailand	6.9	6.1	5.6	6.2	1.8	2.7	2.9	2.1	5.6	4.5	2.0	1.4
Philippines	4.7	6.1	4.7	4.5	3.0	5.5	6.8	4.9	4.3	4.6	2.6	2.0
Malaysia	5.3	7.1	6.0	6.2	1.1	1.4	2.5	2.5	12.9	13.3	13.6	12.2
Newly industrialized Asian economies	3.1	5.5	4.0	4.8	1.5	2.4	2.2	2.3	7.4	7.1	6.8	6.2
Korea	3.1	4.6	4.0	5.2	3.5	3.6	2.9	3.0	2.0	3.9	3.6	2.9
Taiwan Province of China	3.3	5.7	4.0	4.3	-0.3	1.6	1.6	1.5	10.2	6.2	6.6	5.9
Hong Kong SAR	3.2	8.1	4.0	4.0	-2.6	-0.4	1.0	1.1	10.3	9.6	9.4	9.3
Singapore	1.4	8.4	4.0	4.5	0.5	1.7	1.5	1.5	29.2	26.1	23.4	22.9

[1]In accordance with standard practice in the *World Economic Outlook*, movements in consumer prices are indicated as annual averages rather than as December/December changes during the year, as is the practice in some countries

[2]Percent of GDP

[3]Consists of developing Asia, the newly industrialized Asian economies, and Mongolia

[4]Includes Bangladesh, India, Maldives, Nepal, Pakistan, and Sri Lanka

Figure 13.2 *Selected Asian economies: real GDP and other key indicators*

strong growth is projected for India, the NIEs, and the emerging economies of Southeast Asia, underpinned by strengthening domestic demand.[2]

Southeast Asia has been affected by the catastrophic December 2004 tsunami, which left a path of destruction across Indonesia, Sri Lanka, India, Thailand, and several other countries. However, in most cases, the affected areas account for a small portion of total regional output and the adverse effects are being offset by reconstruction activities.

By 2020, Asia's projected population of around 3 billion – about 60% of the world's total – will include 700 million new consumers. If current trends are maintained, these future consumers will be more affluent and even more brand conscious than current buyers. MasterCard, for example, estimates that Asia's "middle-class" population – those earning at least $5000 a year – will grow from 180 million in 2002 to 480 million by 2010, a number greater than the population of the US.[3]

India and China – set to drive the region and the world
India and China are growing so rapidly that they are set to join the ranks of the largest economies in the world, and their global integration is proceeding at speed. The annual growth rate of both countries has averaged 8% to 9% for the last decade. As China has roared ahead as a manufacturing center, and India has developed its service industries, the two economies have taken other countries in the region along with them. Logistics provider Exel, for example, grew its China revenues by 80% from 2004 to 2005, and its Indian business has averaged 25% to 35% growth over the past four years.

While growth is likely to be slower in Japan than in the region's new boom economies, Japanese industry will still be able to take advantage of these fast-growing economies' lower cost base to offshore production and support services. This will result in an unprecedented level of regional economic interdependence for Japan. For example, China is not only a manufacturing center for the West, but also services the manufacturing needs of leading Japanese and Korean corporations.

As noted, China's insatiable appetite for raw materials has played a major part in boosting the economic strength of its resource-rich neighbors, such as Australia, Indonesia, Thailand, and Malaysia, all of which are becoming increasingly dependent on Chinese demand. Chinese and Indian successes are spurring a sharp rise in intra-Asian trade, with China taking in imports at a rapid pace to fuel its boom. Some of the world's fastest-growing shipping routes extend into China from countries such as Singapore. Citibank estimates that from 2002 to 2005, intra-Asian trade rose from 38% of the world total to more than 47%.[4]

REGIONAL CHALLENGES AND CHOICES

High-performance businesses share some common characteristics, and as this book emphasizes, a strong finance capability is among the most important. As discussed in Chapter 1, high-performance businesses are those that effectively balance today and tomorrow. They understand how to focus on long-term success with an eye on short-term costs. They consistently outperform their peers over a sustained timeframe, across business cycles, industry disruptions, and leadership changes. A recent Hackett Benchmark Study analyzed the relationship between world-class businesses and world-class finance organizations. The study's findings highlight the finance function's leadership role in creating and sustaining high performance. Many CFOs agree. "Finance needs to be at the hub of the organization," says Starbucks' Jim Eschweiler. "There cannot be anything that happens in the organization that does not somehow have a path through one of our functions. From the point of view of following the money, whether it is following the cash in and out, approvals for capital expenditure or operating plans, we need to be in the middle of it.

"Philosophically, we strive to have our finance team sitting at the table, setting the agenda and the direction of the business. What this means, in light of Asia's rapid growth and enormous potential, is that I should be able to move with the business and act quickly. It would be very easy for us to become an obstacle and a constraint to growth. If we cannot figure out how to do payroll, get systems in, or get approvals through fast enough, we have set ourselves up to choke off or constrain growth. Likewise, if we aren't in tune with the dynamics of the business, we risk missing opportunities. The biggest thing for us is to be nimble, flexible, responsive, and adapt quickly to demands."

Delivering on the ambitious finance agenda that Jim Eschweiler describes offers some unique challenges. For CFOs, Asia presents several layers of complexity in its plethora of clearing zones; the unevenness of its banking systems and communications infrastructures; varying limits on foreign investment levels; and localized regulations, from pegged currencies to restrictions on the movement and pooling of capital.

Disparate finance operations
Dispersed operations in different countries of the region can result in a

fragmented finance operation, where policies and processes are inconsistent, and controls and standards are difficult to enforce. If communications are poor – for reasons of infrastructure and/or organizational design – strategy can be difficult to implement effectively. Equally serious, critical information from individual countries may never arrive at regional headquarters. With disparate regional operations, it is also difficult for the finance function to scale itself for business growth.

At Exel, Stephen Ferraby says, "All the blocking and tackling is essentially in-country. There is a limited amount that happens through the regional reporting and review process here in Singapore. In terms of balancing risk and legal issues, I probably deal with most of this at the regional level. In-country staff tends to deal with the smaller local negotiations; the more difficult ones or those with global perspectives come through here."

Dispersed operations imply a large accounting group with a primary role to simply deliver transactional services. This is not only costly; it can also present difficulties in sourcing, training, and retaining skilled personnel.

Software giant SAP, for example, has practiced what it preaches to its clients, creating a shared service center in Singapore. "From our regional shared service center, we handle all finances and administration transactions and processes across all lines of business, e.g., software and maintenance contract management and billing, expense and travel management, accounts payable, payroll, time recording for our consultants, course registration and planning for our education business and all month-end closing transactions and processes," says SAP's Colin Sampson. "About forty people in our center do everything, so there are no transactions entered into at the country level. We reduced these resources in the countries and incorporated these functions into our shared services operation."

Prudential, which has operations in 12 Asian countries, also has certain shared regional operations centered in Kuala Lumpur. Regional Finance Director Graham Skeates agrees that the logic behind the regional operations has as much to do with costs as it does with developing robust processes which help to add value. "Policy administration and other volume transactions are the main area, and these are definitely a cost issue as well," says Skeates.

"However, we are not centralizing finance for cost efficiency or staff efficiency. The finance section in a life assurance company is not driven by cost, as it is relatively small in the first place, but it is driven by integrity and reliability of data, which is being effected by new controls such as SOX and changes to international standards along with other external factors. You need to develop reliable controls and processes so that you can sleep at night. Cost savings in the finance area, per se, does not keep me awake."

Inconsistent finance processes

In joint venture situations, the complexities of local tax and compliance across Asia can be daunting. In China, for example, joint ventures must file tax returns in the tax bureau where the joint venture is registered. Multiple joint ventures can also result in inconsistent approaches to implementing standard processes, and in a situation where control breaks down, this can lead to the repetition or reinvention of errors.

Throughout Asia, significant management time is spent on controllership activities, such as the signing of checks. Most finance organizations allocate more than 50% of their resources to delivering transaction processing services, leaving very few resources for financial planning and analysis work. As a result, finance management can be seriously limited in its ability to drive business growth. Ad hoc special projects and initiatives, such as Sarbanes-Oxley Act compliance, systems implementation/ replacement, and mergers and acquisitions are usually handled during the "spare time" of the finance staff. Inevitably, the outcomes of these projects and initiatives are often less than satisfactory.

At a leading global consumer products company, the CFO for the Asian region says that his organization is looking to the rollout of an SAP system anchored around a shared service center to transform its finance capability in Asia over the next three to four years. As the system ramps up, he adds, "I would expect to see a pretty extensive and sophisticated finance function. I would also expect that we would have come pretty far along the shared services front. I would see a far greater use of technology among top people than we have today – not just around analytics, but also around transactional tasks. I would also like to be able to say that we would have progressed to the levels of scrutiny that more mature operating organizations bring to operating key performance indicators (KPIs) from a financial perspective – working capital, asset utilization and all that."

Asia demands great versatility and focus, especially from CFOs whose organizations have operations straddling several countries. Their key challenge is to maintain tight control, while minimizing cost and risk.

This must be done while very closely aligning the finance operation with the business, not only in terms of physical resources but also capabilities.

Exel's Stephen Ferraby says that one of his company's achievements has been the implementation of "consistent systems" across Asia, which puts his finance organization in a "... better position than most of the world. We have a common chart of accounts and, in theory, a common set of processes. As it is rolled out, we have allowed a number of country variations. We are going through a change process now, and few of those variations will be allowed to continue."

THE EMERGING ASIAN FINANCE MODEL

Regional diversity is a constant challenge for CFOs, who face the difficult task of enforcing standardization across disparate business units while providing them with the tools they need to implement strategies appropriate to local conditions. In this environment, scaling up to support business growth, both in terms of cost-effectiveness and capabilities, is also a major problem.

Mindful of these challenges, CFOs from leading organizations in the region have evolved new approaches to building their organizations. As shown in Figure 13.3, the result is an emerging finance model tailored to Asia.

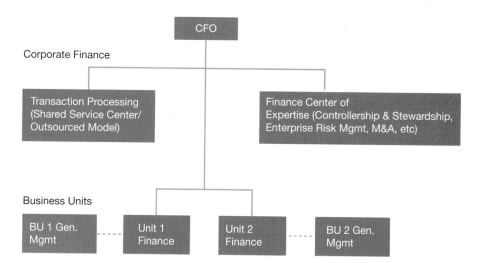

Figure 13.3 *Evolving finance organization model*

CFOs in Asia, like their colleagues around the world who are pursuing high performance, seek mastery in five capabilities: creating a value-centered culture, enterprise performance management, finance operations, capital stewardship, and enterprise risk management. Our research confirms that the shared service center as a foundation for effective, scalable financial operations is just starting to take hold in Asia. This shared services approach is integral to the emergence of the high-performance finance model in the region. In contrast to Western companies, labor cost arbitrage is not a major factor in building a business case for adopting the shared services approach. Instead, CFOs in Asia are wrestling with issues of standardization, robustness of service delivery, and extending capabilities across far-flung markets and geographies.

A key aspect of the evolving Asian finance model is the embedding of processes in business units, such as management report preparation, cost accounting and analysis, and enterprise performance analysis. These are front-line tasks that demand high levels of judgment and proximity to business operations. Asia is full of examples of organizations with variations of this embedded model, structured for their specific regional circumstances.

SAP, as we have seen, has already moved to a shared service model in Asia as part of a tailored response to the region. "In Asia, you need as much transparency and governance as you can get," notes SAP's Colin Sampson. "What we decided to do was to deploy shared services so that we have better control over our destiny, in terms of what we book and how we design processes, than we would have out there in the field.

"Shared services, in particular, has created focus for me as CFO and helped me rethink how we develop the finance organization going forward. High performance is about looking toward the future rather than worrying about what was booked in the past. If you have a shared service infrastructure, you can develop very efficient and effective structures with well-defined processes, so that finance people, both here in the regional headquarters and out in the countries, can concentrate more on decision making."

Sampson says this model enables SAP's people in-country to concentrate on their customers and implementation – the most important aspects of their business. He advises country management teams: "Let the finance people in the country help you focus on what's important to you – closing business, looking at growth opportunities and deciding questions like, 'Should we be in Vietnam, how can we accelerate growth in China and India, how can we expand the business in other areas?'

"That's where high performance comes in," Sampson points out. "Shared services has been an enabler. It has helped finance people move out of their traditional comfort zone. The high performance we're now seeing has only happened since we've really felt the full force of shared services. Our subsidiaries are performing better. Now we're looking more closely at how the whole region is performing and coping with fast growth."

Sampson says that SAP's shared services implementation has delivered measurable savings "... in excess of 40%. Not only that, but we have increased our focus on high value-added decision support provided to the business. These are the critical success factors in a high-performance finance organization."

The move has been so successful that SAP is continuing to expand the scope of operations covered by shared services. "People in the field now come to us and say, 'Would you put that in for us because we think that you could do a better job than we can,' " says Sampson. "That's a sign that they've accepted it and they feel that there's a value add in doing it – and that's good."

CASE STUDY

Taking a "satellite" approach to shared services

A consumer goods company, with revenues of more than $20 billion and an active business presence in 180 countries, wanted to drive operations and process convergence across Asia to reduce operating costs. See Figure 13.4.

Under a strong global directive to deliver operational savings to create shareholder value, the company identified centralized shared services in IT and finance processes as potential areas for creating synergies and increasing efficiency.

The company reorganized its finance and accounting operations in three phases. In phase one, it designed business and operating models for the new finance organization, including the implementation of a shared service center. Phase two involved launching the model operationally and testing it in a pilot country. In phase three, the shared service center was rolled out to eight other business units across four countries.

The next step was to migrate the finance and accounting operations of other country offices in Northern Asia to the "satellite" center, which ultimately supported nine business units in four countries through a fully integrated enterprise resource planning (ERP) platform. In the future, the satellite center will be part of an exist-

Shared Services Vision

- Three SSC "satellite" centers providing 24-hour operational support
  - Asia Pacific - Singapore (GMT 2300–0700 hrs)
  - Europe (GMT 0700–1500 hrs)
  - Americas (GMT 1500–2300 hrs)

- Satellite centers to be part of an existing large operating company
  - leverage existing know-how and finance expertise
  - location chosen should have characteristics similar to Singapore (e.g., labor, language & infrastructure advantages)

- Operations to be "insourced" initially
  - leverage internal resources who understand the business & customers' needs
  - accrue the synergy benefits gained from shared services

- When operations stabilize, outsourcing arrangements may be considered
  - achieve further benefits through increased economies of scale

European Center

Asia/Pac Center

Americas Center

Figure 13.4   *Global consumer goods company – shared services vision*

ing large operating company leveraging existing know-how and finance expertise. While operations will be "insourced" initially, outsourcing arrangements may be considered once operations have stabilized.

The implementation successfully reduced the cost of IT operations in areas such as bank fees, audit, and the duplication of resources. The company has also benefited from an increased focus by its strategic finance professionals on specialized functions, such as tax and treasury. Overall, it now has better information visibility and control across its entire finance organization.

CASE STUDY
Opting for a single shared service center

A global manufacturer of network and mobile equipment, with annual revenues of more than $25 billion and a strong presence in Asia, was facing an increasingly competitive environment and needed to become more market responsive. As part of that process, the company had reorganized itself from a product-oriented company to one that was more customer-focused. To accomplish this, business units were consolidated and realigned to provide end-to-end solutions to customers and leverage cross-selling opportunities. Facing the need to transform back-office operations to increase efficiency, the company launched an initiative to reduce the cost of finance and accounting operations through the use of shared services.

The company established a transaction center in Tianjin, China to handle accounting operations and maintenance resource operations purchasing, as well as ERP functional and technical support to all country offices in Asia. See Figure 13.5. The foundation was built through the initial consolidation of four existing processing operations in Shanghai, Guangzhou, Tianjin, and Beijing in a phased migration. The Tianjin center rolled out its services to all country offices in the region over two years.

Several years later, the company has benefited from China's cost advantage and the language capabilities of its workforce. The center has seen a support function transformed into a customer-focused accounting business delivering a cost-effective service, while streamlined processing capabilities have led to a more efficient distribution of finance resources.

Shared Services Vision

All the back office operations in Asia Pacific would ultimately be consolidated into a single shared service center in Tianjin, China.

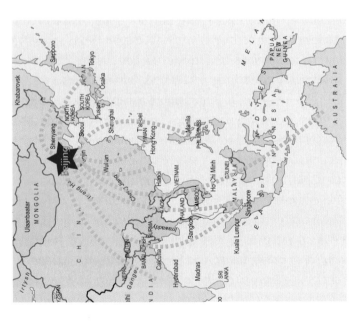

Figure 13.5   *Global network and mobile equipment manufacturer – shared services vision*

CASE STUDY
Developing a multilevel shared services program

A large global electronics company was besieged by cost pressures in both Europe and Asia. Its accounting functions were handled through numerous widely dispersed finance departments and lacked the critical mass required for maximum efficiency. The company's move to restructure its accounting system was driven by a desire to comply with US GAAP. Beyond this, accounting was under pressure to shift from an internal/statutory viewpoint to a sharper focus on responding to shareholders and analysts.

The company evaluated its options based on its existing technology and application infrastructure, skills, and capabilities. It also factored in the legal, tax, and accounting requirements of each country in which it was doing business. In the process, it formulated a strategy to manage its finance and accounting operations in Asia and created a shared services network in the region. See Figure 13.6.

As part of its shared services vision for Asia, the company set up a regional service center, national transaction centers, and a China operations center. The regional service center is responsible for delivering high-value accounting services and related IT support for corporate consolidation and reporting. The national transaction centers located in various countries focus on delivering low-cost, high-quality accounting services, such as posting transactions in payables, receivables, fixed assets, etc. The China operations center covers activities including local consolidation and tax reporting, and the reconciliation of reporting data.

This new structure simplified and standardized accounting. The company succeeded in streamlining transaction processing, resulting in the redistribution of finance resources. More significantly, savings in the total cost of information delivery have been achieved. Other benefits include a reduction in reporting events and closing time through an alignment of closing-cycle time to international standards.

REGIONAL PRIORITIES TODAY – AND IN THE FUTURE

During our interviews, we asked senior executives in Asia to evaluate how important each of the five extended finance capabilities were today,

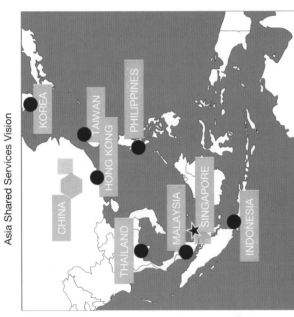

Asia Shared Services Vision

Regional Service Center
Deliver high value accounting services and related IT suppc

- Accounting experts pool for Asia
- Task force for new location transition
- Corporate consolidation and reporting
- General ledger maintenance
- Training on accounting and reporting matters
- Applications support and maintenance
- Service management tools and processes

National Transaction Centers
Deliver low cost & high quality accounting operations

- Post transactions in payables, receivables, fixed asset
- Service line and key account management
- 1st level applications support
- Relationship to local regulatory / tax authorities

China Operations Center
Additional roles are added to the transaction center

- Local consolidation and tax reporting
- Reconciliation of reporting data
- 1st and 2nd level applications support
- JV transition team
- IT fall-back location for disaster recovery

Legend

★ Regional FSSC Center   ▮ Operations Center

● National Transactions Center   ⬡ Servers

Figure 13.6   *Global electronics company – shared services vision*

and how they expected their priorities to evolve over the next three to four years. As in the rest of the world, the ultimate goal of these CFOs is to create a value-centered culture. CFOs across Asia are aligning the other four capabilities with the goal of achieving a value-driven finance model. According to these CFOs, about 50% of their finance resources are focused on financial operations and they continue to view this function as critical. However, it is not necessarily a differentiator.

As a result, many organizations have already implemented, or plan to implement, models such as shared services to support finance operations. Their goal is to free finance managers to focus on capabilities which link strategy and value, such as enterprise performance management. These forward-looking CFOs are implanting standard processes and systems through ERP implementations in order to drive the savings and process efficiencies that deliver value.

Starbucks' Jim Eschweiler says the word "values" resonates right through his company's culture and is central to all its activities, including finance. "As a finance team, we understand the company's values and try to link them to the concept of creating shareholder value. You take the company aspirations that have been laid out and connect them to each person's individual actions. Then you show how those same actions drive financial value. It makes it so much easier to execute financial strategy when we tie it to our guiding principles and our bigger picture objectives. You get buy-in so much faster because people say, 'Oh, I get it, this is consistent with our culture and values.' "

Eschweiler also rates enterprise performance management (EPM) as a "hot" area. On a scale of one to five, with five being maximum importance, he rates EPM as a "four." He explains: "It is a common need and it fits with the whole idea of what we are trying to train people to do and how we are building our finance culture. We try to get teams engaged with their peers in a different function and help lay issues and processes out and teach end-to-end. These are the actions we want to measure, this is what drives value and what does not, and this is how you make it happen. This is the operational report you need to see at this time to help you make a better decision, versus producing one three weeks later. It makes a very clean link to the value center, the culture. It is almost as if this is the vehicle to realize the value-centered organization."

At the Singapore Exchange (SGX), CFO Seck Wai Kwong says that his organization is two years into a transformation that may take five years, with enterprise performance management at its core. As noted earlier, this initiative helped drive a doubling in the enterprise value of the SGX within only 18 months. "When I first came here we didn't really have much – only very rudimentary management reports. So we started out by putting together a road map to value-based management; along the way we needed to put in place a profitability management system," says Seck. "We're trying to segment it by product and by customer, slicing and dicing it as part of the journey towards value-based management."

The executives in Asia with whom we spoke generally rated finance operations and capital stewardship lower on their agendas. SAP's Colin Sampson says that currently, finance operations are a "low priority" largely because the company has already implemented its shared services center. "It's not a focus in terms of where I spend a lot of my time right now because it's not in the development phase, it's in the maintenance phase." Sampson notes that capital stewardship hasn't been a focus in the past, but the "trend is a growing one," largely due to efforts to promote growth through brand investment and other vehicles. "I think SAP has done a tremendous job of building brand recognition over the last few years. Brand is so critical and can shift so quickly if you're not careful," he adds. "The current priority we give capital stewardship is a 2, but going forward it will increase to a 4."

Enterprise risk management is high on the CFO agenda in Asia, mainly because the region's diversity makes the ability to assess and minimize risk an ongoing concern. At logistics provider Exel, for example, Stephen Ferraby says that his challenge is operating in countries that are low cost and low margin. "Indonesia is a classic example," he points out. "If we work for a consumer goods company in Indonesia, our turnover and our margin – which tends to be pegged to the turnover – will be about a fifth of what it is for a European company of the equivalent size. However, an Asian consumer goods company is going to expect us to take on the same sort of liabilities that we assume in Europe and the US.

"One of the more difficult messages to get across to our customers is that their corporate risk management approach is pushing down a standard set of contract terms. We have to turn around and say, 'Well, hang on, a two million dollar liability for Indonesia – we'd have to be in business for fifty years to approach that kind of profit. I can't manage that risk down to zero, so how are we going to compromise on that? That is quite a tough debate …'"

CFOs are embracing the Asian finance model described earlier in this chapter to help manage risk in such key operational areas as these.

- *Finance operations* – by moving toward standard processes and systems (such as ERP), and leveraging shared services with defined processes and metrics, all of which help reduce the risk involved with disparate operations and markets across the region.

- *Enterprise performance management* – by understanding what drives value for the enterprise and then embedding these value drivers in a cycle of planning, budgeting, forecasting, and reporting. This approach enables CFOs to deploy resources to manage risk more effectively.

Pursuing high performance in Asia

Companies operating in Asia have been looking for a "one size fits all" model as a solution to address the region's diversity and complexity. However, our research shows that this is definitely not the answer to long-term success in this exciting and diverse part of the world. Organizations need to find the structures and approaches that best suit their operations in the region – and then implement them innovatively and flexibly.

The "ideal" high-performance finance organization model, however, does share some features with the tailored Asian model that is emerging. The trend is firmly toward a greater consolidation of transactional and specialized processes, skills, and capabilities, with financial analysis and decision-support embedded within geographies and business units where key decisions are made. Overall, the outlook for finance in Asia is exceptionally bright. CFOs can reap the benefits of the region's enormous growth potential by leveraging skills and attributes on a country by country basis to build their finance capabilities.

REFERENCES

1 UBS, *Prices and Earnings: A Comparison of Purchasing Power Around the Globe*; 2003.

2 International Monetary Fund, Chapter 1: Economic Prospects & Policies, *World Economic Outlook*, April 2005.

3 Dr. Yuwa Hedrick-Wong, Economic Advisor, Asia/Pacific Region, Understanding the New Asian Travelers, *MasterCard International*, September 8, 2005.

4 Arthur Clennam, Trading Up, *CFOEurope.com*, December 2004. http://www.cfoeurope.com

CHAPTER 14

High-Performance Finance in Japan

For Japan, the 1990s will be remembered in the minds of many as the "lost decade." This long period of economic recession saw company profits plummet, non-performing loans soar, and government deficits balloon – all of which led to widespread economic malaise. Only now is this period drawing to a close. But while there is relief worldwide that a recovery is at last taking hold, a sense of apprehension still runs deep, both in Japanese businesses and among consumers. Feelings of despair and pessimism may no longer be so common, but the brimming confidence once so closely associated with Japan Inc. has yet to return.

Upon closer examination, however, CFOs among others soon realize that there is more to this picture than meets the eye. The past 15 years or so have been a time of contrasting fortunes for many Japanese companies. They have emerged from this period of polarization either as winners or losers. While a number of Japanese companies have been driven to ruin and bankruptcy (Long-Term Credit Bank of Japan, Yamaichi Securities, Daiei, to name a few), others have strengthened their competitive footing, including Toyota, Canon, and the Mitsubishi Corporation, as described later in this chapter.

One of the characteristics of the winners cited above is robust financial management. For most Japanese companies of the postwar era with their focus firmly on manufacturing, finance was almost the forgotten function. Some high-profile, globally recognized companies did not even acknowledge the relevance of the cost of capital. However, a number of companies realized the importance of financial management and implemented many of the best practices commonly used in the West, such as the quarterly rolling forecast, shared services, and global cash management. With this rapid evolution in working methods, Japanese companies have entered a new era. The recent fight for control of Nippon Broadcasting System between Livedoor, a relatively unknown start-up enterprise, and Fuji TV, a listed enterprise of the First Section of the Tokyo Stock Exchange, will be talked about for years to come as an event that epitomized the transformation of Japanese business culture.

However, it is still misleading to assume that this passing of an era signifies a clean break from traditional Japanese-style management and the embrace of a completely Western management style. The two models now co-exist – much more easily than they did in the past – and successful companies are using features of both models to drive their growth. Nissan Motors, for example, has changed its management approach under Carlos Gosn's leadership, but it also retains its Japanese-style corporate genetic makeup as a legacy of the past.

JAPAN THROUGH THE LENS OF THE CFO

Japan is a nation whose national character, corporate behavior, and economic mechanisms are extremely difficult for many Western executives to decipher. However, for companies seeking to understand the dynamics of a high-performance business in this part of the world, it is essential to gain insight into Japan's unique characteristics. Key features of the Japanese approach to management are these.

The belief that something is wrong with shareholder value
Ask a question in Japan about who owns a company, and "shareholders" will almost certainly not be the answer. The concept of shareholders owning a company makes many Japanese feel uncomfortable, not because it clashes with their theories of management, but because it challenges many feelings deeply rooted in their society. Japanese people would be much more likely to say that the company is owned by its employees or by "the company itself" as a community.

Despite the relentless changes taking place in Japanese business practices, human resource management in Japanese companies is still based on the concept of lifetime employment. A new recruit does not simply "take employment" but becomes part of a community – a member of the "group of those who share the same destiny." The seniority system, in which wages are increased in response to the increasing financial needs of an employee as he or she moves forward through the stages of life, from marriage to childbirth to the education of children, gives support and reassurance to the lives of employees. As a consequence, firing employees for the sake of shareholder value – as occurs in the West – is incomprehensible to many Japanese. This thinking is hard to change, since it is not a matter of logic, nor of emotions, but of culture.

This is why arguments giving priority to the enhancement of shareholder value are not received with enthusiasm by Japanese management. Their attitude on this issue places Japanese companies at a great disadvantage in the global economy, where speed and flexibility are of paramount importance. This is true mainly because the Japanese approach of asking how employee value can be balanced with value for shareholders and others can lead to answers that are much less straightforward and quantitative than asking what is best for shareholders, which is the stance common to Western companies. As a result, managing value creation in Japanese corporations can be a daunting task.

The major banks and keiretsu
Many Japanese corporations have cross-shareholding relationships with banks and affiliated companies in an organizational arrangement called *keiretsu*. While the popularity of such practices has diminished in recent years, this cross-shareholding has traditionally been another reason why Japanese corporations have underestimated the concept of shareholder value. Shareholders were not external beings who pressured corporations by asking for returns. In this sense, it could even be said that the concept of "shareholders," as understood in Western countries, did not exist for Japanese corporations until very recently.

The relationship between Japanese corporations and major partner banks, called "main banks", is very tightly knit. A structure has been established in which corporations focus on business operations (manufacturing and marketing) while banks take care of everything on the finance side. As a result, the banking industry plays the role of CFO for many Japanese corporations. This means that banks, which also provide funds as they do in the West, are deeply involved in the financial and corporate management functions of the companies in the same *keiretsu*. The funds provided by the main bank include stocks (risk money) as well as loans and corporate bonds.

Since finance managers are providing both capital and liability, there is a potential conflict of interest between the financial management role that banks have assumed in Japan and their traditional banking role. One of the unfortunate consequences of this dual role was excessive lending and real estate investment during the bubble economy years of the 1980s.

This tight relationship between banks and corporations, however, has none of the hierarchical features associated with rulers and subjects. It is a partnership based on trust, as evidenced by the practice of cross-share-holding. This relationship is apparent in the Japanese word for "finance." In the Japanese language, financial business, such as banking, is called *kinyu*. On the other hand, the finance functions inside a corporation using these institutions are referred to as *zaimu*. While the word *kinyu* rather directly corresponds to the word "finance," the word *zaimu* is more nuanced. It literally means a business operation to "deal with" financial institutions that perform *kinyu*. This might upset those in the *zaimu* department, but the word indicates the strong tradition in which the finance functions of Japanese corporations have largely been dependent on, and performed by, external financial institutions, most particularly main banks.

Another beneficiary of cross-shareholding is *keiretsu*. A *keiretsu* is a partner company in a value chain that extends from parts to completed products, and a value network that encompasses procurement, manu-facturing, sales, logistics, and finance. However, connection with this partner company is not based on a contract stating the nature of the alliance relationship. Instead, this partnership is one based on a trusting relationship that often springs from the historic ties between organiza-tions. Therefore, it is extremely difficult for a newcomer to join a *keiretsu*. The practice of cross-shareholding is, as noted earlier, tangible evidence of this tight-knit relationship of trust.

Strong *keiretsus* are mainly those rooted in *zaibatsu*, some of which go back several hundred years. *Zaibatsus* were dissolved after World War II, when Japan was under the control of Allied forces, but re-emerged in a new form as part of Japan's post-war economy and still exist today. Mitsui and Mitsubishi, names well known to all Westerners, are major *keiretsus*. Since they have close business relationships with each other, *keiretsus* rarely act as pure shareholders. A recent notable example of this was the Mitsubishi *keiretsu* led by Tokyo-Mitsubishi Bank and the Mitsubishi Corporation coming to the rescue when the Mitsubishi Motor Corporation almost collapsed under the weight of repeated scandals. The development of shareholder-conscious value management in Japan would thus be largely affected by the future of main banks and *keiretsus*. Their historically strong connection persists even today – an important point to keep in mind.

Consensus-based decision making

Some observers have asserted that Japan does not have leaders. It is true that few foreigners would know the names of the presidents, let alone the CFOs, of Japan's leading companies, despite the fact that these are outstanding corporations in a major economy with the second highest gross national product (GNP) in the world. Of course, the low profile of its senior executives does not mean that Japan lacks leaders, only that its leaders lack visibility. Japanese corporations evaluate one's qualifications as a corporate senior executive in great detail during a lengthy screening process. GE is famous for its multi-year screening process. Japanese corporations have a similar approach and every employee is aware of the progress of such screening.

Why are Japan's outstanding corporate managers invisible to those on the outside? Primarily because the decision making process in Japan values consensus building. To Japanese corporations, the best decision making is decision making without having to take a vote. What is desired as an ideal is a situation of which everyone approves, or at the very least, to which no one proactively objects.

It cannot be denied that this consensus-based decision making puts Japanese corporations at a competitive disadvantage internationally. Above all, it slows down their ability to act and respond to the market (although, once a decision is made, action is quick and there is not much adjustment). A unanimous vote means trying to achieve 100% accuracy in the decision process and implies a need to satisfy or placate everyone. In modern economic terms, such a practice requires more cost and time than can be justified by the value it delivers. Overall, the end result is that Japanese corporations often lose out to foreign rivals who challenge them with speed-conscious decision making that is not dependent on unanimous support. Sony's failed attempt to break Apple's dominance of the market for MP3 downloaded music is one example of how this behavior harms performance when different aspects of a product/service solution are deeply embedded in separate divisions, each having its own position in the decision making process.

Attaching great importance to consensus is a national trait and is so engrained that it could well be the last business behavior to change in Japanese society. Given this attitude, it is not natural for Japanese corporations to have CFOs who stand out from other senior executives and who exercise strong leadership hand-in-hand with CEOs.

Balance-oriented mind set: "What goes up comes down ..."
There is an expression in Japanese, *"hougan biiki,"* which means to take the side that is facing eventual defeat in a righteous battle. It is often said that the Japanese are inclined to exercise this tendency in most decision making or conflict situations. Japanese people dislike extremes in almost everything. This includes levels of income and education – all 120 million people in Japan are in effect "stuck in the middle."

This does not necessarily mean that prominent individuals are not favored. If overall balance is attained as a result of including these individuals, the situation will be welcomed. Similarly, the reckless are seen to pose no problem if the attentive are also present. The point is to achieve overall balance in a certain grouping of people or things.

The Japanese find it psychologically hard to come to a decision using a single yardstick. In light of this national trait, scorecarding as a tool to measure balance among multi-stakeholders is something that many Japanese find too trivial to use in business.

A saving-oriented mind set and the spirit of diligence
The Japanese word *mottainai* expresses the feeling of regret for spending or using more than was necessary, thereby creating waste. One feels *mottainai* when something has been wasted without exercising its potential value. It is hardly possible to find any English words that will provide an accurate translation of this feeling. It is neither just "wasteful" nor "redundant." The focus is on the unrealized value that could have been obtained if the resource had not been consumed in excess.

The term "resource" includes human factors, such as a person's time and effort including consideration and thoughtfulness. Time and effort should not be overused for unproductive activities. After identifying those areas of overused time and effort, it is not enough to minimize them to the justifiable level. In the spirit of *mottainai,* you should think of the best use of the excess time and effort that have been extracted from the process. This concept is not solely about saving. In fact, no effort is spared in the spirit of producing valuable outcomes. This can be seen as the secret of the strength of Japanese manufacturing.

It is almost second nature for many Japanese to identify anything "wasteful" in terms of work tasks or materials in the production process and try to make improvements or *kaizen,* the well-known philosophy of improvement that originated with Toyota Motors. Thus, streamlining the business process would be the easiest task for someone in a CFO position in Japanese companies.

Distinctions between "insider" and "outsider"

It is often said of the Japanese that concepts of "insider" and "outsider" are rooted in its island-nation mentality and stem from the fact that Japan is not part of a continent or physically joined to other nations. However, the "insider" vs "outsider" mindset is not limited to the notion of Japanese versus foreigners. It exists at all levels and in all areas: family versus outsiders, relatives versus others, in-house versus external, and so on.

Once you are recognized within a Japanese organization as an "inside person," a relationship of mutual trust is established. This in turn inhibits reciprocal checking to monitor results, leading to a dramatic reduction of what economists call "transaction costs." In an "inside" situation, relationships of reciprocal cooperation – which are much stronger than those of a contract-based alliance – come to exist among constituent members.

The language barrier is a unique factor that widens the distinction between Japanese and non-Japanese. This barrier exists among many nationalities, but the Japanese are probably one of the world's peoples who – in general – are the least competent English speakers. Given this reality, foreign corporations are rarely able to find a way to gain acceptance as "insiders." The consequences can be far-reaching. Without a long-standing business relationship, operating a business with lower transaction costs is not easily possible for foreign corporations.

The recent move by Sony to appoint Howard Stringer as chairman attracted a great deal of attention. This was a singular event for a major company that is far from bankruptcy, and Sony's move inspired much debate in the media. A palpable degree of wariness was felt over the fact that the chairman, "the face of the company," was no longer someone "inside." This public reaction epitomized the Japanese mind set on this issue and demonstrated that it won't be easy for Japanese companies to "transplant" non-Japanese CFOs as a silver bullet to inject Western-type financial discipline.

Existence of inexpensive labor

That labor in Japan is inexpensive may not be the perception held worldwide. However, this is actually the case. First of all, Japanese housewives perform low-paying work. While Japan is no exception in witnessing equalization in the status of women, it is still common for a woman to pursue employment on a part-time basis. If she is not working in a full-time job, she may often not aspire to expand her role or seek a pay rise.

Many women are employed to perform tasks for which the unit price paid would be too low for permanent employees.

Then there are college students. The college-attendance rate in Japan is very high, but at the same time the actual college education and graduation criteria are not rigorous when compared with the tougher entrance criteria. This gives rise to a situation where many students, instead of attending college courses, work to cover their living costs or to save up for leisure activities. In an economic system where, once a student is out of college, employment for life is still the norm, college years are regarded in a positive manner as a time for individuals to experience employment of various kinds. In principle, students do not stay with a job for a long period; as a result, their labor is inexpensive.

Japan's third source of inexpensive labor is known as "freeters." "Freeter" is a Japanized English word that derives from the word "free." It denotes members of the younger generation who live on part-time jobs and seek no fixed occupation after graduating from high school or college. Employment patterns of these workers vary from part-time employment to employment as temporary staff dispatched by personnel agencies. Over four million "freeters" are said to exist in Japan, and their lifestyle is beginning to attract national attention. The number of these non-permanent employees has grown to a significant level and this is viewed with great concern. However, since they are working, "freeters" are distinguished from NEETs (Not in Education or Training).

What housewives, students and "freeters" all have in common is the fact that they have a basic income provided by a husband or a parent. These are individuals who can make ends meet even if their earnings are insufficient to support themselves fully. On average, the educational levels of these groups are very high. One estimate projects that this inexpensive and well-educated labor pool will constitute over 30% of Japan's total workforce by the year 2010. As shown in Figure 14.1, a decrease in the numbers of full-time employees is forecast through 2015.

Due to the abundance of such inexpensive labor, the need for foreign workers is low and progress in receiving overseas workers is not being made in Japan. In this context, it could be said that Japan is one of the nations where "outsourcing" is now rather advanced. As a result of Japan's indigenous low-cost labor, the opportunity to reduce costs further through Western-style outsourcing is often unexpectedly small. However, as a practice, Japan's distinctive form of outsourcing doesn't alleviate management workload, since the processes are still managed internally.

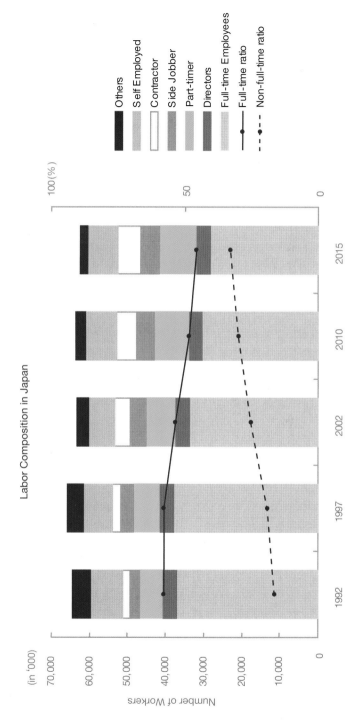

Figure 14.1 *Rapidly decreasing full-time employees*

HIGH-PERFORMANCE BUSINESSES IN JAPAN: THE IMPACT OF GROWING POLARIZATION

Since 1990, the contrast in competitiveness between successful and under-performing businesses in Japan has become increasingly apparent. Various industries are now seeing a clear division between winners and losers. The competitiveness gap is also becoming visible between different industries. Export-based industries with a higher proportion of their sales in overseas markets – such as the automobile, high-tech manufacturing, infotainment, and computer games industries – are generally more competitive. In fact, successful Japanese corporations in these export-oriented industries are proving to be extremely strong competitors in global markets.

This gap between industries suggests that Japan's domestic market is not a fully competitive one. In the domestic market there are still many regulations or less explicit "administrative directives" issued by government agencies; these externally imposed strictures control corporate activity and critical competitive factors, such as new entry into a market. In industries with a higher proportion of their sales in the domestic market, such as manufacturing, retail or infrastructure, there are noticeably more uncompetitive companies than there are global players. In the retail industry, for instance, the industry giant Daiei has been declared "not self-sustaining" and put under an industry revitalization program.

At the same time, the last 15 years have seen the emergence of a wide range of start-up companies. Many of these start-ups which surged in number during the "dot-com bubble" years of the mid-1990s have disappeared. However, some powerful ones, such as Rakuten, have survived and have grown to have a significant impact on the Japanese economy. Most of Japan's successful start-up companies have not yet entered overseas markets, but it is conceivable that they may grow to be corporations on par with such global dot-com era successes as Google.

Since the bubble economy peaked in 1989 before beginning its rapid demise, the Japanese economy has gone through three major stages, which are shown in Figure 14.2.

Between 1990 and 1994, companies could not adjust their operations quickly enough to cope with the rapid bursting of the bubble, and they ended up plunging into the red as they burned up cash flow. Companies slammed the brakes on capital investment. Some were even forced to draw from internal reserves, but their cash inflows dwindled faster due

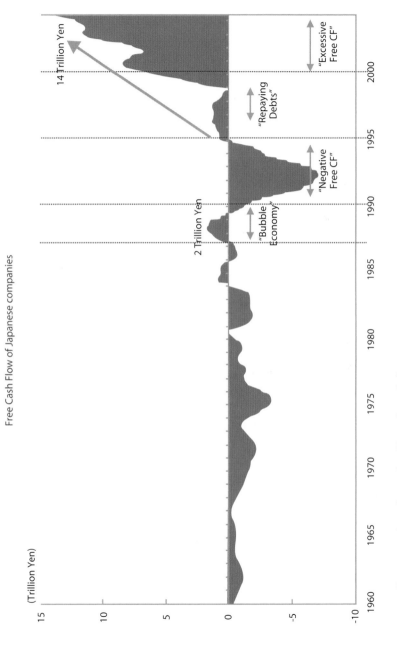

Figure 14.2 *Resurrection from the "lost decade"*

to diminished consumption and investment. During this period, interest-bearing debts continued to accumulate, ballooning until they finally peaked at 641 trillion yen in 1995.

From 1995 to 1999, companies cut back on aggressive investment activities due to unprecedented deflation, and the massive downward pressure of interest-bearing debts became an important issue to resolve. Most surplus cash flow was used to repay the interest-bearing debts, resulting in very low levels of free cash flow. During this period, internal reserves recovered at a gradual pace. The reforms introduced by Carlos Gosn at the Nissan Motor Co. Ltd date from this period, and the company managed to achieve virtually debt-free business operations within a few years after he took the helm. These years, when salary levels were frozen, inspired a deeper sense of anxiety in Japanese citizens than was actually warranted by economic reality and saw a major dampening of consumer sentiment and demand.

Most recently, the period from 2000 to 2004 has been a time of excess cash generation. Free cash flow recovered rapidly, due to reforms initiated by corporations and was aided by the general recovery of the economy. Internal reserves of corporations reached a record 25 trillion yen in 2003. But the corporations failed to find good investment opportunities for their free cash flow, causing increased dividend distributions to be paid out under the name of "returns to shareholders." One exception, as shown in Figure 14.3, was expansion in the investment area of M&A – a trend that continues today, and will be explored later in this chapter.

HIGH-PERFORMANCE BUSINESSES IN JAPAN

An unprecedented number of listed companies – 61 in total – had consolidated profits of more than 100 billion yen in FY2004, up about 60% from the 38 in FY2003. The members of the "100 Billion Yen Club" are listed in Figure14.4. In addition to the automobile and high-tech manufacturing industries, primary industries such as steel and chemicals posted increased profits due to skyrocketing resource prices, along with trading firms. Industry-leading regulars such as Toyota, Nissan, and Honda (automobile), Denso (automobile parts), Canon (high-tech), JFE and Nippon Steel (steel), and Mitsubishi and Mitsui (trading) top the corporate performance rankings. In the chemical industry, Shin-Etsu Chemical, with turnover of about 970 billion yen, is ranked number one in profits, surpassing Mitsubishi Chemical, which has the largest turnover in the industry.

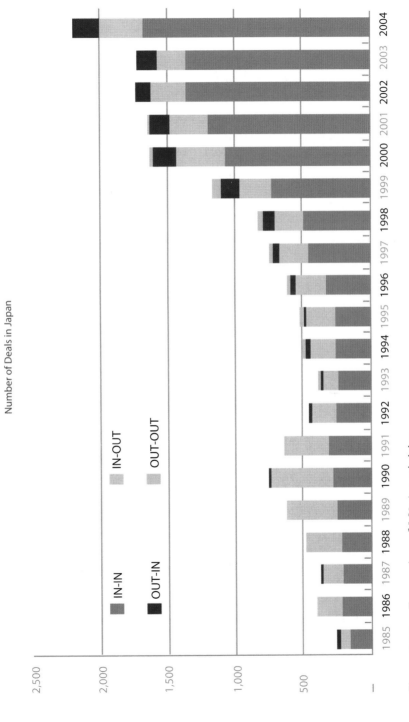

Number of Deals in Japan

Figure 14.3 *Expansion of M&A activities*

Companies with profit exceeding 100 Billion Yen

Auto/Auto Parts	Profit (Oku Yen)	Change (%)	Ranking
Toyota Motor Corporation	17,546	-1	1
Nissan Motor Co. Ltd.	8,557	6	4
Honda Motor Co. Ltd.	6,568	2	5
DENSO Corporation	2,247	15	17
Bridgestone Corporation	1,815	9	23
Kubota Corporation	1,615	496	29
Suzuki Motor Corporation	1,095	15	55

High-Tech	Profit (Oku Yen)	Change (%)	Ranking
Canon Inc.	5,521	23	6
Hitachi Ltd.	2,645	12	14
Matsushita Electric Industrial Co. Ltd.	2,469	45	16
Fuji Photo Film Co. Ltd.	1,623	-2	28
Sony Corporation	1,572	9	31
Sharp Corporation	1,405	26	39
Nintendo Co. Ltd.	1,400	179	40
Ricoh Company Ltd.	1,353	-5	42
Fanuc Ltd.	1,237	37	46
Dai Nippon Printing Co. Ltd.	1,204	24	48
NEC Corporation	1,156	-28	51
Toshiba Corporation	1,105	-24	53
Kyocera Corporation	1,075	-7	56
Sega Sammy Holdings Inc.	1,040	-	60
Mitsubishi Electric Corporation	1,023	21	61

Resouces	Profit (Oku Yen)	Change (%)	Ranking
JFE Holdings Inc.	4,606	111	7
Nippon Steel Corporation	3,714	115	10
INPEX Corporation	2,586	173	15
Nippon Oil Corporation	2,124	272	18
Sumitomo Metal Industries Ltd.	1,732	152	27
Shin-Etsu Chemical Co. Ltd.	1,515	21	34
Mitsubishi Chemical Corporation	1,480	79	36
Nippon Mining Holdings Inc.	1,480	176	37
Asahi Glass Co. Ltd.	1,356	-	41
Sumitomo Chemical Co. Ltd.	1,234	86	47
Kobe Steel Ltd. (Kobelco)	1,160	128	50
Asahi Kasei Corporation	1,128	110	52

Trading/Liner	Profit (Oku Yen)	Change (%)	Ranking
Mitsubishi Corporation	2,097	40	20
Mitsui & Co. Ltd.	1,756	98	25
Mitsui O.S.K. Lines	1,749	93	26
NYK Line	1,548	107	33
Sumitomo Corporation	1,513	39	35
Ito-Chu Corporation	1,199	-	49
Kawasaki Kisen Kaisha Ltd.	1,072	71	57

Food/Pharma/Retail	Profit (Oku Yen)	Change (%)	Ranking
Takeda Pharmaceutical Company Ltd.	4,421	-1	8
Japan Tobacco Inc.	2,702	27	13
Ito-Yokado Co. Ltd.	2,082	4	21
Seven-Eleven Japan Co. Ltd.	1,782	5	24
AEON Co. Ltd.	1,560	19	32
Kao Corporation	1,253	2	45
Astellas Pharma Inc.	1,101	12	54
Kirin Brewery Co. Ltd.	1,065	13	58

Communication/Utility	Profit (Oku Yen)	Change (%)	Ranking
NTT Corporation	17,233	13	2
NTT DoCoMo Inc.	12,882	17	3
Tokyo Electric Power Company	4,082	33	9
The Kansai Electric Power Co. Inc.	2,978	59	11
KDDI Corporation	2,863	4	12
East Japan Railway Company	2,123	-6	19
Chubu Electric Power Co. Inc.	1,951	6	22
Kyushu Electric Power Co. Inc.	1,599	40	30
Central Japan Railway Company	1,423	9	38
Tokyo Gas Co. Ltd.	1,328	1	43
Vodafone K.K.	1,270	-30	44
Tohoku-Electric Power Co. Inc.	1,043	-6	59

Figure 14.4 *Companies in "100 Billion Yen Club"*

As shown in Figure 14.5, there is significant overlap in the ranking of total market capitalization and profit ranking. Toyota has the best total market capitalization among Japanese corporations, at slightly less than 13.9 trillion yen, far surpassing the second-ranked NTT Docomo. In the high-tech manufacturing industry, Canon has the highest total market capitalization and ranks fourth overall, but ranks tenth in terms of economic value added.

Particularly noticeable among those corporations with large gaps between total market capitalization and current economic value added is the Mitsubishi Corporation. It is 16th in the total market capitalization ranking, the best among trading companies, despite being 109th in the current economic value added ranking. This suggests that the trading company business model's future value is expected to be very high by the market. In fact, this trading company business model does not exist in Western countries – and represents a worthy research subject in itself. The basic new model of a trading company is one that finds potential new business and makes investments in it, creating a new business/cash flow and making an income from the business flow or the capital from sales of stocks or assets. Its competitiveness depends on its ability to create and develop new business.

Another way of looking at Japanese corporations is to view their rankings in terms of the growth rate of total market capitalization. Despite the fact that the 2005 Nikkei average remains lower by 70% or more than its average level at the end of 1989 when the bubble economy peaked, there are some robust companies that have increased their total market capitalization. The high-tech company, Nihon Densan, for example, ranks first against this criterion – and increased its total market capitalization almost ninefold between 1989 and 2005. The company has been boosted by the acquisition of more than 20 companies, but the market is evaluating its acquisitions as higher than the acquisition costs incurred because they have actually created consolidated values. In the chemical industry, Shin-Etsu Chemical, which has continued to post record profits for the last ten consecutive years, ranks 17th.

Organizational capability still seems to be the "secret of success" for some of Japan's successful corporations, such as Toyota Motor and the Mitsubishi Corporation. In many other corporations, it is the leadership skills of managers that have proven to be a major factor in improved business performance. The names of these managers may not be internationally well recognized, but they are outstanding leaders by any measure. Fujio Mitarai of Canon, Chihiro Kanekawa of Shin-Etsu Chemical, and

Market Value and Economic Profit Ranking

	Company	Market Value (Oku Yen)	EP (Oku Yen)	EP Rank
1	Toyota Motor Corporation	138,985	18,587	2
2	NTT DoCoMo Inc.	81,329	10,034	6
3	NTT Corporation	69,261	1,585	87
4	Canon Inc.	50,086	7,001	10
5	Honda Motor Co. Ltd.	47,813	5,915	14
6	Nissan Motor Co. Ltd.	47,332	6,800	12
7	Takeda Pharmaceutical Company Ltd.	45,776	4,176	27
8	Sony Corporation	39,511	1,739	76
9	Matsushita Electric Industrial Co. Ltd.	38,930	6,011	13
10	Tokyo Electric Power Company	34,701	22,201	1
11	Yahoo Japan Corporation	33,221	533	267
12	Japan Tobacco Inc.	27,800	3,833	29
13	Seven-Eleven Japan Co. Ltd.	25,016	2,711	39
14	Astellas Pharma Inc.	22,629	1,427	102
15	East Japan Railway Company	22,000	12,493	4
16	Mitsubishi Corporation	21,975	1,289	109
17	Denso Corporation	21,660	5,762	15
18	Hitachi Ltd.	21,186	4,404	25
19	KDDI Corporation	20,738	7,033	9
20	The Kansai Electric Power Co. Inc.	20,361	12,761	3
21	Central Japan Railway Company	19,421	7,437	8
22	Chubu Electric Power Co. Inc.	18,864	11,075	5
23	Sharp Corporation	18,582	4,164	28
24	Nippon Steel Corporation	17,970	4,996	18
25	Fuji Photo Film Co. Ltd.	17,806	1,947	60

Market Value Growth Ranking

	Company	1989 12/29	2005 5/13	Growth (times)
1	Nidec Corporation (Nihon Densan)	1,011	8,671	8.58
2	Toyota Boshoku Corporation	531	4,072	7.67
3	Rohm Co. Ltd.	1,900	11,761	6.19
4	J.Bridge Corp.	159	808	5.08
5	Hisamitsu Pharmaceutical Co. Inc.	590	2,731	4.63
6	Shimamura Co. Ltd.	776	3,101	4.00
7	Keyence Corporation	2,778	10,575	3.81
8	Canon Inc.	13,354	49,730	3.72
9	Keihin Corporation	333	1,233	3.70
10	HOYA Corporation	3,469	12,830	3.70
11	Kibun Food Chemifa Co. Ltd.	190	694	3.65
12	Shinkou Electric Industries Co. Ltd.	466	1,676	3.60
13	Nitto Denko Corporation	3,099	10,530	3.40
14	Nissen Co. Ltd.	214	699	3.27
15	ORIX Corporation	4,103	13,349	3.25
16	Arisawa Manufacturing Co. Ltd.	365	1,093	2.99
17	Shin-etsu Chemical Co. Ltd.	5,732	16,474	2.87
18	Commuture	141	393	2.79
19	Murata Manufacturing Co. Ltd.	4,436	12,164	2.74
20	Honda Motor Co. Ltd.	17,420	47,535	2.73
21	Ibiden Co. Ltd. Corporation	1,121	2,995	2.67
22	Tokyo Electron Limited	3,918	10,060	2.57
23	Unicharm Corporation	1,348	3,215	2.39
24	Advantest Corporation	3,169	7,464	2.36
25	Diamond City	505	1,177	2.33
26	Hirose Electric Co. Ltd.	1,840	4,262	2.32
27	Takeda Pharmaceutical Company Ltd.	20,240	46,865	2.32
28	Namco Ltd.	741	1,703	2.30
29	Tokyo Seimitsu Co. Ltd. (Accretech)	612	1,381	2.26
30	Suzuki Mortor Corporation	3,974	8,948	2.25

Figure 14.5 *Companies valued by the capital market*

Shigenobu Nagamori of Nihon Densan are all good examples.

In the discussion that follows, we highlight the factors that distinguish these leading corporations and excellent managers from less successful ones. In particular, we explore the finance and performance management capabilities that they exhibit.

HIGH-PERFORMANCE FINANCE IN JAPAN

Are Japan's successful companies becoming identical to Western-style global businesses? Or are they succeeding through a mysterious, uniquely Japanese approach? The answer lies somewhere in between these two extremes. While safeguarding their Japanese identity, many successful companies are adapting and using the methods of Western global companies. In addition, they are leveraging practices that have been embraced for a long time by *both* Japan and Western companies, such as a focus on intangible assets. It is a mistake to view the adoption of such practices as an either/or issue. Even when Western companies are competing in the Japanese market and using Japanese employees to provide services to Japanese customers, it is difficult for them to succeed by applying a purely Western approach.

Below is an analysis of how companies in Japan are using the finance mastery framework we introduced in Chapter 3.

Value-centered culture

Which stakeholders do Japanese companies consider when creating value? As noted earlier, their primary concerns in this area are employees, the continuation of the company, and the *keiretsu*. Additionally, Japanese companies are quite comfortable with the philosophy of creating value for customers; many of these companies have adopted the slogan "customer first." However, they do not feel comfortable with the idea of creating value for shareholders.

Becoming a high-performance business will be difficult as long as management remains reluctant to adequately promote the creation of value for shareholders as a key business principle. Creating a culture that recognizes the importance of shareholder value is among the greatest challenges that Japanese companies face. However, Japanese high performers are exceptionally successful in building and sustaining this type of culture through human resource initiatives, such as compensation design and training, or through clear communication from top management.

These required changes are not simply a matter of switching over from the current negation of shareholders to an exclusive focus on them. What is required is an appropriate awareness of shareholders that achieves a balance with the other stakeholders who have traditionally been important to Japanese companies.

CASE STUDY
Developing a value-centered culture

Canon Inc. is a high-tech manufacturer whose core products comprise a full suite of office equipment. In recent times, the company's sustained performance has been excellent. It has posted record profits for four consecutive years up to FY2003. Canon's net income is the fifth largest among Japanese corporations behind Toyota Motor Corporation, NTT Docomo, Inc., Nissan Motor Co. Ltd. and Honda Motor Co. Ltd. Canon ranks above such high-tech powerhouses as Sony, NEC, and Fuji Photo Film Co. Ltd.

The guiding philosophy of Fujio Mitarai, president of the company since 1995, is that "Profits make employees happy." In his view, "The firmer your financial standing is, the more capable you are of making appropriate investments when necessary. You can continue doing what you love because you make profits."[1]

In fact, since Mitarai assumed his post, Canon has improved its financial results and its market performance has also improved considerably. The company's level of dependency on interest-bearing debt has been reduced from nearly 34% (when Mitarai took the job) to less than 5% today, making Canon almost a debt-free business.

As executive director in charge of administrative functions (e.g., accounting, human resources, and general affairs) at the company's headquarters, Mitarai successfully put strategic control into the hands of the accounting department, having pushed through his budget reforms in the face of strong resistance from Canon's business departments. He succeeded not merely in revolutionizing the company's operating systems, but also in hammering home to Canon's different business departments his view that any company, including its subsidiary companies, should be unified through consolidated accounting. This was the starting point for the corporate reforms he has been introducing since he became president.

Some of Canon's reforms have provoked resentment among its employees. Examples include the withdrawal from under-performing businesses such as PC manufacturing, the introduction of a reward system based on merit that could lift the salary of top employees by as much as 100% by the age of 40, and the abolishment of a flexible time system. Despite the controversy he has provoked, Mitarai is bullish about the changes: "Doing something when you are cornered by poor performance and left with no other choice and have everyone's consensus, is not a true reform."

This is not to say that Canon undervalues its employees; at the root of this bold decision making is a conviction that employees are assets. Mitarai also pledges to maintain lifetime employment. Since its founding, the corporate ethos of Canon Inc. has been that of the "Spirit of 3 Selves," comprising "self-motivation, self-governance, and self-awareness." Mitarai has revived this tradition by introducing a policy where each employee explores and evaluates his or her role within the company. To aid this process, new proposals for employee action guidelines have been formulated and training has been re-evaluated.

"The moral sensibility not to betray others, human compassion, and homogeneous abilities are Japanese strengths," Mitarai says. "But the weakness of Japanese companies lies in the fact that the abilities are not brought together." Canon's president says that he is searching for a new business model under which the maximum potential of individuals is realized, both in terms of their individual creativity and their contribution to the seamless functioning of a team. This new model is one that is neither exclusively Japanese nor conventionally Western.

Enterprise performance management (EPM)

Historically, Japanese companies have always been conscious of the need to balance the present and the future with an eye to the continuation of the organization. The issue for performance management in Japanese companies is its speed of execution. The business management cycle for most Japanese businesses is overwhelmingly yearly. In typical Japanese companies, yearly planning and budgeting processes take from three to five months – comparable to the time frame required in the West. These planning and budgeting activities demand an enormous investment of time by employees. Like their Western counterparts, most Japanese companies are hamstrung by this cumbersome process.

Performance management carried out by Japanese companies does not go beyond point solutions, such as the introduction of a balanced scorecard or of economic profit and other economic value-added indicators. Even now, few companies actually undertake a real review of the end-to-end performance management cycle. In contrast, Japan's high-performance companies are implementing performance management on quarterly, monthly, or at times, even shorter cycles. The frequency of these cycles is a source of these companies' competitiveness. They have exhaustively compressed and streamlined their yearly planning and budgeting efforts and are changing over to a forecast-centered performance management process.

Many companies are also dealing with the issue, which arises in the later stages of the performance management cycle, of disclosing information to shareholders and capital markets. Although companies listed on the Tokyo Stock Exchange have at last been required to issue business results on a quarterly basis, the details required for disclosure in Japan remain inadequate when judged by Western standards of reporting, transparency, and governance.

Investor relations (IR) is a relatively new business issue in Japan. In Japanese companies, investor relations activities have not been seen as a core management responsibility. In many cases, investor relations functions are being incorporated into general affairs or administrative departments which are responsible for annual shareholder meetings – despite the fact that they lack full financial knowledge. Although there has been a recent increase in the number of companies with dedicated investor relations departments, the reality is that many of these are just window dressing. Successful Japanese companies, on the other hand, are more effective in the IR area than ordinary companies. They ensure that each quarter their presidents or CFOs attend road shows, including those overseas, and that they disclose a considerable amount of detail about the drivers of their business performance.

CASE STUDY
The importance of effective forecasting

Shin-Etsu Chemical holds significant global market share in products such as vinyl chloride and silicon wafers for semiconductors. The business performance of these products is subject to the commodity market, yet Shin-Etsu Chemical posted record profits for ten consecutive years until 2004. Despite the small scale of its operation, the total market value of Shin-Etsu Chemical exceeds 1.6 trillion yen, making the company one of the top five in the industry worldwide after major global players such as Dow Chemical Company and Bayer. Among Japanese chemical producers, Shin-Etsu Chemical's market capitalization is more than double that of the second largest company, Sumitomo Chemical.

The strength of Shin-Etsu Chemical lies in its ability to accurately forecast market fluctuations. Its shrewd analysis of data has enabled the company to predict changes in market conditions and given it a competitive edge in price negotiations and the adjustment of supply to demand. By the time its competitors become aware of such changes, Shin-Etsu Chemical has already left them far behind.

This ability to look ahead comes from Chihiro Kanekawa, the president of the company since 1990. Kanekawa bases decisions not on intuition, but rather on the accurate analysis of information. He personally examines and analyzes the sales report that arrives every morning from Shintech, Inc., a subsidiary vinyl chloride company based in Houston. Without delay, he provides instructions based on his analysis. "Mr. Kanekawa is very quick to arrive at a decision and always takes action to move forward in the future," says Frank Popoff, independent director and retired CEO of Dow Chemical.

In the reports that he receives, Kanekawa does not allow words such as "generally" or "broadly;" instead, he insists that these reports be put together on the basis of specific, concrete facts. He personally keeps track of a wide range of information so he can analyze and make predictions about the market situation. He takes particular note of trends in orders from customers. Any changes to "regular" monthly or weekly orders, any postponement or cancellation of a contract – everything is considered. Such developments may well signal a more far-reaching change in overall market conditions. Akira Kaneko, special advisor to the company, says, "President Kanekawa does not have the words 'monthly closing' in his dictionary. What he has is 'daily closing.' " Kanekawa completely changed the EPM capabilities of Shin-Etsu Chemical and they are now embedded as an indispensable part of its daily operation.[2]

Capital stewardship

As a people, the Japanese prize thrift. Reducing waste is almost instinctual for Japanese businesses, and reducing capital waste should in theory be an easy task for Japanese companies to accomplish. However, in reality, a lot of waste remains in their settlement and payment processes. The still common use of promissory notes slows down the collection of receivables, reducing capital efficiency. Many Japanese companies do not understand how to optimize capital flow due to the fact that, while they focus on "business" (manufacturing and management), they entrust their "financial" operations to banks.

Japan's most successful organizations have dramatically reduced the payment of interest and commissions by using pooling, in-house banking, and the netting of receivables and liabilities for companies within consolidated groups. There is great variation in the size of businesses within such consolidated groups: There are large companies with good credit ratings and small-to-medium-sized companies that can only attain low ratings. In these diverse situations, cash management initiatives such as pooling can be very effective in reducing costs. An increasing number of successful businesses are carrying out these measures, not only domestically but globally.

CASE STUDY
Relentless discipline in capital management

With a consolidated profit for FY2004 in excess of 1.7 trillion yen, the highest in Japanese industry, Toyota Motor Corporation has exceptional profit-generating capabilities. This profitability is driven by a relentless pursuit of cost reduction. Interestingly, there is no term for "cost reduction" in the vocabulary of unique Toyota words that pertain to management – a list that includes the globally-famous kaizen, which denotes a managerial striving for continuous improvement. Instead, Toyota management speaks of "reducing waste." Cost should be incurred when required, but waste should be reduced as much as possible.

Toyota does not use the formal title of CFO. Takashi Araki is one of the most famous CFOs in Japan, but he is reluctant to be addressed merely as a CFO. As he puts it, "At Toyota, the awareness of the importance of finance capabilities permeates the company as a whole through the Toyota Production System, and there is no extra need to emphasize it."

Toyota's success in comprehensively eliminating waste is not restricted to the factory floor. The company is also removing waste in the management of capital. Since 1999, Toyota has been working in cooperation with Citigroup in Japan, North America, Europe, and throughout Asia to introduce a cash management system for the centralized management of subsidiaries' funds. Within Japan, Toyota has been managing the inflow and outflow of cash for its subsidiaries, netting receivables and liabilities among them, and carrying out in-house banking where necessary. As a result of these measures in eliminating waste in all its companies, Toyota has achieved cash flow in excess of 2.2 trillion yen and has even been given the nickname "The Toyota Bank."

There is criticism from capital markets that having such a large cash reserve is reducing capital efficiency, but Toyota is indifferent. Araki has stated that, "We need both short-term returns, and long-term growth." He considers this cash reserve a "safety measure" that allows Toyota to swiftly make strategic investments – such as investments in fuel cells, information technology, and environmental measures – that require several hundred billion yen. President Fujio Cho says: "We have achieved sound profits through the daily, continuous use of kaizen. This doesn't have the flashiness of the violent ups and downs beloved of investors. However, we are increasing profits just as we promised to do for them. Some people may say that having large sums of cash at hand is inefficient, but Toyota's core values won't change, even with a change in top management."[3]

Enterprise risk management

Handling risk quantitatively is an area in which Japanese companies are weak. Managing uncertainty is an integral part of business, yet the majority of Japanese companies handle business risk qualitatively, not by relying on figures. Arguments such as "because the same case happened in the past," "because it feels right," or "because we will be OK even if it fails" are some of the rationalizations that inhibit quantitative management.

Even financial institutions are significantly lagging behind the West when it comes to their abilities in quantitative risk management. Instead of making credit decisions based upon independent risk evaluations, banks follow the custom of giving credit based upon collateral. It could be said that the reason that Japanese businesses are so far behind in their use of quantitative risk management is that there wasn't much of a need for it. On the purely domestic front, the Japanese economy has a risk reduction system in it, consisting of reciprocal arrangements in a closed community. However, because this system cannot be applied to overseas markets, export-based industries have taken the lead in using robust risk management practice such as foreign exchange risk hedging. The same can be said about trading companies in that they deal with the flow of goods on a global scale, including importing and exporting.

When compared with market risk and credit risk, it is relatively easy for manufacturing-oriented Japanese companies to appreciate the necessity and value of operational risk management. Recent scandals at Snow Brand and Mitsubishi Motors, combined with the move towards SOX compliance, have created a sudden increase in interest among Japanese companies in managing operational risk. Moreover, apart from regular market risk, credit risk, and operational risk, Japan faces many other economic uncertainties, such as the politics of its relationships with other Asian countries (where the question of Japan's acknowledgement of its history is a perennial issue), and Japan's natural phenomena (earthquakes, climate). Coping with these risks is a continuing issue for Japanese companies.

CASE STUDY
Measuring risks and rewards

With 200 million yen net operating profit for FY2004, and more than 2 trillion yen in total market capitalization, the Mitsubishi Corporation is by far the largest trading company in Japan. Mitsubishi is pushing a change in its business model from that of a traditional trading company that lives on commission to one that focuses on business investment. In 2002, slightly under 70% of its profits came from investment-related activities.

Mitsubishi included in its 2003 mid-term business plan a policy of comprehensive management of its business portfolio in order to return to a healthy balance sheet. CFO Ichiro Mizuno states, "In this time of severe deflation, we need more solid assets and balance sheets if we are to achieve a continuous expansion in earnings. Making that happen is the role of the CFO."[4]

A look at the details of Mitsubishi's business portfolio management reveals several important initiatives.[5][6]

1 *Four areas were selected as strategic business fields in which Mitsubishi will concentrate its investments: energy and resources, food and food products, information and communication, and project development.*

2 *Mitsubishi has introduced a business unit system to allow detailed management of each area of focus. The whole enterprise is divided up into approximately 190 business units. Performance accounting is carried out for each unit, which is classified into one of three types depending on its mission. Specifically, these categories are "expansion" – already existing businesses that are to be maintained or expanded; "growth" – good future prospects to which priority should be given for investment of resources; and "restructuring" – businesses which, if not fundamentally restructured, should be withdrawn.*

3 *Mitsubishi's 2003 annual report stipulated that "the first step to returning our assets to a healthy status is to accurately measure risks and to carry out continuous reforms in order that there are healthy returns in line with this." In keeping with this policy, Mitsubishi has introduced its unique "Mitsubishi Corporation Value Added" measure of economic profit. This measure, MCVA, is calculated as operating profit minus (maximum expected loss – shareholder capital costs). Rather than simply looking at the difference between profits and capital cost, MCVA also takes risk into account.*

4 *As an enhanced risk management measure, Mitsubishi has introduced exit standards, such as "three consecutive years in the red." In the four years since 1999, 123 companies have been removed from the business portfolio based on this standard, resulting in a 300 billion yen reduction in assets.*

Traditional intermediary-type business in Japan has been low-risk, low-return. However, Mitsubishi and other trading companies, which are focusing upon the investment business, are taking on broader risk and require rigorous business portfolio management based upon sophisticated risk-analysis techniques. Looking back, trading companies' history shows that they have always spearheaded a new paradigm in the Japanese economy. Mitsubishi's efforts may well be the key required for Japan to reclaim its growth potential.

Finance and accounting operations

Streamlining back-office functions, including finance and accounting (F&A), is one of the reforms that has been undertaken by many Japanese companies. In a wide range of industries, companies are undertaking the improvement and standardization of their back-office functions. Transactional operations are being centralized into shared service centers, and economies of scale have brought about a cost reduction effect. Teijin Ltd and Omron Corporation are some of the best-known examples of enterprises involved in this practice.

A major issue in Japanese business is how to maintain the impetus to drive such reform initiatives. In Japanese companies, it is rare for prominent leaders to offer top-down direction and to push reforms across departments. In successful companies, such leaders do exist, but a more common solution is to set forth clear-cut target numbers. For example, if consensus is reached on the establishment of a quantitative goal of 25% streamlining, then all that remains is executing a series of initiatives – a task at which Japanese companies excel.

Another issue is whether individual companies have a growth strategy in place. In Japan, even in the event of streamlining, most surplus employees are not laid off. As reforms continue to streamline F&A operations, questions arise as to where to place these staffers and how to re-utilize them. The absence of a growth strategy and failure to reassign surplus staff often put the streamlining process on hold.

Another finance capability – M&A expertise

In addition to the finance mastery capabilities mentioned above, another area is rapidly increasing in importance for Japanese companies: their merger and acquisition (M&A) abilities. M&A is still novel among many Japanese companies as a proactive, strategic capability. Japanese companies have strong employee loyalty and many employees will leave in the event of a hostile takeover, making success difficult. This is not to say that Japan hasn't experienced M&A activity. For the most part, however, these efforts have been carried out through long-term, gradual increases in controlling shares or through bail-outs of failing companies. As such, these actions are based upon trust and reciprocal arrangements. Overall, in Japan, M&A numbers have been small.

We are seeing significant changes in these circumstances in the excess cash era of the 2000s. There have been very few hostile takeovers, but M&A is situated as a strategic measure, and there is a movement to look at it afresh as something to engage in positively and actively.

CASE STUDY
The art of the M&A deal, Japanese style

In the last 15 years, Nihon Densan (Nidec Corporation) has experienced the highest growth of all Japanese public companies in terms of market capitalization. Aspiring to become "the world's No. 1 manufacturer of drive-unit technology," the Kyoto-based company, which has only been in business since 1973, had a turnover of slightly less than 500 billion yen in FY2004. In 2005, its total market capitalization surpassed 860 billion yen.

It is the strong personality of Shigenobu Nagamori, founder and president of the company, that has driven Nihon Densan's rapid growth. Nagamori has a grand vision for Nihon Densan. He says: "First, [we would like to achieve] sales of 1 trillion yen, an operating profit of 100 billion yen and 100,000 employees by 2010. That should certainly qualify us as a major corporation to be reckoned with in the minds of many. After achieving the goal, we will expand the company to become a group with 10 trillion yen in sales by 2020. Some may call me a dreamer, but it is our company policy to dream big dreams."[7]

The key factor in the exponential growth of Nihon Densan is its policy of mergers and acquisitions. Its first major acquisition was the Torin Corp., a major US fan manufacturer. Since then, and up until the acquisition of Sankyo Seiki Mfg. Co. Ltd in 2003, the company has been involved in 23 M&A operations at home and abroad. An aggressive M&A policy is central to the company's future plans. Faced with the challenge of increasing sales from slightly less than 500 billion yen in FY2004 to the ambitious target of 1 trillion yen by 2010, the company envisions reaching the 800 billion yen level through "organic growth" and achieving the remaining 200 billion yen through its M&A activities.

Contrary to common Western practice, Nihon Densan does not appoint presidents to the companies it acquires. After investing in a company, Nihon Densan lets the company keep its own president, thereby allowing it to preserve its corporate culture. Even when divesting overlapping businesses, Nihon Densan is careful to ensure that the better one, not necessarily Nihon Densan's unit, is retained. The bottom line for Nihon Densan is efficiency – that is, and has always been, the Nihon Densan way. On the other hand, until an acquired company becomes self-reliant, Nihon Densan will send several officers there as "missionaries" so that the principles of the Nagamori brand of management philosophy can be fully communicated to the incumbent management.

"I only look at their technology when I buy a company," says Nagamori. "I have always believed that if the technology is good, it is not so serious if there are problems in other areas. I consider it my job as a corporate manager to fix these problems. Even if a company is not very profitable, I can tell whether or not the company is worth buying by looking at its technologies or products."

The success of Nihon Densan is largely the result of Nagamori's rigorous management underpinned by his unique personality. The sustainability of that success depends on whether any of Nihon Densan's employees can become as successful a manager as Shigenobu Nagamori.

Japanese corporations operate in a unique business environment. High-performance businesses in this market face challenges that differ significantly from those of their global competitors. And they are coping with those challenges by virtue of their excellence in finance capabilities. Some aspects of these capabilities are comparable with those of Western high-performance businesses, others are not. But to become a high-performance business in Japan, is it enough for companies to merely strengthen their finance capabilities? The answer is no. In order for their enhanced finance capabilities to produce results, companies must address one very important issue: The need to establish the position of CFO.

Japanese companies do not have a single person who is responsible for the tasks that are typically carried out by the CFO in Western companies. In quintessential Japanese companies, with the exception of the CEO, all senior executives are on a par with each other: the CFO is no more important than any other member of top management. The Western idea of having the CEO and CFO working in harmony at the head of a company does not exist. The very title of CFO has only recently come into being, and in reality it means the "head of the F&A department," or the "chief lobbyist for the F&A department." In many cases, the CFO is not recognized as having a role in leading the company from a financial perspective.

As finance capabilities are increasingly recognized, the position of the CFO as a leader will gradually become more accepted in this part of the world. But creating top-caliber finance capabilities without an effective CFO will be difficult. The result is a chicken-or-the-egg puzzle. The solution is to systematically create effective CFOs. Ironically, in Japanese companies, the most important item on the agendas of CFOs is establishing their own position.

REFERENCES

1 Hiroyuki Arai, *Canon's High Turnover System*, Pal Publishing, April 2005.

2 Nikkei Business, *Energized Companies*, April 2003.

3 Nihon Keizai Shimbun Inc., *Toyota System*, April 2005.

4 Japan CFO Association, CFO, *Diamond Inc.*, May 2004.

5 Iwao Kubo, Challenge for *"New Functions"* Management at Mitsubishi, *Jitsugyo No Nihonsha*, November 2001.

6 Koji Okuda, Now is the time for Mitsubishi Corporation, *Nikkan Kogyo Shimbun Ltd.*, March 2003.

7 Nihon Keizai Shimbun Inc., *Nagata-ism at Nidec*, December 2004.

CHAPTER 15

High-Performance Finance in China

The dragon has stirred. China's stunning rate of growth and rapid integration with the world economy is a story with global impact. Home to more than 1.3 billion people, the world's most populous country represents a vast and incredibly varied consumer market. Propelled by an annual growth rate that has averaged between 8% and 9% for the last decade, China is poised to play a dominant role in global economic development. Goldman Sachs estimates that by 2050, China will be a $45 trillion economy – the world's biggest – with the US a distant second at $35 trillion.[1]

China's leaders have set ambitious targets for growth. In May 2005, for example, Chinese President Hu Jintao told the Fortune Global Forum that China's goal was to quadruple gross domestic product (GDP) by 2020.[2] Current gains make this a distinct and impressive possibility: what took 100 years for the West to achieve in terms of economic maturity, China is on a trajectory to achieve in a tenth of the time.

Given this torrid development pace, China presents enormous opportunities for corporations. It also poses significant risks. Managing an enterprise in a hypergrowth environment requires responding to volatility, adapting to constant market shifts, and keeping a close eye on regulatory and policy issues.

According to Steve Guse, CFO of Caterpillar Inc's Asia Pacific operations, one of the main issues he faces is the "sheer scale and pace of growth." Like many other enterprises doing business in China, Guse's company is facing both supply and demand pressures. It is struggling to develop the human and physical resources necessary to support the growth in the region.

In many leading organizations, CFOs like Steve Guse are playing a defining role in responding to these pressures. Success depends not only on developing strong finance capabilities, but also on building a performance management framework that aligns finance with business functions and delivers timely, transparent information. Just as risk management is a crucial finance function in China, its alter ego of performance management is a key area for development. As organizations embrace a more comprehensive approach to risk, performance management must keep pace.

A finance executive of a global bank predicts: "The finance function will become more and more important – and more relevant to our bank's overall growth as we begin to offer support beyond just numbers to our management or board. We will be providing insight, interpretations, and mapping the implications of decisions." He adds that doing business in China requires a strong focus on risk.

"Risk management is far more dynamic in fast-growing economies like China," he points out. "We must constantly adjust our long-term portfolio mix to ensure that it is well balanced, and that each type of loan reflects commercial sensitivities. In China, the economy is growing exceptionally fast; some sectors may be expanding too quickly. In fact, the government would like to moderate this growth rate. Given this environment, banks must monitor their portfolios very closely to ensure that things don't get out of hand."

While risk management is a universal concern among CFOs in China, the specific risks they face vary by company and industry. Starbucks, for example, is a relatively new multinational market player with rapid expansion plans.[3] Its risk outlook differs from an organization like Air China, which has evolved from a wholly state-owned organization to a publicly listed company with international investors. Other domestic Chinese enterprises are expanding from their home base into Greater China – a strategy that poses yet another set of challenges. Still other organizations, such as a provider of IT services to China's air travel and tourism industries, face risks stemming from deregulation and rapid integration.

In our interviews across China, leading CFOs described their responses to this challenging environment. A global bank's finance executive described his company's plan to move toward risk-adjusted pricing with activity-based costing as the backbone. Fan Cheng, executive director of the board and CFO at Air China in Beijing, told us how his company is rising to the challenge of expanding beyond China to become a major international airline – a transformation with major implications for its approach to capital stewardship and risk management. These examples, explored in more depth later in this chapter, typify the rapidly expanding management capabilities of the leading companies in the region.

CHINA THROUGH THE LENS OF THE CFO

In 2002, China became the first country since the 1980s to attract more foreign direct investment (FDI) in a year than the United States. By the end of 2004, China had generated a total of $562 billion in FDI and had 500,000 foreign funded enterprises. Fueled by this rapid inflow of investment, China will soon become the world's dominant manufacturer. China currently accounts for approximately 25% of world manufacturing output, a figure that is likely to rise to 50% by 2050. Its growth in this area is backed by a disciplined, low-cost labor force, a large cadre of technical personnel, attractive tax incentives for investors, and an infrastructure robust enough to support rising manufacturing operations and exports.

China's home market of 1.3 billion consumers is expected to grow briskly, and represents one of the most attractive markets in the world. Morgan Stanley estimates that China's retail sales will rise from $625 billion in 2005 to $2 trillion by 2014.[4] The country is already the largest consumer of cell phones in the world, with four to six million new cell phone subscribers signing up every month. Demand for personal computers remains strong, and internet usage is spreading more rapidly than in any other country. Over the next 10 years, the world's automakers are looking to China to generate approximately 20% of their global sales growth. During 2005, 30% of all new McDonald's outlets will be opening in China. Starbucks is predicting that China will soon become its second largest market outside of the US. From almost every viewpoint, China represents the world's most promising economic opportunity.

But China's complexity remains a significant challenge. There are the well-documented problems in joint ventures (JVs), logistics, strategic sourcing, and distribution. For example, Jim Eschweiler, Starbucks' VP of Finance for Asia Pacific, says that the regulatory maze is one of the main features of doing business in China. "Regulations differ widely from city to city or even district to district. The number of legal entities and the permits required to do business is a major challenge. China is a far more complex and highly regulated environment than we are used to."

In framing an effective response, Eschweiler says that a "big element" is having the resources and discipline to "... make sure we are doing it right. We have had to enlist more support from our corporate resources just for setup and infrastructure. China has required more help from legal, tax, and financial reporting groups than we typically need in other markets."

Along with such complexity, there are a host of recent developments that companies doing business in China must contend with. Among the most important are the rise of Chinese multinationals; an urgent need for raw materials, energy, and infrastructure; inefficiencies of financial systems; and a talent crisis.

The rise of Chinese multinationals

The rush into China by multinationals from abroad has its own Chinese parallel. Over the last decade, Chinese companies have gained in strength and expanded beyond their borders. Many can legitimately be called multinationals in their own right. Currently, there are 15 Chinese companies on the Fortune Global 500 list, including several telecom operators, the country's four major banks, China Life, State Grid, BaoSteel, and SAIC, the Shanghai-based automaker. Within the next 10 years, several dozen more Chinese companies may join the exclusive Fortune Global 500.

Leaders among this new breed of Chinese companies have already succeeded in capturing foreign market share. Huawei, a Chinese telecom manufacturer, entered the international market with prices 30% lower than its competitors. It currently does business in more than 70 countries and generates more than 40% of its $5 billion 2004 revenues from abroad. Haier Group in Qingdao is China's number one household appliances maker. Domestically, its market share exceeds 70% for most home appliances. Haier also exports products to more than 100 countries – and has succeeded in gaining first place in the United States market for sales of compact refrigerators and wine coolers.

Not only have many Chinese companies firmly established themselves overseas, they are also buying into overseas companies. Lenovo, the leading personal computer (PC) brand in China, became the world's third largest PC business by acquiring the PC arm of IBM in 2004 – an operation three times its size – for $1.25 billion. Lenovo is a state-owned enterprise with no previous international experience. Despite facing stiff competition from Dell and Hewlett-Packard, it is now the top PC maker in Asia, excluding Japan.

With its acquisition of IBM's PC business, Lenovo's growth possibilities are multiplying, and its market reach extends well beyond China and Asia. The three big Chinese oil companies – PetroChina, Sinopec and CNOOC – are also on a buying spree. They are investing in Indonesian oil and gas fields and looking at acquisitions outside of the greater Asia Pacific region.

Air China's transformation story is typical of many leading Chinese enterprises. Beginning life in the 1950s as the airline operator of the Civil Aviation Administration of China, Air China became a stand-alone company in 1988. When China's aviation market was deregulated in 2002, Air China consolidated with China Southwest Airlines and absorbed CNAC Zhejiang Airlines. The company listed its shares on the Hong Kong and London Stock Exchanges in 2004, selling over 20% of its equity. It holds stakes in Air China Cargo, Dragonair, Air Macau and Shandong Airlines. Air China is currently growing at 1.3 to 1.5 times the rate of China's overall GDP. According to Fan Cheng, "... this hypergrowth is creating some unexpected new issues ..."

One travel industry IT provider that was first listed on the Hong Kong Stock Exchange in 2001 is among the Exchange's top five performers in terms of total returns to shareholders. In the last year, annual revenue increased from 14.7% to 44%. The company's CFO told us that, "2004 was a remarkable year. Bookings processed by our electronic travel distribution system broke through the $100 million threshold for the first time and climbed to $132 million.

"Following the People's Republic of China's accession to the World Trade Organization, we need to take steps to deal with both new opportunities and new challenges. We have to improve our efficiency in responding to diversified customer demands, the increasingly heated market, and the opening up of our industry to international competition. At the same time, our traditional distribution value chain is rapidly evolving into a new business model as we cope with deregulation in global data services (GDS) as a result of e-commerce and new technology."

Hunger for raw materials, energy, and infrastructure

A fast-growing consumer and export economy requires energy and infrastructure – and China has significant needs in both these areas. It also has major expansion plans that are straining its resources. As the world's second largest energy consumer, China is already experiencing shortages. In turn, its energy consumption is driving up oil, gas, and coal import levels and has triggered massive overseas investment by

China's national oil companies. These companies are active in more than 50 countries around the world, from Kazakhstan and Chad to Australia. A recent fifth upgrade of Australia's massive Northwest-shelf liquefied national gas project – in which China National Offshore Oil Corporation (CNOOC) is a partner – was made largely to supply additional Chinese demand.[5][6][7]

In the modern equivalent of the Maoist era's development programs, China has a five-year, $86 billion infrastructure plan for its central and western provinces, plus another $25 billion plan to complete the massive Three Gorges Dam and Reservoir by 2009. When these projects are fully operational, China will have one of the world's most sophisticated transportation networks.

China's shipping industry and ports are also undergoing major expansion. Where there were no container terminals along the upper Yangtze River in 2000, by 2006 there will be eight. Already, Shanghai has passed Rotterdam as the world's top overall cargo-handling port, processing 380 million tons of goods in 2004. China's cargo capabilities will only increase as a new port is built at nearby Yangshan over the next 15 years.[8][9]

With China's rail system under pressure and carrying record volumes of freight almost every month, the Chinese government is inviting new foreign investment in rail infrastructure. There is a plan to extend the current 73,000 kilometer rail network to 100,000 kilometers by 2020 at a cost of 2 trillion yuan. These funds are expected to flow largely from offshore investors.[10]

Inefficiencies in the financial system

Even as foreign investment dollars pour into China, its domestic financial system remains beset by oversupply, deflation, and bad loans. The Chinese government controls and allocates individual savings via state-owned banks, which direct most of their funds to state-owned enterprises (SOEs). These SOEs have consistently used state-owned bank money to expand capacity. Over time, this has resulted in an oversupply of output, declining retail prices, and rising loan defaults.

State-owned bank resources, and their non-performing loans to other SOEs, are estimated to total close to $500 billion. In April 2005, the government injected $15 billion into the country's largest lender, the Industrial and Commercial Bank of China (ICBC), with a view to preparing it for an initial public offering (IPO) by 2009. This followed earlier infusions of $22 billion each into the Bank of China and the China Construction Bank in 2003. But even these recapitalization sums are not considered adequate. Standard & Poor's recently gave a conservative estimate of $110 billion for recapitalizing two banks, the ICBC and the Agricultural Bank of China. A more realistic figure may be greater than $150 billion.

State-owned banks are not alone in the challenges they face. There are clear signs that the Chinese government is losing patience with its thousands of under-performing SOEs. It recently announced, for example, that it will soon implement a policy of compulsory bankruptcy. Between 1994 and 2004, just under 3500 SOEs were closed; in total, their debts were $237 billion. In the next four years, another 2000 SOEs are expected to enter bankruptcy.

Looming over its domestic financial sector is the urgent need for reform precipitated by China's accession to the World Trade Organization (WTO) in 2001. Under the China-WTO agreement, foreign banks will be able to compete on an equal footing with Chinese banks from 2006 onward. To counter this threat, local players have been scrambling to improve their systems and performance. Managing this transition will be difficult since it increases the risk of financial instability. Already, local banks face a certain degree of competition. Foreign banks have been allowed to undertake renminbi-denominated transactions with domestic businesses since 2004, and will be able to offer this service to Chinese individuals from early 2007. The 2004 deal in which HSBC paid $1.75 billion for 19.9% of the Bank of Communications is a sign of things to come.

The talent crisis

Attracting much-needed talent back to China is a major challenge for this fast-growing world power. In recent years, the number of Chinese students and researchers who study abroad and never return has swelled to 600,000. This outflow of talent has been a long-standing problem. In 2004, the Chinese Ministry of Education reported that from 1978–2003, over 75% of those who left the country to study overseas, especially in the United States, did not come back.

Economic growth spurs the need for superior skills – and companies in China are entering the global war for talent. Demand is fueled by both domestic enterprises and overseas companies seeking to launch or expand their Chinese operations. Overseas companies typically depend on local Chinese to help them in building their businesses. As far back as 1999, for instance, Motorola had approximately 15,000 employees in China, only 150 of them expatriates. Multinational companies like Motorola are often in a better position to offer attractive packages combining higher salary and better training, which lure talented executives from state-owned enterprises.

Starbucks' Jim Eschweiler cites the human resources shortage as one of his major challenges in supporting the expansion of retail operations. "Our jobs grow faster than our people," he commented. "We are going to be in a new world – with new size, new scale, new challenges, and a new level of maturity. We need to bring in exceptional people or their jobs will outgrow them. If you cannot grow the people, the structure you create is going to be obsolete in 24 to 36 months."

Once in a multinational environment, local talent is often carefully nurtured. One leading multinational, for example, has a formal leadership program, personally sponsored by its CEO in which nominees join in weeklong sessions on leadership held in the US. At a lower level, junior executives who are considered leaders of the future attend regionally based sessions. This program will be extended to China for the first time in 2005.

According to a survey of Chinese state-owned enterprises, the loss of local talent exceeds 15% and consists mostly of professionals from middle management and above. Not surprisingly, the talent exodus is most severe in cities like Beijing, Shanghai, and Guangzhou. Most of these employees are highly educated, skilled in English, and have a good knowledge of local markets.[11]

There are signs that this "brain drain" is slowly being reversed as the explosive Chinese economy begins to offer career opportunities once found only overseas. For example, a number of talented and experienced Chinese professionals have recently moved to state-owned organizations. After spending many years in foreign enterprises, they are now attracted by the opportunities for advancement that SOEs offer. A new mindset also appears to be developing among young people, as more Chinese students consider pursuing careers at home rather than abroad.

APPLYING THE ASIAN FINANCE MODEL IN CHINA

Shaping a successful approach to the vast China market depends on the interplay of many factors. Chief among them is an understanding of both a company's overall objectives in Asia and the specific advantages that gaining a foothold in China can provide. Some multinationals, for instance, have large sales and distribution operations in other Asian countries and are using China mainly as a manufacturing center. In contrast, a global retailer is building an entry strategy around the Chinese market as a gateway to the entire Asian region. Yet another IT services company has a different agenda: to become a major exporter by using China as a "local" base of support operations for its globalization plans.

In China, the types of organizations with finance functions fall into three distinct categories:

- multinationals specifically targeting the Chinese market, basing man-ufacturing operations in the country, or using China as a beachhead for entering Asia;

- Chinese state-owned enterprises; and

- local independent Chinese enterprises.

To deliver optimal results, each of these types of organizations requires a different variation of the Asian finance model presented in Chapter 13. One regional retail chain, for example, is developing a three-pronged structure for its finance function by 1) establishing a consolidated coun-try center, 2) setting up regional and city centers, and 3) embedding specific capabilities in business units.

1 The consolidated country center is predominantly responsible for transaction-based activities, such as invoice processing, travel and expenses, general ledger, and fixed assets accounting. Centralizing these largely routine activities is delivering valuable economies of scale. The consolidated center receives documents from the regional and city offices by courier for processing, while imaging technology is used to transmit scans of original source documents, such as VAT invoices.

2 At the regional/city center level, activities focus on tax and regulatory affairs, along with some local statutory reporting and tax return prep-aration. Ultimately, the goal is to move tax and regulatory affairs to the consolidated center as legal and statutory requirements evolve to favor this approach.

3 Activities embedded in the business units are those that require prox-imity to operations on the ground. These business-related functions require a high level of judgment and strict controls are imposed. Although they are generally centralized at the country level, such activities can also be undertaken at a local level (by region, city or even store) where justified by business needs.

MULTINATIONALS IN CHINA

One dangerous temptation for multinationals is failing to rigorously assess the risks they face in their rush to exploit China's market potential. This is one region where the opportunities are so vast, they can be overwhelming. Addressing them strategically requires balancing evaluations of projected benefits with large doses of fiscal caution. In our discussions with corporate executives, another caveat emerged: in the drive to take advantage of China's growth trajectory, companies must remain firmly grounded. Adapting practices to the Chinese way of doing business is important to success, but this process must be carefully monitored.

Multinationals in consumer products and services or manufacturers, particularly those just entering the Chinese market, or planning to, can leverage either out-of-country or in-country capabilities. One CFO told us that he is looking at potential locations for a shared service center in China. As his company continues to roll out SAP Enterprise Resource Planning (ERP) modules in Asia, his goal is to harness centers of excellence in delivery and support. By 2010, he expects that his firm will have a full-scale shared services program under way. However, this same executive notes that his company currently draws clear lines between transactional and non-transactional activities in the finance function. This same CFO questions whether this is appropriate. Over time, he contends the distinction between transactional and non-transactional roles will blur and finance professionals across the board will be involved in high-value analytics.

For companies choosing the in-country option of relying on local talent to build their finance teams, China is not just a market, but also a reasonably priced talent pool where wage arbitrage can be a significant factor. As noted earlier in this chapter, multinationals' higher wages help them attract local finance professionals hungry for experience with international organizations. However, it is often difficult to retain these people because a chronic shortage of top finance talent creates enormous demand for their skills among other multinationals and, increasingly, among domestic enterprises.

In structuring the finance function, many organizations already have global solutions in place. They have the option of adding transaction processing for China to the tasks of existing shared service centers or outsourcing. Other organizations are taking a different approach and attempting to build legacy solutions only for China.

In either case, adapting the shared services model can help promote excellence in execution and delivery, save labor and technology costs, enforce standardization, and deliver consistent reporting. Shared services can also help get an effective operation up and running more quickly. Leveraging or scaling up existing operations or outsourcing relationships minimizes the capital investment required for market entry. In many situations, the "office in a box," with transaction processing and back-office support delivered from another geography, presents the most effective solution when entering China.

The shared services model can also help limit organizational risk. Given China's vast size, it is often difficult to impose corporate policies and ensure compliance if finance capabilities are decentralized. Wage arbitrage to take advantage of low-cost locations is only part of the shared services story. The real advantage flows from concentrating technology and skills in order to deliver seamless service to operations on the ground.

CASE STUDY
Centralizing the finance function

We have already seen the strong inroads that Starbucks is making in China. As part of its market entry strategy, the company has reorganized its finance group around its Hong Kong regional office. "Originally, the finance team was structured by function," notes Jim Eschweiler, VP of Finance for Asia Pacific. In the new finance organization, people wear multiple hats to support geographies and act as points of contact for finance people on the ground. Notes Eschweiler: "This is life in a high-growth environment. You never leave the office with your inbox empty, but at the same time you can't overbuild because there is too much of a premium on being nimble."

In terms of human resources, Eschweiler says that Starbucks is "pretty thin" in the regional office in Hong Kong. "There are three managers, as well as three analysts to senior analysts. We also have a fourth manager who is not dedicated to development support, but to the capital side. It is in large part a consulting and influencing role, because at the holding company level, we are not directly operating our markets. We might be approving the investments and the overall direction they are taking, but it's really at the country level that people are creating the plans and executing them. There is a governance aspect to the role too, because the region conducts business reviews and approves business plans and pro formas for new stores. The idea is that the regional team is tapped into the knowledge, expertise, and history we have in Seattle. They have peers in the North America group whom they access to learn and then share our experience from the domestic business. In opening 1500 stores a year worldwide, we generate great learnings that we want to take and share directly with the partners throughout the region."

In terms of Starbucks' finance model for Asia, Eschweiler explains that there are two levels: "One is within any given market and the second is at the system level. There is a support team in each major city responsible for running that market. It has all the functions represented: store development, operations, marketing, human resources, and finance. The mission of the team on the ground is to do the back-of-house support while helping the operations team to develop and execute the business strategy. Long term, shared services is one of the topics we are looking at. We are not there yet, but I cannot imagine that we will not be there within a few years. It just makes way too much sense.

"We want the mission of each market's finance team to be fully integrated with the business – integrated with the operators and district managers, so that finance knows what is going on in the field, understands what the marketing and product category teams are all about, and is in tune with what the store development team is seeing and experiencing in terms of pipeline. We want finance to be at the table with those teams as they are making decisions."

With rapid growth, however, there is a risk that the company can "disconnect" its functions and "quickly waste a lot of money," Eschweiler cautions. "You get into situations where you are pulling at opposite ends of the same rope. Operations may be focusing on deploying labor in an efficient fashion. At the same time, the marketing and category teams are coming up with new beverages or products to drive incremental sales. And, guess what? They are all highly labor intensive. The incremental sales they generate create operational complexity – and that in turn will drive labor up instead of down. Just like that you have two capable functions doing what is 'best' for the business – only their objectives are at odds with each other."

Part of the response to these issues is developing capabilities in the area of enterprise performance management, which Eschweiler ranks as four – out of a maximum of five – in terms of current importance, just behind the creation of a value-centered culture. "EPM is a thread that runs through every market," he says. "It is a common *need and fits with the whole idea of how we are trying to build the finance culture. We try to get teams engaged with their peers in different functions and lay out our business processes end to end. We tell them, 'These are the actions we want to measure, this is what drives value and does not. The most relevant operational report we can provide is the one that gets to you in time to make a better decision.' EPM offers a very clean link to the value center. It is almost as if this is the vehicle to execute the value-centered aspiration."*

Steve Guse, Caterpillar Inc's Asia Pacific CFO, says that the company's implementation of a common ERP package is key to configuring its finance organization. This package is allowing Caterpillar to "... split transactional reporting from decision-support reporting. It also allows us to move more of our financial transactional reporting out of places like Hong Kong, Singapore, and Australia to India, and out of our China facilities into shared service centers."

CASE STUDY
Building a regionally-tailored finance structure

"In looking at setting up regional shared services, while we do benefit from lower labor costs, the more important goal is to concentrate similar activities in ways that foster continuous improvement in our processes. In the region, we've set up one group focused just on marketing, one group focused on operations, and a third group for monthly product line-type reporting," notes Steve Guse, Asia Pacific CFO. "Their primary role is to provide product managers with visibility on profitability and to slice and dice data to find out where there are islands of profit and where there are holes or losses. They also create dialogue between separate marketing and operations groups."

Guse highlights a continuing issue: "Because we have a relatively simplistic, cost-based competitor base, we need to have discussions between marketing and operations very frequently. But data has been lacking and this has been a problem. It is straining our resources to get an enterprise view of how Caterpillar's investment in China is performing. We aspire to be more value-added, but organizationally, we're trying to address the fact that we have two roles to play and we want to separate those two roles. I spend very little time right now on technical accounting, and most of my time trying to put in place the service center structure, which is a critical role, while also providing decision support."

While Caterpillar will leverage India for most regional work, language differences will lead the company to establish a satellite center in China which will handle the company's China accounting. "There's going to be a group of people in every plant – a business manager and a couple of cost accountants – who make decisions at the plant level," explains Guse. "There will be another team that does decision-support work at the division level consolidating plant data, and helping first-level line managers at multiple facilities understand profitability versus expectations.

"Then there will be a transactional reporting capability that we hope will be invisible. It's going to be Sarbanes-Oxley compliant. It's going to provide all the data needed to run the profit center, but will be measured locally on core things like cost per transaction, quality and customer satisfaction. Although internal, after we have streamlined our processes through common systems and collocation, our service groups will operate as, and continuously be measured against third party alternatives. This will ensure we sustain both effectiveness and cost efficiency."

The joint-venture dilemma

Doing business in China involves some unique complications. As a result of historical regulatory requirements, for example, multinationals have entered into a large number of joint ventures with Chinese business partners. Many subsequently find it difficult to cut through cultural differences, respond to different regulatory and reporting requirements, and monitor the competence of local management teams. In turn, this makes it difficult to enforce the use of Western standards of corporate governance and internal control mechanisms. There is no magic formula for joint ventures, but there is a set of general rules to keep in mind. These can be summarized as follows:

- clearly define the objectives you want to achieve;

- set the ground rules early and closely monitor their implementation; and

- if you are in a joint venture and clear ground rules have not been set, then establish them as quickly as possible. If this is not possible, then the best course may be to simply exit.

STATE-OWNED ENTERPRISES (SOES)

Chinese SOEs face several obstacles when compared with multinationals from overseas and with major domestic companies. Their salary levels for finance staff are low and there is limited room for career development for some of the best and brightest. As a result, SOEs have traditionally had difficulty recruiting and retaining qualified finance professionals in China's very tight skills market.

ERP systems have gained momentum among China's largest SOEs as a result of a government policy that provides tax deductions on the interest on loans taken out for ERP implementation. However, many organizations are still using local software packages. The IPO route has been a catalyst for many SOEs in this area – at least in theory. Several have indicated that they would implement a world-class ERP system as part of their transition to a public company. In some cases, however, this commitment has been ignored after the IPO was completed.

We have already described Air China's decision to take the IPO route, list its shares internationally, and transform itself from a traditional SOE into an international company. Fan Cheng told us that with a new corporate governance and managerial approach introduced along with the IPO, Air China has been able to abandon the old state-decreed strategy of diversifying into areas such as tourism and real estate. Fan Cheng says the company now concentrates on what it does best: "... focusing on airline operation such as passenger and cargo services."

In finance, Fan Cheng says that Air China's main priority is to "identify risks, manage risks, and lead our way through these to our destination. We have to strike a balance between performance and the risks associated with achieving it. The end result is measured in terms of how to maximize profits." In plotting its path, the CFO notes, Air China now has more freedom than ever to plan its own strategic course. "Enterprises have been given more control than in the past, when they were all controlled by the central government," observed Fan Cheng.

Central to Air China's response to this new freedom has been the decision to look toward the business practices and financial management models of Western companies. Implementing the lessons they offer will be its next big step. On the agenda, adds Fan Cheng, are tools to better forecast revenue and evaluate costs "... in order to deliver better returns for our shareholders. Currently Air China is importing overseas practices step by step and learning by ourselves."

Risk management, he says, is the finance function's main priority. On a scale of one to five, with five being maximum importance and one the least, Fan Cheng says risk management should be "... scored the highest – a five. Without risk management, the enterprise cannot get the profitability it needs," he says.

Asked how he would tell Air China's five-year "future history" today, Fan Cheng says hindsight will show that in 2005, Air China was in a transformation stage: "... not just the structural transformation, but also concept transformation and management transformation. So there are still a lot of things to do," he says. "The airline industry is so uncertain. Since China has entered the WTO, we are now facing foreign airline competition for the first time."

In general, SOEs tend to focus on their financial operations capability, with some attention on the planning and budgeting activities as part of a nascent enterprise performance management capability. When structuring their own version of the finance framework, SOEs may assemble large teams of accountants and accounting clerks to perform transaction processing tasks. Even though they are much more top heavy in their manual approach in this area, it still makes sense to consolidate these teams regionally (by province or by a group of provinces), or even to consolidate them nationally.

SOEs still have problems in handling residual staff after any consolidation. They risk causing political unrest if they attempt a major redundancy program. Nor is it easy to retrain or redeploy residual staff, because the skill requirements for financial analysts are different from the previous duties that residual employees may have held, which generally have been limited to accounts payable and data entry.

While SOEs are beginning to put more resources into their planning and budgeting capabilities – and their processes and systems – as part of the IPO journey, their finance capabilities are likely to take some time to improve significantly.

LOCAL INDEPENDENT CHINESE ENTERPRISES

While many of China's rapidly developing local enterprises excel at manufacturing and technology, they tend to lag behind in areas such as corporate governance and financial management. They do have an advantage, however, in their attractiveness to local financial professionals, many of whom are interested in joining local enterprises because they have flatter hierarchical structures than SOEs and offer more opportunities for advancement.

This sector is also moving towards a finance model similar to that used by multinationals. Many local independent Chinese companies with international ambitions are acutely aware that they need to improve in this area if they are going to compete globally. One example is the case that follows.

CASE STUDY

Adopting a multinational-style finance model

One global bank has embraced Western-style concepts of transparency and governance as it attempts to establish corporate credibility in an increasingly competitive environment.

A finance executive explains that, although the organization differs slightly from Western corporations in valuing consensus over more executive decision making by the CEO, it is consciously attempting to replicate Western best practices in many aspects of its finance model. The bank is well advanced with its Basel II compliance, a milestone it is attempting to reach by the end of 2006. It has also launched an enterprise performance management project – comprising a balanced scorecard; planning, budgeting and forecasting; and multidimensional profitability analysis.

Under the pressures of compliance and governance requirements, the bank is also embracing a comprehensive approach to risk on an enterprise-wide level. "In the past, each type of risk was managed separately; now we have set up the post of chief risk officer to manage most of these risks centrally. We also have a risk committee as part of our governance structure. It oversees all major risks to ensure that they are managed coherently."

The bank is also implementing activity based costing as it seeks to identify cost drivers, allocate costs by those drivers, and apply the results to pricing. The executive indicates that the bank is adopting a statutory business unit (SBU) system, with two SBUs – one in the retailing banking area and the other in the corporate bank. "Each SBU has its own finance people, but we have a central finance function. There is a functional reporting line, SBU finance to central finance, but we always provide guidance. Central finance sets policies, procedures, and standards."

This bank has seen significant change over the last few years; for example, that people are paying close attention to relevant key performance indicators. Process changes have also resulted in cultural changes. Before a significant merger, "... there were a number of small banks under a larger umbrella," he recalls. "Each sister bank had a unique culture. After the merger, we built up a new culture and this has led directly to better performance."

At another leading Chinese corporation, the transformation of its finance organization has centered on standardization for reasons of compliance and performance. This company is focused on three core issues: 1) leveraging national policies, 2) improving customer relationships, and 3) exploiting advanced technology from abroad. Internally, this IT service provider to the travel industry is working to integrate two separate business platforms into one, organizationally and operationally. Its goals are to grow stronger and expand while preserving low-cost advantage.

The growth of e-ticketing in the travel industry has put pressure on the company's finance organization to rapidly standardize all processes, from planning, accounting, and reporting to risk management. To achieve this, finance needs a single enterprise management information system that provides a solid platform for delivering services to all the company's customers. This requires consolidating many resources that are currently distributed across different operations in multiple geographic locales. Its major finance challenge is quickly achieving both process and system standardization on one platform. The CFO believes that full-scale restructuring will take from three to five years to complete.

ACHIEVING HIGH-PERFORMANCE FINANCE IN CHINA

Whether a company is foreign or Chinese multinational, an SOE or a local independent Chinese enterprise, the impetus for building a high-performance finance function is apparent as organizations attempt to capitalize on "the China opportunity."

There are well-recognized challenges and obstacles along the path to high performance – from layers of regulation and government, to undeveloped finance resources, to a dearth of talent. Despite these constraints, leading organizations are moving toward a finance function model that leverages their strengths while preserving and promoting their unique business cultures.

Whether configuring transaction functions in an outsourced service center in China, or even in India, most leading organizations are being driven by on the ground insights and needs. Many of these enterprises are implementing technology and processes with the dual goals of improving speed and upgrading decision making. To do this, they are combining decision making and reporting at ground level with regional and global support, backed where possible by "single instance" procedures that not only eliminate duplication, but also promote transparency and limit costs.

For companies pursuing high-performance finance in China, enterprise-wide risk and performance management processes are crucial. These capabilities must be closely aligned with business through relevant metrics. This requires not only deploying and integrating technology to leverage scale and function, but also building a vigorous value-centered culture.

REFERENCES

1 Dominic Wilson and Roopa Purushothaman, Global Economics Paper No. 99, *Dreaming with BRICs: The Path to 2050*, Goldman Sachs, October 2003.

2 BBC Monitoring Asia Pacific, *China to Quadruple GDP by 2020*, May 16, 2005.

3 Starbucks Ventures with China Will Taste Like Java Too, *Seattle Times*, June 10, 2005. http://www.seattletimes.com

4 Andy Xie, *Global Economic Forum, China: Profit from Consumption*, Morgan Stanley, September 7, 2004.

5 The Hindu, *China and Asean: India's Energy Markets*, May 6, 2005. http://www.thehindu.com

6 AFX Asia, *IEA Raises China Oil Demand Forecast*, June 10, 2005.

7 Philip Andrews, China's Oil Companies Making Waves Abroad, *Straits Times*, June 11, 2005. http://www.straitstimes.com

8 William Arbruster, World Trade Spotlight on China/Asia Pacific, *Shipping Digest*, June 13, 2005. http://www.shippingdigest.com

9 Shanghai Vaults into Third Place Among Global Container Ports, *Canadian Sailings*, June 13, 2005. http://canadiansailings.com

10 Rail Freight and Passenger Volume Hits Record, *Xinhua China Economic Information Service*, June 8, 2005.

11 Chinese Talent Development Report, Social Science Literature Publisher. http://www.cpirc.org

Biographies

CHAPTER 1

R. Timothy Breene

Tim Breene is Accenture's strategy and corporate development officer, and the company's group chief executive – Business Consulting. He also serves on Accenture's Executive Leadership Team and numerous other management committees. As strategy and corporate development officer, Mr Breene has companywide responsibility for Accenture's: overall strategy; mergers and acquisitions; and incubation and development of new businesses. He also developed and leads Accenture's High Performance Business program, a major research and capability-building initiative. As group chief executive, Business Consulting, he leads Accenture's Business Consulting Capability Group, which comprises five service lines: Customer Relationship Management, Finance & Performance Management, Human Performance, Strategy, and Supply Chain Management.

Michael Donnellan

Michael Donnellan is an executive partner in the Accenture Products operating group, which covers both the outsourcing and consulting businesses. Mr Donnellan has more than 20 years of experience in the professional services industry. He has also worked extensively on the research, development, and deployment of innovative operating models. An engineer by background, Mr Donnellan has spent the last decade focusing on the new role of finance in the modern corporate enterprise. In 1997, he co-authored *CFO: Architect of the Corporation's Future*, which resulted in the adoption of new finance and accounting organizational models by numerous corporations around the world. In 2004, he co-authored *CFO Insights: Achieving High Performance through Finance Business Process Outsourcing.*

CHAPTER 2

Michael Sutcliff

Michael Sutcliff is the managing partner of the Accenture Finance & Performance Management service line. Mr Sutcliff has extensive experience in strategy, business architecture, systems integration, business transformation and outsourcing engagements across multiple geographies and industries. His responsibilities include developing new service offerings and alliance relationships, and managing Accenture's consulting services of interest to senior finance executives. Since joining Accenture, Mr Sutcliff has specialized in large-scale finance transformation programs involving financial and strategic planning, enterprise performance management, finance operations and reporting, shared services and outsourcing, and tax compliance. In addition, Mr Sutcliff was involved with launching Accenture Finance Solutions as a new outsourcing business unit.

Scott Mall

Scott Mall is an executive partner with the Accenture Finance & Performance Management service line. Mr Mall specializes in finance strategy and global finance change programs. Mr Mall has deep expertise in shared services, outsourcing and finance function restructuring. Over the past three years, he has been responsible for shaping and executing three large, global finance function transformation programs, which collectively included the post-merger integration of two distinct finance organizations, the implementation of two separate global financial systems, the outsourcing of more than 1000 full-time equivalents of finance function work, and the reengineering of scores of finance function processes. Mr Mall has extensive international experience and was part of the leadership team that opened the Accenture operations in Chennai, India.

CHAPTER 3

Paul Boulanger

Paul Boulanger is an Accenture executive partner with responsibility for the Finance & Performance Management service line in the Resources operating group, which consists of energy, chemicals, natural resources and utilities industry segments. Mr Boulanger has more than 17 years of experience in assisting organizations in finance and accounting transformation, as well as helping organizations with evaluation and business planning phases of large-scale initiatives. Mr Boulanger specializes in finance function strategy, restructuring and reengineering of financial organizations and processes, and enterprise performance management.

Gordon Stewart

Gordon Stewart is a partner in the Accenture Finance & Performance Management service line. Mr Stewart has 19 years of international finance experience with in-depth knowledge of business transformation, finance operational excellence, finance and accounting outsourcing, and enterprise performance management. He is recognized as an expert in enterprise performance management, including planning, forecasting, reporting, and the use of scorecards.

CHAPTER 4

Christopher Rutledge

Christopher Rutledge is an executive partner in the Accenture Finance & Performance Management service line. Mr Rutledge has responsibility for developing the assets and offerings addressing finance functional and organizational strategy. Since joining Accenture, Mr Rutledge has focused on global finance transformational efforts across industries and functional areas. He has expertise in finance visioning and strategy, finance and accounting shared services and outsourcing, and enterprise performance management.

CHAPTER 5

Daniel London

Daniel London is the North American managing partner for the Accenture Finance & Performance Management service line and has overall responsibility for the Accenture Enterprise Performance Management market offering. Mr London oversees engagement teams that enable successful enterprises to make extensive use of business insight, to identify the best value-creation opportunities within and outside the organization. Since joining Accenture, he has focused on global finance transformational efforts across industries and functional areas. Mr London has expertise in finance visioning and strategy, enterprise performance management, shared services and outsourcing, financial management, billing and payment, and procurement.

Brian McCarthy

Brian McCarthy is an executive partner in the Accenture Finance & Performance Management service line. Mr McCarthy has more than 12 years of experience in value and performance management and financial reengineering engagements. He is responsible for developing thought leadership and is one of the global leads of the Accenture Enterprise Performance Management market offering. Mr McCarthy's primary focus is helping clients address key performance management challenges and align their organizations around increasing shareholder value. He has also led recognized primary research projects, written extensively for publications including *Outlook*, *Journal of Business Strategy, CFO,* and *Business Finance* and has presented at multiple industry conferences. He has led a number of performance management engagements with companies across a variety of industries.

CHAPTER 6

Tony Masella

Tony Masella is a Montreal-based executive partner in the Accenture Finance & Performance Management service line. Throughout his career, Mr Masella has focused on financial process design and implementation, cost management, and performance management. Mr Masella specializes in the design and implementation of shared service centers. He has extensive international experience and has assisted companies in many industries including retail, consumer goods and industrial products. He currently leads the Finance & Performance Management service line in Canada.

Stefania Bassi

Stefania Bassi is a Milan-based partner in the Accenture Finance & Performance Management service line. During her career, Ms Bassi has focused specifically on treasury and finance organizational modeling and related performance management, finance operations transformation, organization design and implementation, and shared service architecture implementation combined with best practices utilization and related performance reporting. Ms Bassi also has significant European experience in different industries including communications and high technology, retail, consumer goods, industrial products and natural resources. She currently leads the development of the Treasury market offering in Italy and related knowledge capital in Italy.

CHAPTER 7

John Ballow

John Ballow is an executive partner in the Accenture Finance & Performance Management service line and an executive fellow with the Accenture Institute for High Performance Business. Mr Ballow has more than 25 years of experience as a corporate finance officer, advisor and strategist in corporate and finance management across multiple geographies and industries. He specializes in enterprise valuation and performance management, corporate strategy, restructuring, mergers and acquisitions, financial management, and finance operations. Mr Ballow has led Accenture research on valuation, strategy and intangible assets and has authored numerous articles appearing in publications such as *Outlook*, *Journal of Business Strategy*, and *Journal of Applied Corporate Finance.*

Robert Smith

Robert Smith is a partner with the Accenture Finance & Performance Management service line. Mr Smith specializes in finance transformation and strategy, including capital planning, shared services design and implementation, business process outsourcing design and implementation, and planning and budgeting. Mr Smith is also a qualified UK chartered accountant and has experience as an investment analyst at an investment bank. He has worked across a broad range of industries including banking and capital markets, insurance, chemicals, oil and gas, consumer goods and security.

CHAPTER 8

Maged Fanous

Maged Fanous is an Accenture executive partner with responsibility for the Finance & Performance Management service line within the Financial Services operating group in the United Kingdom. Mr Fanous leads the Accenture Treasury & Risk Management market offering, and is a leading expert in risk management, asset and liability management, and risk-adjusted performance. He has assisted major financial institutions, in Europe, Asia and the United States, with the implementation of risk management solutions and regulatory compliance programs covering Basel ll, International Accounting Standards and other regulatory requirements. He has also led large delivery programs starting from the high-level design phases to the solution implementation and system rollout. Mr Fanous has published a number of articles on risk management and compliance solutions.

David Rombough C.A.

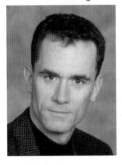

David Rombough is a senior manager in the Accenture Finance & Performance Management service line in Toronto. Mr Rombough is a chartered accountant with a wealth of experience in finance transformation, particularly in risk and performance management. Working with a variety of major global organizations, he has helped clients improve their finance and controllership processes and translate their business issues into robust performance models. These models support management decisions related to profitability improvements, process performance and control, and business risk analysis.

CHAPTER 9 - SEE CHAPTER 1

Michael Donnellan

CHAPTER 10

Rowan Miranda Ph.D.

Rowan Miranda is a partner in the Accenture Finance & Performance Management service line. Dr Miranda specializes in working with government and non-profit organizations to improve financial management through the use of benchmarking, advanced budgeting and planning processes, and the implementation of ERP systems. Prior to joining Accenture, he was Director of Research and Consulting at the United States Government Finance Officers Association. He has also served as a CFO and Budget Director of several local governments.

CHAPTER 11

Steven Culp

Steven Culp is the executive partner responsible for the Accenture Finance & Performance Management service line across five European countries (United Kingdom, Ireland, Austria, Switzerland and Germany). He is involved in both initiating and delivering a wide array of projects across the CFO agenda for pan-European clients. Since joining Accenture, Mr Culp has focused on financial process design and implementation, cost management, and performance management. Mr Culp is experienced in the design and implementation of shared services as well as programs to deliver enterprise performance management solutions. He has extensive international experience and has assisted companies across many industry segments.

Manfred Ebling

Manfred Ebling is a senior manager in the Accenture Finance & Performance Management service line. Based in Zurich, Switzerland, Mr Ebling focuses on improving the effectiveness of finance operations. With more than 15 years of business experience in international finance and financial services, he has a strong background in finance strategy, enterprise performance management, mergers and acquisitions, shared services, and investor relations. Prior to joining Accenture, Mr Ebling was senior vice president for multiple finance functions at a global industrial group. Currently, Mr Ebling leads the Accenture Revenue Assurance, Credit & Collections market offering in Austria, Switzerland and Germany.

Karsten Schlageter Ph.D.

Karsten Schlageter is a senior consultant in the Strategy service line in Germany. Dr Schlageter is an expert in corporate and finance strategy at Accenture. He has more than six years of experience in consulting, and obtained his doctorate in the field of Strategic Management/International Economic Policy in the Americas at the University of Tübingen, Germany. His work focuses on helping clients to define and implement growth and finance strategies, as well as enabling value-oriented IT strategies and governance structures to help clients achieve high performance.

Luiz Ferezin

Luiz Ferezin is an Accenture managing partner based in Sao Paulo, Brazil. Mr Ferezin has more than 20 years of experience in supporting transformation in large companies. He has been involved in many shared services projects and was responsible for establishing the Accenture Shared Services Center for Latin America that manages processes in finance, human resources, and IT. Mr Ferezin has extensive experience with companies in different industries throughout Latin America.

CHAPTER 12

Mauro Marchiaro

Mauro Marchiaro is the executive partner of the Accenture Finance & Performance Management service line responsible for Italy, Greece, and emerging markets including Russia, Poland, the Czech Republic and Hungary. Mr Marchiaro has more than 16 years of experience in large finance transformation programs for clients in the consumer goods and services, automotive, travel and transportation, and pharmaceutical industries across multiple geographies. He has extensive experience in financial process reengineering, value and performance management, post-merger integration, financial systems design and implementation, shared services, and activity-based management. Prior to joining Accenture, Mr Marchiaro served as group CFO of an industrial company, gaining experience in finance and accounting operations, tax planning and optimization, and mergers and acquisitions.

CHAPTERS 13 &15

Matthew Podrebarac

Matthew Podrebarac is the executive partner responsible for the Accenture Finance & Performance Management service line in Asia Pacific. He advises CFOs and other senior executives of multinational and large organizations on large-scale organizational change programs. His expertise includes finance organization strategy, financial processes, shared services, outsourcing, and enterprise performance management. Mr Podrebarac has led some of the largest and most complex finance programs undertaken in Asia as well as in the United States and Europe, and currently leads several regional finance programs across Asia Pacific.

Andy Hui

Andy Hui is the partner responsible for the Accenture Finance & Performance Management service line in Greater China. Mr Hui has extensive experience working with finance executives of multinational organizations and Chinese enterprises on system implementation and organization change programs. His expertise includes finance organization strategy, enterprise performance management, risk management, finance process reengineering, and enterprise resource planning (ERP) system implementation. Mr Hui has led a number of system implementation and organization change programs for companies in the United States, Europe and across Asia Pacific.

CHAPTER 14

Mitsuo Isaji

Mitsuo Isaji is the executive partner responsible for the Accenture Finance & Performance Management service line in Japan. Mr Isaji has been helping Japanese companies and their CFOs to enhance their finance, accounting, business intelligence and performance management capabilities. Mr Isaji also has a strong background in business strategy formulation and business architecture renovation. He has assisted companies from various industries, including automotive, retail, chemical, utilities, and energy with their performance improvement initiatives.

CHAPTER 15 – SEE CHAPTER 13

Matthew Podrebarac
Andy Hui

The Hackett Group

Richard T. Roth

Chief Research Officer, The Hackett Group

Richard Roth is responsible for The Hackett Group's overall research methodology and is a member of its executive team. With extensive experience in benchmarking and best practices, he is responsible for the quality of the firm's analysis and published research, and for building its benchmarking methodology. Mr Roth has more than 20 years of experience working with executives to achieve world-class performance in all areas of the sales, general, and administrative functions, and has employed his expertise to guide employees at a wide range of companies, including GE, Hewlett-Packard, Cisco Systems and Citigroup.

Index